ALSO BY STEVEN VERRIER

*Professional Wrestling in the Pacific Northwest:
A History, 1883 to the Present* (McFarland, 2017)

Gene Kiniski

Canadian Wrestling Legend

STEVEN VERRIER

Forewords by Nick Kiniski *and* Kelly Kiniski

McFarland & Company, Inc., Publishers
Jefferson, North Carolina

LIBRARY OF CONGRESS CATALOGUING-IN-PUBLICATION DATA

Names: Verrier, Steven, author.
Title: Gene Kiniski : Canadian wrestling legend / Steven Verrier.
Description: Jefferson, N.C. : McFarland & Company, Inc., Publishers, 2019 | "Table of Contents Forewords Preface Introduction: The Historical Backdrop 1. The Kiniskis of Chipman, Alberta 2. Edmonton and Tucson: Tale of Two Cities 3. Arizona Wildcat 4. Learning the Ropes 5. Return to the Gridiron 6. Long Road to Hollywood 7. Hot in California 8. Breakthrough Years 9. Indianapolis and Minneapolis 10. Vancouver Territory, 1961/1963 11. Julia Kiniski 12. 1964 ... a Very Good Year 13. More of a Very Good Year 14. Height of His Career 15. Passing the Torch 16. Passing of Nicholas And Julia 17. Still Going Strong, 1969/1973 18. The Only Woman He Ever Loved 19. Focusing on Home 20. Kiniski/Tomko: An Uneasy Alliance 21. Slowly Winding Down 22. Endgame 23. "You couldn't help but love the guy" 24. A Largely Retired Life 25. Final Decade 26. Celebration of Life Selected Bibliography Index." | Includes bibliographical references and index.
Identifiers: LCCN 2018054650 | ISBN 9781476674834 (softcover : acid free paper) ∞
Subjects: LCSH: Kiniski, Gene, 1928–2010. | Wrestlers—Canada—Biography.
Classification: LCC GV1196.K625 V47 2019 | DDC 796.812092 [B]—dc23
LC record available at https://lccn.loc.gov/2018054650

BRITISH LIBRARY CATALOGUING DATA ARE AVAILABLE

ISBN (print) 978-1-4766-7483-4
ISBN (ebook) 978-1-4766-3427-2

© 2019 Steven Verrier. All rights reserved

No part of this book may be reproduced or transmitted in any form or by any means, electronic or mechanical, including photocopying or recording, or by any information storage and retrieval system, without permission in writing from the publisher.

Front cover: NWA World Heavyweight champion Gene Kiniski shows off his championship belt (Kiniski family archive).

Printed in the United States of America

McFarland & Company, Inc., Publishers
  Box 611, Jefferson, North Carolina 28640
    www.mcfarlandpub.com

To all whose memories, effort, and insight
made this project possible and pleasurable

Table of Contents

Foreword by Nick Kiniski	1
Foreword by Kelly Kiniski	3
Preface	5
Introduction: The Historical Backdrop	9
1. The Kiniskis of Chipman, Alberta	13
2. Edmonton and Tucson: Tale of Two Cities	19
3. Arizona Wildcat	25
4. Learning the Ropes	28
5. Return to the Gridiron	32
6. Long Road to Hollywood	37
7. Hot in California	43
8. Breakthrough Years	51
9. Indianapolis and Minneapolis	71
10. Vancouver Territory, 1961–1963	79
11. Julia Kiniski	89
12. 1964 … a Very Good Year	95
13. More of a Very Good Year	101
14. Height of His Career	109
15. Passing the Torch	123
16. Passing of Nicholas and Julia	133
17. Still Going Strong, 1969–1973	138
18. The Only Woman He Ever Loved	153
19. Focusing on Home	159
20. Kiniski–Tomko: An Uneasy Alliance	164

21. Slowly Winding Down	177
22. Endgame	187
23. "You couldn't help but love the guy"	192
24. A Largely Retired Life	201
25. Final Decade	218
26. Celebration of Life	229
Bibliography	233
Index	239

Foreword by Nick Kiniski

Since childhood, people have asked what it was like to be raised by my father, Gene Kiniski, otherwise known as "Canada's Greatest Athlete." I told them, and continue to tell them, that this question is difficult for me to answer as he was the only father I had. Looking back, I realize how lucky I was to be his son. Growing up, I lived like a celebrity. My father supported our amateur sports careers but did not want his boys to follow in his footsteps as professional wrestlers. Later, I became successful through my own decisions and efforts. Throughout the 80s and 90s, I owned two of the largest bars in the state of Washington. I became involved in emergency services many years ago in my local community and that led to becoming a fire chief. Today, I give back by working as a battalion chief and paramedic. However, nothing has opened more doors in my life than being the son of Gene Kiniski.

We've all heard of charisma. Some have it and some don't. My dad had it and, I would say, worked it until the day he passed away. When I was younger, I recall that he would tease me for buying Mercedes and Corvettes. He would say that I was so insecure that I needed a fancy car. I would reply, "Dad, I'm not on TV every week like you...." He was known for telling it like it was and he could read people and situations in an instant. He had charisma in the ring, during interviews and in the grocery store. Even as he aged and wasn't necessarily recognized by face or name, he still exuded charisma—he could say and get away with just about anything (sometimes as I backed away in embarrassment…)!

From a young age, my brother and I observed my dad chatting it up with anyone, including the reserved and seemingly unattainable people, and he could walk into any environment and command the room. From my perspective, sometimes he was definitely over the top. However, he was a good father. Since I was 12, he raised me and my older brother on his own. The house was always clean, he cooked breakfast and dinner every night (excellent cook!), didn't date much and made sure we weren't partying as teenagers. Until the age of 18, we had a strict curfew on school nights and weekends. Also, we had to kiss him goodnight and have a conversation with him every single night (in retrospect, probably to ensure we weren't drinking).

I am amazed at how much information Steve accumulated about my dad. When I received his draft, I teasingly stated that he knew my dad better than I did. It was so great to hear history about my father that I never knew. It was a reminder that we sometimes take things for granted. I had forgotten how much traveling and hard work my dad put into the wrestling business. Whether sick, injured or beyond exhausted, the Show Must Go On. He was affectionate and present, and he was also tough. I never noticed any signs of fear whether in the stadium or out, including competitors, crowds, media, authority figures, mean dogs, etc. Steve's book made me realize the sacrifices my father made to provide for his family. To me, he was not only Canada's Greatest Athlete but World's Greatest Dad.

Steve, thank you for doing all the research necessary to write this book. I truly appreciate the time and effort you took to write such a great book. My father would have approved of it if he were still alive.

P.S. Readers, I hope you enjoy this book. If you'd like to check out some memorabilia, take your picture next to a life-size cut-out of Gene Kiniski (very popular thing to do, apparently), read some fan mail and hate mail, and/or possibly meet me, visit the family-friendly Kiniski's Reef and Tavern in Point Roberts, Washington, visit our website at www.KiniskisReef.com or like us on Facebook @KiniskisReef.

The younger son of Gene and Marion Kiniski, Nick Kiniski followed his father into amateur wrestling and won the Canadian amateur superheavyweight championship in 1980. After graduating from Simon Fraser University, Nick wrestled professionally across North America and internationally before returning to the Pacific Northwest. He has been a fire chief and paramedic and owner of The Breakers.

Foreword by Kelly Kiniski

I think my mom and dad, before Nick and I were born, had a marvelous time on the road. I know my mom was a really fast driver. She drove back after the matches, and my dad sat in the passenger seat. Once my mom had Nick and me and couldn't go on the road, things definitely changed.

I think all the wrestlers' wives had it pretty tough moving to new areas, getting the kids in school, and being a father and a mother. Just because it was a birthday or a wedding anniversary didn't mean Dad would come home. Wrestling came first no matter what.

My dad didn't want to travel when he was home. He just wanted to stay in his sweatpants and relax and not have to be under any time restraints. All those years of being champion, he had to make airports and the matches. It was go go go all the time. My mom was home all those years wanting to go out to a nightclub or where the action was. Dad didn't want to leave the house. They were both right, but for different reasons. That made it tough on the relationship.

When Mom was gone, Dad always kept the house immaculate. He would always make all the meals. I mean, here was a guy who was a star and everything else, and he's now making beds, folding sheets, and doing all the laundry. Nick and I went through a lot of football gear. He washed all that, even though he didn't even know how to use a washing machine at first. The towels would have so much bleach in them I'd go to dry my back with a towel and I'd rip it in two. Champions would have that lifestyle—hotels, going out at night, partying—and now he's just washing clothes, hanging them on hangers, putting them in our closets, making all the beds, vacuuming the shag carpet, and shopping for groceries. Most people don't understand he didn't know how to do any of that. He was always gone, and all of a sudden he had to learn how to be a mom. He never missed a lick. I sometimes tried to help out, but he would have none of that.

He was mentally tough. You didn't wrestle hour-long championship matches night after night without being mentally tough. I never saw Dad scared of anything. He could stay calm in a riot. There could be a whole carload of teenagers, and if he had to, Dad would chase them down and pull them all out of their car. My dad had no fear.

If my dad thought night was daylight, you couldn't sway him. It was daylight. It didn't matter who told him different; it would be daylight. My dad never had indecision.

He taught me you always worked hard. Don't take the night off just because you have a 103-degree fever. Show up on time and work hard in the ring. Like my dad said, for every dollar the people pay they get a five-dollar value. My dad said the harder he worked, the luckier he got.

Right up until he was in his 80s, if a wrestling fan came over to the table, Dad stood up and said, "Glad to meet you, Mr. So and So" and "Where are you from?" and "What do you do?" He always, no matter what, made a point of shaking the person's hand, even after he'd been out of wrestling for years and years.

Dad impacted a lot of people. He loaned out money to a lot of people who needed a few extra bucks here or there. You wouldn't believe how many people Dad loaned money to, though we never even knew about that until after Dad died. Dad told all the kids around him they needed an education and were idiots if they didn't quit their jobs and go back to school. Even today, I meet all kinds of people who have some kind of story about Dad. Before I know it, they'll be talking for an hour—and they won't say one word about wrestling. Dad was a great, great wrestler for sure, but people who knew him remember him as a lot more than that.

Kelly Kiniski is the older son of Gene and Marion Kiniski. He played college football in Texas before kicking off a professional wrestling career in 1980 that took him across North America and overseas. Following his retirement, Kelly worked as an electrician in Texas before returning to the Pacific Northwest. He is now a resident of Point Roberts, Washington, where he owns a construction business, Kiniski & Co.

Preface

This book grew out of research for my 2017 McFarland book, *Professional Wrestling in the Pacific Northwest: A History, 1883 to the Present*, which helped clarify—at least, in my mind—the relationship between wrestling in its various forms and the regions, cultures, and time periods it often played a key part in illustrating. Research for that earlier book also helped me see how certain wrestlers have transcended their sport and lived lives that serious biographers and readers—regardless of their views on wrestling—should find fascinating and full of unexpected twists and details. Without a doubt, one such wrestler is Gene Kiniski, a former professional wrestling world heavyweight champion who was known to a generation of Americans and especially Canadians—and to this day is fondly remembered by millions—as Canada's Greatest Athlete.

I grew up watching Gene Kiniski on television, as he was a featured performer and heel (or "bad guy") for many years on *All-Star Wrestling*, which originated in British Columbia and, during much of its 1960s–1980s run, could be seen across Canada. Growing up in Southern Ontario, I made a ritual of tuning in to CKCO-TV on Saturdays and getting lost in an entertaining world of body slams, grudges, wacky characters, and—traveling the airwaves from a small television studio in Burnaby, British Columbia—plenty of hype concerning the main event of an upcoming Monday night arena show in Vancouver, which, as I lived about 2,500 miles away, I never got to attend.

Kiniski, with his razor wit and aggressive style, was always one of my favorites. He was a well-traveled wrestler, though, and wasn't always on the show. But when he was, whether lavishing compliments on announcer Ron Morrier; sparring verbally with the likes of John Tolos, Bob Brown, or Dutch Savage; or mixing it up physically with rivals like Don Leo Jonathan, Mark Lewin, or Steven Little Bear, Kiniski delivered entertainment in spades to a national audience that was supposed to hate him but often found that impossible to do.

Research for *Professional Wrestling in the Pacific Northwest: A History, 1883 to the Present* dispelled some misconceptions I'd had about Gene Kiniski. For one, I learned his part in the pro wrestling game wasn't limited to what fans saw in the ring. I learned he was a player behind the scenes as well, as an owner of the Vancouver wrestling promotion he was so closely associated with. I learned he was a shrewd and capable businessman, an avid reader and surprisingly complex individual, and someone people from all walks were as drawn to in real life as on television or in arenas. I was surprised to learn Canada's Greatest Athlete—always a proud Canadian—lived in the United States for more than four decades until passing away in 2010. As far as the other end of Kiniski's life was concerned, while I'd always heard ring announcers or TV commentators introduce him as hailing from Edmonton, Alberta, I learned Kiniski was in fact born in rural central Alberta, about 45 miles east of Edmonton, and spent his early years in a village called Chipman.

When it became apparent that Gene Kiniski was well deserving of a serious biography, the first phone call I made was to the village office in Chipman, Alberta. Within seconds I was advised to contact Steven Eleniak, an Edmontonian who'd lived in Chipman during the Depression and knew much about the village's history. He'd also known the Kiniski family and had some interaction with Gene over the years.

I quickly contacted Steven, and as it turned out, he could not have been more gracious—then or during the entire time I worked on this project—in sharing his knowledge about central Alberta and the background that played a big part in making Gene Kiniski what he was. Steven generously shared memories and documents, answered every question I threw at him while touching base over the course of the entire time I spent working on this book, and directed me to several other individuals who were able to provide important insight into the formative years of Gene Kiniski. One of the highlights of my working on this book came when I met Steven in Edmonton and he took me for a visit to Gene Kiniski's boyhood home in Chipman.

Gene's sons Kelly and Nick Kiniski were nothing but supportive when I brought to their attention my interest in writing a book about their father. They were always gracious in providing information and insightful comments about growing up as the sons of Gene and Marion Kiniski, and they thoughtfully answered every question I asked about many aspects of their father's life. Also extremely helpful were other members of the Kiniski/Kinisky clan, who generously shared information and memories of Gene, his parents, and his siblings.

While I had the pleasure of interviewing friends of Gene Kiniski's spanning a period of nearly 70 years, special mention must be made of Benny Grabow, who was a close friend of Kiniski's in Edmonton in the 1940s and 1950s before both migrated to the West Coast in the 1960s. Benny Grabow and Gene Kiniski remained steadfast friends until Kiniski's final days, and Benny's memories were an invaluable contribution to this book.

Also exceedingly generous were key figures from the wrestling and broadcasting worlds—many quoted in the pages that follow—who offered insightful comments and honest appraisals of Gene Kiniski the athlete, the entertainer, the celebrity, and the man. Some of those names will be instantly recognizable to many readers, but one that stands out is Don Leo Jonathan, a ring rival of Kiniski's for many years and a close Kiniski friend for twice as long. I had enjoyed interviewing and meeting Don Leo Jonathan previously, and this time around it was a pleasure listening to recollections of Gene Kiniski shared by the only other wrestler ever to have settled permanently in the Pacific Northwest whose footprint in the wrestling world is equal to Kiniski's.

Several well-qualified readers were kind enough to look over all or part of this book's manuscript at various stages of completion. One reader in particular—Richard Vicek, author of the impressive and entertaining Crowbar Press biography of Dick the Bruiser (*Bruiser: The World's Most Dangerous Wrestler*, 2016)—needs to be acknowledged for giving the entire manuscript a meticulous reading and for offering valuable comments and suggestions. Thanks also to Vance Nevada, Jason Beck, Tim Hornbaker, Herb Simmons, the late Larry Matysik, Nick Kiniski, and Kelly Kiniski for taking time to read and comment on the manuscript.

On November 23, 1928, Gene Kiniski—the youngest son of hardy Polish immigrants to rural Alberta—was born into a family of memorable characters. During his teen years he gravitated to sports, especially football and amateur wrestling, and after a brief professional football career he set about making his name as a professional wrestler. Billed at times early in his career as a Polish heavyweight champion—though he never set foot in Poland—Kiniski main-evented almost everywhere he appeared en route to reaching the pinnacle of his profession by winning the NWA World Heavyweight championship from Lou Thesz in St. Louis on January 7, 1966. *Gene Kiniski* chronicles Kiniski's ring career from beginning to end—from coast to coast and beyond—including his role as an active part-owner of the Vancouver All-Star Wrestling promotion for 15 years.

But while the wrestling-related part of Kiniski's story is fascinating in itself, it is more the memorable nature of the man that I hope will stand out to readers. Though every effort has been made to do justice to the legacy of Gene Kiniski the athlete, this is perhaps less a wrestling book than a book that illustrates how a rugged, one-of-a-kind child of the Canadian prairie used wrestling as his means of rising from humble roots and carving out a path to success, notoriety, and celebrity—a path marked by tragedy, triumph, and some amazing stories by people who knew Kiniski along the way.

Introduction: The Historical Backdrop

During most of the 19th century, the land now comprising Alberta gave little indication of what Canada's westernmost Prairie province would later become. While the Hudson's Bay Company—architect of a major share of the history and development of Canada, especially in the West, for more than two centuries—had established a few trading posts in what is now Alberta in the 1700s, change came slowly to the region during most of the 1800s.

In the early 1800s the population of the area now comprising Alberta was sparse and predominantly represented by peoples such as the Blackfoot, Sarcee, and Cree. The few nonnatives populating the region were almost entirely fur traders and explorers, the latter largely occupied with trying to figure out the best overland and freshwater routes to link Upper Canada/Lower Canada—now Quebec and Ontario—to the Pacific coast, much as Lewis and Clark set out to do in the United States in 1804.

Neither "Canada" as it is understood now nor "Alberta" as a separate entity yet existed. Canada as a nation would not exist until 1867 and, during its first few years, would consist only of the central and eastern provinces of Ontario, Quebec, New Brunswick, and Nova Scotia. And while Manitoba—the province directly west of Ontario—and British Columbia, Canada's westernmost province, would join the Canadian Confederation in 1871, it would be more than another three decades until the two provinces sandwiched between British Columbia and Manitoba—Alberta and Saskatchewan—would join Canada simultaneously as the eighth and ninth provinces in the Confederation.

Alberta—the more rugged and challenging of the two provinces-to-be—attracted explorers, mappers, fur traders, and missionaries to its expansive frontier during the early and middle decades of the 1800s. According to historian Robert M. Stamp at TheCanadianEncyclopedia.ca, the middle of the 19th century also saw the arrival of fur traders from the American Montana Territory who had a special interest in exploiting highly profitable bison hides. This resulted, by the late 1860s, in "a mass influx of free traders across the border. These traders used 'whiskey,' a deadly combination of alcohol, dyes, medicines, and poisons, as their primary trade item." In a scenario calling to mind the abuses British traders and forces heaped on Chinese "customers" during the 19th-century Opium Wars, the Alberta natives—especially the Blackfoot—suffered greatly.

The new nation of Canada—definitely with its own slant on Manifest Destiny—saw something desirable in what is now Alberta and acquired the huge territory from the

Hudson's Bay Company, whose license was terminated in 1870. The Canadian government of Sir John A. Macdonald established the Northwest Territory—in whose jurisdiction what is now Alberta would remain for more than three decades—and established North-West Mounted Police posts at Fort Macleod and in what would become the major cities of Edmonton and Calgary. The Macdonald government also set out to stop the "whiskey" trading to natives and to work out land and treaty arrangements with the Blackfoot, Cree, and other native groups.

Regarded as key in bringing the new Northwest Territory up to the standard of being a valuable addition to the Canadian Confederation was the building of a transcontinental railroad, one of the main goals of John A. Macdonald's inaugural national government. The first American transcontinental railroad, completed in 1869, had played a vital role in making development of the American West and true Atlantic-to-Pacific nationhood a viable venture, and many Canadians—especially those who populated the West Coast region when British Columbia became Canada's sixth province on July 20, 1871—saw the same road ahead for Canada. British Columbians, as a condition for joining the Confederation, insisted that the Canadian government complete the building of a transcontinental railroad, all the way to the West Coast, within a decade of British Columbia's joining the Confederation. Macdonald himself promised British Columbians that the coast-to-coast railroad would be completed by 1881.

A glance at a map would indicate such a railroad would have to pass through the part of the new Northwest Territory comprising what is now Alberta. But the terrain was often difficult and the land largely unsettled. The Dominion Lands Act of 1872—similar in nature to the U.S. Homestead Act of 1862—helped provide low-cost homesteads and spurred some settlement in Alberta, but it did not aid greatly in boosting the building of a railroad to join points in Eastern and Central Canada to points in the West. The Macdonald government issued land grants to companies and developers seen as able to contribute substantially to the building of stretches of railroad—and, of course, some companies were eager to get in on the land-grab in order to help build the railroad and, in the process, rake in some handsome profits. As a result, government officials were bribed in an effort to get them to issue land grants to certain companies and developers.

This resulted in the Pacific Scandal, which brought down the Conservative Macdonald government in 1873. The Liberal government of Alexander Mackenzie—in power for the next five years—did not place similar priority on building and completing the transcontinental railroad; and partly due to lack of funding, difficulties determining the best routes, and challenges stemming from plans to take the railroad through native lands, progress in building the railroad—especially in the challenging western terrain—was limited during the Mackenzie administration.

When Macdonald and the Conservatives returned to power in 1878, completion of the railroad was placed back on high priority, although finishing the job by 1881 as originally proposed was out of the question. But with the key eastern leg of the transcontinental railroad—the section joining Nova Scotia and New Brunswick to Quebec and Ontario—having been completed during Mackenzie's watch in 1876, the Macdonald government set out on what Pierre Berton, in the opening words of his Canadian classic, *The Last Spike: The Great Railway, 1881–1885*, calls "[t]he bitterest and longest parliamentary wrangle in the history of the young Canadian nation" (6). The result of the parliamentary debate—which occupied much of the winter of 1880–1881 and reflected serious division in the country, "consumed its major participants, and left the capital dazed and exhausted" (6)—saw the official recognition and founding of the Canadian Pacific Railroad (CPR).

Though the founding of the CPR in 1881 fell within the ten-year window British Columbians had insisted on as a condition for joining the Confederation, there was still major work to be done. While about a third of the proposed railroad—the Nova Scotia-to-Ontario stretch—had been operating for a few years, "now it was simply a matter," as Berton puts it, "of driving the steel west to the Pacific" (6).

There would be nothing simple about that, however, as the task would involve some difficult planning and execution in the West, especially across several hundred miles of rugged mountain terrain. Some of the most challenging terrain lay within the section of the Northwest Territories that in 1882 was renamed the District of Alberta—after a daughter of Queen Victoria—and comprised much of present-day Alberta, including Edmonton, Calgary, and points west and south. The District of Alberta's topography posed serious engineering challenges, and construction was further challenged by inclement weather, work stoppages due to pay delays, and continued issues regarding funding and plans to cross native land. Yet the railroad extended to Calgary by 1883, and two years later, on November 7, 1885, the last spike on the Canadian Pacific Railroad's transcontinental line was driven at Craigellachie, BC, effectively providing what was a modern transportation connection between Alberta of that era and key points in Western, Central, and Eastern Canada.

Change did not come quickly to Alberta, however, after the completion of the railroad. While the building of the CPR had brought a small flood of Central Canadian and immigrant workers to the District of Alberta, few chose to plant roots in the area, and few outsiders from anywhere were enticed to ride the rails to establish permanent residence in Alberta during the years immediately following the completion of the railroad. As Stamp reports, "In 1881, just before the arrival of the railway, only about 1,000 non-native settlers resided within [what is now] the province of Alberta; a decade later, in 1891, that number had grown, but only to 17,500," and the "arrival of hundreds of thousands of settlers that had been expected in 1885" would not get underway until about a decade after that.

1

The Kiniskis of Chipman, Alberta

Researcher Erica Gagnon, at the Canadian Museum of Immigration website, says "Canada thirsted for settlers"—particularly to the Western Prairie region—following the challenges of the 1870s and 1880s, which included a lengthy recession. But after the accession to power of Canada's first francophone prime minister, Sir Wilfred Laurier, in 1896, Interior Minister Clifford Sifton set out to populate the West. According to Gagnon, "Sifton is known for promoting the immigration of nontraditional immigrants [and] strongly believed that sturdy European immigrants were the best settlers for the challenging Prairies, because of their familiarity with agriculture, rural lifestyles, and harsh climates.… Sifton disliked the idea of urban populations settling the Prairies, for they would congregate in cities, instead of developing Prairie homesteads. Instead, he promoted the immigration of groups like the Ukrainians, Hungarians, and Mennonites over the more ethnically 'desirable' British immigrants."

While advertising and recruiting efforts had sought to bring immigrants into what is now Alberta ever since the land had been acquired by the Canadian government, immigrant communities prior to the 1890s had been small and scattered, consisting mainly of a small French community near St. Albert, pockets of Chinese around Calgary, Mormons in Cardston, and Icelanders in Markerville.

The 1890s—particularly after the Laurier-Sifton regime came to power—saw the District of Alberta welcome tens of thousands of new arrivals from Europe, many from the eastern part of the continent, drawn to the Canadian prairie by the lure of free homesteads of 160 acres, or about a quarter of a square mile. Many of the settlers from Eastern Europe—eager to flee poverty and meager prospects in their homelands—came from countries such as Romania, Hungary, the Ukraine, and Poland. Proven farmers in their homelands, many of those immigrants were attracted to the Canadian prairie in particular, according to Stamp, "as a result of the development of fast-maturing varieties of hard spring wheat, the exhaustion of good available land in the American West, the easing of the 22-year economic depression that had gripped North America and the aggressive immigration policy of the federal government under the direction of Minister of the Interior Clifford Sifton."

Pawel Romanowski, at PolishHeritage.ca, reports that while "the first recorded Polish settlers in Alberta arrived in 1895," it appears likely that Polish settlers—hailing from southern Poland, which was noted for coal mining—had arrived earlier to work in mines in the southwest part of the Territory of Alberta. Polish miners and their families played a role in helping establish several settlements, including Banff and Canmore, as growing communities.

Other Polish immigrants to Alberta, according to Romanowski, consisted of agricultural settlers who "came as part of Minister Clifford Sifton's plan to populate and cultivate the vast regions of Western Canada. These Poles came mainly from the Austrian-controlled province of Galicia, as it had the most relaxed policies on emigration, and were almost invariably of the peasant class. This made them suitable candidates for farming the land surrounding Edmonton, which is where the majority settled. Some of the earliest Polish settlements include Wostok/St. Michael, Rabbit Hill/Nisku, Skaro and Mundare. All are situated within a hundred kilometer radius of Edmonton and all were settled by the turn of the century.... Other Polish communities established in this region in the early 1900s include Chipman, Round Hill, Waugh, Kopernik, Flat Lake and Naples."

As far as Chipman was concerned, the village website indicates "settlers first arrived around 1892, [and] supplies were brought from Edmonton by team and wagon, or by settlers on foot carrying their supplies on their backs." The settlement grew by a trickle until 1905, the year Alberta became a province, and the small settlement 45 miles east of Edmonton got a new railway station and a name—"Chipman," in honor of Clarence Campbell Chipman, a railroad official.

A few businesses and services sprang up in the area, and homesteaders started pouring in from Central Canada, the United States, and Europe. Many of the new settlers represented persecuted minorities such as Jews, African Americans, Mennonites, Mormons, and Doukhobors. Others were primarily economic refugees—many from Eastern Europe—eager to bring their agricultural know-how to the Canadian prairie. Along with the Ukrainians, a key immigrant group from Eastern Europe spurring the development of Chipman were arrivals from Poland—among them, the family of Julia Warshawski, a girl of 12 or 13 when she and her family set out from Poland in 1912; made a long sea voyage possibly originating in Naples, Italy; traveled west on the Canadian Pacific Railroad; and followed that up with a short trip on the Canadian Northern Railroad to Chipman, which, in 1921—one year before Chipman was incorporated as a village—"had a population of 175 ... one blacksmith shop, one chopping mill, one elevator, one hotel, two implement agents, one insurance office, two livery and feed stables, one lumber yard, one real estate office, two stock yards, three stores, a Methodist church, a school and a railroad station," according to the Village of Chipman website. But more importantly—from a hungry immigrant's perspective—Chipman also had "land [that] could be purchased for $12 to $15 per acre, and only 20% of the land was under cultivation." Clearly, there was opportunity for settlers committed to succeeding in a harsh climate and austere environment—and those who proved robust and dedicated enough to overcome the challenges of living in a small, bootstrapping prairie community such as Chipman in the early 1900s would be well positioned to breed remarkable children and to demonstrate unusual persistence paying off, at least in some cases, in well-deserved success and recognition later in life.

While many of the early Polish settlers in communities like Chipman were well equipped for the challenges they would face, their lives, according to Romanowski, "were difficult to say the least. Although they had received that most cherished of all possessions—land—they lacked tools, supplies and co-operative networks. Homesteaders often had to clear great swathes of forest and parkland in order to establish farms. Once land was cleared (an arduous task in itself), many settlers began mixed farming and lived at a subsistence level off their various crops and livestock. To supplement the food supply, women and children would pick berries and mushrooms in the summer. The harsh Canadian winters and lack of outside support would test these early settlers, but the vast majority managed to survive and progressively improve their lot."

As the Warshawskis settled into a life of new challenges, Julia, just into her teen years, apparently joined the household of her uncle John Warshawski, who, according to the Alberta Rose Historical Society's *Pride in Progress*—at about 800 pages, by far the most detailed account of the Chipman area's history in print—was "the first of the Warshawski family to leave his homeland" when he immigrated to Canada from Poland in 1899 (775). After working for the CPR in British Columbia for about two years, John Warshawski married Ukrainian immigrant, Chipman resident, and family friend Anna Molchan, and the couple lived in Fernie, British Columbia, and Fort Saskatchewan, Alberta, briefly before settling in Chipman in 1905 with their first two children (*Pride in Progress*, 776). There would be a few more children in John and Anna's homestead by the time John's niece Julia Warshawski apparently joined the household in 1912 or 1913.

While John Warshawski—described as "an enterprising person" in *Pride in Progress* (776)—appears to have been a hard worker who increased his landholding and was owner or part-owner of a few small businesses, the Polish community around Chipman faced challenges during World War I—underway for Canadians by August of 1914—as immigration was largely halted for the duration of the war and Poles were viewed with suspicion by some Canadians. Though there is no indication that John Warshawski's household was adversely affected by the war, there were few educational opportunities around Chipman for Polish immigrant children like Julia, who didn't make it past the seventh grade.

When she was 16, Julia married Nicholas Kiniski, a young fellow immigrant from Poland who had come to Canada with his brother before the two siblings got separated. It is uncertain whether Julia and Nicholas' marriage was arranged. According to *Pride in Progress*, Nicholas worked on a railroad section gang and lived for a time in the home of Tom Achtemychuk, one of Chipman's prominent citizens, and his wife Anna. *Pride in Progress* reports that Nicholas and Julia Kiniski's wedding took place in the Achtemychuk home in 1915, and *Edmonton Examiner* writer Joe Ranger reported 85 years after the wedding that Julia's mother passed away that same year. According to Ranger, Julia's father died two years after his daughter's wedding.

After leaving the railroad, Nicholas Kiniski is remembered primarily as the Chipman village barber, although he would be active in other lines of work as well.

According to Nicholas and Julia's grandson Bruce Kinisky (correct spelling), after leaving railroad section gang work, Nicholas began trying his hand in small-town business. "He had a store in Lamont," seven miles northwest of Chipman, says Bruce Kinisky. "I think it was a general store."

According to Bruce, Nicholas and Julia apparently started their married life in Lamont and remained there until Nicholas' store in Lamont burnt down.

Describing his grandfather as a "jack of all trades" who "did whatever he had to do to survive," Bruce Kinisky says the young couple moved to Chipman, where Julia had spent a few years prior to getting married.

Arthur Roberts, another grandson of Nicholas and Julia Kiniski's, reports that Nicholas maintained his entrepreneurial spirit in Chipman, where he owned a small grocery store. Those who remember Nicholas mainly as a barber say his grocery and barbering businesses were in the same modest building. According to Allen Thomas, whose mother was a first cousin of Julia Kiniski's, Nicholas Kiniski, whose presence was well known in Chipman during the Depression, "used to play the Jewish harp all the time."

This photograph, apparently from 1926, shows (rear) Nicholas and Julia Kiniski; (middle, left to right) Julia's cousin Helen Warshawski, who was staying with the Kiniskis; Fred Kiniski; Dorothy Kiniski; and (front row) younger siblings Mary and Rudy Kiniski. Julian Kiniski was born later in 1926, and Gene Kiniski would come into the picture two years later (thanks to Steven Eleniak).

Recalling the Chipman village barber as "Old Man Nick," Walter Melnyk, born about five years after Nicholas and Julia Kiniski's wedding, says, "He cut my hair.... I'd come in there with long hair because I couldn't afford it. And one time he told me, 'Listen, I'm going to charge you 35 cents next time if you come in with long hair.'"

Melnyk, who would get to know several members of the Kiniski family well, does not speak fondly of Julia—at least as far as her years in Chipman are concerned. When he attended school across the road from the Kiniski home, Melnyk says, Julia came across as a harsh woman. But he acknowledges that, years later, "after she went to Edmonton she changed her way of thinking."

Nicholas and Julia averaged about a child every two years during their first 13 years of marriage. Of the couple's first five children, the most prominent would turn out to be Julian, who, like his mother, would become a public figure in Edmonton after the family moved there following the Depression.

But it was the Kiniskis' sixth and youngest child, Eugene "Gene" Nicholas, born November 23, 1928, apparently at the area hospital in Lamont, who would make an impact in Chipman—where he spent his early years—as well as in Edmonton and far beyond during his storied life. That didn't seem a likely prospect, however, to Melnyk, who recalls, of the young boy he says was sometimes called "Baby Nick," "Up to the time he was six years old, he had wet pants.... He'd come out there every day at dinner time in wet pants. I'll never forget that"—though Melnyk acknowledges no one would have dared bring that up to Gene Kiniski in later years.

While Julia Kiniski's Edmonton City Government biography indicates Julia and Nicholas Kiniski moved to Edmonton from Chipman in 1936, Thomas, Gene Kiniski's second cousin—who says, "We only lived a block apart"—recalls the Kiniski family living in Chipman as late as 1940 or 1941, when Gene was about 12. Thomas recalls of the young Gene, "He was a tough little bugger.... He was not a bully, but he was tough."

The Kiniski family in 1939. Pictured are (back row, left to right) Mary, Rudy, and Dorothy Kiniski, and (front, left to right) Julian, Nicholas, 10-year-old Gene, Fred, and Julia Kiniski (thanks to Bruce Kinisky).

About two decades later Gene's brother Julian wrote, in a magazine article titled "My Brother Is a Brute!," "Gene was the baby of the family.... He was a sissy, slow to get started and not at all prone to doing his share of work around home." But a turning point in Gene's young life, Julian wrote, came when a boy moved to town and "set about terrorizing all the children—boys and girls alike. Then Gene got to him and that was that."

Thomas reports none of the toughness Gene exhibited as child during the Depression ever played itself out on an athletic field, ice rink, or gym in Chipman. While sporting opportunities were limited, Thomas says the local boys often played hockey in winter and baseball in summer. "I don't recall [Gene] participating in anything," he says.

Thomas says, while Kiniski would sometimes visit the local swimming hole, he showed no signs that an athletic career lay ahead. As far as the gridiron was concerned, Thomas recalls, "We never played football in town there. We never had football teams or anything like that."

While Thomas remembers the young Kiniski as a relatively quiet boy who would not slip into his gregarious persona until years afterward, he recalls, "We'd have a little crown and anchor game. We'd make a little wheel, a crown and anchor—we had one at Gene's place, in his backyard—and we were always trying to win money from the other guys."

Though Julia and Nicholas Kiniski may already have laid the groundwork for such a move—and one or two of their older children may already have departed for the city—it was not until Canada's attention was focused on World War II that Gene Kiniski's parents completely pulled up the roots they had put down in Chipman and moved the family 45 miles west to Edmonton. Nicholas and Julia had seen significant changes and events in the village during their years there—including an influenza outbreak following World War I, slow but steady growth during the 1920s, the introduction of electricity to the village during that same decade, a fire in 1931 that razed much of the business district, and severe challenges stemming from the Great Depression.

The Chipman village website reports, "the [D]epression was felt in every home. Grain and livestock prices fell so low that farmers could no longer make the payments on their farms, pay their taxes, buy machinery or even pay for their groceries. Businesses went under one by one, until the entrepreneurial spirit was virtually destroyed. Young men could no longer get jobs, and some rode the trains from city to city looking for work. Often when a freight train stopped in Chipman, numerous unemployed men scattered throughout the village looking for handouts of food. Seldom if ever were they refused, for most families shared willingly what they had, even if it was only bread and butter. To make things worse, the dry years came and lasted for most of the 1930s." Thomas says, of Chipman, both during and after the Depression, "unless you were farming or had a store in town, there wasn't a heck of a lot of opportunities." As a result, he says, "a lot of people moved to Edmonton."

Thomas says Gene Kiniski was 12 or perhaps 13 when his parents made the call to move the entire family from tiny Chipman to the provincial capital of Edmonton. And while Julia was seen around Chipman from time to time afterward, Thomas, who saw more of Gene Kiniski several years later after making the move to Edmonton himself, says, as far as Chipman was concerned, "I don't remember him coming back."

2

Edmonton and Tucson
Tale of Two Cities

In 1894, about a century after it was established as a Hudson's Bay Company trading post, Edmonton was incorporated as a town of about 1,000 residents. Within a few years the town became a popular transit point for ambitious travelers heading off for the Klondike Gold Rush. By 1904, with a population approaching 10,000, Edmonton was incorporated as a city, and a year later, in 1905, it became the capital—selected over the similarly sized city of Calgary, 185 miles to the south—of the newly established province of Alberta.

The Canadian Northern Railway, which helped boost the growth of Chipman in 1905, did likewise to the new provincial capital, although on a much grander scale. Spurred by construction and the founding of new businesses, the introduction of streetcars to city streets, the establishment of the University of Alberta, and the steady arrival of new residents, Edmonton's population grew, by the start of World War I, to 70,000—though it dipped during the war and did not reach 70,000 again until about the start of the Depression. And while Edmonton—like just about every other North American community large or small during that era—faced its share of difficulty during the Depression, the city saw its population rise by a trickle in the 1930s as new residents moved in from smaller towns in northern and central Alberta where Depression-time prospects looked a lot bleaker than they did in the provincial capital. Migration to Edmonton from outlying areas continued into the 1940s, and among those deciding to make a go of a new life in the city were the family of Polish immigrants Nicholas and Julia Kiniski, arriving from Chipman.

Since September of 1939, following Germany's invasion of Poland, Canada had been a participant in World War II, and the period from 1939 until the mid-1940s saw a large number of enlistments of young Alberta males in the Canadian Armed Forces. But young Gene Kiniski, a new kid in town nearly or barely into his teens, apparently was not directly affected by the war, though he had an older brother serving in the military. By all accounts Gene had a relatively normal youth in Edmonton, which, despite wartime enlistments, continued to grow steadily during World War II, topping 100,000 residents midway through the conflict. By that time, Gene was often in the company of two friends he met in Edmonton and would remain close to in later years, Benny Grabow and Steve Paproski. Grabow, a close friend for decades, recalls, of his early association with Gene Kiniski during World War II, "We met many, many times in boxing and wrestling clubs." Grabow, who is Jewish, says, "Edmonton was a very anti-Semitic city, and Jewish kids weren't fighters," although Grabow himself had a background in boxing. "[If I learned] that somebody was picking on them ... I'd get a hold of Gene, and Gene and myself would go down, pick up the guy, and ... Gene would keep the bullies back, and I would take the guys one-on-one." Grabow also recalls learning there was at least some degree of Jewish background in the Kiniski family, though it may have been slight and buried well in the past.

Paproski, of Ukrainian origin but born in Poland, also was a strapping teenager during the wartime era in Edmonton. Grabow says the three friends sparred regularly—in boxing and wrestling—and, while Kiniski could be outboxed, he was never outwrestled. When Kiniski was in high school, Grabow says, he weighed well over 200 pounds, topping out at about 225. "In those days," says Grabow, "he was big compared to everybody else."

The war was still far from over when Kiniski, who clearly had athletic potential, enrolled at St. Joseph Catholic School, which in 2018 is the oldest Catholic high school in Edmonton. St. Joseph, built in 1931, was an all-boys' school during its first two decades, and perhaps its most distinguished graduates, on an international scale, during that period were actor-singer Robert Goulet and Gene Kiniski.

Presumably, a lack of girls on campus helped provide an optimal training ground for aspiring young male athletes. In any event, Kiniski threw himself into sports, particularly wrestling and football, while at St. Joseph. Six feet tall with a powerful build, Kiniski excelled in both, at least to the extent that opportunities in central Alberta would allow. As far as wrestling was concerned, Kiniski won the Alberta provincial heavyweight championship in 1947—without having to compete in a single match. Although Alberta amateur wrestling records from that era are spotty, Mike Eurchuk, a prominent figure in Alberta and Canadian amateur wrestling for many years, says, "I know he was the champion, but I also know he was the only guy in the weight class."

It is widely remembered that Kiniski, besides wrestling at the collegiate level, wrestled at the YMCA during his teen years. According to Eurchuk, "The YMCA was a bit of a center for wrestling. We used to have the city recreation club too. They both had active teams."

Kelly Kiniski, the older of Gene's two sons, recalls his father telling him that his wrestling trainer at the YMCA, Leo Magrill, could barely see. "But he knew how to teach wrestling," Kelly says.

In a November 19, 1971, feature by John Kirkwood in *The Province* (Vancouver, BC), Gene Kiniski said of Magrill, "He was the rasslin' coach there, a fine rassler and he never got a cent for it. That's a person I'd have to say I have a great deal of respect for because he really gave me my foundation. He was my guiding light."

In the February 2004 Point Roberts, Washington, *All Point Bulletin*—well over half a century after his seminal days as a wrestler—Gene Kiniski would reflect on his experience on the amateur mat back in Edmonton, telling writer Tavish Bradbury, "At 15, I was bigger and stronger than everyone else. I would be wrestling 30 and 40-year-old men at the YMCA, and I cleaned the mats with 'em.... I would wrestle anybody, and I usually won. No one wanted to get out there with me. So I began wrestling local coaches, older men, and I beat them. They couldn't believe my strength and endurance and wanted to know who this kid was."

Kiniski began competing in tournaments at the provincial level, and at least once, in 1947, he was listed as a competitor in the dominion amateur wrestling championship, which that year was held, apparently outdoors, in Athabasca, Alberta. While the name of the tournament suggests the competition was Canada-wide, entrants were limited to participants in programs in Montreal, Winnipeg, Vancouver, Calgary, and Edmonton. Kiniski was slated to compete in the 191-pound division along with two other competitors, though it is unclear where Kiniski placed in the tournament.

At the provincial level, meanwhile, Kiniski took anywhere from two to four provincial titles in amateur wrestling in the late 1940s, depending on the source. An Alberta Amateur Athletic Union of Canada certificate declares Eugene Kiniski the winner of the open class championship in wrestling at the provincial competition held in Calgary on April 23, 1949.

Although professional wrestling had become a regular attraction in Edmonton in 1948 under the promotion of Al Oeming, in association with Stu Hart, there are no strong indications Kiniski seriously considered a career in pro wrestling in the wake of his Alberta amateur wrestling career. Given his size, background, and local roots, there is little doubt Kiniski would have been given an opportunity in the pro wrestling ring; but not yet the charismatic figure he would become, he chose another route into pro sports.

While it is uncertain how many amateur championships Gene Kiniski earned prior to becoming a professional wrestler, he was a dominant heavyweight—and often the only competitor in his weight class—during his years in Alberta amateur wrestling. Months after being awarded this provincial championship certificate, Kiniski would join the Edmonton Eskimos as a bruising tackle (Kiniski family archive).

His choice was not a big surprise, as Kiniski, since high school, had combined his success in Alberta amateur wrestling with some prominence on the football field. There are records showing Kiniski was, first, an alternate and then, by age 17, a key player—as a tackle wearing number 5—on the Edmonton Maple Leafs junior football squad, which lost an exhibition to the older, larger University of Alberta Golden Bears squad by only two touchdowns and made it to the provincial junior championship game during at least one of Kiniski's four seasons with the team.

In 1949 Kiniski moved up to a defensive lineman position with the Edmonton Eskimos during that football team's inaugural season in the Western Interprovincial Football Union (WIFU), a forerunner of the Canadian Football League (CFL), which would come into existence a decade later. Playing on the line with Kiniski on the 1949 Eskimos team—which had a losing season under rookie head coach and future Canadian Football Hall of Famer Annis Stukus—was Steve Paproski, who had been a teammate of Kiniski's on the Maple Leafs squad. Also playing for the 1949 Eskimos was future Alberta premier Peter Lougheed.

While Kiniski, wearing number 50, performed solidly with the Eskimos despite suffering an apparent shoulder dislocation while attempting a tackle in the ninth game of the season, it was well known that he was far from satisfied with the level of compensation he was receiving. As local reporter Joe Carbury would later write, "Local boy Gene [Kiniski] couldn't have bought a complete wardrobe of clothes for the money he received for playing for the [Eskimos] in 1949." As Kiniski himself later put it in an unidentifiable news clipping from his personal collection, "Those lousy Eskimos paid me a stinkin' $200 in 1949."

Happy or not, it appears Kiniski was a participant during the Eskimos' spring training exercises the following year. According to an unidentified clipping from Kiniski's collection, another participant was Gene's brother Julian, who was "not as tall as kid brother Gene but ... weighs about the same, 225." It is not certain whether the brothers' joint participation in the exercises took place in 1950, but that seems a likely scenario. And, while Julian, like all of Gene Kiniski's siblings, had size going for him, he did not seem to have Gene's competitive nature when it came to football, and it is unclear whether he had any serious ambition to make the team.

Julian, described in the August 26–September 1, 1961, edition of Edmonton's *TV Week* as a "pipe-smoking sportsman," was already several years into a successful meteorological career and well into married life by the time he and Gene apparently worked out together with the Eskimos. According to *TV Week* writer Dick MacLean, Julian, who was two years older than Gene, had already worked in the northern British Columbia town of Fort Nelson for several years as a meteorologist—though not the type that appeared on television, which Julian would later do for six years-plus back in Edmonton. MacLean also reports that Julian took a short break from his duties in Fort Nelson in 1947 to marry Alice Thompson in Edmonton.

Another clipping from Gene Kiniski's collection—written by Hugh Watson but otherwise unidentifiable—indicates Kiniski, following the 1949 Eskimos season, was considering job offers from an oil company that would have taken him to Peru. It appears Kiniski, by his early twenties, had an interest and some experience in power generation and engineering, as his Eskimos biographical sketch in an unidentified local paper (though likely the *Edmonton Journal*) in 1949 records his non-football profession as "Engineer, City Power House." In a Canadian Press article written about a dozen years later, Stephen Scott reports Kiniski "was working in the Edmonton thermal electric plant" in the late 1940s or early in 1950, and in the 1971 *Province* feature, Kiniski told Kirkwood, "I'm fascinated by heavy equipment.... I enjoy thermo-electric plants, you know. I'll go out of my way to visit one any time I have the chance." As far as the Peru offers were concerned, Watson reports they "are said to be out of this world." If that was the case, chances are they warranted serious consideration in Kiniski's mind on the heels of his low-paying 1949 season with the Eskimos.

But as it turned out, both Kiniski and Steve Paproski would accept athletic scholarships to the University of Arizona, where they were Arizona Wildcats teammates under freshman coach Frank Sancet during the 1950 season. According to a mainly unidentifiable article from Kiniski's collection, Paproski came to Arizona in February of 1950, stayed several weeks, and then, after returning to Edmonton, persuaded Kiniski to attend university with him in sunny Tucson later that year.

Between stints with the Edmonton Eskimos, Kiniski had success as a freshman and sophomore lineman for the University of Arizona Wildcats from 1950 to 1951. In Arizona Kiniski caught the attention of pro scouts and became a strong NFL prospect (Kiniski family archive).

The article says Kiniski didn't need a lot of convincing because "it gets down to 35 degrees below zero in Alberta in winter." Multiple sources credit Bill Radovich, a former NFLer who later rose to fame for getting a ruling in U.S. courts subjecting professional football to antitrust laws, with recommending the two young players from Alberta for their scholarships. In 1949 Radovich, blackballed from playing in the NFL after trying to jump teams, worked as a line coach for the Eskimos.

The article reporting Paproski's visit to Tucson in February of 1950—titled "Football Puzzles Frosh Gridders"—also makes much of the fact that, in Canada, Kiniski and Paproski had played a form of football more akin to rugby and, in many ways, had to learn to play football again after arriving at the Wildcats' training camp in Huachuca, Arizona, about 70 miles southeast of Tucson. Yet the two soon caught on and became strong members of Arizona's 1950 undefeated freshman squad. As far as Kiniski was concerned, he had two productive seasons as a Wildcats lineman and, wearing number 76, became a strong NFL prospect.

In an article from Kiniski's collection likely from the *Houston Chronicle* a few years later, in August of 1956, Benjamin "Boo" Odem—identified by Kiniski in a February 2002 interview with Canadian journalist and author Greg Oliver as a former next-door neighbor (Oliver, Files)—characterizes Kiniski as "the most penalized lineman in the history of Arizona." According to Odem—who in the article confirms he occupied a room next to Kiniski's in a University of Arizona athletic dorm in 1951 and says he once came out on the short end of a scuffle with his neighbor—Kiniski, prior to arriving in Arizona, "was touted as one of the roughest and meanest tackles ever produced in Edmonton." Odem reports Kiniski received most of his penalties with the Wildcats for unnecessary roughness and "was tossed out of three games for this type of play."

Another hard-to-place article from Kiniski's collection, likely published about a quarter century after his college years, indicates that when the young Wildcat's parents came down from Edmonton to watch him in a game—probably in Eugene, Oregon, as Kiniski, in his February 2002 interview with Oliver, spoke of such a visit (Oliver, Files)—Kiniski had a bad day as "he was smeared and stepped on by opposing players." The article continues, "After the game Mrs. Kiniski looked at her battered son and suggested he might find something better to do."

In a sense that's exactly what happened, as Gene Kiniski would never play another down of collegiate football following his otherwise strong 1951 sophomore season.

3

Arizona Wildcat

Looking back on the three semesters he spent at the University of Arizona, Kiniski, in an unidentified article marking his return to Tucson in 1971, said, "Living in Tucson and attending the university was the highlight of my life. Those are memories I'll always cherish." On at least several occasions, Kiniski publicly acknowledged Wildcats head coach Bob Winslow—who left the University of Arizona at about the same time Kiniski did—as a key influence who helped prepare him for success.

While Grabow says, "I don't think he ever attended a class," Kiniski, who Scott says concentrated on studies in mechanical engineering before switching to physical education, in later years would credit a speech course he took at Arizona with helping him develop the verbal skills he would become so noted for. In the same 1971 article, Kiniski said, "I learned to express myself. That's important. You have to be able to go on the radio and television and motivate people. You have to sell yourself."

That is just one illustration of how it appears Kiniski had more than an inkling while in college of what career path would bring him to fame afterward. Another such illustration is that Kiniski, while careful to meet all his football obligations, also made some time to keep up with his wrestling.

Though it appears he never talked about it with his sons, clippings indicate Kiniski did some competitive amateur wrestling in Arizona and decisively earned a state heavyweight title while attending university. Some sources indicate Kiniski took the state title twice and owned the Border Conference Heavyweight title while attending Arizona. In some circles over the following decades, he was recognized as the only individual ever to have won both a Canadian provincial and a state amateur heavyweight championship. Whether or not Kiniski actually was the first or only person to have done so, newspaper accounts and anecdotes from the time do indicate Kiniski pulled off the rare double feat he was credited with.

Yet numerous reports indicate that, as far as wrestling was concerned, even while in college Kiniski gave most of his attention to wrestling of the professional variety. And while he had become acquainted in Edmonton with future Alberta Sports Hall of Famer Stu Hart, Al Oeming, and a few others who were already known in professional wrestling, it was in Tucson that Kiniski seemed to have his first serious introduction to the sport.

The manner in which he did so is notable.

In an unidentified newspaper article from Arizona in the early 1970s, Tucson promoter Rod Fenton—an Edmonton native himself who knew the Kiniski family—looked back about two decades and recalled, "These two kids from the University of Arizona tried to sneak in the back way into the [Tucson] Sports Center and they were caught by a couple of our wrestlers. They threw the kids out ... not bodily, of course. Later I heard a ruckus out front and there they were. The two kids were hollering, 'Bring those wrestlers out here. We'll fight 'em.'"

Fenton continued,

> One thing led to another and they admitted they were broke and needed jobs. That started it all off. Gene Kiniski and Steve Paproski started to work as ushers at the wrestling matches, and they also brought down eight or 10 other kids from the University.
> Kiniski had been a pretty good wrestler up at Canada and when he entered the state meet in Arizona he cleaned up on everyone. He flattened one opponent after another in a matter of seconds.
> Meanwhile, Kiniski had advanced to selling programs for me and he and the football players were doing a great job. We had a lot of pretty mad spectators at the wrestling matches in those days and the big football players did a good job handling the fans.

Patrice Fenton, Rod's daughter, recalls that the football players hired on by her father served as bouncers as much as ushers. "They were called the Goon Squad," she says.

In a Vancouver (BC) *Columbian* article by Glyn Lewis, apparently from 1962, Fenton said that when he took Kiniski on as an usher, "I put him on the payroll at $2.50 a night."

That payment paid off for Fenton when young usher Gene Kiniski quickly got involved—as Tony Tselentis reports in an otherwise unidentified clipping, though almost certainly from the *Tucson Daily Citizen*—when "tempers flared at the Sports Center last night" and wrestler "Monte LaDue was waylaid ... by a fan with a steel chair and was saved only by the quick action of an usher as a minor riot broke out."

Tselentis writes, "Big Gene Kiniski of the Arizona football squad hustled LaDue into the auxiliary dressing room while other ushers pounced on the would-be assailant and his cohorts."

In later years Kiniski would be more noted as an instigator of riots.

Besides earning his stripes and a few dollars as an usher and program-seller at Tucson's Wednesday night wrestling shows, Kiniski also took whatever opportunities he had to work out with Fenton and with wrestlers who were in town for the shows—most notably, Dorrance "Dory" Funk, Sr., an extremely tough Texan who cast a strong influence on the wrestling business for decades; Lorigo

Pierre LaBelle had already been wrestling for about 16 years when he gave Kiniski some attention as the younger wrestler was trying to break in and make a name in the early 1950s. Though never a major name in the wrestling industry, LaBelle had a solid career that took him to numerous territories before he finally hung up his wrestling boots in the late 1960s (Kiniski family archive).

"Tony" Morelli, more of a journeyman but one Kiniski always acknowledged as a trainer who helped pave his way to becoming a wrestler; and Pierre LaBelle, another solid journeyman whose career, like Morelli's, began during the Depression and lasted until the 1960s.

While many details are difficult or impossible to confirm, there are numerous accounts suggesting Kiniski's contact with professional wrestling during his period of attendance at the University of Arizona went beyond ushering, selling programs, working out with wrestlers, or saving wrestlers from irate fans. Most such accounts involve fellow Wildcat and usher Paproski, suggesting the pair did some professional wrestling while attending university in Tucson. In an article from Kiniski's collection, likely from late 1979 or early 1980, Jim Kearney, who interviewed Paproski before writing the article, says the pair wrestled outside Tucson in order to protect their identities and their status as collegiate footballers.

Kearney writes,

> The outside assumed-name wrestling, so that they could keep themselves in pocket money, ended when a picture of the pair as Canada's contribution to the Arizona Wildcats appeared in a Tucson paper.
>
> After a few phone calls from wrestling fans in the boondocks identifying the 290-pound guy on the left [Paproski] as Killer Mike Murphy, the coach called them in and ordered them to cease and desist. Otherwise, they would be turned into pillars of salt by NCAA headquarters.

Kearny goes on to quote Paproski: "At university we'd do anything to make a buck. Gene and I then got a job unloading cartons of Purina dog chow from boxcars. The pay was to have been $1.50 an hour, but we made a deal to do it by contract—$75 a carload. Because we were a couple of pretty big and strong kids, it really paid off. In eight hours we could unload five cars."

Due to a family emergency back in Alberta, Paproski's stay at the University of Arizona lasted only about a year, and in 1951 he was back with the Eskimos. It is unclear whether Gene Kiniski may have seen things differently had his friend been able to stay longer in Tucson, but as it turned out, after playing out his strong sophomore season with the 6–5 Arizona Wildcats, Kiniski made a decision his parents could not talk him out of. In an article by Lou Pavlovich in what appears to be an early 1952 edition of the *Tucson Daily Citizen* or the *Arizona Daily Star*, Kiniski said, of his parents, "They disapprove of my [decision to wrestle professionally]. They hate that. Even if I drove up to the house in a Cadillac, they still wouldn't like it."

But by now a known local commodity coming into his own as a confident spokesman of the emerging Kiniski brand, Kiniski was not about to change course once his decision was made, and, as the *Daily Citizen* reported on February 8, 1952, "Gene Kiniski trades his gridiron togs for a pair of wrestling shorts to make his professional mat debut at the Sports Center next Wednesday." The report goes on to say, "Promoter Rod Fenton, who has been training the young grappler, predicts big things for him in the mat world."

4

Learning the Ropes

According to a January 16, 1952, Lethbridge (Alberta) *Herald* report four weeks before his pro wrestling debut, Kiniski "said in a letter to an Edmonton friend that he has been approached by coach Frankie Filchock of Edmonton's football Eskimos. But he says he doubts if [the] Eskimos can match the lucrative professional wrestling contract he has been offered in Tucson."

As Kiniski had learned in 1949, pro football was no sure ticket to a healthy salary. Pro footballers in that era, even in the NFL, were not the high earners they would later become, and there are numerous stories about all-star caliber football players returning to their hometowns during the off-season to work at menial jobs in order to pay the bills. A few who were skilled enough in both sports—most notably, football Hall of Famers Bronko Nagurski and Leo Nomellini—would alternate between football season and a wrestling-heavy off-season. It was even common for some pro footballers to wrestle during the football season, as would be evident in Edmonton during the early 1950s.

While an unidentified clipping from Kiniski's collection indicates Honolulu wrestling promoter Al Karasick had considered using him as a special referee when the Wildcats were in Hawaii for the final football game of Kiniski's collegiate career, there seems to be no evidence that Kiniski set foot in a wrestling ring during his late 1951 visit to Hawaii. What *is* well reported is that his debut as a pro wrestler took place on February 13, 1952, in Tucson. Kiniski was featured on the cover of the official program sold that night for a dime at the Sports Center and billed as "probably the roughest man ever to don an Arizona football uniform." As the *Daily Citizen* reported the next day, Kiniski's debut "proved a roaring success as he rode Curly Hughes to the mat in 12 minutes to take last night's one-fall special attraction at the Sports Center."

The *Daily Citizen* continues, "Hughes managed to open a cut over one of Kiniski's eyes before the fall. Gene set up his win with a series of body blocks. After the decision, Hughes wouldn't quit, so Kiniski gave him a few more jolts for good measure."

Little is known about Hughes except that his wrestling career appears to have begun in Arizona more than a decade before his encounter with Kiniski. Few records seem to exist that document any matches Hughes may have been involved in between an undercard appearance on a show in Phoenix on May 20, 1940, and Kiniski's debut on February 13, 1952.

Kiniski's second documented professional wrestling match took place five days later in Albuquerque, New Mexico. His opponent was Ivan the Terrible, played by a veteran wrestler also known as Daffy Don Lee. Kiniski was victorious in their midcard encounter and followed it up with a midcard victory over Ace Abbott the next night in El Paso, Texas.

During the early months of his wrestling career, Kiniski wrestled mainly in Tucson, Albuquerque, and El Paso, scoring wins over some still-familiar names including Tom Renesto, Sam Menacher, and Bob Geigel. But, while cast as a credible heavyweight who could go toe-to-toe with any opponent, Kiniski lost more documented matches than he won during the early stretch of his career in Arizona, New Mexico, and Texas. Among opponents who got the better of the rookie Kiniski were ring veterans Danny Savich, Ace Freeman, and Dory Funk, Sr.

Savich, a Utah native, had been a successful wrestler dating back to the Depression, briefly holding a version of the World Junior Heavyweight title in 1938. He went on to wrestle throughout much of the United States, often in main events, although he was never a nationally known wrestling star in the United States or in Canada, where he appeared at times in the 1930s and 1940s. From 1950 until the end of his career more than a decade later, Savich wrestled primarily in the southwestern United States, becoming a regional star as a heel, or villain, in Texas and Arizona. In Texas he was recognized as the state's heavyweight champion in 1951, and in March of that year—simultaneously holding the National Wrestling Alliance (NWA) Texas Heavyweight championship and a share of the NWA Texas Tag Team title—Savich unsuccessfully challenged NWA Heavyweight champion Lou Thesz in the Dallas Sportatorium.

Savich was a known wrestler in Tucson when he first faced, and defeated, Kiniski there on March 12, 1952, four weeks into Kiniski's career, on a show on which one of the wrestlers on the card, "Dr." Lee Grable, was scheduled, according to that night's Sports Center program, to give "his famous demonstration of mass hypnotism." While a Kiniski-Savich return match at the Sports Center the following week went to a no contest, Savich—playing a vicious heel testing a rugged but fair-minded youngster—earned further victories in singles and tag team encounters with Kiniski during the following weeks in Tucson, El Paso, and Albuquerque. The April 2, 1952, *El Paso Times* reports that nearly 5,000 fans had turned out the previous night to watch Kiniski maul Savich in a losing effort in what the paper says was the first main event of Kiniski's career. In all, Savich and Kiniski appear to have met at least seven times during Kiniski's initial months as a pro wrestler, with Savich apparently never losing a decision to the newcomer yet helping establish Kiniski in the Southwest as a tough youngster who could battle it out on nearly even terms with a proven veteran of championship stock.

Zoltan "Ace Freeman" Friedman was a Hungarian native and a quick, ground-based "scientific" wrestler who had been semi-successful, appearing from coast to coast in the United States for about a decade before becoming a regular in the Tucson and Amarillo, Texas, promotions during the late 1940s and staying there well into the 1950s. By the time Kiniski debuted as a wrestler in 1952, Ace Freeman was an established performer in the Southwest, and it was hardly a surprise that he was booked to have the upper hand in the only singles meeting it appears he had with the rookie Kiniski. Friedman and Kiniski also had a few tag team encounters in Texas and Arizona, and the pair found themselves on the same side during a six-man (three-against-three) main event in Tucson on April 30, 1952. In all likelihood, Freeman was a veteran Kiniski could learn from, as, several years later, Freeman settled in the Pittsburgh, Pennsylvania, area, where he is credited with training East Coast and international wrestling legend Bruno Sammartino, who would face Kiniski numerous times from 1962 to 1965.

Among wrestlers Kiniski faced during his 1952 rookie year, the most impactful over the long term undoubtedly was Funk Sr., one of his trainers. An Indiana native and ex-amateur wrestler, Funk had wrestled mainly in the Midwest for several years before becoming a regular in the Southwest in the late 1940s. Funk was between Amarillo-territory Southwest Junior Heavyweight title runs when he engaged in an opening-match singles draw with Kiniski and a main-event three-on-three loss to the team including the Kiniski-Freeman duo—with both matches occurring on the same Tucson show on April 30, 1952. Six weeks later, in what would turn out to be one of Kiniski's last matches of his rookie year, Funk, who apparently wrestled in three matches on the show, earned a singles victory over Kiniski.

But perhaps Kiniski's most potentially intriguing opponent during his time based in Arizona was a wrestler billed as the Masked Marvel, one of many such-named competitors in the history of professional wrestling. While it is unclear how many times this Masked Marvel and Kiniski met in the ring, Canadian Parliamentarian (later Quebec premier) Jean Charest, quoted at openparliament.ca, said, on the floor of Parliament on January 20, 1994, "[The Masked Marvel] would from time to time wrestle against a gentleman named Gene Kiniski. Of course Gene would win on one day and [the Masked Marvel], if you can believe the coincidence, would always win the next day and so on it would go. In some matches they in fact became a tag team."

Charest's tribute to the Masked Marvel took place shortly after Parliament convened in early 1994 following the death of Steve Paproski, who had spent a quarter-century as a Member of Parliament until his death in December of 1993. Charest confided that Canada's Governor General Ray Hnatyshyn, a friend of Paproski's who shared his Ukrainian roots, had been the one to reveal, while delivering a eulogy at Paproski's funeral, that Paproski, while attending the University of Arizona on scholarship more than four decades earlier, "had very little means [and] supplemented his revenue" by wrestling on the side. Presumably to protect his status as an amateur athlete in the United States, "he became known as the Masked Marvel."

Although a documented match between Gene Kiniski and a Masked Marvel took place in El Paso on June 17, 1952, it was not Paproski behind the mask that night but Herbert "Buddy Knox" Knotts, who had a long career and, for a few years in the late 1940s and 1950s, enjoyed a successful run in several territories as the Masked Marvel. No records seem to exist of any professional wrestling appearance by a Masked Marvel in the U.S. Southwest that would correspond with the period when Steve Paproski attended the University of Arizona.

But the story takes a slightly different turn when Pat Paproski, a son of Steve's now living in Vancouver, is asked by telephone to comment. Pat Paproski says he is familiar with stories about his father's brief wrestling career and suspects Kiniski and his father sneaked in a little wrestling on the side while both were amateur footballers at Arizona. "At least that's the story," Pat Paproski says. "This is what I was told—that they would slide into Mexico and team up as a wrestling duo when they were playing football down in Arizona. I don't know that the coaches knew that, [but] I remember my dad saying they had a few nights with a lot of fun going down [to Mexico] and tag teaming."

Meanwhile, Grabow, though unaware of any professional wrestling Steve Paproski may have done in Mexico, backs up the story of Kiniski wrestling professionally while attending university. On a visit to Tucson when Kiniski was a Wildcat, Grabow says, "I went across the border [to Mexico] with my ex-wife. We were on our honeymoon."

In Nogales, Mexico, he says, he had occasion to see Kiniski wrestle under a mask as the Hooded Terror. Asked what he figured put his friend up to that, he says life was not easy back on campus even for a star athlete on a football scholarship. At the time Kiniski was crisscrossing the border for wrestling matches before hiding his mask and slipping back into the college dorm, Grabow says, of whatever paydays his friend could wangle out of wrestling a match here and there under the radar of the coaches at Arizona, "That's the only money he had."

5

Return to the Gridiron

As Kiniski wrestled in Arizona, New Mexico, and Texas during the late winter and spring of 1952, typically earning about $300 to $400 a week, he had the attention of pro football scouts interested in securing the services of a large, rugged lineman who had performed well as an Edmonton Eskimo and a major college standout.

Among scouts wanting to take a close look at Kiniski was Ed Kotal of the Los Angeles Rams, who had a talk with Kiniski when he came to Tucson to scout football talent. According to the March 17, 1952, *Tucson Daily Citizen*, "Kotal was impressed with Gene's size and liked what he heard from Bob Winslow about his defensive possibilities." The *Daily Citizen* reports, "[Kotal] would like to see Kiniski show up at the Los Angeles camp when practice opens late this summer." A letter to Kiniski from Rams owner Dan Reeves, dated March 20, 1952, confirms the Rams' interest in signing Kiniski for the coming season provided NFL Commissioner Bert Bell would waive, in Kiniski's case, the league requirement that signees who dropped out of college had to wait until four years after starting college to play in the NFL. When special dispensation apparently was not forthcoming, Kiniski continued wrestling in the Arizona, New Mexico, and Texas circuit until early summer.

But while showing unusual promise as a rookie in the pro wrestling ranks, it was clear he had not lost interest in football—and though the 23-year-old Kiniski was a legitimate NFL prospect, it was not with the Rams or any other NFL franchise that the next and final stage of his pro football career would play out.

The *El Paso Herald-Post* reported, on June 3, 1952, "Gene Kiniski, the former Arizona gridder now making wrestling his life's work, will leave late this month for training with the Edmonton, Canada football team." In fact, Kiniski wrestled in Arizona, Texas, and New Mexico through June and into early July before returning to Alberta, getting in a little football training during the Eskimos preseason camp, and kicking off the regular season with the Eskimos on August 23.

The 1952 season was a relatively successful one for the Edmonton Eskimos, as the team compiled a 9–6–1 regular season record and won a two-game total-points Western Interprovincial Football Union semifinal series and a best-of-three WIFU final before representing the WIFU in the single-game Grey Cup championship, losing to the Interprovincial Rugby Football Union's (IRFU's) Toronto Argonauts. A few years later the WIFU and the IRFU would merge and take the lead in forming the Canadian Football League (CFL).

But while the 1952 season was a good one overall for the Eskimos, it was disastrous for Kiniski, who suffered a serious injury during the first game, August 23 in Regina,

The Los Angeles RAMS

REPRESENTING LOS ANGELES IN THE NATIONAL CONFERENCE OF THE NATIONAL FOOTBALL LEAGUE

7813 BEVERLY BOULEVARD
LOS ANGELES 36, CALIFORNIA
WEbster 3-8291

April 28, 1952

Mr. Gene Kiniski
1540 N. First Avenue
Tucson, Arizona

Dear Gene:

Thank you for your letter of April 22nd, explaining your decision to sign with the Canadian Club.

We would appreciate your returning the contract which we sent you and are enclosing herewith stamped, addressed envelope for your convenience.

Wishing you the best of luck, I am

Very truly yours,

THE LOS ANGELES FOOTBALL CLUB

Joseph Stydahar
Head Coach

JS:mh

Following a productive season with the Edmonton Eskimos and two seasons of college football at Arizona, Kiniski was a strong NFL prospect who earned a contract offer from the Los Angeles Rams. When technicalities related to dropping out of college stalled his NFL chances, Kiniski continued wrestling for a few months before returning to Canada and rejoining the Eskimos (Kiniski family archive).

Saskatchewan, when he reportedly ruptured a ligament in his right knee—which some reports indicate was broken—while attempting to block a member of the opposing Roughriders. It was quickly determined that Kiniski would be out of action for the season, and there was plenty of speculation that his football days would be over entirely. But Kiniski, instead of throwing in the towel, threw *himself*, almost immediately, into rehab as it was understood at the time. Grabow says, "You can't imagine what he went through with this knee injury…. His knee was virtually shattered. They said he would never play football or wrestle again, and this guy got into a gymnasium. He worked eight to ten hours a day strengthening a totally damaged knee [until] that bad knee became better than his regular knee."

A few 1952 Eskimos who fared better that season than Kiniski did would remain close friends of his for decades afterward. One was Paproski, who had rejoined the Eskimos in 1951 after his collegiate season in Arizona. According to Pat Paproski, his father cut short his stay in Arizona and returned to Alberta in order to help support his family when Steve's father was battling cancer. Steve Paproski would be a star lineman with the Eskimos until 1954 before running a construction business and, in 1968, beginning a 25-year political career, representing his Edmonton riding in Parliament until his death.

Two other teammates of Kiniski's on the 1952 Eskimos roster would, like Kiniski, become more noted for their achievements in the wrestling world than for what they achieved on the gridiron.

Wilbur Snyder, a 240-pound tackle and kicker originally from California, spent the 1952 and 1953 seasons with the Eskimos before becoming a nationally known young, clean-cut wrestler—noted for an assortment of basic "scientific" wrestling moves with a few football tackles thrown in—during mid-1950s broadcasts of wrestling from Chicago's Marigold Arena on the DuMont Television Network. Snyder had debuted, in California, as a wrestler in 1952 prior to joining the Eskimos later that year. Following his rookie season with the Eskimos, he returned to California to wrestle during the off-season. He also wrestled in Utah, where he had attended college, prior to rejoining the Eskimos for the 1953 season, and in July of that year—very early in anyone's career for such an opportunity to take place—Snyder challenged Lou Thesz in Salt Lake City for the National Wrestling Alliance Heavyweight title. Then, during the height of the 1953 Canadian football season, Snyder participated in several Edmonton main events for the Oeming-Hart promotion before heading back to California once his football commitments in Alberta were over, wrestling full-time, and never looking back.

Meanwhile, Joe Blanchard, a teammate of Kiniski's who was with the Eskimos from 1951 to 1953, also had a successful wrestling career. Like Snyder, Blanchard appeared with Big Time Wrestling—the forerunner of Calgary-based Stampede Wrestling—during his stay in Alberta and would wrestle in numerous territories over the next quarter century. Originally from Oklahoma, Blanchard would also become an owner-promoter when he established the San Antonio-based Southwest Championship Wrestling promotion in the late 1970s, and, like Snyder, he would cross paths with Kiniski many times following their stint as Edmonton Eskimos teammates.

Not fully over the effects of his knee injury, Kiniski, according to a March 4, 1953, Canadian Press report, informed the Eskimos that he was planning to retire from football to return to wrestling, which figured to be easier on his knee. But as it turned out, CFL/WIFU records show Kiniski's knee was sufficiently rehabilitated to allow him to turn in some strong play while appearing in 13 regular-season games for the Eskimos in 1953.

On September 22, 1953, just short of the midpoint of a healthy 12–4 regular season for the Eskimos, Kiniski returned to the pro wrestling ring at an Edmonton show promoted by Oeming, who would leave the wrestling business a few years later and gain some fame as a zoologist and naturalist—according to people who knew him, his true calling in life, which his years in wrestling promotion enabled him to fund. Edmonton was a weekly stop on the circuit run out of Calgary by Stu Hart, a former Eskimo himself, and on the September 22 show Kiniski quietly disposed of veteran journeyman Toar Morgan in a match that appears to have drawn surprisingly little interest or press coverage.

5. Return to the Gridiron

Kiniski (50), Wilbur Snyder (63), and Joe Blanchard (60) were Edmonton Eskimos teammates under coach Darrell Royal in 1953. Kiniski, Snyder, and Blanchard would go on to achieve fame as wrestlers, and Royal would become best known as the football coach at the University of Texas, where he won three U.S. national championships (Kiniski family archive).

It is unclear whether, prior to his match with Morgan, Kiniski had the opportunity to work out with Saskatchewan native Earl McCready, one of the great amateur and professional wrestlers of the late 1920s–early 1950s era, who frequently appeared on shows in Alberta in the 1950s prior to retiring late in the decade. In any event, Kiniski, in his February 2002 interview with Oliver, named McCready, along with all-time great Ed "Strangler" Lewis, as a highly respected grappler who took the time to pass some of the finer points of wrestling on to him. Of McCready, Kiniski said the veteran "showed [him] a lot of moves" (Oliver, Files).

After his September 22, 1953, match with Morgan, Kiniski, perhaps not wanting to test his knee too much yet—or perhaps in keeping with a general understanding that footballers, as the playoffs got near, ought to concentrate solely on the gridiron—did not wrestle again until the Eskimos' season was over following a loss in the WIFU final series against the Winnipeg Blue Bombers.

Before his August 1952 injury on the football field—which Bruce Hart, a son of Stu's, says his father reported Kiniski blamed on "heat" (or bad blood) he had with Roughriders star tackle Martin Ruby—Kiniski had been scheduled to appear on a wrestling show the following month promoted by Oeming at Edmonton's Sales Pavilion, according to an *Edmonton Journal* clipping from Kiniski's collection. The clipping pictures Kiniski in his

Eskimos uniform and is hand-dated August 23, 1952—the same day he suffered his injury. It is unclear whether Kiniski had plans to wrestle steadily during the Eskimos' 1952 season, but it seems likely he would have gotten back into the ring during the off-season, likely in the Tucson loop—as he indicated he would do, prior to rejoining the Eskimos—had his knee been up to it.

Dave Meltzer, editor of the *Wrestling Observer Newsletter*, reports in the April 28, 2010, *Observer* that Kiniski sought a $1,000 raise to return to the Eskimos in 1954 but was turned down. As Kiniski, who earned in the range of $7,000 to $8,000 in 1953, put it himself a few years later in an article by Maurice Smith,

> You'll remember that in 1953 Darrell Royal was coach of the Edmonton Eskimos. He thought that I was a pretty good lineman and at the end of the season told me he'd probably be able to get me more money next year.
>
> Well, you know what happened! Royal didn't return to Edmonton. Instead he accepted a coaching job at Washington State. After Pop Ivy took over as coach, the club wouldn't give me the increase I wanted, so I quit.

Shortly after the Eskimos' 1953 season-ending loss to the Blue Bombers, Kiniski packed his bags again and headed south; and while the Eskimos won the Grey Cup—Canada's equivalent to the Super Bowl—the following season, it is unlikely Kiniski had any regrets about his decision to close the curtain on his football career. As Smith writes, "Kiniski says he'll thank Darrell Royal to his dying day for accepting the job at Washington."

6

Long Road to Hollywood

In December of 1953 Kiniski was back in Arizona, where he appeared weekly on wrestling shows in Tucson until April of 1954. Records also exist of Kiniski appearances in Phoenix and Mesa, Arizona, and El Paso, Texas, during this period in which Kiniski renewed friendships and acquaintances and retraced some familiar paths on his wrestling journey.

But as familiar as parts of the journey were, this time around it was, in a big sense, completely different. Kiniski was no longer setting his own course—a course for one—but was now making his way through the wrestling circuit and through life with a bride some observers have characterized as the most fetching beauty ever to come out of Daysland, Alberta.

On December 7, 1953, Gene Kiniski and Marion "Bunny" Weller were married at St. Mary's Cathedral in Edmonton. The best man was Gene's older brother Julian, and ushers were Paproski and Mario DeMarco, both teammates of Kiniski's on the Eskimos.

While it is unclear exactly when Gene and Marion first met, it was apparently during Kiniski's second run with the Eskimos that Marion showed up in Edmonton from Daysland, a village about 70 miles south of Chipman.

Chipman native Steven Eleniak, who as a youngster knew the Kiniskis in Chipman and, like Gene Kiniski, made the move to Edmonton during his youth, kept in some contact with the Kiniski family after relocating to the city. Eleniak also made the acquaintance of Marion "Bunny" Weller, new in town and an employee at the Canadian Bank of Commerce. "She lived [in a basement suite] in my wife's sister's place," Eleniak says. While unsure when it took place, Eleniak recalls a conversation he had with Gene Kiniski. "I think it was one Saturday we were talking, and he didn't have a girlfriend," he says. "Bunny was relatively new in town," although, says Eleniak, she had been dating a pool shark known locally as "the Minnesota Fats of Edmonton."

Eleniak arranged a meeting between Gene and Marion, to his best recollection, at the Rainbow Ballroom in Edmonton. "That's pretty fuzzy stuff," Eleniak says more than six decades after that meeting took place, "but I think that's where they first met."

According to Eleniak, Marion, 5'9" with a model's looks, did not take immediately to the rugged young man she was introduced to. "For whatever reason, Bunny didn't seem to like him. I don't think she went with him for a while."

As Kelly Kiniski puts it, "My dad was an ugly pro football player, and she didn't want anything to do with him."

Even so, it wasn't long until Marion fell under the spell of Gene Kiniski—as he had fallen under hers. They became a couple, apparently while Kiniski was rehabilitating his knee, and Eleniak says the couple may have lived together briefly in Edmonton after Marion left, unannounced, from her suite sometime in 1953. According to Eleniak, his sister-in-law Mary, Marion's landlord, contacted Marion's bank and was told she had left her job on short notice. "There was about a month there," says Eleniak, "where Mary was upset because she didn't know what happened to her."

Barely a week after the couple's marriage, Gene Kiniski was back in Tucson, headlining his share of shows mainly at the Tucson Garden, the venue Fenton moved his Wednesday night cards to near the end of 1953 when his Sports Center lease expired. With his base reestablished in Tucson, Kiniski set off for matches in a few other centers in the Southwest. Kelly Kiniski says, "Mom and Dad went on the road [and] had a great time.... My dad would drive during the day, and at night Dad would drink and my mom would drive."

Kiniski's roughly half-year stay back in the Southwest was especially notable for a couple of reasons. One was the opportunity for Kiniski to get reacquainted with wrestlers who had been generous in giving him time and attention when he was just breaking into pro wrestling.

Tony Morelli was already a 19-year ring veteran in his mid-forties when he faced Kiniski in a Tucson tag team match on February 10, 1954. Morelli, who would wrestle in a second match later on that same show, continued his career until his mid-fifties, appear-

December 7, 1953. Newlyweds Gene and Marion Kiniski on their wedding day in Edmonton (Kiniski family archive).

6. Long Road to Hollywood 39

December 1953. Gene relaxes with a cigar in Las Vegas while en route with bride Marion to Tucson, Arizona (Kiniski family archive).

ing across much of the United States as well as in a small promotion based in North Bay, Ontario, and in Alberta during the latter years of his career. Though he was a headliner only in smaller promotions, Morelli was a respected professional, and probably one nobody respected more than Kiniski did.

Dory Funk, Sr., had worked out with Kiniski and faced him several times on shows in 1952 prior to Kiniski's return to the Eskimos. After Kiniski returned to Alberta in July of 1952, Funk wrestled primarily in Texas and Arizona, and he was the reigning Southwest Junior Heavyweight champion—a title associated with the Amarillo wrestling territory Funk anchored for many years—when Kiniski returned to the U.S. Southwest in December of 1953. On the night of Kiniski's first pro wrestling match after retiring for good from pro football—December 16, 1953—Funk appeared in the main event on the same show, following Kiniski's semifinal match victory in Tucson over veteran John Cretoria with a losing challenge to NWA World Junior Heavyweight titleholder Baron Michele Leone, a well-traveled Italian wrestler best remembered as a headliner in Southern California in the 1950s and a traveling NWA World Junior Heavyweight champion during that same decade.

Within a month, Funk and Kiniski reversed the order of their appearances on a Tucson wrestling show, as Kiniski rapidly worked his way up to the main events. By February of 1954 the two had participated jointly in several Tucson main events, all but one a tag team encounter. In the pair's only singles meeting since his rookie year, on January 20, Kiniski earned a victory over Funk via disqualification. While Funk and Kiniski wrestled in the same territory for only about two months in 1954, Funk apparently continued to make himself accessible to Kiniski and spent time helping him develop as a wrestler; and in later years Kiniski would readily acknowledge that Funk had been a key figure in training him to be a championship wrestler.

There is a two-month gap, during the spring of 1954, in the documented record of Kiniski's career. That is at least partly accounted for by a turn of events a young Canadian advancing his career in the United States almost certainly would not have predicted.

In between losing a match on April 7 in Tucson to Elmer Larsen and turning up in Southern California in June, Kiniski, as reported in the April 8, 1954, *Daily Citizen*, was scheduled to report for U.S. Army examination in Phoenix and then for duty in Fort Bliss, Texas, near El Paso, "if his 'football knee' passes physical examination" and it was determined Kiniski was fit for military service. While it was well known around Tucson that Kiniski was from Canada and did not have U.S. citizenship, Kelly Kiniski, born in 1957, says his father faced the draft mainly because of pressure on the army from wrestling fans who believed that even a rugged Canadian known to bend the rules in the wrestling ring would stand to benefit from military service.

Some of that may be the stuff of wrestling legend because Kiniski in fact, while known to rough it up with opponents and to cause a little mayhem among spectators, was a popular wrestler at that point in his career—particularly around Tucson, where he was regarded much in the manner of a local college hero and hometown boy. In fact, during the early part of his career Kiniski was as noted for coming to the ring in an Arizona Wildcats jacket as he would later be noted for wearing a blue "Canada" warm-up jacket before his matches.

Although the *Daily Citizen* reported Kiniski was looking at serving a two-year stint in the U.S. Army as a fast track to gaining U.S. citizenship—which Gene Kiniski never acquired even after living in the United States throughout most of his wrestling career and for many years afterward—the army ended up turning Kiniski away from any obligation to serve. It is unclear whether his citizenship status, concerns about his

Early 1954. Gene Kiniski (left) and fellow Albertan and Tucson wrestling promoter Rod Fenton. Fenton paved the way for Kiniski to become a pro wrestler while the latter attended university in Tucson, and the two had a close association in Arizona in the 1950s and in British Columbia in the 1960s (Kiniski family archive).

Top: May 30, 1954. Gene and Marion Kiniski (at right) enjoy an outing in Ciudad Juárez, Mexico, with friends Tom and Betsy Stolhandske as Gene nears the end of his brush with the U.S. Army across the border in Fort Bliss, Texas. Stolhandske, a teammate of Kiniski's on the 1953 Eskimos, went on to play briefly in the NFL (Kiniski family archive). *Bottom*: June 4, 1954. A note in the Kiniski photograph album identifies this occasion as the night of Gene's discharge from the army. Ten days later, following a two-month halt to his wrestling career, Gene would make his debut in Southern California. Gene and Marion are in the center; the two other men are unidentified (Kiniski family archive).

knee, or both, most influenced that decision, but an unidentified clipping from Kiniski's collection says Kiniski at one point wrote to Al Oeming to tell him he'd passed his army physical. The *Daily Citizen* reports that, had Kiniski been obligated to serve, "Gene estimates his cash slash as from $15,000 to $20,000 a year down to $120 a month."

According to the *Daily Citizen*, Kiniski—whose weight had risen to 260 pounds, up from the 220 to 225 pounds he had been listed at during his football days in college and with the Eskimos—hoped "to 'get in a little wrestling' while in the service.... And as for getting out, it'll probably be 'pro wrestling if I can stay in shape. Unless I can get in an awfully good football offer. And I'll be 27 then.'"

Another unidentified clipping quotes Kiniski: "I wanted to serve in the army, but the doctors kept examining that knee almost every day and they finally decided to discharge me because of it."

Kiniski's military career appears to have lasted about seven weeks. Once his brush with the army was over, his reputation and connections would certainly have allowed him to resume his wrestling career in Arizona, Texas, and other areas in the region where he had begun his career and already earned an excellent reputation, but instead, he and Marion set out for another location, one that would give him an opportunity to become a major star in professional wrestling. And, while many followers of Kiniski's career have observed that he did not have the sort of face normally associated with success in Hollywood—though, by all accounts, Marion did—that was precisely where Kiniski headed for the next stage of his career.

7

Hot in California

Los Angeles-Hollywood had been at the forefront of television production for a national audience since the late 1940s, and L.A.-Hollywood also played a key role in establishing the marriage between professional wrestling and television, which has remained strong ever since. Los Angeles' KTLA-TV became the first station in the United States to broadcast a weekly television wrestling program in 1945, and the success of that show quickly led other TV stations across the United States to produce their own weekly programs in association with local and regional wrestling promotions. Such arrangements were seen as obvious win-win situations, as the channels could attract large local audiences with an action-packed product that was relatively easy and inexpensive to produce, while wrestling promoters learned that an entertaining, compelling hour or two of television wrestling could raise the profile of wrestlers, drive attendance to arenas, and increase profits significantly.

Johnny Doyle, a promoter in the Hollywood-Los Angeles market in the 1950s, was one of the first wrestling promoters in the United States to get TV clearance on a national scale during the early years of American network television. After a couple of years of producing wrestling shows for the local L.A.-Hollywood market, Doyle saw his *Wrestling from Hollywood* program picked up for a time by the Paramount Television Network, a major U.S. network during a brief period in the late 1940s and 1950s. The Paramount Television Network had well over 100 affiliated stations during its short lifetime, reaching the significant population centers in almost every state and spilling over into Canada—especially via Paramount affiliates in Montreal and Winnipeg—and most of the Paramount network affiliates, including the two in Canada, carried *Wrestling from Hollywood*. Doyle also supplied wrestling programming to some ABC-TV affiliates, and by early 1954, as wrestling historian Steve Yohe reports in a post at www.wrestlingclassics.com, "CBS was running a Saturday network show out of the Hollywood Legion Stadium … with national stars like [Buddy] Rogers, [Bill] Longson, and [Antonino] Rocca being brought in to L.A. just for the show and it seems to have been shown in every market."

Doyle left the promotion at about the same time, and according to Tim Hornbaker at www.legacyofwrestling.com, "around May 1954"—the month before Gene Kiniski debuted in Southern California—"the national CBS-TV deal to present professional wrestling from Southern California every Saturday … was cancelled despite a six-year contract." As Hornbaker reports, "There was a clause in the contract that said if the show didn't have a sponsor to pay the $70,000 a week bill for production costs and network time by the 13th week, the program could be cancelled by CBS. And that is precisely what happened."

Despite the loss of the CBS deal and greatly reduced exposure on Paramount, the promotion still had a strong regional television presence when Kiniski had his first recorded match in Southern California on June 14, 1954, facing veteran Vic Christy on the undercard of a show at the Hollywood Legion Stadium. The show was headlined by a main event pitting 27-year ring veteran Karl Davis against former Edmonton Eskimo Wilbur Snyder. Kiniski and Snyder both won their matches.

Snyder, unlike Kiniski, had benefited from the presence of Doyle and the abundance of television opportunities prior to mid-1954. With roughly the same amount of pro wrestling experience as Kiniski, Snyder had already headlined major shows and appeared repeatedly on network television. Since signing a contract with Doyle in March of 1953, Snyder had been featured in matches against name wrestlers such as Fred Blassie, Baron Michele Leone, Danny McShain, and Mr. Moto. After taking a few months off to play his second and final season with the Eskimos—during his off-time, managing to squeeze in several wrestling matches in Edmonton—Snyder returned to Southern California as a full-time wrestler, apparently convinced that a career on the mat would pay significantly more than the reported $8,000 per season he had earned with the Eskimos.

Snyder enjoyed several regional title reigns in the NWA Hollywood territory in 1954, and on March 27, 1954, he wrestled NWA champion Lou Thesz to a 60-minute draw on the CBS network program. According to Yohe in his www.wrestlingclassics.com post, "The great showing made Snyder a national star."

By the time Kiniski debuted in Hollywood in June—with the approval of Rod Fenton, who continued to hold his contract—the promotion's profile had slipped a bit, as Doyle's presence was more of a memory and loss of the CBS show significantly reduced opportunities for grapplers in the territory to make national names. Yet Kiniski got the first television exposure of his career on *Wrestling from Hollywood* and generally won his early matches in the promotion—except sometimes on occasions when he was matched with established stars.

During his second week in the promotion, Kiniski suffered his first loss in California when he teamed with veteran Hans Schnabel to face Snyder and Bobo Brazil. At that point Snyder already had some national recognition and was positioned ahead of Kiniski; Brazil clearly was on the rise toward major stardom after several years as an African American trailblazer in American wrestling; and Kiniski, while generally booked to lose to wrestlers of that caliber during his eight-month-long stay in Southern California, was never made to look weak or overmatched. While losing in singles matches to Snyder and Brazil, Kiniski earned victories over nearly everyone else he faced in Southern California, including former Eskimo teammate Joe Blanchard and former world champion Sandor Szabo.

Kiniski proved a reliable hand and a credible main eventer during his early months in California, and by August he was rewarded with a share of the NWA Inter-

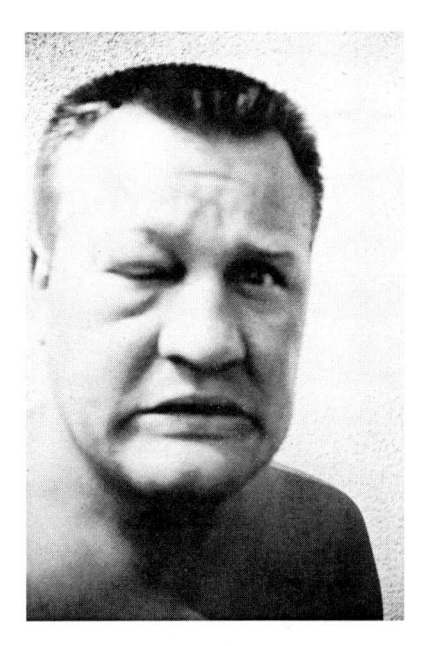

The Kiniski album labels this photograph "Souvenir from Bakersfield"—one of the cities Gene hit while making the rounds in the NWA Hollywood territory in the mid-fifties (Kiniski family archive).

national Television Tag Team championship. His partner was fellow Canadian John Tolos, a Hamilton, Ontario, native who was just 21 when he and Kiniski took the title from Brazil and Snyder in a best-of-three-falls main event on October 13, 1954, at the Grand Olympic Auditorium in Los Angeles. Like Kiniski, Tolos had made a big impression in wrestling, also kicking off his career in Tucson before migrating, at age 20, to California in 1953. During his rookie year Tolos made a name by earning some big victories in both the Southern California and Northern California promotions. In the San Francisco-based Northern California territory, Tolos won his first professional title, just five months into his career, when he and older brother Chris Tolos captured the Pacific Coast Tag Team title.

The Kiniski-Tolos tandem was positioned strongly, reeling off an impressive series of wins over teams consisting of proven wrestlers such as Snyder, Brazil, Szabo, Mike DiBiase, James Blears, Tom Rice, Warren Bockwinkel, and Warren's son and future international headliner and American Wrestling Association (AWA) World Heavyweight champion Nick Bockwinkel. Although Kiniski and Tolos held the title for barely a month, television exposure with a major promotion's title definitely gave their young careers a boost. In Kiniski's case, he continued to lose in singles matches to top competitors such as Brazil and Snyder, but he was clearly positioned near the top of the NWA Hollywood promotion's pecking order.

Wilbur Snyder (left), Warren Bockwinkel (center), and Gene Kiniski meeting out of the ring when all were key players in the NWA Hollywood promotion. Kiniski would later develop friendships with Snyder's and Bockwinkel's sons, Mike Snyder and Nick Bockwinkel (Kiniski family archive).

While still based in Southern California in early 1955, Kiniski made a few appearances in Phoenix, Arizona—one of the cities to which promoter Fenton had branched out from Tucson—twice teaming with Danny "Golden Terror" Plechas to split victories with the team of Dory Funk, Sr., and Bobo Brazil. Kiniski also lost his second-ever NWA Heavyweight title challenge, in Phoenix, to Thesz on January 31, 1955. His first challenge for the NWA title had taken place about three months earlier, on November 3, 1954, when he lost in straight falls to Thesz in a match at the Grand Olympic Auditorium that was televised in the L.A. market. Nearly half a century later, in February of 2002, Kiniski would recall, of Thesz, "He could look at you and hurt you" (Oliver, Files).

Besides Tolos, a tag team partner of note during Kiniski's 1954–1955 stay in California was James Blears, a British native who had held a version of the World Light Heavyweight title from 1947 to 1948. By the time Kiniski got to Southern California, Blears had been a name wrestler there for several years and had earned some national exposure on the

DuMont Television Network's *Wrestling from Marigold* broadcasts from Chicago and on NWA Hollywood broadcasts during the Doyle era. Best known nationally as Lord Blears—a haughty, aristocratic Brit whose character seemed at odds with Kiniski's more rugged, straight-ahead, meat-and-potatoes persona—Blears was a regular tag team opponent during the brief Kiniski-Tolos NWA International Television Tag Team championship reign as well as a partner of Kiniski's both before and after the latter's pairing with Tolos. Blears was a capable wrestler and heel who, while just a few years older than Kiniski, definitely knew the ropes of the wrestling business both in and out of the ring and had plenty of knowledge and experience to pass on to Kiniski.

As Blears recounted of his early impression of Kiniski in Greg Oliver and Steven Johnson's *The Pro Wrestling Hall of Fame: The Heels*, "He was great, knocking people down, knocking the posts down, the big giant. So I said, 'That's the man for me,' and we teamed up" (Oliver and Johnson, 73).

While wrestling in the NWA Hollywood territory, Blears was also a headlining wrestler in the Northern California NWA San Francisco territory run by Joe Malcewicz, a highly regarded wrestler and, like Kiniski, the son of Polish immigrants. Malcewicz had been promoting shows in Northern California since the Depression, and by the early 1950s he was running the San Francisco territory. But in contrast to fellow 1950s promoters such as Doyle, Chicago's Fred Kohler, Toronto's Frank Tunney, and Portland's Don Owen, Malcewicz apparently had no desire to feature his wrestling promotion or its entertainers on television—though he finally came around and produced a TV wrestling show in the 1960s when competing promoter Roy Shire forced his hand before putting him out of business.

Even without television in the 1950s, Malcewicz, as a National Wrestling Alliance promoter, had access to many of the leading wrestlers of the era. Appearing on wrestling shows in San Francisco, Oakland, Sacramento, San Jose, Fresno, and other stops on Malcewicz' circuit were names including Gorgeous George, Bobo Brazil, Leo Nomellini, Bob Orton, Sr., Rikidozan, Mike and Ben Sharpe, Blears, and—making his debut in the territory, in Sacramento, on February 7, 1955—Gene Kiniski.

Kiniski fared well in singles matches during his nine-month stay in Northern California from February to November of 1955—rarely losing except to established stars such as Brazil, Nomellini, Enrique Torres, and Cyclone Anaya—but he made his name in Northern California primarily through continuing his successful tag team partnership with Blears.

Gene Kiniski backstage at the Grand Olympic Auditorium in the summer of 1954. Early in Kiniski's career, his "Arizona" warm-up wear was as much a part of his wrestling attire as his famous "Canada" jacket would later become (Kiniski family archive).

7. Hot in California

As Blears recalled in *The Heels*, "We were attacked every night. In California, Gene and I, I'm not kidding you, had to fight our way out of the ring. We couldn't get out of the ring. The fans wanted to kill us" (Oliver and Johnson, 73).

The rugged Kiniski and the more finesse-oriented Blears held the San Francisco version of the NWA World Tag Team championship three times between May and November, turning back challenges by brother teams Ben and Mike Sharpe, Steve and Gene Stanlee, and Vic and Ted Christy and teams consisting of prominent names in the territory such as Nomellini, Torres, Anaya, Johnny Barend, Ron Etchison, and Bobby Bruns. Kiniski's stay in the San Francisco territory is also notable, in retrospect, for numerous encounters he had with Hungarian native Sandor Kovacs, whose greatest impact on the wrestling business—years later—would be closely associated with Kiniski.

On September 23, 1955, Kiniski was matched in an Oakland main event against NWA Heavyweight champion Thesz, with Thesz apparently winning the deciding fall by disqualification. Another Kiniski disqualification loss followed when he met Thesz in Santa Rosa two weeks later. At that point in his career, while not yet breaking through to the top tier of singles attractions on the West Coast or top contendership for the NWA world title, Kiniski was solidly positioned on the list of regional stars a traveling world champion would likely have to face when traveling the circuit for a week or two in a territory where Kiniski was wrestling.

Bill Radovich (left), pictured with Kiniski, was a former NFLer who successfully took the NFL to court before becoming an Edmonton Eskimos line coach when Kiniski played for the team in 1949. Radovich, credited with paving the way for Kiniski to play football at the University of Arizona, turned up in California after leaving the Eskimos and became a "tough guy" actor in Hollywood films (Kiniski family archive).

In the middle of Kiniski's 1955 Northern California run, he returned to the NWA Hollywood territory, apparently for a single appearance, July 13 at the Olympic Auditorium, against one of the most successful and visible wrestlers in the United States at the time, Buddy Rogers. Rogers was already a much-decorated and nationally known wrestler, and, like Kiniski, he would go on to be a nationally and internationally recognized world champion in the 1960s. In 1955 Rogers, seven years Kiniski's senior and the more established wrestler, headlined shows in Southern California for a few months before taking his arrogant, bleached-blond "Nature Boy" persona to several other territories and to New York's national television platform later that year. Kiniski, back in the Hollywood territory only briefly but remembered there as a young wrestler rising near the top of his profession, lost his July 13 encounter with Rogers two falls to one.

While it appears Kiniski, when he was based in Northern California, did not attract the degree of press attention he had attracted in Alberta, Arizona, or Southern California, there is a report in his hometown newspaper at the time, the *Santa Cruz Sentinel-News*, outlining an incident that took place in November of 1954, when Kiniski was off the road nursing a minor injury. Santa Cruz was one of the cities on Malcewicz' circuit, but to wrestling fans there, Kiniski was no hometown boy but a dastardly villain they loved to hate. Yet the *Sentinel-News* reported, "Gene Kiniski, usually one of the villains during the wrestling shows presented here, has proved he's a hero in real life."

According to the report, "During a walk on the municipal wharf he spied a dog near drowning in the surf. He calmly climbed down the pier and swam out to rescue the animal"—not surprisingly, to people who knew Kiniski.

The following month, along with fellow West Coast wrestlers Ben and Mike Sharpe, Kovacs, Barend, and Nomellini, Kiniski and Blears headed for the NWA Hawaii territory. Noted for short travel distances, a relatively easy schedule, and an abundance of outdoor activities to enjoy during off-hours and off-days, the Hawaii territory—promoted at the time by Al Karasick—provided a setting in which many wrestlers aspired to work. Some referred to a stint in Karasick's territory—or even a brief stopover in transit to or from

Left: San Francisco, June 1955. In the midst of his nine-month stay in Northern California—where he battled the likes of Bobo Brazil, Leo Nomellini, Enrique Torres, and the Sharpe Brothers—Kiniski obviously had something other than wrestling on his mind at times (Kiniski family archive). *Right*: August 1955. Gene Kiniski and older brother Fred (right), who settled in California after serving in the Canadian Navy in World War II, spend a sunny day in Pacific Grove, California (Kiniski family archive).

7. Hot in California

Japan—as a working vacation. Kiniski would spend five months there, from December 1955 until April 1956, no doubt enjoying many activities that would have been unthinkable when he was growing up in central Alberta, with its long and brutally cold winters.

In Hawaii Kiniski and Blears got off to a blazing start, winning the NWA Hawaii Tag Team championship from Barend and Kovacs in Honolulu on December 4, 1955, in what appears to have been the Kiniski-Blears team's first match in the territory.

While occasionally wrestling in singles matches, though never against each other, the ex-linebacker Kiniski and the 190-pound Blears were cast as a dominant tag team in Hawaii. Holding the title for nearly five months, they turned back teams composed of established wrestlers such as Nomellini, George Bollas, Hans Schnabel, Great Togo and Tosh Togo, and Billy Varga and emerging superstars including Dick Beyer and Rikidozan. Also present in the territory—although it appears he never faced Kiniski on a wrestling show there—was the veteran Tony Morelli, who had mentored Kiniski a few years earlier.

Gene Kiniski and "Lord" James Blears (right) were a top tag team of the mid–1950s, holding titles in Northern and Southern California and in Hawaii. After disbanding the team in 1956, the two would remain close lifelong friends (Kiniski family archive).

Kiniski's most notable singles match during his stretch in Hawaii was a February 24 encounter with Schnabel billed in a newspaper ad from Kiniski's collection as "30 falls to a finish"—unless one wrestler took three consecutive falls or was unable to continue. Schnabel was a well-traveled wrestler who had some national TV exposure during the 1950s from both Hollywood and Chicago. According to what appears to be a February 24, 1956, clipping from the *Honolulu Advertiser*, "A couple of months ago these two grapplers engaged in a match that lasted until midnight. Elapsed time was almost two hours. Tonight they will meet in a 'finish' match." Schnabel—like Kiniski, noted for the backbreaker finisher—won the February 24 meeting, though it is unclear how many falls it took him to do so. Kiniski, meanwhile, would follow up with victories over Schnabel in March and April.

After losing the Hawaii Tag Team championship to the Togos near the end of April, the Kiniski-Blears combo returned to Northern California. Though still booked as a top team in the territory, they did not win any championships this time around, and Kiniski broadened his ring experience by facing a variety of opponents in singles matches. But he continued to focus primarily on tag team encounters during his brief stay back in the

San Francisco territory—partnered at times with Blears and at other times with Bill Miller, a skilled amateur wrestler and "shooter" (legitimate grappler and submission specialist) who would hold many major wrestling titles throughout his career, including the AWA World Heavyweight title in the 1960s, which Kiniski also would hold during that decade. Notable opponents of Kiniski's in the Northern California tag team ranks in 1956 included Nomellini, Kovacs, Blanchard, the Sharpes, and "Yukon" Eric Holmback, who four years earlier had seen his fame skyrocket when one of his cauliflower ears was removed from his head during a match in Montreal against Killer Kowalski—who himself would be a notable opponent and partner of Kiniski's during the late 1950s and early 1960s.

Kiniski and Blears went their separate ways midway through 1956, with Kiniski heading for Texas and Blears spending another year in California, where he headlined some shows in both the Southern and Northern California territories before returning to Hawaii during the summer of 1957. It was in Hawaii that Blears—who enjoyed a strong 30-year career—would have his greatest career success, both in the ring and as a booker (planning matches and programs and setting the overall direction of the promotion) during the 1960s and 1970s "golden age" of wrestling in Hawaii. Over the years, other members of the Blears family would pick up on Lord Blears' avid interest in surfing, and two—son Jimmy and daughter Laura—went on to reach the highest levels in competitive surfing.

After dissolving their tag team, Blears and Kiniski would reunite on occasion and maintain a friendship that spanned over half a century—during which time, according to Kelly Kiniski, his father could count on receiving a photo of the Blears family almost every Christmas.

8

Breakthrough Years

Following his two-month stay back in Northern California, Kiniski returned to Texas early in the summer of 1956 as a featured performer for promoter Morris Sigel's Houston Wrestling, which at the time ran shows in much of the Lone Star State. Over the course of four months in Texas, Kiniski did not wrestle under his already-familiar name but as Gene Kelly, namesake of a popular Hollywood actor. "Gene Kelly" had brief turns with both the NWA Texas Heavyweight title, which he won from Pepper Gomez, and a share of the NWA Texas Tag Team championship with partner Lenny "Len Crosby" Passaforo, better known during much of his career as Lenny Montana. Frequently during his 1956 stay in Texas, "Kelly" was associated in storyline with Count Pietro Rossi, a veteran wrestler who doubled as a manager who liked to get involved in his clients' matches.

Among notable opponents Kiniski faced in Texas in 1956 were Gomez, who had more than 50 regional title reigns over the course of a nearly 30-year career; Duke Keomuka, another wrestler with championship credentials en route to a 30-year career; tough journeyman and former Kiniski partner Danny Plechas, also on course for a career spanning about 30 years; Mike DiBiase, father of 1990s World Wrestling Federation (WWF) star Ted DiBiase; 1960s–1970s Southeast U.S. mainstay Len Rossi; Ray Gunkel, an ex-amateur wrestler who would go on to hold many titles in Georgia from the late 1950s to early 1970s; and Ed Francis, who would have a long association with Lord Blears as the promoter of record in Hawaii in the 1960s and 1970s. Traveling around Sigel's Houston Wrestling circuit, Kiniski also had opportunities to face some all-time legends of pro wrestling: Johnny Valentine, a Seattle-area native who was an international star for many years; The Sheik, Michigan native Ed Farhat, widely considered one of the top heels in professional wrestling history; Buddy Rogers, a future NWA and WWWF (World Wide Wrestling Federation) champion widely remembered as one of the best performers of his era; Lou Thesz, generally considered one of the top grapplers and champions ever in professional wrestling; and Whipper Billy Watson, who was the NWA Heavyweight champion when he defended the title against Kiniski in what appears to have been their first meeting, in Galveston on August 16, 1956. While Kiniski held his own against that elite group, with recorded victories over Rogers and The Sheik, he fell just short in his NWA title match against Watson, whose name, like Thesz', is closely linked with Kiniski's in the record books.

Quoted in an April 14, 2010, *SLAM! Wrestling* report by Greg Oliver, Kiniski claimed he wrestled as Gene Kelly in Texas in 1956 because his antics had earned him a suspension in California. "I used that name [Kelly]," he said, "so I could wrestle in Texas." But even in the 1950s, given Kiniski's notoriety and the nature of wrestling storylines, it seems more likely there was another reason there were two Gene Kellys going strong for a time

51

in 1956. According to Kelly Kiniski, his father wrestled in Texas as Gene Kelly because Sigel or someone else with authority in the promotion believed "Kiniski" was too difficult or unusual a name for fans in the territory to pronounce or relate to—even though "Gene Kiniski" had been a recognizable name in Texas for some time. The *SLAM!* report quotes Kiniski further: "I was Gene Kelly, but everybody knew who I was." An unidentified clipping from Kiniski's collection—from either an area newspaper or a local wrestling program published shortly before Kiniski's mid-1956 arrival in Houston—points out that "Gene Kelly" was not an Irishman and then quotes him as toeing the party line: "My name sounds so much like Kelly that everyone has always called me Kelly because they couldn't pronounce it. Why fight City Hall. They want to call me Kelly so I'm Kelly."

As to how he came to acquire the ring name his father had used in Texas—or what special meaning the name "Kelly" may have had to Gene Kiniski—Kelly Kiniski is unsure. But Pat Paproski sheds a little light on why Gene Kiniski's elder son may have inherited the name at birth. "One of the things that I heard growing up," says Paproski, "was that Gene and my dad had made a vow that when they married and had boys, Gene's boy was going to be named Kelly, and Steve's boy was going to be named Patty. And so it came to be."

Following an October 23, 1956, loss to Gomez at the Dallas Sportatorium in Kiniski's final match before leaving Sigel's promotion in Texas, Kiniski arrived in Buffalo, New York, about a week later to report for work with promoter Pedro Martinez. Kiniski debuted in the Buffalo territory in the semi-main event of a November 2, 1956, Friday night show at the Buffalo Memorial Auditorium, facing journeyman Roberto Pico, who over the course of a 27-year career won about a dozen titles in the United States and Canada as Bobby Lane and Pancho Villa. The main event of that November 2 show saw Whipper Billy Watson defend the NWA Heavyweight title against Mr. Hito. Hito—not to be confused with 1970s–1980s Stampede Wrestling star Katsuji "Mr. Hito" Adachi—was the Buffalo-territory working name of Robert "Kinji" Shibuya. Shibuya, a native of Hawaii, was a successful Japanese heel across the United States and Canada for many years, a mainstay up and down the West Coast during most of the 1960s and 1970s, and a frequent opponent and occasional tag team partner of Kiniski's during several tours of the Pacific Northwest in that same period.

Though Kiniski was capable of speaking for himself and was seldom associated with a wrestling manager over the course of his career, Count Pietro Rossi (right) was sometimes in his corner during Kiniski's successful Texas run in 1956. Here, the two enjoy a lighthearted moment outside a pool in Houston (Kiniski family archive).

8. Breakthrough Years

"Bulldog" Danny Plechas (left) was both a tag team partner and a tough opponent early in Kiniski's career. While not normally a main-eventer, Plechas had a long career that intersected with Kiniski's in several territories (Kiniski family archive).

The night after Kiniski's Buffalo debut, he reported to the local WGR-TV studio for his first television taping in the area. With a wrestling tradition dating back to the 1880s and live televised shows from the Buffalo Memorial Auditorium dating back to 1948, Buffalo was a major wrestling center in 1955 when Martinez—formerly a part-owner of New York City's National Wrestling Alliance promotion—took over the Upstate New York wrestling office. Martinez had been a headlining wrestler and regional world champion—as recognized by the Boston wrestling office, which extended to Buffalo—prior to getting into wrestling promotion in the 1940s. Martinez, who promoted shows all over western New York and in western Pennsylvania and, later, eastern Ohio, remained associated with wrestling in that region until 1974. In early 1955, the year before Kiniski migrated to Buffalo, Martinez and Kiniski crossed paths for the first time when both were wrestling in Southern California, and presumably, Martinez—soon to leave the ring altogether in order to give full attention to his owner-promoter duties—saw major drawing potential in Kiniski.

As Martinez explained it a few years later in an unidentified article in Kiniski's collection from a newspaper somewhere in Upstate New York, "I found a kid wrestling in Texas under the name of Gene Kelly. His real name is Gene Kiniski, but they told him there weren't any Poles in Texas so he'd have to make it Kelly."

In contrast, advertisements for Kiniski's matches in the Buffalo area sometimes played up his Polish heritage and even billed him at times as a Polish champion, though it doesn't appear that "title" was ever on the line.

Kiniski's primary wrestling destination during the period he was associated with Buffalo was the nearby Toronto territory, and his first recorded match there, a victory over New Zealander Ken "Ken Kenneth" Schiscka, actually took place Wednesday, October 30—two days before his debut in Buffalo—in Hamilton, Ontario, a weekly stop on the Toronto circuit and the second-largest city in the loop. A week later in Hamilton, Kiniski bested Frank "Tex" McKenzie, a 6'9" Washington State native who made an international name over a 22-year career as a "cowboy" wrestler. The two would meet again—with a similar result—six days later, when Kiniski made his wrestling debut in Montreal. The night after that, Kiniski made his Toronto debut, defeating Kenneth at Maple Leaf Gardens.

For a number of months, Gene and Marion Kiniski lived just across the Canadian border from Buffalo, and from their base in the Crystal Beach-Ridgeway area (now part of Fort Erie) in Ontario's Niagara region, Gene was well situated to make his mark in the Buffalo and Toronto territories.

November and December of 1956 saw Kiniski holding down a busy schedule of appearances in western New York State and Southern Ontario, facing a wide variety of opponents and going nearly undefeated except for disqualification losses. And while Kiniski was not generally in main events in the region yet, several of his opponents stand out.

McKenzie, like Kiniski, had started his career in the early 1950s and spent time in Texas before arriving in Southern Ontario and Upstate New York in the middle of the decade. While still rising toward the main events, he was a popular wrestler in the Martinez territory, portraying a gentleman from the Alamo and winning the vast majority of his matches. Charleston *Post and Courier* columnist Mike Mooneyham, following McKenzie's death in 2001, reported on his website that McKenzie had main-evented "in most of the top territories in the country, including the Carolinas, Detroit, Los Angeles, Amarillo, Omaha and Buffalo, as well as overseas in Australia, Canada and Japan." McKenzie's greatest career success was probably when he held the (Australian) IWA World Heavyweight title in 1967 and 1968, when that promotion was on fire and was luring many leading North American wrestlers away from regional promotions around North America. As far as Kiniski was concerned, Tex McKenzie, while considered more an attraction than a skilled grappler, would prove a worthy adversary, facing Kiniski on several dozen occasions over the course of 15 years, particularly in the Pacific Northwest, and picking up a respectable number of vic-

Paul Boesch (right), whose career as a wrestler was cut short due to injury, had a distinguished promoting career, first in Washington State and then in Texas, where he ran a successful territory for several decades. When Gene Kiniski appeared in the Houston circuit (which covered much of Texas) in 1956, Boesch was the assistant to head promoter Morris Sigel (Kiniski family archive).

Kinji Shibuya, pictured with Marion Kiniski, was a top Japanese heel in several territories from the early 1950 to the mid–1970s. His career intersected with Kiniski's in territories around the United States and Canada as the pair engaged in dozens of wild battles and occasionally joined forces as a potent team (Kiniski family archive).

tories. Looking back at McKenzie in a 2006 interview with Oliver, Kiniski recalled, "Big old Texie. Fuck, he was a big, likable person. He could draw, but his athleticism left a lot to be desired." Elaborating slightly, Kiniski added, "He was a klutz" (Oliver, Files).

Billy "Red" Lyons was a Dundas, Ontario, native who had some early success in Texas, the Mid-Atlantic, Ohio, and a few other regions or territories before facing Kiniski several times in Southern Ontario in November and December of 1956. Lyons went on to have a well-traveled, 30-year career but is best remembered as a "scientific" Toronto-territory wrestler who eventually became a television commentator and interviewer for that promotion, often imploring viewers, after hyping a coming major arena show, "Fans, don't ya dare miss it."

James "Shag" Thomas was an opponent of Kiniski's during a December 1956 encounter in Maple Leaf Gardens. Though that match lasted less than three minutes before Kiniski was disqualified and it appears the two met in the ring only about twice afterward—in the Pacific Northwest a decade later, at the height of Kiniski's success—Thomas, like Kiniski, would go on to become a legend in the Northwest.

Originally cast as a heel in Don Owen's Oregon territory, Thomas went on to become one of the most popular wrestlers in Pacific Northwest Wrestling during the U.S. Civil Rights era and is credited, at www.onlineworldofwrestling.com, with appearing in what may have been the first interracial professional wrestling match in Georgia. Besides appearing in the Toronto-Buffalo region, Georgia, and the Pacific Northwest over the

November 1956. After three years of making a name in the Southern United States, Kiniski moved back north just in time for winter in the area around Buffalo, New York. Here, he shovels snow for probably the first time in several years at what appears to have been a short-term lodging in Crystal Beach, Ontario (Kiniski family archive).

course of his long career, Thomas—a short, stocky ex-footballer remembered more as a performer than a skilled grappler—enjoyed runs as a featured wrestler in other areas including California, Alberta, Texas, Hawaii, and the Midwest.

Bobby Managoff, who wrestled Kiniski to a draw in the semi-main event of a November 20, 1956, Hamilton card featuring a Lou Thesz NWA World Heavyweight title defense against Buddy Rogers, was a skilled wrestler and headliner around the United States and Canada who held three versions of the world heavyweight championship, including the National Wrestling Association (not National Wrestling Alliance) title, during the decade and a half preceding his first encounter with Kiniski in Hamilton. A second-generation wrestler widely recognized as a legitimate grappler, Managoff is described by Lou Thesz, at the National Wrestling Hall of Fame website, as "a terrific wrestler and ... a top-class guy all the way." While perhaps not as well remembered by modern fans as other wrestlers of his day with lesser skill, Managoff definitely had all the credentials to make an impression on Kiniski, and the two would face each other again in several territories in later years. Nearly half a century after the Kiniski-Managoff match in Hamilton, Kiniski would assist *Chicago Tribune* reporter Rick Hepp in writing Bobby Managoff's obituary, which appeared in the April 20, 2002, *Tribune*, and afterward, Hepp would send Kiniski a handwritten note to thank him for sharing his memories of Managoff.

It was only a week after Kiniski's debut in Buffalo that he would face the wrestler many old-time fans associate most closely with the 1950s heyday of professional wrestling in Buffalo. Ilio DiPaolo, a native of Italy, had done some wrestling in Latin America

8. Breakthrough Years

before arriving in New York State in 1951 and, the following year, marrying into Pedro Martinez' family. Throughout the 1950s DiPaolo had some success in a variety of territories from the East Coast to the West Coast, but his success and popularity hit a peak in Southern Ontario and western New York. While DiPaolo was never considered a top-tier wrestler of his day, he enjoyed strong fan support especially in Buffalo—where he made his home until he died in 1995—western New York, northern Ohio, and Southern Ontario. During his career DiPaolo earned victories over some of the top wrestlers of his era, including Gorgeous George, Bill Miller, Fritz von Erich, Hans Schmidt, and Kiniski—though, as far as Kiniski is concerned, most of DiPaolo's victories came in tag team matches. DiPaolo retired from the ring in the mid–1960s and became a popular restaurateur in Buffalo, establishing an Italian eatery that family members continue to run more than half a century after Ilio DiPaolo's Restaurant was established.

On December 26, 1956, Kiniski faced Toronto native Whipper Billy Watson in the main event of a show at the London, Ontario, Arena. Watson, holder of the NWA World Heavyweight championship for eight months until dropping the title to Thesz on November 9, 1956, had defended the championship in Texas against Kiniski in August.

Watson was a celebrity in both Canada and the United States as a result of holding the NWA title and having appeared on nationally televised broadcasts of *Wrestling from Marigold* in the United States and the CBC's *Saturday Night Wrestling* in Canada. He had spent most of the early part of his career, in the late 1930s, in the British Isles before returning to Ontario and becoming a huge attraction in the Toronto area and remaining

Kiniski's quick rise up the ladder in Pedro Martinez' Buffalo territory put him into an enviable income tax bracket. The Kiniski photograph album identifies the occasion for this photograph as Gene Kiniski's "first 'g' payoff" as Kiniski proudly holds the first $1,000 check of his wrestling career (Kiniski family archive).

a local institution there until his death in 1990. To this day Watson, who retired from the ring in 1971 after his leg reportedly was nearly severed by a car, remains the name most closely associated with the height of Toronto wrestling in the 20th century.

Another wrestler with championship credentials to whom Kiniski was introduced in Southern Ontario in late 1956 was Texas native and three-time NCAA Heavyweight wrestling champion Dick Hutton. Hutton, a four-time All-American at Oklahoma A&M University, narrowly missed being a four-time champion, as www.legacyofwrestling.com reports he lost a close decision in the 1949 NCAA tournament final to University of Minnesota standout and future professional wrestling great Verne Gagne, whose career would intersect with Kiniski's for a few years beginning in 1958. Before losing that match to Gagne, Hutton took fifth place in heavyweight freestyle wrestling at the 1948 Olympics, with Gagne an alternate on the same team.

Hutton was well established in the Buffalo-Toronto region as a no-frills, rugged grappler when he and Kiniski first teamed, on December 3, 1956, in Kitchener, Ontario, against Utah natives Guy Brunetti and Joseph Tangaro, wrestling as Guy and Joe Brunetti. The Brunetti Brothers had twice held the Toronto-territory Canadian Open Tag Team championship earlier in 1956, but the debuting Kiniski-Hutton combo fought to a draw against the more experienced team. Kiniski-Hutton remained a regular tag team in Ontario for more than a year—though both continued mainly as singles wrestlers during that time—and while never winning a title together, Kiniski-Hutton often split victories with teams consisting of other big names such as Watson, DiPaolo, Pat O'Connor, and Yukon Eric. Kiniski and Hutton continued to team with some regularity until the night before Hutton's November 14, 1957, victory over Thesz for the NWA Heavyweight title, but from that point on—at least, as long as Hutton held the title—they would be booked as rivals, and often bitter ones.

Texas native Dick Hutton was a skilled amateur wrestler and an outstanding partner and opponent of Kiniski in the late 1950s. While Hutton, NWA World Heavyweight champion from late 1957 to early 1959, was usually a straightforward, gimmick-free wrestler, he was cast as a cowboy while wrestling in Southern California. California-based photographer Dr. Mike Lano—who has been photographing pro wrestlers and pro wrestling internationally since the early days of Kiniski's NWA world title reign in 1966—recalls, "Dick Hutton *hated* having to play the cowboy gimmick in L.A." (photograph courtesy Mike Lano's collection, photographer unknown).

Although Kiniski did not match Hutton's feat of capturing a major wrestling organization's world title in 1957, it was nonetheless a stellar year for Kiniski, who would headline many of the weekly shows at Buffalo's Memorial Auditorium, setting attendance records in the process; wrestle main events in Canada's four westernmost provinces while attracting major attention for the first time as a professional wrestler in his native Alberta; headline shows in

Canada's Atlantic provinces; start making a name in St. Louis, at the time considered by many the leading center of American wrestling; hold key singles titles in the major Canadian promotions based in Toronto and Montreal; and rise to the status of a legitimate drawing card everywhere he wrestled and a bona fide celebrity in Canada.

While the majority of Kiniski's success in 1957 was the result of his imposing presence as a singles wrestler and a compelling speaker who always seemed prepared for interviews, he also enjoyed continued success as a tag team wrestler in 1957. Kiniski and Hutton were regular partners in Southern Ontario during much of the year and joined forces that summer in Alberta and Saskatchewan, most notably facing the teams of Whipper Watson-Pat O'Connor and Italian native Giacomo "Al Costello" Costa and Australian Roy Heffernan, who would become known across Canada and the United States and internationally as the Fabulous Kangaroos. Hutton and Kiniski were already familiar with the Watson-O'Connor pairing, having faced that team several times in Ontario during the first half of 1957, and while Kiniski's career is not linked to the Fabulous Kangaroos' to any great degree, he would face the Costello-Heffernan team again on a few occasions while partnered with two legends of the wrestling industry—Fritz von Erich and Don Leo Jonathan—who would remain lifelong friends of Kiniski's.

Sandor Kovacs was a capable wrestler who got to know Kiniski well in California, Hawaii, Buffalo, and Toronto before the two converged in Vancouver in the early 1960s to play key roles behind the scenes for promoter Rod Fenton. In 1967, when Fenton sold out of the promotion to return to the United States, Kovacs, Kiniski, and Don Owen joined forces to take over ownership of All-Star Wrestling (Kiniski family archive).

Von Erich—Texas-born Jack Adkisson—had a background in football at Southern Methodist University before gravitating to pro wrestling in the early 1950s. He debuted as a wrestler in Dallas in early 1953 and spent most of that year wrestling around Texas before making some appearances, as German heel Fritz von Erich, in Quebec that same fall. In 1954 he wrestled mainly in Texas and the Midwest, continuing to appear under his own name throughout Texas but further honing the Von Erich character during his travels outside the Lone Star State. In February of 1955 he arrived in Alberta to kick off a five-month stay in Hart's Big Time Wrestling.

While reports suggest Adkisson was a member of the Edmonton Eskimos in the early 1950s—some indicating he was on the 1953 team with Snyder, Blanchard, and Kiniski—such reports seem to be part of the same wrestling lore suggesting Adkisson played in the NFL, which he never did. It does appear, however, that he signed a contract with the NFL's Dallas Texans in 1952 only to get cut before playing in a game. As far as the Eskimos are concerned, Adkisson is not listed on the roster at any point in the team's history, but in between recorded wrestling appearances in Texas by Adkisson prior to the 1953 Canadian football season and wrestling appearances by Fritz von Erich in Montreal and Adkisson in Texas once the Canadian football season was well underway there is a gap of about three months—coinciding with the Eskimos' 1953 training camp and the first half of the regular season—without any apparent records to confirm Adkisson's whereabouts. As a result, it is entirely possible Adkisson worked out or tried out with the Eskimos in 1953 and made the acquaintance of Kiniski at that time.

Dave Meltzer, editor of the *Wrestling Observer Newsletter*, reports in the March 1, 1993, *Observer* that "Jack Adkisson was a back-up offensive guard at Southern Methodist University and set a school record in the discus. But he lost his scholarship by violating team rules and getting married to the future Doris Adkisson. The two took off for Canada, where he played Canadian football with several future wrestling superstars including Gene Kiniski and Wilbur Snyder. In 1954, he learned wrestling from Stu Hart in Calgary, and he, Doris and son Jackie Jr. lived in a trailer park on the Hart property."

While parts of that account are hard to verify, multiple reports suggest Hart and Adkisson were well acquainted before the latter ventured north from Texas—where he had been wrestling in late 1954—to become a featured performer with Big Time Wrestling from February to July of 1955. The Calgary-based territory was noted by wrestlers of that period—and long after—for bitter cold winters and sometimes blizzard-like conditions. While wrestlers of any renown would often act as their own booking agents and simply telephone and work out arrangements with promoters they wanted to work for, there is an excellent chance that Adkisson and Hart were not strangers when Fritz von Erich made what appears to have been his Alberta wrestling debut on February 1, 1955. And while Kiniski was busy wrestling in California during von Erich's 1955 stay in Alberta, it seems possible that they had met a year or two earlier and that their friendship was already well underway.

As Fritz von Erich, Adkisson became what Meltzer describes as a "6–3, 275-pound powerhouse with the agility, charisma and a certain demonic sneer that exuded toughness and danger [and] became one of the country's biggest drawing cards." The 1950s, on the heels of World War II, saw no shortage of hated German heel wrestlers, but the most prominent among them were Fritz von Erich and Hans Schmidt, played by Quebecer Guy Larose, who rose to prominence a few years earlier than Fritz von Erich, defeated von Erich in a German heel vs. German heel encounter in Chicago in 1954, and perhaps passed on a few of the finer points of playing a despicable World War II-era German heel.

By 1955—the year he became Fritz von Erich full-time—Adkisson was a legitimate headliner in a several territories. That year, he won his first titles: the Calgary territory's NWA Canadian Tag Team championship with Minnesota native Lou Sjoberg and the Toronto territory's Canadian Open Tag Team title with the same partner, renamed Karl von Schober. Von Erich also debuted in the Buffalo territory in 1955, teaming at times with von Schober and at other times facing off as a singles wrestler against the likes of DiPaolo, Watson, Rocca, and Yukon Eric. The following year, 1956, von Erich continued to headline in Calgary, Toronto, and Buffalo, teaming frequently with von Schober in the Toronto-Buffalo region and reclaiming Big Time Wrestling's NWA Canadian Tag Team title with the same partner, back in Alberta and wrestling again under his own name of Lou Sjoberg.

In 1957 von Erich was a successful singles attraction in the St. Louis, Minneapolis, Toronto, and Buffalo territories, facing major names such as Watson, Gagne, O'Connor,

8. Breakthrough Years

Rogers, and NWA titleholder Thesz. Von Erich also continued his success as a tag team wrestler in 1957—early in the year with von Schober and then, regularly starting in July, with Kiniski, whose successful partnership with Dick Hutton overlapped with his better-remembered pairing with von Erich, at least until Hutton captured the NWA World Heavyweight title from Thesz on November 14, 1957. Two weeks before Hutton's world title win—on October 31, 1957—Kiniski and von Erich won the NWA Canadian Open Tag Team championship from Watson and O'Connor at Maple Leaf Gardens.

Kelly Kiniski was born in Buffalo in late 1957 after Gene and Marion left Crystal Beach-Ridgeway and moved across the border to the central part of the city, about a mile or two east of the Buffalo Zoo, earlier in the year. Kelly, who came into the world while his father and von Erich were one of the top teams in wrestling, recalls Fritz von Erich as one of the few wrestlers who remained a lifelong friend of Gene Kiniski's. Both would rise to the top of the wrestling world—each holding the AWA World Heavyweight title in the early 1960s and making a major name in the United States and internationally during that decade—and the two faced off in the ring regularly in the late 1960s. And though it appears they never wrestled each other or teamed after that, they kept in touch and remained "tight," according to Kelly.

Fritz and Doris von Erich experienced the tragedy of losing a young son while Fritz was a headlining wrestler in Buffalo and Toronto in 1959. Although Kiniski and von Erich had disbanded their tag team shortly before the tragedy, they would continue to cross paths in later years and would remain friends for life (Kiniski family archive).

Shortly after Kiniski and von Erich dissolved their team in February of 1959, von Erich's six-year-old son Jackie drowned after being electrocuted in Niagara Falls, New York. That sad incident, in retrospect, seems a precursor for a great deal more tragedy that would come the von Erich family's way in the 1980s and 1990s. According to Kelly Kiniski, his father provided moral and financial support to the von Erichs as they grieved the loss their first child in March of 1959. In a handwritten card mailed to Gene and Marion Kiniski at their Stockbridge Avenue, Buffalo, address that same month, "Doris and Fritz" express heartfelt thanks "for your friendship and loyalty when we needed you so desperately." They continue, "We would surely have fallen apart without your strength, Gene, and we will be forever grateful."

During much of the 1960s von Erich, as Meltzer reports in the March 1, 1993, *Wrestling Observer*, was "a phenomenal drawing card in Texas for promoters Ed McLemore and Morris Sigel." But Meltzer reports von Erich "pulled his big power play" in 1967 and "rallied all the North Texas wrestlers and pulled out the rug from under McLemore to start his own company." Established as the top babyface (or popular hero) in the promotion he secretly owned, von Erich faced Kiniski from time to time and settled into playing a Texas-born hero, though he continued to go professionally by his German-themed name for the rest of his life. He had a brief run as NWA president in the mid–1970s, but to fans of 1980s wrestling von Erich is best remembered as the owner of Dallas-based World Class Championship Wrestling (WCCW). Featuring several of von Erich's sons, WCCW at its peak could be seen on television around the United States and, in many viewers' minds, set the standard of the day when it came to producing a wrestling television program aimed effectively at a young, eager—and largely female—audience. But sadly, the von Erich name would become synonymous with tragedy when Fritz and Doris von Erich lost four of their five remaining sons—three by suicide—over the course of nine years, from 1984 to 1993.

Kiniski's highest-profile singles matchups in 1957 were against many top wrestlers of the day, including Watson, Rogers, O'Connor, Thesz, Yvon Robert, Killer Kowalski, and Hutton—with former heavyweight boxing champion Jersey Joe Walcott often brought in as a special referee to keep Kiniski in line. While Kiniski's rise to the top of his profession was not yet complete, he was booked to hold his own against top-caliber competition and took victories against most of the wrestlers on that list in 1957. And though not yet positioned at the level of Thesz, Watson, or O'Connor, Kiniski earned victories over the latter two in 1957 and was positioned as a legitimate threat to Thesz' NWA World Heavyweight title in both the Buffalo and Toronto territories.

Kiniski drew plenty of notoriety in 1957 as the result of a highly publicized $500 fine and four-week suspension in Toronto levied by Ontario Athletic Commissioner Merv McKenzie stemming from Kiniski's actions on a Thursday night show early in the year in the Toronto suburb of East York. Events of that night reportedly also led to the suspension, for at least six months, of promoter Frank Tunney's license to hold shows in East York.

An unidentified article from Kiniski's collection reports, "The facts which brought this about were that Kiniski, as Dick Hutton's second, jumped in and out of the ring at East York, took part in the bout which he had no business doing, and, by waving chairs and making threatening gestures, incited the crowd."

Kiniski kept busy during the suspension, wrestling in other Ontario cities and in Buffalo. An unidentified article, apparently published not long after the Toronto suspension, reports Buffalo promoter Martinez as saying, "Kiniski today is the biggest thing I've ever had."

Martinez continued, in the article, "Kiniski stood up to a microphone on my TV show and insulted a million people. 'All these idiots are watching to see me get beat,' said my boy. The sponsors nearly died. But now I got 11,666 people paying to see him in the flesh."

Back in Toronto on May 2, 1957, Kiniski won his second career singles title by defeating O'Connor for the British Empire Heavyweight title in a 21-minute Maple Leaf Gardens main event. O'Connor—a New Zealander who would go on to hold the NWA world title—was a high-profile wrestler in the United States and Canada through national television appearances in both countries during the 1950s, and capturing a major title from O'Connor constituted a significant breakthrough for Kiniski as a singles wrestler. Though perhaps featured less prominently or memorably on the CBC's national television broadcasts in the late 1950s than wrestlers like Watson, O'Connor, and the flashier, TV-friendly Sweet Daddy Siki, Kiniski was beginning to make a national name in Canada on the back of his rising success as a major singles wrestler in Toronto, the center of Canada's anglophone media.

Kiniski's notoriety carried all the way to the Canadian Maritimes, and he was a featured performer, facing the likes of Watson and O'Connor, during visits to Newfoundland and New Brunswick in 1957. A clipping from Kiniski's collection—unidentified but likely from a mid–November edition of the St. John's (Newfoundland and Labrador) *Telegram*— also confirms that the Kiniski-von Erich team appeared at least once in St. John's while holding the Toronto-based Canadian Open Tag Team title. Many of the wrestlers working shows—some held in stadiums—in Atlantic Canada in 1957 came from the Toronto circuit, and Kiniski was a main eventer who drew good crowds and hit fans' nerves in cities such Moncton and Saint John, New Brunswick, and St. John's—where, according to an August 25, 1957, newspaper report by John Wood, Kiniski said he would never wrestle again "due to unfair treatment." Wood continues, "[Kiniski] called people of this province displaced persons, and worse off than Hungarian refugees."

While he held the British Empire title for only a month before losing it to Watson, Kiniski remained strong in Ontario during the remainder of 1957, both in singles matches against the likes of Watson and O'Connor and in tag matches paired with Hutton or von Erich. Kiniski was also positioned strongly in Quebec during much of 1957, earning a victory—leading to a near-riot when Kiniski continued beating on his opponent after the match—April 24 at the Montreal Forum against Quebec legend Yvon Robert. Then, on June 12, just days after relinquishing the British Commonwealth title in Toronto, Kiniski captured the Montreal version of the world heavyweight championship from Édouard Carpentier.

The lead-up to Kiniski's program with Carpentier in Montreal had gotten underway six weeks earlier, on May 1, when, according to an unidentified clipping likely from the *Montreal Gazette*, Kiniski, following a victory on the undercard before the evening's Kowalski-Carpentier main event, "invaded the ring ... and promptly attempted to ridicule Carpentier before his home throng. He sneered ... at Carpentier's size, and inherited a well-placed boot for his trouble. He pleaded with the crowd for a few seconds free time on the public address system, but was roared down. He argued with the referee ... and finally rounded off his invasion of the ring by elbow smashing Carpentier and fleeing from the scene, bowling over obstacles on his spirited dash to the dressing room."

After winning the title from Carpentier, Kiniski dropped it six weeks later to Kowalski. But while Kiniski's July 17, 1957, best-of-three-falls title loss, via countout, to Kowalski at Delormier Stadium drew nearly 22,000 fans, it was a Kiniski appearance three weeks later at the same stadium that really marks Kiniski's place in the history of wrestling in Montreal. The main event was a Kowalski-Carpentier rematch, and this time Kiniski came to the ring, when the match was squared at a fall apiece, to challenge the winner. An article from Kiniski's collection titled "Flying Chairs Halt Ball Park Program" begins, "Wednesday, August 7 will go down in Montreal wrestling history as the night of the Great Chair hurling Riot." According to the article, after Carpentier chased him from the ring, "Kiniski grabbed the nearest chair and hurled it at Carpentier." After a few chairs were swung and thrown, "chairs came flying into the ring, hurled by some of the 14,789 [in attendance]. Kiniski [already clocked by a chair] arose groggily, was hit twice by the steel missiles, and fled, running through a broken field, pursued by flying chairs. He made for the wrong exit [and], after leaping the infield fence, was forced to retrace his steps [and] again raced through the hostile crowd. His right hand was hit and badly swollen. Bruised and battered, Kiniski made his escape into the dugout. Later, police rescued him from a waiting, angry crowd."

A second report, without any identification, says, "Kiniski started the wildest riot in local mat history [and] there were fully 40 to 50 chairs on the ring floor when the wild scenes were over. Both main-bout wrestlers, Kowalski and Carpentier, were knocked out by chairs [crashing] to their heads [and] several spectators were beaned by the flying missiles." A third report puts it this way: "Confusion reigned at Delormier Downs last night and ex-Edmonton Eskimo footballer Gene Kiniski wound up with enough chairs to start a furniture store."

As Kiniski himself reported to Greg Oliver nearly half a century later, on February 3, 2006, "The fucking chairs are coming down like a fucking snowstorm. I ran up into the stands because the fucking people were beating me with chairs. At least I just got punched and kicked up in the stands. Finally, they got some security to me and I got back to the dressing room with a broken thumb after being hit with a chair" (Oliver, Files).

Kiniski returned to Montreal several more times in 1957, usually to mix it up with Carpentier or to team with Kowalski.

Back in Buffalo, Kiniski put in strong performances throughout 1957, usually in highlighted singles matches against opponents such as Watson, DiPaolo, Yukon Eric, Ron Etchison, and 1957 reigning NWA Heavyweight champions Thesz and Hutton. Kiniski also had matches that year in the Buffalo territory against Joe Blanchard and Sandor Kovacs.

Late in the year, barely a week after falling to Hutton in an NWA title challenge at the Memorial Auditorium, Kiniski rebounded by causing a reported near-riot after charging the ring in his street clothes and attacking Watson, who appeared on the verge of beating von Erich. Former boxing champion Rocky Marciano, on hand that night as a special referee, called for a disqualification as a result of the interference. An unidentified article from Kiniski's collection—likely from the *Buffalo News*—indicates "Joe Masters, deputy commissioner for the New York State Athletic Commission, announced he would recommend that Kiniski be suspended." While it appears Kiniski did not wrestle again in Buffalo until nearly three months later, it is difficult to confirm whether he was in fact suspended.

In 1957 Kiniski also returned to his native Western Canada—three and a half years after his departure from the Eskimos and his only previous verifiable professional wrestling match in the region—as a big-time wrestling star. Kiniski's football background in Alberta and his wrestling exploits in Central Canada were well known to Western Canadians, and particularly to Albertans. Kiniski made his first Vancouver wrestling appearance in 1957, bringing his feud with Whipper Billy Watson to the city Kiniski would call his professional home several years later. Kiniski brought another well-known rivalry to Winnipeg in 1957, facing off late in the year against O'Connor. Kiniski also brought both of those rivalries to Alberta and Saskatchewan, where he managed to fit in several mini-tours while touching base with family members and old friends. In Hart's Alberta territory in 1957, Kiniski repeatedly faced off in main events against Watson or O'Connor or—while teaming with Hutton—both. In July Kiniski challenged NWA Heavyweight champion Thesz on consecutive nights in Edmonton and Regina, Saskatchewan.

It was probably during the local buildup in Edmonton to the July 10 Thesz-Kiniski title match—though possibly during the buildup earlier in 1957 to one of several Kiniski-Watson matches that took place in the city—that an incident happened that Alberta Sports Hall of Famer Bill Manson—active for many years in the highest levels of provincial, national, and international amateur wrestling—says he recalls vividly about 60 years later. The incident involved Gene's brother Julian, a popular meteorologist on Edmonton's CFRN-TV who also had some involvement for a time in wrestling, according to Julian's son and Gene's nephew Bruce Kinisky.

As Manson recalls, "His brother had him on TV.... He was interviewing him ... but they got into a big argument right on TV. You know, Gene gets up and grabs his brother, who was also a big man ... and he flattened him right on the television."

Manson continues, "I know wrestling because I'm a wrestler. I know that Julian hit the floor pretty darn hard. Whether it's show or not, he hit the floor hard."

Julian, who was known to stand up to his younger brother during their adult years, did not in any way live in the shadow of Gene Kiniski. Julian was a knowledgeable meteorologist with a high-profile platform, and Julian's son Bruce reports that his father also did some local promoting and refereeing on wrestling shows in Edmonton "in the early days when Gene was starting out." In "My Brother Is a Brute!" Julian reported he was one of Gene's training partners—going to the mat for repeated five-minute sparring sessions with his brother—when Gene was getting back into wrestling shape following his 1952 knee injury.

Bruce recalls, at age six or seven, watching a tag team match on television, refereed by his father, in which Gene Kiniski was one of the participants and Julian got involved in a skirmish in the ring. "They were beating the crap out of Dad," recalls Bruce. Speaking specifically of his uncle and his father, he says, "They mixed it up."

Bruce continues, "Dad was all bloody ... [his] shirt was torn ... and I was quite worried."

An unidentified article from Gene Kiniski's collection reports another incident in which Kiniski "pulled another trick out of his already well-filled and much-used bag during Tuesday night's wrestling match. At one point during the proceedings, when the giant 'badman' was at the end of Whipper Watson's business, Edmonton's genial weatherman and Gene's college-educated little brother [actually, older brother], Julian, jumped into the ring to, as he put it, 'help my brother who is being unfairly treated by that Watson.'"

While it was no secret to the public that Julian Kinisky was Gene's brother, Julian was a local celebrity in his own right who had made his own name in Edmonton and central Alberta. In fact, Julian's desire to stand on his own had contributed to his decision to change the spelling of his surname to "Kinisky" from "Kiniski." As Bruce Kinisky explains, "The name change [had] something to do with him distancing himself from the large family who used the *i* at the end of the name. Dad always wanted to be a bit different, to stand out so to speak."

While Kelly Kiniski reports that brothers Gene and Julian fought or argued when they were together almost as long as they lived, Gene Kinisky, Julian's other son, says, of his uncle and father as adults, "They were close. They visited from time to time. They had their difficulties, like any brothers do, I suppose, but you know, they visited from time to time and communicated by letter quite often." Bruce Kinisky adds, of his father and his uncle Gene, "There always seemed to be a competition between the two of them."

Regardless of where the line separating storyline from reality may have lain, there is no doubt that any public sibling tension Manson or Bruce Kinisky may have seen was simply another wrestling angle Gene Kiniski brought to life for the sake of drawing fans to his matches. Whatever part Julian may have had in planning or carrying out the angle, Gene Kiniski was certainly one who understood that fans would pay to see a nasty villain who roughed up his own brother on television get the beating he deserved.

But even relatively early in his career, Gene wasn't taking a lot of beatings in the ring. He followed up a superb 1957 by continuing to headline shows in several territories throughout 1958. While he lost matches from time to time—particularly to career nemesis Watson, still in the afterglow of his 1956 NWA World Heavyweight title run, and reigning NWA champion Hutton—1958 was another strong year that saw Kiniski solidify his standing as one of the top wrestling attractions in North America.

May 1958. Proud father and son five months after the birth of Kelly Kiniski in Buffalo, New York (Kiniski family archive).

Kiniski made his U.S. East Coast debut in 1958, losing to Watson via disqualification on a Boston show loaded with wrestling stars including O'Connor, Rocca, Carpentier, and Haystack Calhoun and a main event pitting regional world heavyweight champion Killer Kowalski against Yukon Eric. While the door was certainly open for Kiniski to follow up his Boston debut with further matches on the East Coast, it would be a full six years until he did so.

Kiniski was a regular challenger for Hutton's NWA title throughout 1958, facing the champion for the title multiple times in the major U.S. wrestling centers of St. Louis—headed by long-time promoter and Ukrainian native Sam Muchnick—and Indianapolis, largely run at the time by the equally legendary Jim Barnett, who controlled a territory spanning much of the United States until he headed for Australia with partner Johnny Doyle and established the wildly popular World Championship Wrestling (no connection to the Atlanta-based promotion of the same name in existence from 1988 to 2001) in that country in 1964. In 1958 Kiniski also had victories in St. Louis over former National Wrestling Association (not National Wrestling Alliance) World Heavyweight champion Bill Longson, who, like Kiniski, is remembered as one of the legends of St. Louis wrestling.

As far as St. Louis was concerned, that was the center most closely associated with the nickname "Big Thunder" by which Kiniski was known over the course of much of his career. But while there are differing accounts of how or when Gene Kiniski adopted or got the nickname, a June 1957 article, by Earle F. Yetter, in *Wrestling Life* magazine confirms Kiniski was known in the wrestling world as "Big Thunder" before he ever set foot in a St. Louis ring.

Though still based in Buffalo, Kiniski wrestled only occasionally in western New York in 1958, facing familiar opponents such as Bobo Brazil and Watson. Although Kiniski preferred to maintain his residence in the United States in order to protect his and Marion's green card status, the majority of Kiniski's matches in 1958 took place in Canada. Only a single recorded appearance, however, was in British Columbia. Two days after teaming with Ivan and Karol Kalmikoff in a February 19 main event in Vancouver, Kiniski wrestled on the undercard of a show in Calgary before continuing east to Central Canada, where most of his in-ring attention was focused in 1958. In June Kiniski returned to Alberta for a brief tour highlighted by a pair of matches against former tag team partner Bill Miller, with each man earning a victory.

In a 2004 interview with Oliver, Kiniski said, of Miller, who practiced veterinary medicine in his native Ohio after cutting back on his wrestling in the 1970s, "He was just a great, great wrestler. He was a 290-pounder. He was about the same size as me. A very, very fine competitor.... A highly intelligent individual."

Kiniski was active in the Montreal-Ottawa region during much of 1958, teaming with Kowalski to face, at least one time, Ben and Mike Sharpe and, several times, teams comprising any combination of Gagne, Carpentier, and O'Connor. As a singles competitor, Kiniski faced off in Montreal against notable opponents such as Watson, Bearcat Wright, and Lyons. In the Toronto territory, meanwhile, Kiniski was a top performer the entire year and, as in Montreal, one who sometimes played a big part in helping drive attendance for major shows.

Memorable opponents of Kiniski's around the Toronto circuit in 1958 included reigning NWA champ Hutton, ex-champions Watson and Thesz, and Rocca, Brazil, Yukon Eric, and Dara Singh. Singh, while never a major wrestling star in North America, was a megastar in his native India who achieved major success in wrestling, film, and politics.

Kiniski also kept busy as a tag team wrestler in Southern Ontario during much of 1958, holding the Canadian Open Tag Team championship with Fritz von Erich until mid-February, when the powerful heel team's 10-week reign came to an end at the hands of Watson and Eric. Later in the year, Kiniski teamed on occasion in the Toronto territory with partners including von Erich, Longson, Fred Atkins, and Bob Orton, Sr., facing a familiar lineup of opponents including Snyder, Singh, Brazil, and Yukon Eric. Kiniski also faced notable tag teams Bill and Ed Miller, Joe and Guy Brunetti, and Stan and Reggie Lisowski (the latter morphing later into future AWA superstar The Crusher) during 1958 tag team encounters in Ontario.

The following year, 1959, saw Kiniski follow a similar schedule as in 1958. Wrestling mainly in the same territories he had frequented or visited the previous year, Kiniski had multiple singles matches in 1959 against the likes of Carpentier, Managoff, Watson, DiPaolo, Kowalski, Yukon Eric, and O'Connor, who held the NWA Heavyweight title from January 9, 1959, until mid-1961. On April 17, 1959, in Toronto, Kiniski defeated Watson via disqualification to win the British Empire Heavyweight title for the second time before losing it back to Watson two months later in Toronto.

Kiniski continued his tag team success in 1959, teaming early in the year in the Toronto territory with Fritz von Erich and then, on a few Maple Leaf Gardens shows in late summer, with Don "Hard Boiled Haggerty" Stansauk. Hard Boiled Haggerty was a memorable heel of the 1950s and 1960s who had teamed with Kiniski on a Calgary show in 1957 and would go on to have several successful tag team runs with Kiniski in the early 1960s. Kiniski also teamed at least twice in 1959, fairly early in the year in Toronto, with Gorgeous George, one of wrestling's megastars in the 1940s and 1950s, who spent a few months touring Ontario in 1959.

But Kiniski's primary success in 1959 tag team competition was with a wrestler better remembered as a frequent opponent of Kiniski's over the course of most of their careers. Kiniski had a 20-year professional association with Don Leo Jonathan—like Kiniski, a top wrestler worldwide from the 1950s to the 1970s—and it was on an August 25, 1959, show in Hamilton, Ontario, that Kiniski and Jonathan apparently debuted as a rugged team composed of two large imposing and accomplished wrestlers.

Jonathan, who has to rival Watson as the fellow wrestler most readily associated with Kiniski's ring career, was the son of a 1930s–1950s wrestler who is described on the Professional Wrestling Hall of Fame Museum website as the "hymn-singing Brother Jonathan, who tossed opponents from pillar to post while in the midst of a Bible quotation." Don Leo Jonathan, a native of Utah, served in the U.S. Navy before debuting, while still a teenager, in 1950 and often teaming with his father in Colorado and California during the first year of his career. Throughout the 1950s Jonathan was a headlining wrestler in many parts of the United States and Canada, and prior to joining forces with Kiniski in the summer of 1959, he had enjoyed successful title runs, especially in Texas and Montreal; been featured on national TV while based in the Midwest in the mid-1950s; and established himself as a regular challenger for the NWA World Heavyweight title.

The Kiniski-Jonathan team's earliest recorded matches appear to have been a series of encounters in August and September of 1959 with Whipper Billy Watson and, depending on the show, Watson's partners Yukon Eric, Jack Laskin, and Sam Steamboat. Cast as a bruising, give-no-quarter pairing and playing the part to perfection, the Kiniski-Jonathan tandem quickly earned a reputation for riling audiences by laying a beating on

8. Breakthrough Years

fan favorites and defying anyone to do anything about it. Some fans seemed eager to take the newly dominant heel tag team up on that challenge, especially when Kiniski and Jonathan took it upon themselves to leave the ring and address fans from the arena floor.

The *SLAM! Wrestling* website, in an April 30, 2008, overview of Kiniski's career, reports on the aftermath of a Kiniski-Jonathan match, about two months into their partnership, on October 19, 1959, in Niagara Falls, Ontario: "Wrestler Gene Kiniski is arrested after a 'rumpus' at a wrestling match and charged with assaulting a police officer.... Constable Robert Gillies said Kiniski pushed him around when he ordered Kiniski to return to the ring with Don Leo Jonathan.... The two wrestlers had gone to the floor of the arena to argue with spectators." An unidentified article from Kiniski's collection leads off its report on the incident by saying, "Wrestler Gene Kiniski lost his match last night—to a police officer." As the incident played out over the course of about six weeks, Kiniski ended up paying a fine and court costs totaling $99—fairly small potatoes compared to the fine imposed on him two years earlier in East York/Toronto.

Despite their trouble that night in Niagara Falls—or because of it—Kiniski and Jonathan returned to headline a show in the city a week later, and three days after that, on October 29, they captured the Canadian Open Tag Team title from Watson and Yukon Eric in a Maple Leaf Gardens main event. Though the Kiniski-Jonathan title reign lasted only until New Year's Eve, when they dropped the title to Watson-DiPaolo, it would be difficult to deny the pair—despite their teaming for a relatively brief period during the first decade of their careers—a place on the list of top tag teams of the late 1950s–early 1960s era.

According to Jonathan, the two met in Texas earlier in the 1950s and, when put together as a tag team, seemed to click from the start.

"We wrestled as a team in Toronto and Buffalo and Chicago," he said the initial period in which he and Kiniski teamed, as the pair would have another notable run as a tag team in British Columbia a few years later. "I never had to do too much," Jonathan said. "He always seemed to get things done. We were a good team, though. There wasn't any bad shows with Gene and I.... The matches were always good.

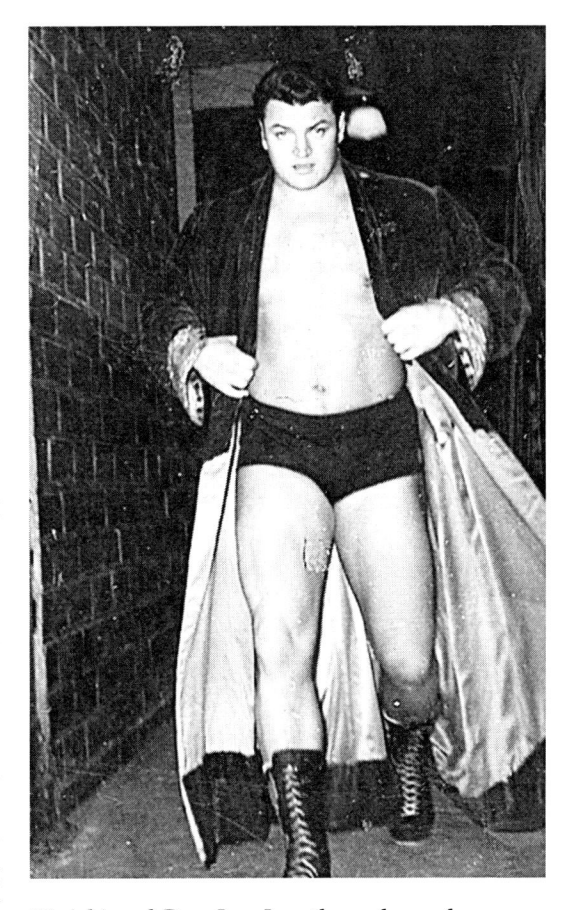

Kiniski and Don Leo Jonathan, shown here, met in Texas in the 1950s and became a top team in Ontario during the latter part of that decade. Both settled in British Columbia in the 1960s, setting the standard for wrestlers in the Pacific Northwest for two decades and remaining good friends after leaving the ring (Vance Nevada collection; thanks to Terry Dart).

"We had riots every place we went," Jonathan continued. "London, Ontario, was a bad place," he said, echoing a similar comment Kiniski had made years earlier about the normally quiet Southern Ontario city. According to Jonathan, Southern Ontario fans in the late 1950s were so rambunctious that "they finally had to put a bridge from the dressing room to the ring" so that wrestlers could safely travel to the ring for their matches. Elevated ramps of that sort are especially well remembered as a staple of the era at wrestling events in Toronto and London.

In the United States during their brief run as a top tag team, Jonathan said, the pair sometimes shuttled between Buffalo and Chicago by train. Jonathan recalled a trip in which "Gene and I were coming back from Chicago. We were on the train, and he was sitting across from me so we could stretch out and have a little sleep."

Jonathan continued, "This gentleman came up and sat down and started talking.... I was sitting in the seat on the edge of the aisle, and this guy was inside, and he was talking to me, and Gene, every once in a while, he'd go like he was having a nightmare. He'd kick this guy upside his head."

The man, Jonathan said, would "back off and rub his head, talk to me a little bit more, and [Gene's] foot would come upside this guy's head. Well, you know, it took about six or seven times for him to finally get the drift of what was going on, and he got up and left. Man, he took some awful kicks to the side of his head. Poor guy. He was trying to be serious, and I was having a hard time to keep from laughing. And just when I would about have myself contained, Kiniski would whack him upside the head again with them [size] 14s."

While Kiniski and Jonathan—who passed away in 2018, at age 87—would team up on occasion in 1960, the two largely went their separate ways for a few years in the wake of their December 31, 1959, loss of the Canadian Open Tag Team championship to Watson and DiPaolo. As far as Kiniski was concerned, it had been a memorable three years of raising the ire of fans all over Ontario—drawing rabid crowds in some northern towns and all over the south of the province—and attracting the attention and concern of numerous journalists and a few politicians and guardians of the public good who seemed to see him as a threat. But now, reportedly in the wake of being named 1959 Heel of the Year by Toronto's shoe repairmen, it was time to move on and turn his focus primarily to drawing considerable money and attention in other regions and territories.

9

Indianapolis and Minneapolis

In Jim Barnett's Indianapolis territory in early 1960, Kiniski formed a potent tag team with William "Dick the Bruiser" Afflis, a former Green Bay Packer lineman and one-of-a-kind wrestling personality who, especially during the early part of his career, had a knack for earning suspensions and instigating riots. The two tough ex-footballers teamed for the first time in late January and within two weeks won the territory's version of the world tag team title from future San Francisco promoter Roy Shire and his fictional brother Ray Shire, better remembered as legendary 1960s–1980s wrestler Ray Stevens.

Kiniski and Bruiser headlined several shows in Indianapolis before dropping the title back to the Shire Brothers in April of 1960. While Kiniski and Bruiser never shared another tag team title, they did team again in later years—particularly in Detroit, where both were featured at times during their long careers; in Indianapolis, where Bruiser would become an owner-promoter and the most popular wrestler ever in the territory; and in St. Louis, where both were among the top wrestling attractions for many years. More often than joining forces, however, Kiniski and Dick the Bruiser were opponents—kicking off their singles rivalry the same month their only tag title reign ended and continuing to face off at times through much of the 1960s—although, in the latter part of their careers, the two would please long-time fans by teaming again twice in St. Louis.

During his run in Indiana and neighboring Michigan during the first half of 1960, Kiniski sometimes shared billing with his friends Snyder, Blanchard, and von Erich. Snyder and Blanchard were notable opponents of Kiniski's in the territory, as were Cowboy Bob Ellis, Johnny Weaver, Yukon Eric, and Nick Bockwinkel, wrestling as Nick Bock. Although Kiniski and von Erich apparently never teamed while both were in the Midwest in 1960, Kiniski partnered at least twice in Indianapolis with The Sheik, splitting victories with Snyder and Ellis.

Kiniski was a frequent headliner in St. Louis before, during, and after his stay in Indianapolis in 1960. Usually in main events, Big Thunder faced off multiple times at the Kiel Auditorium against St. Louis icons Longson, Watson, and reigning NWA Heavyweight titleholder O'Connor, along with fellow top contenders Snyder and Ellis. Toward the end of the year, following a loss on November 18 at the Kiel Auditorium with partner Taro Miyaki against Watson and John Paul Henning, Kiniski was suspended for 60 days by the Missouri Athletic Commission for "mauling" Watson outside the ring, as an unidentified clipping from Kiniski's collection puts it.

On several occasions in 1960, Kiniski also took his hard-hitting matches against O'Connor and Watson to Alberta and Winnipeg. Late in the year, Kiniski was back in Toronto for a few appearances, including two matches against Watson.

Kiniski's schedule in 1960 also included main-event appearances, sprinkled throughout the year, in British Columbia against top names including O'Connor, Jonathan, Carpentier, Sandor Szabo, Hutton, and Watson. In the spring he played a key role in helping kick off what is generally overlooked as the first incarnation of Vancouver wrestling to hit the airwaves—a series called *The Manly Art of Mayhem*, which had a brief 11:30 p.m. Monday-night run on CBUT-TV two years before the much more famous *All-Star Wrestling* debuted on CHAN-TV. In a March 12, 1960, column in *The Province*, Eric Whitehead credits Rod Fenton, recognized in the column as the co-promoter of British Columbia wrestling with partner Cliff Parker, as being the force behind the series.

For his part, Kiniski, who the previous year had been brought in to help give a boost to a new show, *Chicago Championship Wrestling*, on the Windy City's WBBM-TV, recognized the importance of television in bringing interest in his brand to the masses. In an otherwise unidentified newspaper article written by Robert Anderson in connection with the WBBM debut, Kiniski said television had "renewed interest in the sport." He added, "TV has speeded up the matches and made the defensive wrestler obsolete."

Not much is remembered about *The Manly Art of Mayhem*, which, as British Columbia journalist Doug Peck reported in an otherwise unidentifiable "Television" column apparently in the spring of 1960, "ended a 10-week run of cockeyed foolishness this week." According to Peck, the series' final episode included a panel discussion whose participants included Kiniski and Curtis Iaukea—like Kiniski, one of the wilder wrestlers of his time—along with "a prim-looking lady in the front row of the audience who kept hurling insults at Kiniski" and "a short wrestling bout ... which incidentally looked more 'legitimate' than the panel talk."

Discussing the program's chance of getting renewed by CBUT—which apparently did not happen—Peck wrote, "If it doesn't return next spring ... it will be a pity." He continued, "I am not a wrestling fan and for this reason was a little surprised to find myself thoroughly enjoying the show," which, he said, "quite literally pulls the leg of wrestling as a sport, but makes the most of its value as entertainment."

As far as Kiniski's ring career in 1960 was concerned, a significant development was his summertime arrival in the Minneapolis-based American Wrestling Association (AWA), established earlier that year by Verne Gagne.

Among pro wrestlers of his day—or any era—Gagne had rare credentials as a legitimate athlete. Like Kiniski, he was a champion wrestler in high school. Attending the University of Minnesota in the 1940s, Gagne was an All-American football player, a four-time Big Ten heavyweight wrestling champion, and a two-time NCAA wrestling champion. After earning an alternate spot on the 1948 U.S. Olympic freestyle wrestling team behind Dick Hutton, Gagne had opportunities to play in the NFL, but as Margalit Fox reports in Gagne's obituary in the May 1, 2015, *New York Times*—and as Kiniski would determine for himself—"there was little money in pro football then, and [Gagne] chose to earn his keep on the canvas."

Gagne had been a major attraction and titleholder across the United States and Canada prior to cofounding the AWA in 1960. In the mid–1950s, Gagne's appearances as a clean-cut "scientific" grappler on nationally televised shows from Chicago and Los Angeles launched him to fame in the United States, while his success as a wrestler in Toronto and, especially, Montreal in the 1950s earned him a strong reputation in Canada. In and around Montreal in 1958, Kiniski and Gagne faced off a few times in tag team matches.

Gagne's establishment of the AWA was the drawn-out response to divisions in the National Wrestling Alliance, which had been the dominant professional wrestling organization in the world dating back to its inception in 1948. Although the NWA increased its membership to more than 30 promotions in the 1950s, it also faced government investigation as a result of alleged exclusionary practices aimed at stifling competition and ensuring the advantages and well-being of NWA promotions and the alliance as a whole. But despite putting up a relatively united front in standing up to allegations and in beating down independent competition, NWA promoters did not always agree about who should be the touring NWA champion. As reported by Greg Oliver in an April 20, 2000, *SLAM! Wrestling* feature on Gagne, "Some members of the National Wrestling Alliance got fed up with Lou Thesz as the world champion." According to Oliver, those opposing Thesz backed Édouard Carpentier as NWA champion following a disqualification victory by Carpentier over Thesz in 1959.

The actual match in question appears to have been a June 14, 1957, encounter in Chicago (two days after Carpentier dropped Montreal's world title to Kiniski) that Scott Beekman, in his book *Ringside*, describes as one leading to "one of the most confusing episodes in the history of professional wrestling" (100). In the match, Beekman reports, Thesz, who had been NWA champion during most of the alliance's existence, suffered a back injury and had to forfeit the match. Although the NWA continued to recognize Thesz as champion, Carpentier was billed at times as the NWA titleholder, and Beekman speculates that "quite possibly [NWA President Sam] Muchnick planned the confusion over the championship to increase revenues by having two champions engaged in title defenses across the continent and to generate excitement for unification bouts" (100). Tim Hornbaker, in his book *National Wrestling Alliance: The Untold Story of the Monopoly That Strangled Pro Wrestling*, offers further clarification: "The decision was spurred by a hunger to make money during Lou [Thesz'] expedition to the South Pacific and Asia in the fall of 1957. With Thesz unavailable for two months, [NWA] members were concerned about losing the sizable gates he'd normally be bringing in" (229).

Beekman continues, "With the NWA not offering the public a clear championship picture, independent-minded promoters recognized they could establish their own championships.... By 1958, promoters in Montreal, Boston, and Omaha established their own 'world' champions through Carpentier" (101).

Omaha promoter Joe Dusek recognized Carpentier as world champion, and as Beekman reports, "Verne Gagne obtained the promotion's version of the world championship in 1958 after defeating Carpentier" (102). From there, Beekman continues, Gagne, armed with well-recognized athletic credentials and a claim to the world heavyweight wrestling championship, "pushed for a chance to wrestle NWA champion Pat O'Connor. After the NWA refused, not surprisingly, to give an 'outlaw' champion a shot at their title, Gagne and Minneapolis promoter Wally Karbo established the AWA in August 1960" (102) and, that same month, brought into the new territory one of wrestling's top attractions, Gene Kiniski.

Kiniski's early months in the AWA saw him compile a strong winning record as he ran off victories against relatively high-level competition such as Roy McClarty, Stan Kowalski, Larry Hennig, Aldo Bogni, and Tiny Mills. Generally positioned as the number two wrestler—behind Gagne—in the AWA from his first day there, Kiniski established himself as a credible challenger for the AWA World Heavyweight title, falling just short, sometimes by disqualification, in several challenges for the title between October and

December of 1960. High in the AWA pecking order along with Kiniski was Wilbur Snyder, and Kiniski defeated Snyder by countout for the AWA United States Heavyweight title on December 13, 1960.

Besides making a big impression in large cities the AWA was running at the time—among them Detroit, Cincinnati, Columbus, Denver, Winnipeg, and especially Gagne's home base of Minneapolis-St. Paul—Kiniski was a key attraction when it came to bringing mayhem to rabid audiences in smaller cities all around the loop, including Brainerd, Mankato, Duluth, and Rochester, Minnesota; Hope and Evansville, Indiana; Mellen and Hurley, Wisconsin; and Fargo, North Dakota. Kiniski's travels to outlying areas often came amid a good measure of fanfare. An unidentified clipping from Kiniski's collection announcing his arrival in Hibbing, Minnesota, to defend the U.S. Heavyweight title against Leo Nomellini, says, "The champion has crippled more opponents than any man in the game." The same article brings up Kiniski's familiar list of accomplishments over the years in football and wrestling, and—aimed at a readership and potential arena audience in the hockey country of northern Minnesota—adds that "he was also better than average as a hockey defenseman."

The AWA also hit some locales in Canada other than Winnipeg when Kiniski was a top attraction for the Gagne promotion. According to the June 5, 1961, *Fort Frances Times*, Kiniski had come to town a few days earlier "by popular demand. The former Edmonton footballer somehow managed to attract fan mail from Fort Frances that he proudly read during his televised matches in Minnesota." The article says Kiniski started out his match in Fort Frances—a northwestern Ontario town just across the border from Minnesota—as a heavy favorite of the 1,500 fans in attendance but managed to turn the crowd against him over the course of the contest. Yet, says the article, "folks who managed to meet the big wrestler during his visit were impressed by his pleasant [behavior]. Some even suspected his villainous ways in the ring are a disguise to his true, good nature." Later that month Kiniski brought his "villainous ways" to the small Northern Ontario city of Port Arthur—now part of Thunder Bay—where he teamed with Hard Boiled Haggerty to defeat Roy McClarty and George Scott and to rile the crowd. According to the June 27, 1961, *Port Arthur News-Chronicle*, "The 1,000 fans in attendance at the Gardens were in hysterics over the methods used by the bad boys in administering their opponents helpless." Such hysterics were run-of-the-mill during Kiniski's stay in the AWA, as he was known to take abuse from unruly fans and an occasional chair shot to the head—not by a fellow wrestler but, again, from a spectator. One incident in which a St. Paul fan put a lit cigar to Kiniski's leg resulted, in November of 1962, in a $2,000 settlement in Kiniski's favor.

While packing them in with the AWA, Kiniski continued making the rounds, as his schedule allowed, to the Pacific Northwest, Alberta, and Southern Ontario, and his matches in Central and Western Canada against Watson—along with his matches in Minnesota and Winnipeg against Gagne and his matches around the Midwest against Snyder—were among the hottest tickets in wrestling in 1960. Kiniski's reestablished partnership with Haggerty in the AWA was another surefire ticket-seller.

Kiniski was an active United States champion well into 1961, maintaining the credibility of a title traceable to the NWA United States title that had been traded around in Chicago among such major names as Hans Schmidt, Dick the Bruiser, Snyder, and Gagne. When he was NWA United States champion in 1958, Gagne split off from Fred Kohler's Chicago promotion and established his own version of the U.S. title, which would later become the AWA United States Heavyweight title.

Kiniski and Don "Hard Boiled Haggerty" Stansauk teamed off and on for several years and were a top tag team of the early 1960s in the Midwest and on the West Coast. Like Kiniski an ex-pro footballer and leading villain of his day, Haggerty went on to a successful career as a character actor when his wrestling days were over (Vance Nevada collection).

Kiniski turned back a battery of challengers including Mills, Nick Roberts, Jim Hady, Joe Scarpello, and Snyder, who took the U.S. title back from Kiniski in mid–February before losing it back to him six weeks later. Kiniski would go on to hold the AWA United States Heavyweight title until the final weeks of his stay in the AWA, although it appears he may have dropped the title to Snyder and regained it more than once.

In early April Kiniski replaced Len Montana—who, as Len Crosby, had held the Texas Tag Team title with Kiniski in 1956—as a coholder, with Haggerty, of the AWA World Tag Team championship. Montana—who went on to play the role of Luca Brasi in *The Godfather* after serving time in real life for his involvement in organized crime— had apparently suffered a broken leg while holding a share of the AWA tag title, and Haggerty, at least in storyline, chose Kiniski as Montana's replacement. The record shows, however, that Montana—whatever the condition of his leg may have been—was wrestling a busy schedule in Florida just a few weeks later.

The Kiniski-Haggerty duo—composed of two ex-pro footballers and bona fide lead heels in the fledgling AWA territory—performed at a high level, reeling off victories against top teams such as Gagne-Snyder, Eric-Mills, and, in Winnipeg, Watson-Snyder.

But the heel champions were booked as a lucky team as much as a dominant one, as they lost a few matches by disqualification before dropping the title in Minneapolis on May 23 to Snyder and Leo Nomellini. Nomellini, an ex-footballer and former NWA champion—for four months in 1955, between the first two of Lou Thesz' National Wrestling Alliance title reigns—was a major wrestling attraction in California and the Midwest in the 1950s, and Kiniski had faced him numerous times in California in 1955 and 1956.

Two months after losing the AWA World Tag Team title to Snyder and Nomellini, Kiniski and Haggerty regained the championship in St. Paul on July 19, 1961—by which time the professional wrestling career of Gene Kiniski had risen to an altogether new level.

Kiniski's crowning achievement in the AWA came on July 11, 1961, when he defeated Gagne in Minneapolis to capture his first major singles world championship, the AWA Heavyweight title. In between capturing the AWA Heavyweight title and regaining a share of the AWA Tag Team title eight days later with Haggerty, Kiniski faced Watson in a July 13 Edmonton main event that ended in a double disqualification. There are also reports of a meeting between Kiniski and Pat O'Connor in Calgary on July 10, 1961—the night before Kiniski took the AWA Heavyweight title from Gagne in Minneapolis. As Kiniski reportedly lost the Calgary match against O'Connor—who had dropped the NWA title to Rogers just 10 days earlier in a record-breaking show drawing more than 38,000 fans to Chicago's Comiskey Park—it is questionable whether Gagne was aware of the full nature of Kiniski's booking in Calgary.

Though Kiniski defended the AWA World Heavyweight title only a few times before losing it back to Gagne in Bloomington, Minnesota's Metropolitan Stadium on August 8, 1961, his four-week run with the AWA title solidified his reputation as one of the toughest wrestlers in the world, a credible world champion, and an engaging speaker. Gil Hayes, who would become a pro wrestler in the mid-1960s after meeting Kiniski in the Winnipeg bar where Hayes was a bouncer, recalls watching Kiniski on televised matches from Minnesota during the 1960s and says Kiniski made a big impression on him. "He was a real good man on the stick," says Hayes, who would become a star with Stampede Wrestling before joining Kiniski in Vancouver's All-Star Wrestling in the early 1970s. "[If you] put the microphone underneath him ... he put his lips in gear and he could talk your ear off. It's just a thing he had."

Verne Gagne's son and future wrestling star Greg Gagne recalls an AWA television segment during the height of the Kiniski-Gagne rivalry. At the time, Verne Gagne owned a store in Minneapolis, where he sold health products, including Gera Speed vitamins.

"My father sold his vitamins during commercial time," says Greg Gagne. "He was doing a commercial with Marty O'Neill about his vitamins, and Gene came barreling into the interview area, started a big argument with Verne, and hit him with one of the bottles of Gera Speed. And Verne went down and he took him out."

Greg Gagne, who was about 12 years old at the time and working as a hot dog vendor at the show, continues, "[Kiniski] was right next to us where we were selling the stuff, and I was scared. [He] scared the shit out of me. I'm in tears, my dad's down, and what's going to happen?"

The next day, recalls Greg, he went to visit the son of AWA co-owner Wally Karbo. "I went up there for the weekend," says Greg, "and who does [Karbo] have up there but Gene Kiniski."

After describing his fear, Greg says Kiniski took him aside. "I was almost in tears," he says. "[Kiniski] says, 'Come here, young man. You know, your father and I—we're enemies, and I'm sorry what happened. But I want you to understand, I think you're one of the best young men I've ever met in my life.' [That] made me feel like a champ. And him and I went fishing that day, and I had a hell of a time with Gene. After that, we kind of became friends. I always looked up to him over the years."

As far as his father was concerned, Greg Gagne says, despite any illusions that Gene Kiniski was a hated rival, "they were good, close friends. [Verne] and Gene got together famously. The three of them—him and Wilbur Snyder and Verne—they were best of friends." His father's friendship with Kiniski, says Greg, outlasted the relatively brief stay "Uncle Gene" had as a headliner in the AWA. "Gene and Verne stayed close for a number of years."

Of Kiniski's ability as a wrestler, Greg Gagne says, "He was a big and rugged guy. I mean, he was fantastic ... a terrific performer ... fun to be around.... [He] always kept you on your toes." Of the Kiniski-Gagne matches that helped put the AWA on the map in the early 1960s, Greg says, "They were classics."

Though a generation younger than Gene Kiniski, Greg Gagne says, "[Gene] and I became friends over the years, and he was just a great guy and always fun to be around." They would continue to cross paths for years in Winnipeg, a city where Kiniski headlined on occasion long after leaving the AWA. "When he was in Winnipeg whenever we were there," says Greg, "him and I always went out to dinner afterwards and shared some good times together."

In many respects, Wilbur Snyder's son Mike, who wrestled professionally in the 1970s, tells a similar story. Mike Snyder, who says Gene Kiniski was his godfather, considered Kiniski a close friend despite the fact they were a generation apart. "He was a gentle giant of a man with great humor," says Mike. "My relationship with him never wavered as I stayed in contact for many years after I left the business." Of his father's friendship with Kiniski, Mike Snyder says, "They stayed in constant contact throughout their careers and often went on hunting trips together." He adds, "My mother and Gene's wife became very good friends."

Kiniski remained in the AWA for less than two months after dropping the World Heavyweight title back to Verne Gagne in a cage match that saw Kiniski's championship tag team partner Haggerty "accidentally" throw dirt in Kiniski's eyes. The weeks following the loss of the AWA world title were a busy time for Kiniski, who still had two titles to defend—the AWA U.S. Heavyweight championship and the AWA World Tag Team title he shared with Haggerty. But far more was going on in Kiniski's life at the time, as second son Nick had been born, in Minneapolis on January 7, 1961—delivered, according to legend, which Nick doesn't deny, by Dr. Richard Fliehr, father of 1970s–2000s wrestling superstar Ric Flair and at the time a noted Minneapolis obstetrician. Now numbering four, the Kiniski family, by the summer of 1961, had begun a transition toward relocating to the Pacific Northwest, an area Gene Kiniski already knew fairly well. Kiniski had been appearing occasionally on wrestling shows in Vancouver since 1957, and since early 1960 Canada's Pacific Coast had been a regular stop on the Kiniski tour.

Shortly after losing the AWA title, Kiniski captured the British Empire Heavyweight title—the Vancouver promotion's top title at the time and an offshoot of the British Empire title recognized in Toronto—from Whipper Watson before dropping the title back to Watson two days later. Another regular opponent of Kiniski's in British Columbia in 1961 was Dory Funk, Sr., who had been so instrumental in getting Kiniski's career off to a strong start. On August 22, 1961—in the middle of a three-day run of wrestling shows at Vancouver's annual Pacific National Exhibition, with the Watson title changes taking place on the other two shows—Kiniski lost a main event to Funk, who wrestled as The Outlaw.

Back in the AWA a week later, Kiniski followed up on the disharmony stemming from his October 8 AWA World Heavyweight title loss to Gagne after Haggerty threw dirt in his eyes. That was not the first time Haggerty's interference had cost Kiniski a match, and the strongheaded partners dissolved their championship pairing after the title loss mishap—although they reunited briefly across the border in Winnipeg on September 15, defeating Verne Gagne and Karl Krauser, better remembered as Karl Gotch. But both before and after that one-night stand in Winnipeg, Kiniski and Haggerty were embroiled in a wild feud that culminated in Kiniski's losing the AWA United States Heavyweight title and his half of the AWA World Tag Team championship to Haggerty, who would continue his tag title reign with future NWA president Bob Geigel as his partner.

On September 28, 1961, one day after finishing out his run in the AWA, Kiniski was back in Ontario, headlining a Maple Leaf Gardens show and losing via disqualification to Bulldog Brower, a tough wrestler Kiniski would face a few more times over the next several years. A week after their initial meeting in Toronto, where Brower was strongly positioned as a frequent main eventer, Kiniski—a heavy fan favorite when matched up with the psychotic-looking Brower—lost the return match at Maple Leaf Gardens.

Kiniski traveled to Alberta following his stop in Toronto, reconnecting with family and friends and bringing his traveling show with Whipper Billy Watson to Edmonton on October 21, 1961. That match—resulting in the same double DQ finish as their match in the same city three months earlier—would be their last recorded meeting in a singles match in Edmonton, though their singles rivalry would remain strong in other locations for several more years.

Bruce Kinisky recalls, about his uncle Gene, "He always liked to come back to his roots." According to Steven Eleniak, one of Kiniski's favorite gathering places in Edmonton was a popular hotel and watering hole for athletes and sportswriters based at the nearby Edmonton Journal building. "[Kiniski] used to come back quite often and … hang around with the guys at the Selkirk Hotel," recalls Eleniak, who was not a fan of pro wrestling. "On a Saturday afternoon that was common. There would be at least half a dozen of these so-called wrestlers drinking beer."

Eleniak recalls one of Kiniski's visits to the Selkirk after his career was well established: "He had chains around his neck … gold, big chains.… He was really dressed far in advance of the people in the hotel there." Throughout most of his career—especially while holding a major wrestling championship—Kiniski was noted for playing the part of a well-dressed, well-paid athlete. Yet Eleniak recalls that Kiniski was generally approachable in his old, familiar surroundings.

But after catching up a bit in his native Alberta in the fall of 1961 and apparently resting or mending briefly in the aftermath of a shoulder separation suffered during one of his matches in Toronto against Brower, Gene Kiniski—along with Marion and the couple's two sons—would soon head west to take up residence in the area that would become most associated with the life and career of Gene Kiniski.

10

Vancouver Territory, 1961–1963

Kiniski's first match in the Vancouver territory following his departure from the AWA was a November 13 victory over Watson at the Pacific National Exhibition Gardens. That was roughly—and perhaps conservatively—the 200th career meeting between Kiniski and Watson in either singles or tag team matches, and it set the stage for an amazing Kiniski run in Northwest wrestling rings and an association with the region that would remain strong for the rest of his life.

Kiniski's last previous meeting with Watson in Vancouver—January 2, 1961, at the Pacific National Exhibition (PNE) Gardens—had not gone nearly as well. Not only had Kiniski come out on the losing end, but he made headlines by getting stabbed by a fan as he left the ring.

According to a January 4, 1961, Canadian Press report, "Kiniski was jostled by a crowd of fans who invaded the ring after the bout and an unidentified person drove a shiv into Kiniski's side in the melee…. Blood poured from the wrestler's wound and he was rushed to Vancouver General Hospital to have it stitched. The knife wound penetrated right to the ribs."

An unidentified clipping from Kiniski's collection adds, "After a riled zealot hopped into the ring and stabbed him for 14 stitches, Mr. Kiniski demanded that police find the stabber. 'I want that man as a partner in a tag team match,' said Mr. Kiniski. 'He must be the bravest guy who ever lived.'"

The Canadian Press article reports that Kiniski, following his stitching, left the hospital and returned to his home in Minneapolis. But what neither article mentioned was that Kiniski was back in the ring—in Duluth, Minnesota—two days after being stabbed.

In later years Kiniski would take plenty more abuse—including getting shot with staple guns and burned with cigars—in Vancouver as much as anywhere else. "I remember Dad said Vancouver fans are nuts," says Kelly Kiniski.

After his successful meeting with Watson in November of 1961, Kiniski quickly established himself on his new home turf as a top wrestler, top heel, and top attraction who could deliver convincing matches against big names such as Watson and Funk, against mid-level stars of the day, and against wrestlers who filled out the cards but whose names are all but forgotten by modern-day fans. One of Kiniski's frequent opponents was Roy McClarty, a fairly successful wrestler who had faced Kiniski at least a dozen times in Ontario and in the AWA before migrating to the Northwest in 1961. McClarty would wrestle for several years in British Columbia and northern Washington—most notably in tag team matches, partnered with "brother" Don "McClarty" Leeds—before settling into a long-term role as a referee for All-Star Wrestling and maintaining a close association with Kiniski for years.

By the time Kiniski started wrestling primarily in the Pacific Northwest, the British Columbia territory was in the capable hands of co-promoters Cliff Parker and Rod Fenton—with the latter widely recognized as the main force in the day-to-day running of the promotion.

Parker, who had been a popular wrestler in Vancouver's Big Time Wrestling (not the Alberta-based Big Time Wrestling promotion run by Stu Hart) and Pender Wrestling Club promotions in the late 1930s and 1940s, had been promoting in British Columbia's Lower Mainland since 1949 and booking wrestlers out to Washington State promoter Cliff Olson since the late 1950s. Parker had enjoyed a fairly successful decade of promoting when Fenton came in as his partner, and Kiniski—often facing a leading wrestler of the era such as Watson, O'Connor, Jonathan, Hutton, Carpentier, or Sandor Szabo—had been brought in as a featured performer from time to time since 1957. Overall, Vancouver under Parker was viewed as a relatively good place for a wrestler to advance his career.

Fenton—like Kiniski, a product of Edmonton—had taken Kiniski under his wing in 1951 when the latter was transitioning from college in Tucson to the wrestling world. Prior to that, Fenton—though on the small side for a wrestler at a weight ranging from about 150 to 190 pounds—had been known as Lightning Rod Fenton over the course of a successful 18-year career.

While Fenton apparently never won a pro wrestling title (though Oliver reports he was sometimes referred to as the "middleweight champ of Canada"), he appeared in several territories from 1933 to 1951, the year he got into promoting. Noted for a lethal-looking dropkick, Fenton won his share of matches up and down the West Coast, in the Midwest and Gulf Coast regions, and particularly in Texas—where he met his wife Jackie and married her on their second date—before landing in Tucson in 1950.

Fenton's promotional career in Tucson is remembered favorably, no doubt in large part thanks to his role in getting Kiniski's career off to a strong start in 1952. Though Fenton sold the Tucson promotion in the summer of 1957 in order to focus on his avid interest in horse racing, Oliver reports in a June 30, 2010, *SLAM! Wrestling* article that Fenton bought the promotion back from U.S. District Judge D. W. Bartlett and ex-wrestler Karl Sarpolis in February of 1958, telling the *Tucson Daily Citizen*, "I've had enough of a rest." Oliver's June 30, 2010, *SLAM!* account and a report on Fenton by Tim Hornbaker at www.legacyofwrestling.com are in agreement that Fenton, during the time he sat out promoting in Tucson, continued running shows in Phoenix, Mesa, and Yuma, where he had been promoting for a few years. In Phoenix Fenton was also a co-owner of the city's main wrestling venue, named Madison Square Garden but certainly not to be mistaken for its more famous namesake.

According to Hornbaker's report, Fenton had been promoting in Phoenix since 1954, and newspaper reports and arena wrestling programs from the time confirm that. During at least part of his tenure as a promoter in Phoenix, Fenton was a member of the National Wrestling Alliance. Hornbaker, in *National Wrestling Alliance: The Untold Story of the Monopoly That Strangled Pro Wrestling*, says Fenton's application for NWA membership was approved unanimously in 1954 (28). Meanwhile, *Chokehold: Pro Wrestling's Real Mayhem outside the Ring*, a critical examination of the NWA's practices self-published in 2003 by ex-wrestler Jim Wilson and Weldon T. Johnson, reports—apparently incorrectly—that Fenton's application for NWA membership was in 1955, not 1954, and was not approved (261). Hornbaker's www.legacyofwrestling.com report says Fenton was an NWA member but was dropped from the organization in 1956 when he did not pay membership dues or respond to communication from the NWA. Whatever the exact nature or duration of Fenton's association with the NWA might have been, it seems clear he was no longer connected with the organization by late 1956.

Fenton had success in his promoting ventures in Arizona until about the end of the 1950s, when he saw an opportunity to make a name as a wrestling promoter in his native country. It is not clear exactly why he chose to give up his operations in Arizona, but it has been suggested that Fenton, with his longstanding interest in horse racing and perhaps other gambling-oriented activities, had as much reason to want to leave Arizona and the United States as he did to return to his native land. As Vance Nevada reports in *Wrestling in the Canadian West*, "It is [rumored Fenton's] homecoming was directly tied to gambling debts incurred by the veteran matman in the United States" (44). But Rod's daughter Patrice Fenton points out that her father's mother lived in North Vancouver at the time, and that may have contributed to his decision to look seriously at a business opportunity that came up in British Columbia.

According to Patrice Fenton, her father "knew members of the mob [in Arizona], and there was a big scandal that they might have been involved in Rillito Racetrack," a Tucson facility Rod Fenton had rebuilt with a partner and was managing during his tenure as a wrestling promoter in the 1950s. "There were some trials, as I recall," Patrice Fenton says, adding that her father was called to testify. "Dad was exonerated, but there was still kind of a blemish on the track, I think, from that."

Since the trial took place in about 1954 and the Fenton family didn't leave Arizona until near the end of the 1950s, Patrice says, "I'm thinking that wasn't a factor." She is

Rod Fenton owned an acreage outside Tucson, where he raised horses and often hosted Gene Kiniski and other wrestlers who came through Arizona (Kiniski family archive).

quick to add that she doesn't think Gene Kiniski was in any way involved in the racetrack's troubles.

Fenton was well established in his new position as Cliff Parker's partner in running the Vancouver-based wrestling promotion by the time Gene Kiniski took up his position—which he would hold for many years—as the lead heel in the territory.

Kiniski's first full year based in the Pacific Northwest solidified his standing as a dominant singles wrestler, but it was in tag team competition that Kiniski had some of his most notable success in 1962, both in and outside the Northwest. He would reunite in the ring that year with a pair of partners with whom he had earlier formed dominant championship tag teams, and Kiniski and his partners would waste little time in taking their reestablished teams back to the top. But before that would happen, Kiniski, barely after arriving in the Northwest, reunited with another top name from his past—one remembered more than half a century later as a powerful partner and an equally powerful opponent of Kiniski's.

Killer Kowalski—born Edward Spulnik in Windsor, Ontario—was a 13-year wrestling veteran when he arrived in Vancouver in late 1961, right around the time Kiniski arrived there. Kowalski was already a legendary figure to wrestling fans across North America, largely as a result of his appearances on *Wrestling from Marigold* in the 1950s but particularly because of an October 15, 1952, match at the Montreal Forum that helped establish him as a top wrestling villain for a generation.

It was a freak accident during a match against Yukon Eric that set things in motion for the wrestler formerly known as Waldek Kowalski and Tarzan Kowalski to become known as "Killer" Kowalski for the final quarter-century of his career as a full-time wrestler and during his later career as a wrestling trainer.

As Kowalski recounted the incident in a "What I've Learned" feature in the August 31, 2008, digital edition of *Esquire*, published shortly after his death, "I used to jump off the top rope and put my shinbone across my opponent's chest. So I tied Yukon Eric up in the ropes. Then I climbed to the top turnbuckle and jumped. He saw me coming and tried to turn away. But my shinbone scraped his cheek so tight, it caught his cauliflower ear. The ear flew off and rolled across the ring like a little ball."

A few days later, according to Kowalski's obituary in the August 31, 2008, *New York Times*, Kowalski and Eric—who apparently had no hard feelings—were sharing a laugh over the incident in Eric's hospital room when there were reporters within earshot. "The next day," Kowalski said in the *Esquire* piece, "the newspapers were filled with stories of me laughing at the sight of Yukon Eric's missing ear. When I walked to the ring the next week, people were throwing bottles at me. 'You're nothing but a killer!' someone screamed. From that moment on, I was Killer Kowalski."

Kowalski, one of the most-traveled wrestlers of the 1950s and early 1960s, had much in common with Gene Kiniski. Both were larger-than-average wrestlers—often coming across as larger than life—shared a Polish Canadian background, and employed a bruising, relentless, give-no-quarter style in their matches. Their paths had crossed in several territories—occasionally inciting minor riots and at least one major one—prior to their convergence in the Pacific Northwest in November of 1961, and the two knew each other well when they first joined forces as a team in British Columbia in a November 20, 1961, main event at Vancouver's Pacific National Exhibition Gardens to face off, in a losing effort, against NWA Pacific Coast Tag Team champions Watson and Roy McClarty. While the Vancouver wrestling promotion was not formally a National Wrestling Alliance territory at the time, the promotion had a good relationship with the NWA, and its titles were recognized by the alliance.

Kiniski and Kowalski had earlier teamed in the Montreal-Ottawa region in 1957, when both were headliners in the territory and either could have made a strong case for being considered the lead heel. The two partnered at least a dozen times from 1957 to 1958, usually facing teams composed of top babyfaces such as Carpentier, O'Connor, Gagne, or Watson, but also joining forces a few times to participate in wild heel-vs.-heel encounters against teams comprising Japanese stereotypes such as Mr. Hito, Mr. Moto, and Tosh Togo. Kiniski and Kowalski also teamed up in St. Louis on February 3, 1961, to defeat Wilbur Snyder and Bob Ellis on a card headlined by a Pat O'Connor NWA title defense against Johnny Valentine.

A few years before converging in Vancouver, Kiniski and Kowalski also faced off in a few brutal encounters in Chicago, St. Louis, and, most notably, Montreal, where Kiniski's July 17, 1957, regional world title loss to Kowalski drew 22,000 fans to Delormier Stadium. In the Vancouver territory from late 1961 to mid–1962, the two would follow their familiar pattern of mixing success as a tag team with a few tough singles matchups in which many fans no doubt hoped the two top heels in the territory would tear each other apart.

With Kowalski often headlining shows in Alberta during his stay in the Vancouver territory, it appears, at least partly as a result, that the pair successfully defended the Pacific Coast Tag Team title only once—losing via disqualification to Watson and McClarty—during their six-week reign. On March 5, 1962, at Vancouver's PNE Gardens, Kiniski and Kowalski dropped the title to Watson and Ernie "Mr. Kleen" Bemis under controversial circumstances leading to a Kiniski-Kowalski singles main event, won by Kiniski, two weeks later in Vancouver. On May 21 the two would have a rematch in Vancouver, which resulted in a double disqualification. Sandwiched between their two wild singles main events in Vancouver, in an era in which news traveled much more slowly than it does now, Kiniski and Kowalski reunited as a team at least twice in Alberta— once, during an April 3 appearance at Edmonton's Sales Pavilion, where it appears they functioned as a well-oiled unit in putting away Bearcat Wright and Jesus "Mighty Ursus" Ortega in a best-of-three-falls match. In Calgary, meanwhile, Kiniski and Kowalski were declared an "invincible tag team" in an arena program when they made an appearance in the city early in 1962, but by summer they would split up the team again and throw their heavy artillery at each other in a singles match in Calgary.

But it was with another ex-partner that Kiniski had his most notable tag-team success in 1962. In February, while still holding the Vancouver territory's tag title with Kowalski, Kiniski reunited with ex-partner Hard Boiled Haggerty, and the two teamed several times before the Kiniski-Kowalski championship reign ended on March 5. Just three weeks later Kiniski regained a share of the Pacific Coast Tag Team title when he and Haggerty took the championship from Watson and Mr. Kleen on March 26.

During the Kiniski-Haggerty team's initial title run in the Northwest, spanning 15 weeks, the champions had several meetings with the McClarty Brothers, Roy and Don, a top team in the territory at the time. While the McClartys would not take the Pacific Coast Tag Team championship from Kiniski-Haggerty, the fictional brothers did defeat Kiniski and Haggerty in the tournament final for the International Tag Team championship in Winnipeg on July 5, 1962, four days before Kiniski and Haggerty lost the NWA Pacific Coast Tag Team title in Vancouver to Whipper Watson and Bearcat Wright.

But a few weeks later Kiniski would hold not only a share of the Pacific Coast tag title again—regaining the championship, with Haggerty, from Watson and Wright on August 7 in Vancouver—but a share of another prestigious tag team title, with another former partner, half a continent away in Texas. He won his share of that title—the NWA Southwest Tag Team championship—from a team that included another key figure from Kiniski's past.

Dory Funk, Sr., like Kiniski, was one of the top wrestlers in the world in 1962. For more than a year Funk had been dividing his time mainly between British Columbia—wrestling under a mask as The Outlaw—and the Amarillo territory, where he had won numerous titles as the centerpiece and, since the mid–1950s, part-owner of the promotion. After reuniting with Funk upon settling primarily in the Pacific Northwest, Kiniski began making short-term excursions to northwest Texas, where his reputation was still fresh, to engage in high-profile matches, often against Funk.

During much of 1962 Kiniski was recognized in the Amarillo territory, though not elsewhere, as the NWA World Heavyweight champion, supposedly as a result of a series of victories over Buddy Rogers; and for about a year, from early 1962 to early 1963, Kiniski occasionally defended the "NWA World Heavyweight title" in the Amarillo territory.

On July 19, 1962, Kiniski faced Funk in a tag team match at the Amarillo Sports Arena. For the occasion, Kiniski was reunited with his former partner in the Toronto-Buffalo region, Fritz von Erich, to challenge NWA Southwest Tag Team titleholders Funk and Ricky Romero. According to amarillowrestling.wikia.com, the match lasted about 50 minutes, with Kiniski and Funk trading the first two falls with their backbreaker and spinning toe hold finishes and von Erich pinning Funk to win the third fall and the title for his team, wrestling together for the first time in more than three years.

Kiniski and von Erich would not team again until four weeks later, when they successfully defended the Southwest tag title against Funk and Romero in an Amarillo rematch. In the interim Kiniski was back in the Northwest, headlining shows around the territory, as was Funk. For Kiniski's part, he faced Lou Thesz in Victoria and apparently in Tacoma, Washington, and headlined a major show in Vancouver, reportedly drawing between 14,000 and 16,000 fans for a match against Buddy Rogers—recognized in British Columbia, as in other places outside the Amarillo territory, as the legitimate NWA Heavyweight champion—during the week immediately preceding Kiniski-Haggerty's August 7, 1962, NWA Pacific Coast Tag Team title rematch against champions Watson and Wright at the PNE Gardens. The Kiniski-Haggerty team's successful August 7 title challenge followed a hot semifinal match in which Funk fought Thesz to a draw.

In mid–October Kiniski traveled back to Texas, where he defended his locally-recognized NWA Heavyweight title against Joe Scarpello in Odessa, dropped a decision to Funk the next night in Lubbock, and then teamed with von Erich at the Amarillo Sports Arena to drop the powerhouse pair's once-defended title back to ex-champions Funk and Romero. In a pattern somewhat familiar to Kiniski, he would travel back from the Northwest to Amarillo a few weeks later to engage in a wild match against a former championship partner, this time von Erich, who defeated Kiniski in a best-of-three-falls "fence" match that apparently did not compromise the promotion's recognition of Kiniski as NWA Heavyweight champion.

Meanwhile, back in British Columbia, Kiniski and Haggerty marked their second title run with multiple defenses against the McClartys and new challengers Bearcat Wright and Sweet Daddy Siki. Their final defense took place October 13 in Victoria with a disqualification loss to Whipper Watson and strongman Hercules Cortez. That match was not only the Kiniski-Haggerty team's final defense of the NWA Pacific Coast Tag Team title but the last time any team would defend that title.

With the phasing out of the Vancouver territory's Pacific Coast Tag Team championship in the fall of 1962 came the introduction of a new title to take its place. A tournament was held in Vancouver on November 12, with six teams vying to become the inaugural NWA Canadian Tag Team titleholders as recognized in the Pacific Northwest.

Haggerty was already gone from the territory, and Kiniski's new partner was Clyde Steeves, a well-traveled veteran who had arrived in Vancouver a few months earlier and settled into the midcard with solid showings against many of the prominent names in the promotion. On October 27 in Victoria, Steeves teamed with Kiniski to defeat Cortez and Roy McClarty, but six days later Kiniski-Steeves lost to Cortez and Dan Miller, real-life brother of Bill Miller. Kiniski and Steeves' next match as a duo took place in the first round of the November 12 Vancouver tournament, when they defeated Winnipeg grappler George Gordienko and Erich Froelich, who over the next two decades would be a prominent preliminary and midcard wrestler in British Columbia. The second round of the Canadian Tag Team championship tournament saw Kiniski-Steeves defeat Watson and Cortez. But in the tournament final, Kiniski-Steeves fell to the team of Dan Miller and Sandor Kovacs. Five days after their tournament final loss, Kiniski and Steeves lost a rematch to the champions in Victoria. Records show Kiniski-Steeves teaming only once after that, on December 6 in Chilliwack, British Columbia, in a losing effort against Miller and Cortez.

Froehlich, whose professional association with Kiniski would last about as long as Don Leo Jonathan's, knew Kiniski from all angles and had a similar reputation among insiders for testing newcomers to the territory in the ring to see what they had to offer. Like many, Froelich says that while Kiniski played his character well, "if you met him on the street he was a different person." Summing up Kiniski's contribution over a quarter century to wrestling in the Northwest, Froehlich says, "He was good for the business."

While Kiniski did not hold a singles title in 1962 except the dubious recognition as NWA World Heavyweight champion in the Amarillo territory, 1962 was nonetheless another outstanding year for Kiniski when it came to singles competition.

Most of his activity that year was in the Pacific Northwest, and Kiniski, recognized as a top heel and top "worker" in the Parker-Fenton promotion, did not need a regional singles title in order to impress on fans that he was

German native Erich Froelich was a capable athlete who arrived in British Columbia in the 1950s before becoming a wrestler and facing Kiniski in the ring many times over the course of nearly two decades (Vance Nevada collection).

a legitimately tough wrestler certain to win the majority of his matches. In the fans' minds, anyone beating Kiniski in a singles match would potentially be elevated to headlining status—and Kiniski did his part to raise the stock of several wrestlers who plied their trade in the Pacific Northwest in 1962.

While it is no surprise that Kiniski lost matches in 1962 to Rogers, Watson, and Wright, other 1962 Kiniski losses in the Northwest definitely gave a boost to several opponents—particularly Dan Miller, Don McClarty, Hercules Cortez, and Mr. Kleen. Of Mr. Kleen, Kiniski recalled, in February of 2002, "The guy had a super, super physique [but] he didn't have anything upstairs and he didn't have any wrestling ability" (Oliver, Files).

Despite those losses, Kiniski was a dominant singles wrestler in 1962, and he likely would have held the regional singles title much of the year had there been an actively-defended singles title in the promotion at the time. As it was, the regional NWA British Empire Heavyweight title, established just three years earlier, was barely on the Vancouver wrestling radar by 1962. Kiniski had held the title for two days in August of 1961, but there appear to be no records suggesting any of Kiniski's matches against Watson in 1962—when Watson held the British Empire title for all but about a week—were for the championship. But even without a title at stake, Kiniski earned singles victories in 1962 over key wrestlers such as Kowalski, Wright, Siki, Gordienko, Brower, and Funk—whose losses to Kiniski in Vancouver on September 18 and Tacoma on October 22 led to the unmasking of The Outlaw in both cities.

Outside the Northwest, Kiniski had great success in singles matches throughout 1962, putting on strong performances against the likes of Funk, von Erich, and Bob Ellis in Texas; Leo Nomellini in San Francisco; Bill Miller and Yukon Eric in Winnipeg; and Bockwinkel, Wright, and Kowalski in Saskatchewan and Alberta. Kiniski also made appearances in 1962 in Toronto, including teaming in a late November Maple Leaf Gardens main event with Bruno Sammartino—who would be a fierce rival of Kiniski's two years later—in a losing effort against Brower and Johnny Valentine.

Except during short visits to Texas, Toronto, and Winnipeg and a brief summer stop in Newfoundland and Labrador—where he had made a big impact six years earlier—Kiniski generally stayed home in the Northwest in 1963. On visits to Texas early in the year he faced familiar opponents such as von Erich, Roy McClarty, Cortez, and Funk Sr., and on March 28 in Amarillo Kiniski had his first career match against Dory Funk, Jr., who was awarded the victory when the referee stopped the match during the third fall. Highlights for Kiniski in Winnipeg included teaming with future AWA legend The Crusher in January and February and earning a main-event singles victory over Sammartino in March. Kiniski had only four recorded matches in Toronto in 1963, one an unsuccessful rematch, with partner Sammartino, against Brower and Valentine, which took place just 13 days after Kiniski's victory over Sammartino in Winnipeg.

Although Kiniski was not a frequent traveler to Toronto in 1963, his reputation in the city scored him an appearance that aired in May on CFTO-TV's *Sports Hot Seat*, a popular panel show that would be picked up nationally a few years later. The show involved a group of sportswriters who would "grill" the guest—in this case, Kiniski, who, according to *Toronto Telegram* columnist Bob Blackburn, "is probably the sharpest and most articulate of the grunters and groaners"—and, of course, the panelists' grilling would involve questioning the legitimacy of Kiniski's chosen sport.

Blackburn continues, "Mr. Kiniski is a very engaging fellow, and it was an entertaining and comical half-hour, but unlike other shows in the series it accomplished nothing. For all his clowning approach to the program, the wrestler admitted nothing at all, and the panel members, who appeared to be fans of his, didn't push it very hard. Thus the umpteenth attempt to 'expose' wrestling went down the drain."

Canadian sports broadcasting veteran Bernie Pascall, who worked for CFTO-TV in the 1960s, says Kiniski was a popular guest who was invited back for a few more appearances on the *Hot Seat*. Pascall, who first met Kiniski when the latter was back in Toronto in the mid–1960s for a return appearance on the program, recalls, "He was just a master and just manipulated the high-profile Toronto media as only Gene could."

With only occasional absences from the Northwest in 1963, Kiniski was the mainstay of the Parker-Fenton promotion at a time when the promotion was reaching new heights in terms of its visibility and popularity throughout British Columbia's Lower Mainland and in areas of western Washington not far from the Canadian border, including Tacoma and a few other towns promoted by Cliff Olson, who booked talent out of Vancouver. The wrestling boom in the Northwest was largely the result of the association Fenton— running the promotion out of the house he rented on Granville St. in Vancouver's Shaughnessy district—had established with Vancouver's CHAN-TV during Kiniski's strong run as a headliner in 1962. Kiniski quickly became a fixture on the popular *All-Star Wrestling* show and, to a large degree, the face of professional wrestling in the Pacific Northwest.

While *The Chilliwack Progress* reported on January 9, 1963, that Kiniski had punched a fan during a wrestling show in the city several nights earlier, Kiniski seemed to suffer no negative consequences as a result of the altercation and went on to enjoy another strong year on his home turf. Many of his early 1963 matches in the Northwest were tag team encounters in which he partnered with Frank Townsend, a semi-successful journeyman who was appearing in British Columbia and northern Washington as Mr. X. After quickly establishing themselves as a contending team, Kiniski-Mr. X took the Canadian Tag Team title from Kovacs and Dan Miller in Vancouver on February 11, but following a few largely forgotten defenses of the title, Kiniski-X fell to the team of Kinji Shibuya and Mitsu Arakawa in what appears to have been booked as a heel team-vs.-heel team encounter a month later in Vancouver.

Shibuya and Arakawa—Japanese stereotype characters who enjoyed long careers in numerous territories—were hot opponents for Kiniski in 1963. From March to July Kiniski teamed with a variety of partners—including Mr. X, Fritz von Goering, Ron Etchison, and Joe Brunetti—to face the Japanese heel team, which also faced off against Kiniski and a variety of partners in Winnipeg during that period. Kiniski also engaged in numerous singles meetings in 1963 against both Arakawa and Shibuya, losing a few matches to Shibuya but often getting cheered along the way.

Other key Kiniski matches or programs in 1963—normally touted but seldom featured on *All-Star Wrestling*—were against the likes of Thesz, Haystack Calhoun, Watson, Siki, Cowboy Carlson, Kovacs, Dan Miller, and, late in the year, Funk Sr. and new arrival Tex McKenzie. Kiniski also faced off in 1963 against a variety of newcomers to wrestling who were passing through the Northwest en route to building successful careers. Some of those included future AWA star and current WWE agent Jack Lanza; James "Great Mephisto" Ault, who would go on to hold numerous titles in the southern and eastern United States; and Dick Garza, who had been wrestling for several years but had not yet morphed into the Mighty Igor, who would hold the AWA World Heavyweight title for a week in 1965 and remain a popular wrestling attraction for years after that.

Native Torontonian Walter Sieber was a veteran wrestler when he debuted in the Northwest in October of 1963 after appearing in the Midwest and on the U.S. East Coast earlier in the year. No stranger to Kiniski, as the two had crossed paths in Southern Ontario and western New York several years earlier, Sieber had been billed in several territories as Fritz von Erich's younger brother Waldo, though Sieber arrived in the Pacific Northwest in late 1963 under a mask as The Great Zimm. As Zimm, Sieber piled up some big wins—even splitting victories with Watson in a couple of Vancouver main events—before losing his mask in a loss to Kiniski in December. While Sieber and Kiniski faced each other in the Northwest only a few other times in late 1963, they would renew their association, across the continent, a year later and enjoy major success as a unit.

Bill Watts—future wrestling superstar and Mid-South Wrestling promoter "Cowboy" Bill Watts—arrived in British Columbia in late 1963, just a year into his career. As Watts notes in his book *The Cowboy and the Cross*, "They dropped the 's' off my last name because they didn't want people to confuse me with 'Whipper' Billy Watson, one of Canada's top wrestlers, so I became 'Big' Bill Watt" (62).

"Watt," obviously being groomed for a top spot in the promotion, went undefeated for a month before winning his only match against Kiniski in the Northwest, on December 16, 1963. But then Watts decided to leave the territory when Fenton refused to pay him what Watts felt he was worth. After losing a match to Don Leo Jonathan—who had moved up the coast from California earlier in the month to take up what would be permanent residence in British Columbia—Watts left the territory never to return, although his career association with Kiniski would be far from over.

As far as titles were concerned, 1963 hardly stands out as a banner year in Kiniski's career. He did not regain a share of the NWA Canadian Tag Team championship after he and Mr. X dropped the title in March. Other than that month-long reign, the only other gold Kiniski held in 1963—at least, after Thesz regained the NWA World Heavyweight title from Rogers in January and Kiniski's claim to the Amarillo territory's NWA "world" title faded into history—was the seldom-defended British Empire Heavyweight title, which he took back from Watson in July before that title effectively faded into history as well. Yet, in almost every respect, 1963 was the year in which Gene Kiniski, thanks to a knack for delivering solid matches and projecting an engaging presence in arenas and on television, established himself as the centerpiece of wrestling in the Vancouver territory.

11

Julia Kiniski

Gene Kiniski was not the only member of his clan to garner public attention in 1963. Back in Alberta, older brother Julian remained a popular figure, although he had given up his broadcast meteorologist's platform to embark on research activities that would occupy his attention for the next several years. But despite the public profiles of the two Kiniski/Kinisky brothers who were well known from years of appearances on television, 1963 was a year in which both were likely outdone by their mother Julia.

Julia Warshawski did not have many advantages after settling near the start of her teenage years in Chipman, Alberta. While some of her grandchildren report that Julia came from a well-to-do background in Poland, education was hard to come by for the daughter of Polish immigrants around Chipman in the early 20th century. After marrying Nicholas Kiniski at age 16, Julia gave birth to her six children over the next 13 years and presumably gave little thought to continuing her education during some challenging years in small-town central Alberta. By all accounts, Julia put aside any personal ambition and focused on her family's well-being during her early years of marriage and motherhood in Chipman. That was especially the case as the Depression set in shortly after the birth of Julia's youngest son, Eugene "Gene" Nicholas.

The Kiniskis moved to Edmonton apparently when Gene was approaching middle school age, and Tom Hawthorn reports in the April 20, 2010, *Globe and Mail* and his book *Deadlines* (268) that Gene's "Polish-born mother sold cosmetics door to door and managed a café." Hawthorn also reports that "when Gene was fifteen, she went back to school to complete her education, interrupted in Grade 7." Most reports indicate Julia did not reenroll as a traditional student to complete further grades or to graduate from school but instead sought to educate herself by enrolling in University of Alberta extension courses in the social sciences. According to Allan Wachowich, former Chief Justice of the Court of Queen's Bench, Alberta, Julia Kiniski also did some teaching at the Little Flower School, in Edmonton's Rossdale neighborhood, that Gene attended prior to enrolling at St. Joseph.

In 1945 Julia Kiniski began a journey that would continue through the rest of her life, although there would be little indication at first—or for nearly two decades—that the path she had chosen was one that would eventually lead to success. By all accounts, it was Julia's persistence more than anything else that was instrumental in that success.

"She was a tenacious woman," says Julia's grandson Bruce Kinisky.

Many others share that estimation, including former Alberta amateur wrestling standout Mike Eurchuk. "The Kiniski family were friends of my family," recalls Eurchuk. "My parents were over visiting, and I went along with them quite a few years ago—many years ago now. The fighter in the family was Gene's mother Julia."

No less a wrestling legend than Don Leo Jonathan concurred. "[Gene and I] were wrestling in Edmonton," said Jonathan. "He took me over and I met his mother ... and I had a nice meal. It was Polish food." But then Jonathan added, with a hint of humor, "They told me not to get mixed up too much with her. She'd straighten me out."

Julia's grandson Gene Kinisky recalls, "Granny was a bulldog. When she got her nose into something, that was it."

What Julia Kiniski "got her nose into" in 1945 was politics—an arena in which she would stay involved for nearly a quarter century despite all odds.

In 1945 Julia Kiniski made her entry to Edmonton city politics with a low-budget run as an independent candidate for city council. While Julia had no previous background in elective politics, she had been known as a supporter—and apparently a member—of the socialist Co-operative Commonwealth Federation party and an Edmontonian who seldom hesitated to express her views on politics and politicians' shortcomings at the city, provincial, and federal levels of government.

Kiniski finished dead last in that 1945 election, signaling what some observers or even candidates in her position might have taken to be the end of a brief political career. But that's not how she saw it.

Steven Eleniak, who would be involved as a volunteer in some of Julia Kiniski's later campaigns for Edmonton City Council, says, "You could call her Mrs. Tenacity because there was no way you could dissuade her. If she lost she'd say, 'Fine. I'll do better next time.' This is what sort of drove her—the fact that she would do better next time. That's what more or less kept her going."

Kiniski did do better next time, in the following year's city election, but only slightly. Though doubling her number of votes, she finished in last place again.

Over the course of several attempts at winning a council seat in annual or biennial city elections from 1945 to 1956, Julia Kiniski usually finished last and never finished better than third-from-last among a usually large slate of candidates. Yet she was gaining recognition as an "underground" candidate—one without the political and business connections associated with many of her competitors in the city elections—and though her support base may have been small, it shared some of Julia Kiniski's tenacity.

While falling short in city elections, Julia sought out other avenues in which to serve her community—most notably as president of the local Civic Rights Protective Association and the Cloverdale Community League—and she was consistently outspoken in her views regarding city politics, political incompetence, and corruption. In an otherwise unidentified letter to the editor from son Gene's personal collection, citizen Julia Kiniski decries the Edmonton mayor's planned trip to Berlin, which, she said, "comes under the heading of foolish spending. No doubt any of us would enjoy a trip to Berlin; but how do you explain to the taxpayer that such a trip will benefit our city?"

Eleniak recalls, "I was with the Jaycees—Junior Chamber of Commerce—[when Julia] was a guest speaker, and she was saying that she has got a real problem because she doesn't have any support. So about 20 of us decided to support her."

Eleniak was chosen to head the Kiniski support team and oversaw an effort that focused on distributing pamphlets, placing yard signs on Kiniski's behalf, and transporting potential Kiniski supporters to voting areas on election day. But the impact of Jaycees and others coming on board did not translate to immediate success for the Kiniski campaign, although things were clearly on a slight upswing; and Kiniski, sometimes running as an independent and other times under the banner of a small alternative party, finished near the middle of the pack in all five city elections in which she ran from 1957 to 1962.

"She wouldn't give up," says Bruce Kinisky, who as a child passed out fliers in support of his grandmother's efforts to get elected to council.

While a fervent believer that government had a key role to play in bettering the lives of the less fortunate, Julia didn't overlook the role private citizens could play. Wachowich recalls, of Edmonton during the 1940s and 1950s, "There was no Catholic welfare. The church was a theological church…. At Christmastime [Julia] collected Christmas hampers and clothes and stockings and everything else for everybody else. She herself was Catholic charities."

Meanwhile, Benny Grabow recalls Julia as "a phenomenal woman with prisoners…. She spent so much money taking gifts to prisoners," particularly at Edmonton's Belmont Correctional Centre, which was established in the middle of Julia's series of unsuccessful runs for council.

According to Joe Ranger's report on Julia Kiniski in the May 12, 2000, *Edmonton Examiner*, in 1948 Julia invested in Leduc oil stocks and, apparently not too many years later, sold her stock for eight times her investment. Ranger writes, "With her windfall, she bought a five-suite apartment, a house, and a ticket to her native Poland."

Though her own financial health had improved from earlier years, by nearly all accounts Julia Kiniski's doggedness to serve on Edmonton City Council was rooted in her support of the poor and working class and her opposition to vested business interests in government. As Eleniak recalls, "She went after the corporate bums … large companies that were getting government grants and things like that, which they didn't really need, according to her. So she was sort of active in the whole financial structure—anything that she felt was overspent…. She went after those people."

All of Kiniski's and her supporters' efforts finally paid off in the October 16, 1963, Edmonton municipal election, when Kiniski earned about three times her previous high number of votes and finished well enough among the pack to earn a seat on council—according to her bio on the Edmonton city government website, after "she [had] tried unsuccessfully to run for a seat 11 times." In a postelection report by Donna Dilschneider of the *Edmonton Journal*, Julia said, "It would have been my last attempt if I had lost. I would have felt people just weren't interested enough." According to journalist Jim Proudfoot, the slogan that swept Julia to her seat was "Edmonton has the finest mayor money can buy."

Bruce Kinisky says, "She became the most popular alderman on city council," echoing John Warren, who in a June 30, 1964, Canadian Press report says, "It took Julia 20 years and 11 elections to win a seat on Edmonton's city council. Once there, in less than two months, she established a reputation as the most outspoken, persistent and energetic alderman in the city of 330,000." Meanwhile, former amateur wrestling standout Eurchuk describes Julia Kiniski, as a result of her persistence and eventual contributions as a member of Edmonton's City Council, as "kind of a legend in the city."

Julia Kiniski's reputation—in evidence to this day—was earned largely through her never-quit attitude en route—after repeated failure, little support, and few signs of hope in the early years—to gaining her seat on city council. But her reputation also stands on what many observers view as a similar doggedness, as alderman or councilor, when it came to supporting the best interests of the proverbial "little guy." While some did not share her views or see her as the most qualified person to serve on council, few ever seemed to question Julia Kiniski's ethics or the strength of her character.

Eleniak recalls, "She was really against those big spenders.... One friend of mine [in local government]—he went over to Japan ... and in Japan he bought a dinner. At the dinner he bought a bottle of wine that was $39. This was [many years ago], so that could have been about a $200 bottle of wine.... When she got hold of his expense account, man, did [my friend] ever get embarrassed. She was that type. She was really for the common laborer type."

Bruce Kinisky says, "When she first got elected as alderman, she was asked ... to represent the city of Edmonton in Ottawa for a conference. And in those days she was given a travel advance. So she had this $300 travel advance, went to the convention and came back, and she had money left over. And she went to the city treasurer and said, 'I have this money left over from my travel advance,' and the city treasurer said, 'Well, what do you want me to do with it? No one's ever done that before—returned the money.' And she said, 'Well, what do you do with it? It's not my money. It's the people's money.' And that kind of gives you an indication of what kind of politician she was.... She didn't want to take people's money that didn't belong to her.

"She was well-loved here in the city."

As Julia Kiniski's bio on the Edmonton city government website indicates, "one of her biggest issues was to fight for household owners with basement suites." According to Bruce Kinisky, Julia and Nicholas Kiniski had a basement suite in their home when Edmonton City Council considered making such rental suites illegal. According to Eleniak, concerns such as overcrowding and fire safety caused some officials to call for an end to rental basement suites, but Kiniski held firm in her belief that such suites provided vital affordable housing to the poor. As Eleniak recalls, Kiniski supported upgraded standards regarding overcrowding and fire standards in basement suites but never wavered in her support of the right of both homeowners and low-income renters throughout the city to share the benefits of basement suites.

Says Eurchuk, "She was the big push to make all basement suites legal, and she kept having big battles with council because they kept, of course, structural requirements to have legal suites in the basements, and she would just say, 'The hell with that. They should have 'em.' She had a respect for the little person."

Kiniski was also staunch in her support of the televising of Edmonton City Council meetings. A December 12, 2015, *Edmonton Journal* "Day in History" feature focusing on December 12, 1965, describes Kiniski as "the main promoter of television coverage," which, despite some hesitation or opposition from fellow politicians, got underway in early 1966. In the *Journal* article, Kiniski is reported as saying, "I talked to 500 [people], everywhere I was—even at the symphony—and they all think it's wonderful."

Transparency of government was high on the Kiniski agenda, and after her initial election to city office in 1963, Julia Kiniski was reelected three times, in some ways as a counterbalance to some of her more polished, more traditional-type peers on the council. Often viewed, as her son Gene was, as a little rough around the edges, Julia, again much like Gene, was known to speak her mind and to command notice. "Her English wasn't very good," says Eleniak, "but her thought process was good."

Warren quotes Julia Kiniski as once telling a heckler who apparently criticized her English, "I may not talk too good but you don't think too good. Your tongue moves so fast it must have put a knot in your brain." Proudfoot quotes Gene Kiniski: "This guy says to [Julia], 'Mrs. Kiniski, for a person in public life, you speak very poor English' and she says 'maybe but I can call you a damned fool in four languages and that gives me a big advantage over you.'"

Proudfoot quotes Gene Kiniski further: "All she's interested in is what she thinks is right. She can be wrong, too, but the important thing is that she speaks up. She cares."

One memorable item from Gene Kiniski's collection of news clippings is a Canadian Press report, titled "Klondike Clean-up Sees Cutie Covered," which begins, "The forces of Alderman Julia Kiniski have covered up a naughty painting in Sue's Saloon, set up outside city hall for Klondike Days, the city's annual summer festival."

The article continues: "'She's completely nude,' said Ald. Kiniski…. 'A thing like that is not to be exposed in a place like city hall. It's a disgrace…. I told the mayor to either remove it or do something or I was going to tear it off myself.'"

As the article reports, this was one more battle in which Alderman Kiniski was not to be denied: "The painting got a quick cover-up painting on Wednesday on instructions from the mayor but it looked like a cross between a bathing suit and old style underwear. This morning the painting was covered by a tarpaulin."

While it appears Julia Kiniski never saw her son wrestle professionally in person, those who knew both—and many who knew only Gene—agree the bond between mother and youngest son was strong.

"He's a good boy. He does what his Mama tells him," Julia said in a mid-1960s *Edmonton Journal* article by Dave White that Gene Kiniski preserved in his collection. For his part, Gene said, in the Proudfoot column, "I remember when I was 22 and weighed 275. If I stayed out after midnight, my mother would punch me on the ear."

After Julia was gone from the scene, the Kiniski Gardens neighborhood—a working-class subdivision in Southeast Edmonton—would be named after her. But based on how she overcame a lack of formal education and reset her life to make a difference in the lives of the underclass in Edmonton, it seems likely she would be prouder of the fact that a public elementary school in Edmonton would bear her name and provide educational opportunities to help children from diverse backgrounds, as the Julia Kiniski School's website says, "develop the skills, knowledge and attitudes necessary to become contributing global citizens."

Aside from indirectly influencing thousands of young students in Southeast Edmonton through the school that bears her name next to a park that bears her name, Julia Kiniski is recognized by her surviving

Gene Kiniski and his mother Julia. Julia's tenacity over many years en route to eventually winning a seat on the Edmonton City Council suggests maybe *she* was the toughest Kiniski to come out of Alberta (Kiniski family archive).

relatives as a major influence on her own children, including youngest son Gene, who is widely believed to have inherited some of his feistiness from his mother. But much of Julia's influence on all six of her children, descendants say, came more from the quiet, nurturing example she set at home while usually leaving the discipline to husband Nicholas, who did not get involved in Julia's political life. According to Julia's grandson Gene Kinisky, his grandmother's nurturing presence remained strong long after her six children were grown.

"I called her Granny," says Gene Kinisky, "and she was just like a mom, always cooking for you, always looking after you, and just a very jolly woman. She was a very heavy lady, and she loved her grandkids. I just always remember her as just sort of that very nurturing kind of grandma."

He continues, "Later in life, my dad [Julian] and I would talk about my grandmother, and she definitely had an effect on my father. There's no doubt about that."

Julia Kiniski's influence on her son Julian would take on a public nature when Julian followed his mother into Edmonton city politics after her death from a heart attack in 1969 at age 70. In fact, Julian's entry to politics came in November of 1970, when he won a by-election to assume his mother's seat on city council—and from there he would be in and out of politics at the city level for nearly two decades. Along the way, despite unsuccessful runs for mayor, the Alberta Social Credit Party leadership, and a seat in the Canadian Parliament as a candidate for the federal Liberal party, Julian Kinisky became a popular political figure in Edmonton in the 1970s and 1980s and was seen by many Edmontonians as the standard-bearer to carry on his mother's political legacy, although Julian's son Bruce Kinisky emphasizes that "[my father] was more center, [while] my grandmother was on the left."

Julia Kiniski's influence on her youngest son may not have been as obvious, but relatives and observers generally saw some overlapping in the feisty spirit and full-bodied presence of mother and son. As Don Leo Jonathan put it, "She'd get after those guys in the council. Gene was the same way."

But Gene Kiniski, despite the rough exterior he often displayed, had a tender side when it came to his mother. As Hawthorn writes in *Deadlines* and in his *Globe and Mail* report, regardless of where Kiniski's wrestling career took him, "every year, on [his mother's] birthday, Gene made sure she received a bottle of Joy perfume. Long after her death, her son said even the slightest rose-and-jasmine whiff of her [favorite] perfume reduced him to tears."

In an unidentified clipping from Gene Kiniski's collection exploring the influence of celebrities' mothers on their children, Gene Kiniski said, decades after Julia's death, "I think of my mother all the time.... I was very, very proud of her.... If it wasn't for my mother, hell, I wouldn't have had such an enjoyable life. I think she had to be the greatest person in the world."

Though she made her mark in the country to which she immigrated as a child, Julia Kiniski remained proud of her Polish roots to her death and visited Poland on a fairly regular basis until her later years. According to her grandson Gene Kinisky, Julia made her annual trips to see relatives in Poland without the company of her husband Nicholas, who, says Kinisky, had no interest in ever returning to Poland. Clearly, Julia Kiniski was never afraid to set her own path in pursuit of any goal or destination she thought was worthy, and by all accounts, her youngest son Gene had a very similar trait.

12

1964 ... a Very Good Year

During the months immediately following his mother's first victory in Edmonton city politics and her assuming a place on council, Gene Kiniski continued to headline shows in British Columbia's Lower Mainland, on Vancouver Island, and across the border in Tacoma and a few other Washington cities where Cliff Olson promoted. Singles opponents of Kiniski's in the Pacific Northwest from January to March of 1964 included Jonathan, Shibuya, Thesz, Bearcat Wright, Bulldog Brower, and pro wrestling sophomore Dory Funk, Jr.

Funk Jr., who wrestled in the Pacific Northwest for a few months in early 1964, suffered a broken knee in the ring shortly before a match in which he was scheduled to face Kiniski. Funk, who was scheduled for surgery, recalls, at www.wrestlezone.com, that when he called Rod Fenton to deliver the news, Fenton advised him to consult Kiniski, who, Funk says, told him to show up for their scheduled match an hour early rather than go ahead with surgery.

Funk continues, at www.wrestlezone.com,

> I had to cover up and sneak in the back door. I was on the main event and couldn't let the wrestling fans see that I couldn't walk. Gene was there one hour ahead of schedule. He taped my leg tight as a cast from top to bottom, then said, "Bend it till you get a slight tear in the tape by your knee." As Gene left the room, he growled, "Okay kid, I will see you in the ring."
>
> Gene Kiniski was there every night that week one hour ahead of schedule to tape my knee before we wrestled, [and] then we would go into the ring and he would whip the heck out of me but leave the knee alone.

Funk concludes, "I owe it to Gene Kiniski that I did not have to have surgery on my knee in Vancouver or ever in my life and Gene may have saved my career in professional wrestling."

Funk Jr. and Kiniski also had at least one encounter—on opposing sides in a tag team match—when Kiniski made a short visit to Texas in early March of 1964. During the same visit Kiniski also faced Funk Jr.'s father Dory Funk, Sr., and pro footballer and future wrestling headliner Wahoo McDaniel.

From his West Coast base in early 1964, Kiniski also set off for two headline appearances in Toronto, including one in which he challenged Thesz for the NWA World Heavyweight title. According to www.wrestlingdata.com, that match ended in a time-limit draw after 35 minutes.

But more notable than Kiniski's achievements in familiar territories in 1964—including Hawaii and St. Louis, where he would appear later in the year—was his first visit to a key region he had not yet set out to conquer.

In early April Kiniski began his first-ever tour of Japan, which lasted 10 weeks and established him as one of the top foreign attractions in a country that, barely a decade after pro wrestling's arrival and its rise to a national pastime, was one of the hottest wrestling markets in the world. During his 1964 tour of Japan, Kiniski wrestled in arenas around the country for the Japan Wrestling Association (JWA), which had been established in 1953 by a native of northern Korea—North Korea after the partition of the Korean Peninsula in 1948—who came to Japan as a teenager around 1940, assumed a Japanese identity, and trained to be a sumo wrestler.

At the time Japan was bent on eradicating Korean culture from the Korean Peninsula, and those who recruited the teenager to sumo, according to author Robert Whiting in *Tokyo Underworld: The Fast Times and Hard Life of an American Gangster in Japan*, believed "the public would not accept a Korean in what was known as the sport of the Emperor and was seen as the epitome of national ethos. It was thus heretical to claim that a Korean, or anyone of any other nationality for that matter, could defeat a Japanese sumoist" (102). As a result, young Korean native Kim Sin-rak became young "Japanese native" Minokichi Momota, learned the language and ways of Japan, and immersed himself in the world of sumo, where, renamed Rikidozan, he achieved moderate success while keeping his true identity from the public.

Professional wrestling was almost unknown in Japan when Rikidozan decided, at age 25, to leave sumo to become a pro wrestler after, as www.legacyofwrestling.com reports, meeting up with "a contingent from the United States ... headed by Joe Louis." After "learning the ropes" for a couple of years mainly in Hawaii and California—in the process, facing a young Gene Kiniski in a few tag team matches—Rikidozan returned to Japan, established the Japan Wrestling Association, and took on the role of a "Japanese" hero defending the nation's honor against a long line of tough and often scary and unscrupulous foreign wrestlers.

Rikidozan's top challengers during the JWA's early years included Mike and Ben Sharpe, the former a regular tag team partner of Kiniski's in the Northwest during the months leading up to Kiniski's first Japan tour; Bobo Brazil, who at the time played a likeable gentleman everywhere he wrestled but in Japan; and Lou Thesz, whose competitive title defenses against Rikidozan and a couple of high-profile losses to the latter helped establish Rikidozan as a bona fide wrestling superstar to the Japanese public. Other top challengers included Don Leo Jonathan, King Curtis Iaukea, Fred Blassie, Killer Kowalski, Haystack Calhoun, and The Destroyer—all giving Japanese fans, including astounding numbers that tuned in via television, fits when facing off against national hero Rikidozan, who usually emerged victorious after unloading his deadly karate chop on opponents.

The formula of "Japanese hero vs. foreign threat" continued after Rikidozan died a week after getting stabbed outside a Tokyo night club near the end of 1963. A key wrestler who took up the banner of Japan's defender was Shohei "Giant" Baba, a gigantic ex-pitcher with the Yomiuri Giants, Japan's equivalent to the New York Yankees. After seeing limited success several years into his baseball career, Baba left the game in order to try his hand at wrestling, under Rikidozan's tutelage.

After starting his wrestling career with the JWA in 1960, Baba went overseas to develop his craft in North America, out of view of the Japanese public, as Rikidozan had done in the 1950s and as numerous Japanese wrestlers being groomed for top spots in Japanese wrestling promotions would do until the 1980s or 1990s. In January of 1964,

Baba and Kiniski both appeared on a wrestling show in Toronto, with Baba winning on the undercard and Kiniski losing via countout to Watson in the main event. Three months after that apparent initial intersection of their careers, Kiniski and Baba would be facing each other on wrestling shows all over Japan.

Baba—about 6'10" and 300 pounds—would go on to become one of the central figures in the history of Japanese wrestling, both as a combatant and a promoter, and Kiniski is regarded as one of the most important figures in helping launch Baba to the heights he would achieve.

During Kiniski's 10-week Japanese tour in 1964, he faced Baba at least 27 times in singles, tag team, and six-man (three-on-three) matches. While Baba was 26 years old at the time, in relatively good condition, and not nearly as limited in the ring as he would become in later years, he was still a somewhat lumbering, sometimes awkward wrestler the quality of whose matches generally depended on the quality of his opponents. Kiniski, at the height of his skills, showed himself worthy of his reputation as a top hand in wrestling by engaging in some exciting matches against Baba.

While the Baba-Kiniski association would become more noted for encounters they would have a few years later, they faced each other in singles matches six times during Kiniski's 1964 tour—with five of those matches going to a draw. At the time Baba was emerging as the JWA's successor to Rikidozan, and Kiniski's job clearly was to help him get there. It was not until Kiniski's last night on the tour that Baba earned a victory—not by pinfall but via countout—over Kiniski.

Though his battles with Baba were a highlight of Kiniski's first visit to Japan, other noteworthy events took place during that tour. Among them were at least two singles victories by Kiniski over Kim "Kintaro Kongo" Il, a Korean native favored by Rikidozan as one of the future standard-bearers for the JWA, along with Baba and Antonio Inoki, who in one order or another would go on to become probably the second and third most important figures in Japanese wrestling history, behind Rikidozan. While Baba's reputation would be based almost entirely on his contributions to wrestling, Inoki, following a very successful wrestling career, would go on to become a nationally known politician, though perhaps one considered more a novelty or entertainer than a serious political force.

From his debut in 1959, Kim Il was positioned as a strong force in the JWA, and by 1964, following Rikidozan's death, he was a top name in the promotion. Yet Kiniski, during his first tour of Japan, was recognized as the greater star and was booked to get the better of Kintaro Kongo.

Most of Kiniski's encounters during his April–June tour of Japan were two-on-two and three-on-three tag team encounters in which he teamed with other non–Japanese wrestlers to face teams composed of a variety of Japanese wrestlers on the JWA roster—most prominently, Baba and Kintaro Kongo, who, for all intents, given the long-term plans the promotion had for him, was accorded the status of a top Japanese star with the JWA. Kim "Kintaro Kongo" Il is widely remembered in the wrestling community as Kintaro Oki, the name he used during much of his successful career in Japan and elsewhere.

Among Kiniski's more prominent partners in Japan during the spring of 1964 were Roy McClarty; Bull Curry, a smallish but tough Texan who had success in several wrestling territories over a four-decade career as a bushy-haired, unibrowed heel who loved to inflict pain on his opponents; Chief White Wolf, played by an Iraqi native who, after wrestling many more years as a Native American character, would become a major star as an Iraqi villain in Verne Gagne's AWA and Vince McMahon's WWF; Benny "The Mummy" Ramirez, who in several promotions in the early 1960s wrapped himself up to look like a mummy in one of the wackier wrestling gimmicks of his day; and Ramon "Calypso Hurricane" Rodriguez, a Venezuelan native who later in his career would be better known as Cyclone Negro. As a two-man unit, Kiniski and Calypso Hurricane won the JWA's All-Asian Tag Team title from Toyonobori—a top Japanese wrestler at the time, an ex-sumo wrestler and associate of Rikidozan's, and the JWA president who succeeded Rikidozan—and partner Michiaki Yoshimura in mid–May before dropping the title two weeks later, in their first title defense, to Toyonobori and Baba.

After leaving Japan following his countout loss to Baba on June 13, it appears Kiniski embarked on a non-wrestling tour of Southeast Asia with Marion, who apparently had accompanied Gene during at least part of his tour of Japan. Kelly and Nick Kiniski both recall hearing about how their mother—an attractive platinum blonde in the aftermath of a Marilyn Monroe craze in Japan not many years earlier—was a curiosity and popular attraction on the streets of Japan during her visit there.

According to Kelly, one of the stops on his parents' Asian tour—likely Singapore, which had its share of conflict in 1964—saw their plane meet machine-gun fire when it came in to land. "I remember either my mom or my dad told me that the jet had to circle … so none of the bullets would hit the plane," he says.

Following their travels in Asia, Gene and Marion touched down in Hawaii, where Gene was well known from earlier visits. Hawaii, a popular stopover among top North American wrestlers heading to or from Japan, provided the opportunity to earn a good payday while working an easy schedule allowing plenty of time to heal from the bumps and grind of wrestling and to soak in some spectacular scenery.

Kelly Kiniski—six years old and attending first grade when the Kiniski family was in Hawaii in 1964—says he and Nick had been staying on the islands with Marion's mother while his parents were in Asia. After arriving in Hawaii near the start of summer, Gene settled into wrestling a match or two per week in a territory that had been running shows regularly since the Depression. In 1962 long-time Hawaii promoter Al Karasick sold the promotion, and, as Cody Metcalf reports at www.onlineworldworldofwrestling.com, "for the next 17 years, Ed Francis promoted wrestling in Hawaii on the highest rated TV program in [the state]." Much of Francis' success during "the Golden Era of Hawaii wrestling," according to Metcalf, was due to "the talented booking of 'Lord' James Blears."

Blears, aside from being a featured wrestler and a key direction-setter in Hawaii wrestling during Kiniski's 1964 sojourn in the Aloha State, had been a regular partner of Kiniski's in earlier years and had played a key part in Kiniski's success in California and Hawaii during the early part of his career. But by the time Kiniski touched down in Hawaii in 1964, he was widely recognized as one of the top wrestlers in the world—a main eventer in every sense who could be counted on to put the Francis-Blears regulars to the test. While there appear to be no records indicating Kiniski and Blears resurrected their highly successful tag team during the summer of 1964, the two were on opposing sides at least once, in a three-on-three main event August 19 in Honolulu, which Kiniski's side won.

Most Kiniski-Blears interaction in 1964 took place far from the arena or the office, and much of it involved the Kiniski and Blears families. The wrestlers' wives and children were all friends, and for the two families to spend a day together at the beach was commonplace.

12. 1964 ... a Very Good Year

Key opponents of Kiniski's in Hawaii in 1964 included Dean Higuchi, Luther Lindsay, and Neff Maiava, a popular Samoan who had been wrestling in Hawaii for more than a decade and would continue to do so for another decade after facing Kiniski in a series of singles matches in Honolulu. During their first match, on July 16, Kiniski took the NWA Hawaii Heavyweight title from Maiava, but four weeks later Maiava regained the title in a best-of-three-falls match.

Higuchi, a Hawaiian native, was a competitive bodybuilder who got to know wrestlers who visited the gym he owned in Honolulu before he decided to get into wrestling himself. After wrestling mainly in the U.S. Northwest and Hawaii during the early years of his career, Higuchi arrived in Vancouver in 1968 and went on to establish a long association with Kiniski.

Lindsay, an African American wrestler from Virginia, was considered by Lou Thesz, Stu Hart, and others to be a top grappler of his era. While not a nationally known wrestler, Lindsay was a key figure in pro wrestling's slow road to integration in the southern United States, and he was the first African American wrestler to complete in integrated matches in Tennessee and Texas. He was also the first African American to challenge for the National Wrestling Alliance World Heavyweight title—which, over the course of his career, he would do many times, against several champions—and in that context Lindsay and Kiniski would cross paths again about four years after going to a draw in what appears to have been their lone singles match in Hawaii.

Also wrestling in Hawaii during Kiniski's stay there in 1964 were two young Hawaiian natives who went on to significant achievement in professional wrestling. One, Japanese Hawaiian Harry Fujiwara—billed as Mr. Fujiwara in the Hawaii territory in 1964—would hold several regional singles titles over the course of a long career. Fujiwara—best known as Mr. Fuji during most of his career—had the majority of his success as a tag team wrestler, holding major titles from coast to coast, most often with fellow Japanese heels such as Haru Sasaki, Toru Tanaka, and Masa Saito. With the latter two Mr. Fuji shared a total of five WWWF/WWF World Tag Team title reigns to go with a variety of other championships Fujiwara/Fuji held over the course of his ring career in the United States, Puerto Rico, Canada, New Zealand, and Japan—all before gaining perhaps his greatest notoriety in wrestling as a heel manager in the WWF for more than a decade.

Curtis Piehau Iaukea III—whose career had intersected briefly with Kiniski's in British Columbia in 1960—also had a long career as a wrestler in the United States and internationally, and he did some managing as well. The 6'3" "King Curtis," described by Rod Ohira in the July 24, 2005, *Honolulu Advertiser* as "one of the headliners who made the 1960s and '70s a golden age of pro wrestling in Hawaii," was an alumnus of the University of California Berkeley, where he majored in economics, and, like Kiniski, a former pro footballer in Canada. Also leaving pro football after a brief career, Curtis racked up an impressive list of wrestling titles in Hawaii, around the continental United States, and in Canada, New Zealand, and Australia. He was known almost everywhere he wrestled as a wild-looking, bloodthirsty brute who led fans through numerous emotional turns over the course of his matches. Daniel Dennis reports, in the February 25, 2011, Sydney (Australia) *Morning Herald* obituary for the 1960s–1970s wrestling headliner and four-time (Australian) IWA World Heavyweight titleholder, "His deeply grooved forehead became as familiar to wrestling fans as his stream-of-consciousness tirades against opponents in post-match interviews, delivered in a deep, menacing growl. With his mastery of crowd psychology and personal magnetism, King Curtis captivated fans."

Few reliable records seem to exist of matches held in the Hawaii territory outside of Honolulu in mid-1964. While www.onlineworldofwrestling.com reports there were monthly stops on Hilo, Maui, and Kauai and in the Kona district during the height of wrestling in Hawaii, there seem to exist no records confirming in-ring meetings between Kiniski and Curtis or Fujiwara during the summer of 1964. Given each man's profile in the territory, however, it seems unlikely Kiniski would not have faced the other two at some point during his 1964 stay in Hawaii.

Shortly after Kiniski dropped the NWA Hawaii Heavyweight title back to Maiava in late August, it appears Marion and the boys returned to Alberta before reuniting with Gene by early fall on the U.S. East Coast, where the Kiniski family set up residence for the next seven or eight months in Ashland, New Jersey, 15 miles southeast of Philadelphia.

13

More of a Very Good Year

When Kiniski arrived on the East Coast, the World Wide Wrestling Federation (WWWF) was firmly in the hands of the McMahon family, as its present incarnation—World Wrestling Entertainment (WWE), towering over every other professional wrestling organization in the world—is to this day. While the modern-day WWE is controlled primarily by Vincent K. (Vince) McMahon, the WWWF in 1964 was under the control of Vince McMahon's father Vincent J. McMahon.

The WWWF's start—at least, according to legend—can be traced back to Jess McMahon, father of Vincent J. McMahon and the grandfather of current WWE chairman and CEO Vincent K. McMahon. When Jess McMahon, whose days as a wrestling promoter in New York City dated back to the Depression, died in 1954, son Vincent J. McMahon supposedly took over his father's promotional organization. In reality, any such transfer of power was not nearly as smooth or automatic as suggested.

While Vincent J. McMahon had assisted his father in New York, at the time of Jess' death Vincent J. was established as a promoter in Washington, D.C. Using, among others, name wrestlers whose movements were largely controlled by fellow promoters Fred Kohler and Toots Mondt, Vincent J. McMahon followed Kohler's lead by securing a television slot on the DuMont network in early 1956, and within six months McMahon's popular program was televised in New York City. The following year McMahon established the Capitol Wrestling Corporation in partnership with Mondt and minority partner Johnny Doyle.

Capitol Wrestling, based in New York, drew generally good crowds in key cities such as Baltimore, Washington, and Philadelphia and often packed 15,000–19,000 fans into Madison Square Garden for major shows. Tim Hornbaker reports, in *National Wrestling Alliance: The Untold Story of the Monopoly That Strangled Pro Wrestling*, that Capitol Wrestling was admitted to the National Wrestling Alliance in 1957 (182).

One of the main attractions all around Capitol Wrestling's northeastern circuit in the early 1960s was Buddy Rogers, who won the NWA World Heavyweight title from Pat O'Connor at Comiskey Park on June 30, 1961. Rogers would go on to hold the title for the next year and a half.

Besides promoting in New York and elsewhere over a period spanning nearly 40 years, Mondt had a long history of managing wrestlers and booking them out to fellow promoters around the United States. Among wrestlers whose schedules Mondt had a strong say in setting was Rogers, who had been one of wrestling's top performers and drawing cards for more than a decade. In the 1950s Rogers' occasional pairing with Kiniski—both as an opponent and a partner—helped facilitate or solidify Kiniski's standing as a top-tier wrestler, particularly in California, Texas, and Toronto. On July 30, 1962, before a Vancouver audience estimated at up to 16,000, Rogers successfully defended the NWA World Heavyweight title against Kiniski.

While Rogers defended his NWA title around the United States and Canada as the NWA from its inception in 1948 had determined the champion was obligated to do, the majority of his matches and the lion's share of his title defenses were in or near the Northeast. On Capitol Wrestling shows in New York, New Jersey, Connecticut, Pennsylvania, Rhode Island, eastern Ohio, and Washington, D.C., between July 1961 and December 1962, Rogers defended the NWA title against a long list of challengers including Antonino Rocca, Johnny Valentine, Sweet Daddy Siki, Crusher Lisowski, Red Bastien, Haystack Calhoun, Art Thomas, Bearcat Wright, Mark Lewin, Bob Ellis, Édouard Carpentier, Arnold Skaaland, Giant Baba, Moose Cholak, Bobo Brazil, Hans Schmidt, Dory Dixon, Killer Kowalski, and Bruno Sammartino. Rogers also faced many other challengers who are not as well remembered.

It did not sit well with the NWA that its champion—counted on to stir interest and spike attendance in member territories by regularly making the rounds to take on regional contenders—confined so much of his activity to a single member promotion based in New York, and it was precisely because Rogers had no title defenses in west Texas that the Amarillo promotion recognized Kiniski as the NWA World Heavyweight champion from early 1962 until early 1963. There are reports that the NWA and wrestlers loyal to the organization vented their frustration by trying to make life difficult for Rogers, who, while a first-rate performer, was not noted as a shooter. Ruling that the NWA Heavyweight title was not being defended as was in the best interests of the alliance, the NWA Board of Directors determined that it wanted Lou Thesz—already a multi-time champion whose credentials were beyond question—back for another world title run.

Facing forfeiture of a $25,000 bond he had been required to put up as security against the title as well as the daunting prospect of angering Thesz, Rogers went along with the NWA's ruling, dropping the alliance's world title to Thesz in Toronto on January 24, 1963.

Vincent J. McMahon and Mondt did not support the title change, however, as Thesz was not considered an attraction in the Northeast who was likely to keep Capitol Wrestling crowds as large as they had been while Rogers traveled the territory during his NWA title reign. Even if Thesz had been regarded as a major potential drawing card in the Northeast, it was clear that he intended to defend the title in numerous other NWA territories and was likely to limit his appearances in the Northeast, especially in the smaller cities in the Capitol Wrestling loop. As a result, the Capitol Wrestling Corporation left the National Wrestling Alliance and McMahon Sr. and Mondt established the new World Wide Wrestling Federation (WWWF), named Rogers the winner of a fictitious tournament in Brazil to become the inaugural WWWF World Heavyweight champion, and had 27-year-old Bruno Sammartino soundly defeat him on May 17, 1963, in Madison Square Garden to kick off a legendary championship run.

Though Sammartino was a main-event wrestler and a popular attraction particularly in the Northeast and Toronto, fans in both regions were aware of how he had fallen short in NWA title challenges against Rogers and Thesz. While Sammartino would go on to successfully defend the WWWF title many times in Toronto—not exclusively a WWWF city but one that sometimes featured WWWF World Heavyweight title defenses on its shows—and throughout the Northeast, it would take some time and a string of strong title defenses to establish him as a credible champion on the level of Thesz or Rogers.

Just two months before winning the WWWF title, Sammartino had also lost a singles match in Winnipeg to Kiniski, though few fans in the areas where Sammartino defended his new world title would have been aware of that.

Among Sammartino's challengers in 1963 were Magnificent Maurice, Hans Mortier, Al Costello, Skull Murphy, Buddy Austin, Johnny Barend, Brute Bernard, Kowalski, The Crusher, Boris Malenko, Gorilla Monsoon, Klondike Bill, Tommy O'Toole, Duke Hoffman, and Kiniski's ex-tag team partner in the Northwest Clyde Steeves, wrestling as The Shadow in the WWWF—certainly a mixed bag of challengers ranging from a few top names of the era to others that modern-day fans would be hard pressed to remember.

In 1964 Sammartino's standing as a strong world champion was solidified with decisive victories to close out series of matches around the WWWF loop against numerous challengers—most notably, Monsoon, Jerry Graham, Kowalski, Mortier, and Fred Blassie. Then, after turning back every challenge he'd faced during 16 months as the WWWF champion, Sammartino was rewarded with the opportunity to face one of his stiffest challenges to date when Gene Kiniski was brought into the territory in the fall of 1964.

In his first recorded appearance in the World Wide Wrestling Federation, Kiniski scored a victory in Washington, D.C., on October 5, 1964, over Klondike Bill, a tough backwoods character with some similarity to Yukon Eric. From there, Kiniski would reel off a series of victories before apparently losing a match on November 2 in Washington to Bobo Brazil, who had lost to Kiniski in Newark, New Jersey, a few days earlier. Moving up the ladder as a challenger for Sammartino's WWWF World Heavyweight title with victories over key wrestlers such as Pedro Morales and Bill Watts, Kiniski would not lose again before challenging for the title in Madison Square Garden on November 16.

That first WWWF meeting between Kiniski and Sammartino ended in either a countout or disqualification victory for Sammartino, who often began championship programs by losing, in unconvincing fashion—not resulting in a title change—to his top challengers. Beginning his program with Kiniski with a victory—albeit not a resounding one—likely helped solidify Sammartino's standing as a champion fans could have confidence in, but it probably did not help set up Kiniski as the ultimate threat to the popular champion.

Kiniski rebounded by racking up some big victories—most notably, over Brazil, Watts, and Fred Blassie—during the four weeks leading up to his Madison Square Garden rematch with Sammartino. He also made visits to St. Louis during that period, appearing on television matches and at the Kiel Auditorium, and, over the course of about two weeks, teamed on one show with Rip Hawk, teamed on another with Fritz von Erich, and beat Snyder in a singles match. Kiniski was clearly the top contender for the WWWF World Heavyweight title when he faced Sammartino for the second time in Madison Square Garden on December 14, 1964—only to lose, this time apparently via pinfall. A few days later Kiniski fell short in another WWWF title challenge, in Baltimore, though he closed out 1964 with impressive victories over Watts and Morales—the latter of whom would enjoy a successful WWWF world title reign several years later.

In the WWWF in late 1964, Kiniski was occasionally involved in tag team matches, paired with Monsoon, Blassie, and, most notably, Waldo von Erich, Fritz' fictional brother who had wrestled in British Columbia as The Great Zimm a year earlier. Kiniski and Waldo von Erich would go on to be a regular tag team during the first several months of 1965.

In January of 1965 Kiniski briefly went home to Western Canada, where he defeated WWWF opponent and fellow Albertan "Klondike" Bill Soloweyko in Vancouver and Edmonton main events, went toe-to-toe with Don Leo Jonathan in a Calgary main event, faced noted shooter Karl Gotch in Winnipeg, and then capped off a whirlwind week by teaming with Jonathan to capture the NWA Canadian Tag Team championship from the Fabulous Kangaroos—one of the most innovative and best-remembered tag teams of their era—in another Vancouver main event.

Within a week of winning the title with Jonathan, Kiniski would appear on two shows in Washington, D.C., teaming on one with Monsoon in a losing effort against Sammartino and Watts. Sandwiched in between the two Washington shows was a loss in St. Louis to Fritz von Erich, the follow-up to a match at the Kiel two weeks earlier—on New Year's Day 1965—that saw Kiniski lose two-on-one (arguably three-on-one, with Whipper Watson serving as special referee) to Pat O'Connor and Fritz von Erich, who had to take turns facing Kiniski.

But it was the other von Erich—Waldo—with whom Kiniski made the most news in 1965. The two had started teaming in early December of 1964, and within two months—after fewer than 10 recorded matches as a unit—Kiniski and Waldo von Erich won the WWWF United States Tag Team championship from the Graham Brothers, Jerry and Luke, at Washington's Capitol Arena.

That victory did not make Kiniski a regional tag team champion on both coasts, because several days before his East Coast title victory with von Erich, Kiniski teamed with Jonathan in Vancouver to drop the NWA Canadian Tag Team title back to the Kangaroos. Two nights earlier, Kiniski had scored a victory over Watson in Winnipeg.

Kiniski and von Erich had a successful two-month championship run in the WWWF, losing occasionally to keep things interesting but managing to hang on to the title until early April. Among teams winning nontitle matches against Kiniski-von Erich were Brazil-Siki and Sammartino-Wahoo McDaniel, and among top teams falling to the champions were Jerry and Eddie Graham, McDaniel-Don McClarty, and Calhoun-Miguel Perez. On March 28 Kiniski and von Erich took their act to Toronto, earning an impressive victory over Watson and Johnny Valentine. But then, on April 8, Kiniski-von Erich dropped their United States Tag Team championship to Watts and Monsoon in Washington.

While holding his share of the WWWF United States tag title, Kiniski remained active as a singles wrestler in the WWWF and elsewhere. Within a week of his title victory with von Erich—and following a quick return to St. Louis for a win over Moose Evans—Kiniski fell short in a pair of title challenges to Sammartino in Trenton, New Jersey, and Baltimore. On visits to Detroit while holding his share of the WWWF United States tag team title—the only WWWF title he would ever hold—Kiniski won singles matches against Ox Anderson, Lupe Gonzales, Snyder, Bill Frazier, and Guy Mitchell. In Toronto, meanwhile, Kiniski faced off with Watson in two tough matches with largely inconclusive finishes, and in St. Louis he earned strong victories over Ilio DiPaolo and Joe Blanchard. In the WWWF during that same period, Kiniski seemed to get the better of all his singles opponents except Sammartino and Wahoo McDaniel.

McDaniel, like Kiniski a trainee of Dory Funk, Sr., had lost to Kiniski in Texas on March 5, 1964, in what appears to have been their only meeting prior to converging in the WWWF. What appears to have been their second career meeting—a nontitle tag team match in Elizabeth, New Jersey, in which McDaniel and Sammartino defeated

Kiniski and von Erich—took place exactly one year later, on March 5, 1965. A five-year NFLer coming off a season with the New York Jets when he faced Kiniski several times in March and April of 1965, McDaniel was the kind of wrestler Vince McMahon, Sr., and Toots Mondt liked to get behind. While a capable athlete, McDaniel was considered an entertaining wrestler of the sort often featured in the WWWF, which generally went more for larger-than-life characters than simply skilled grapplers along the lines of Lou Thesz. After a successful WWWF run in 1965, McDaniel—who Kiniski came to consider a friend—returned to the Jets for the NFL season. When the 1965 season was over he was traded to the Miami Dolphins and, despite enjoying much success as a wrestler during the remainder of his NFL career and for about two decades afterward, never had another run in WWWF/WWF/WWE rings.

As far as Sammartino was concerned, he would spend the vast majority of his career in the WWWF/WWF, in the process becoming the second-longest-reigning world heavyweight champion the wrestling industry has ever seen, behind only Verne Gagne. But while the majority of NWA World Heavyweight champions hopped almost constantly among the various NWA territories—each with its own circuit and its own cast of wrestlers—building up regional heroes as viable contenders for the world title and helping boost business in the territories, Sammartino and Gagne, long-time champions in the WWWF and AWA, operated on a different model. In the WWWF and AWA, it was a revolving-door cast of challengers who would make the rotation while the champion remained a constant presence in familiar arenas, perhaps losing a few early matches in a title program to a tough or crafty opponent but nearly always emerging a clear victor at the end of a program, after which it would be the next top contender's turn to make the rounds. In the case of Kiniski-Sammartino, while Kiniski at times seemed to fall just short of winning the world title, it was clear by early April of 1965 that he was being booked in such a way as to be Batman—though a villainous Batman—to Sammartino's Superman.

According to Nick Kiniski, Gene was unhappy over the manner in which he was booked during his WWWF run—especially given his popularity with Polish Americans in the Northeast and the quality of matches he delivered night after night. But perhaps even more important in Gene Kiniski's mind than the perception that he was playing second fiddle to Sammartino was what Nick describes as "a run-in with Vince [McMahon], Sr., ... over a payoff." Nick says his father felt he was not being compensated fairly for delivering strong matches and helping boost attendance during his stay in the WWWF. When Gene complained, says Nick, McMahon offered him some money and said, "There's some misunderstanding." But his father would have none of that, says Nick.

"Screw me once and I'm out of here. I don't need you," is how Nick puts his father's response.

Though there apparently was some concern that Kiniski would "shoot" on Sammartino—or try to surprise and hurt him in one of their remaining matches—Nick stresses that his father had no such intentions and in no way blamed Sammartino for his troubles with McMahon. Thirty-five years later, in a November 10, 2000, *SLAM! Wrestling* chat, Gene Kiniski seemed to bear that out when he said, "Bruno was a very powerful man. He was always a great gentleman in and out of the ring. He was a very big asset to the world of professional wrestling."

For his part, Sammartino, who passed away in April of 2018, spoke highly of the former top contender for his WWWF championship when interviewed by phone in April of 2017.

"I always had the utmost respect for Gene Kiniski," he said. "I thought he was a tremendous performer. I respected him and appreciated him for always being in shape—that he could go the distance, so to speak. If he had to go a half hour [or] one hour, it didn't matter."

Summing up his view of Kiniski, Sammartino said, "I think he was one of the very top guys in his time."

After cleanly losing a few title matches to Sammartino and dropping the tag title he shared with von Erich, Kiniski wrestled a few more matches in the WWWF—getting no more wins on his way out of the territory—before losing his blowoff match with Sammartino on May 6 in Washington and leaving the WWWF for good. But during the final weeks before his departure from the WWWF, Kiniski was a frequent flier, making appearances in Vancouver, Winnipeg, Toronto, St. Louis, and a variety of Midwestern cities newly promoted by a couple of his friends, Wilbur Snyder and Dick the Bruiser.

According to Dick the Bruiser biographer Richard Vicek, Snyder and Bruiser had begun running shows in Indiana in April of 1964 in opposition to Jim Barnett and Johnny Doyle, major power brokers in wrestling for many years who influenced the industry from coast to coast and controlled a large territory in the late 1950s and early 1960s covering many cities and regions extending from Michigan to California. Months after Bruiser and Snyder started promoting in Indiana, Barnett and Doyle established an Australia-based wrestling promotion that would be one of the most successful in the world for more than a decade. With Barnett and Doyle out of the picture, Snyder and Bruiser settled into running events in cities including Indianapolis, Louisville, and Detroit. By the time Kiniski was winding up his stay in the WWWF in the spring of 1965, Snyder and Bruiser were also running shows in Chicago.

Shortly before concluding his stay in the WWWF, Kiniski traveled to the Midwest to make several appearances in Snyder and Bruiser's Indianapolis-based World Wrestling Association (WWA). There, Kiniski faced both owners in wild singles matches and mixed it up with other major names such as Nick Bockwinkel and Bobby Managoff. After his final loss to Sammartino on the East Coast—or possibly, shortly before—Kiniski set up residence in Indianapolis and proceeded to headline WWA shows during the remainder of 1965 while frequently leaving the territory to wrestle in St. Louis, the Pacific Northwest, Texas, Winnipeg, Alberta, and Tennessee. From May to December of 1965 Kiniski was featured on major shows in a variety of territories, facing an amazing array of talent during a period that would prepare him well for what was to occur early the following year.

If there was any question that Kiniski—despite being booked in the WWWF to come off as less than Sammartino's equal—was on a rapid rise to becoming the top-positioned wrestler in the world, a close look at his schedule and success over the last eight months of 1965 would likely clear any doubts. In May, sandwiched between WWA appearances featuring Kiniski in tag team matches with partners Dick the Bruiser and Johnny Valentine, was a brutal Texas Death Match victory in St. Louis against Fritz von Erich. Then, after wrestling in British Columbia, Indiana, and Texas, Kiniski returned to St. Louis in mid–June to challenge Thesz for the NWA World Heavyweight title. While Kiniski was disqualified in that match, it was clear he was being booked as someone with the potential to step in, when the time came, as a credible world champion. A similar comment could perhaps be made about 24-year-old Dory Funk, Jr., who was booked on that same show.

In the weeks following his NWA title shot in St. Louis, Kiniski alternated between matches in the Indianapolis territory and appearances in British Columbia, Texas, Manitoba, Ontario, and Tennessee—where, collectively, he earned victories over the likes of Valentine and Snyder and, over a five-day period, challenged Thesz two more times for the NWA title.

Kiniski was back in St. Louis in midsummer to participate in a home run hitting contest, along with a lineup of other St. Louis sports celebrities, before a Cardinals-Dodgers game at Busch Stadium. Larry Matysik, a close associate of Sam Muchnick's in the 1960s who later became a commentator on St. Louis' *Wrestling at the Chase* television program, recalled over the phone that Kiniski—decked out only in wrestling trunks, wrestling boots, and a baseball cap—"did very well." Muchnick, a former baseball writer and a strong backer of amateur wrestling, made every effort to present his professional wrestling product to the public and to the St. Louis sporting community as legitimate sport, and he tried to foster a close relationship between his St. Louis Wrestling Club and the wider sporting community in his city—particularly the baseball Cardinals. As far as Kiniski's relationship with mainstream athletes in the batting contest and the St. Louis sporting community at large was concerned, "They all loved him.... He knew about their sports. He talked about how they trained.... He got over with them probably as much as he got over with the fans," said Matysik, who passed away in November 2018.

Kiniski closed out a busy summer by continuing his pattern of travels from Indianapolis with appearances in Ontario, St. Louis, the Pacific Northwest, and Winnipeg. In Winnipeg and Vancouver, Kiniski challenged Thesz twice in a 48-hour period, with neither man taking a victory. Thesz at the time was tiring of the grueling schedule an NWA titleholder was expected to maintain, and clearly, Kiniski, a proven draw who could deliver generally athletic and realistic-looking matches—and who had the backing of Thesz himself—was under serious consideration as a candidate to take up the torch from Thesz when the right time came. But while Kiniski was respected, there was concern about wrapping the NWA title belt around the waist of someone who in recent months had fallen short in challenges for Sammartino's WWWF World Heavyweight title. Sammartino's matches in the Northeast were closely covered in the wrestling newsstand magazines of the day, and NWA directors did not want fans to perceive the alliance's champion as anything other than the best wrestler in the world.

For his part, Kiniski, with seven-year-old Kelly about to start a new year at school, seemed more than content to stay for a time with his friends Snyder and Bruiser in Indiana. When his father was back in Indianapolis between trips to Ontario, the Northwest, Manitoba, Texas, Alberta, and St. Louis, Kelly says, "Dad would bring wrestlers home at night. It would be two, three, four in the morning."

On August 21 in Indianapolis, Kiniski won the WWA Heavyweight title—billed as a world heavyweight title—from Bruiser, who had been the only WWA Heavyweight champion since the promotion was established the previous year. For the remainder of 1965, Kiniski would headline shows mainly around Indiana and Illinois, drawing generally good crowds while defending his title against the likes of Snyder, Managoff, Moose Cholak, Bob Ellis, and Bruiser. In between matches in the WWA, Kiniski would continue to rile crowds in some of his other favorite territories.

Kiniski's autumn was as busy as his summer with his schedule of WWA title defenses and repeated visits to Toronto, St. Louis, Texas, Alberta, and the Pacific Northwest. Among notable opponents Kiniski faced outside the WWA during the fall of 1965 were Watson and Johnny Powers in Toronto; O'Connor in St. Louis; Jonathan in Winnipeg; Bill Dromo in Vancouver; and Fritz von Erich, Wahoo McDaniel, Funk Jr., Antonio Inoki, and Bob Geigel in Texas.

On Christmas Day 1965, Kiniski had his last WWA Heavyweight title defense—a losing effort, as it was time to drop the title back to Bruiser before heading off for bigger and better things. As Kelly recalls, WWA co-owner Snyder, thrilled about the great adventure on which his good friend and fellow former Eskimo was about to embark, handed Kiniski the keys to a new Chrysler Imperial. Kelly says that when his father responded, "I can't pay for this," Snyder explained, "I'm not asking you to, Gene. You go, and you'll never have to look back."

Kiniski did, however, return to Indiana the following year, drawing strong crowds for encounters with Bruiser, Snyder, and Ernie Ladd. But as it turned out, his 1965 WWA title run—especially in combination with his busy schedule facing top wrestlers in several other territories—served much as a dress rehearsal for what was about to happen, beginning with a defining moment in Kiniski's career that took place less than two weeks after he dropped the WWA title to Dick the Bruiser.

14

Height of His Career

Lou Thesz' plan to drop the NWA World Heavyweight championship came to fruition early in 1966 in St. Louis. Among wrestlers considered as potential successors to Thesz were the rugged Johnny Valentine and Fritz von Erich, but Kiniski was regarded as a reliable and legitimate athlete who was short on gimmicks and could deliver excellent matches. More important was that he had the backing of Thesz and NWA president and St. Louis promoter Sam Muchnick.

The Thesz-Kiniski title match at the Kiel Auditorium on January 7, 1966—Nick Kiniski's fifth birthday—had been built up over the course of four weeks, beginning during a December 11, 1965, television show from the Chase Park Plaza Hotel that saw Kiniski—who had put together a strong winning record in St. Louis since losing by disqualification in an NWA title challenge to Thesz at the Kiel in June 1965—appear under a mask as Marauder #2, partner of Bobby "Hercules" Graham, who was appearing as Marauder #1. Kiniski and Graham, without masks, had been a successful team in St. Louis on previous shows, and in a comprehensive audio series conducted with Gary Cubeta, Larry Matysik said it was obvious to fans who the wrestlers under the masks were. Facing Guy Mitchell and Bobby Managoff on the December 11 *Chase* show, the Marauders injured Mitchell—who could not continue—and roughed up Managoff until Thesz, scheduled to appear on the show, could stand no more and got involved in the action. After clearing the ring of Marauder #1, Thesz, with Managoff's assistance, unmasked Marauder #2 to reveal beyond any doubt what everyone already knew: that Gene Kiniski was up to no good.

On *Wrestling at the Chase* the following week, Thesz closed the book on the Marauders by defeating and unmasking Marauder #1 as Graham. On the same show it was confirmed that Kiniski would be challenging Thesz for the NWA World Heavyweight title three weeks later at the Kiel Auditorium.

In the interim Kiniski made a swing through Texas and then dropped the WWA title to Bruiser in Indianapolis before returning to St. Louis and defeating Angelo Poffo on an episode of *Wrestling at the Chase* that aired on New Year's Day 1966. And then, six days later, came the match fans had been primed to see. As Hornbaker reports at www.legacyofwrestling.com, "Thesz appeared at the Kiel Auditorium on January 7, 1966 … [and] 11,612 watched Kiniski battle the champion through three falls and strap the NWA World Title around his waist at the end in victory. He was pinned in the initial fall in 18:08 and tossed over the top rope during the second fall. The official disqualified Thesz, thus evening the match. After 1 minute and 17 seconds of the third fall, Kiniski pinned Thesz and was declared the winner. Kiniski became the first man to have held the AWA World Title and the NWA World Title." According to Matysik in the audio series with Cubeta, during the third fall Kiniski "was on [Thesz] like a panther" and put him away with three backbreakers. Following Kiniski's victory, Matysik reports, the NWA title belt was handed over to the new champion by the Missouri State athletic commissioner—highlighting Muchnick's emphasis on giving his promotion and its wrestlers an air of legitimacy to fans and others in the St. Louis sporting community.

Inheriting an NWA World Heavyweight champion's busy schedule of title defenses, Kiniski immediately set off on a long road trip that would essentially see him shuttle from territory to territory for the next three years to take on a long list of worthy challengers—most well remembered to this day—and occasionally return to his new home base in the St. Louis area or, more frequently during the latter stages of his NWA title run, return to the permanent home base he would establish in the Pacific Northwest.

The night after defeating Thesz for the title in St. Louis, Kiniski faced Dick the Bruiser in a Chicago main event. The match, billed as a "Congo Death Match"—essentially, the same as a Texas Death Match or no-disqualification "fight to the finish"—apparently was for the NWA title but not for the WWA championship Bruiser had reclaimed from Kiniski two weeks earlier. Vicek, in his 2016 biography *Bruiser: The World's Most Dangerous Wrestler*, reports that Chicago promoter Bob Luce, in the buildup to the January 8, 1966, International Amphitheater main event, warned, "Wrestling fans who watch the Bruiser-Kiniski match are urged to keep calm and cool. This match could bring on a heart attack to any fan who cannot control his nerves" (128).

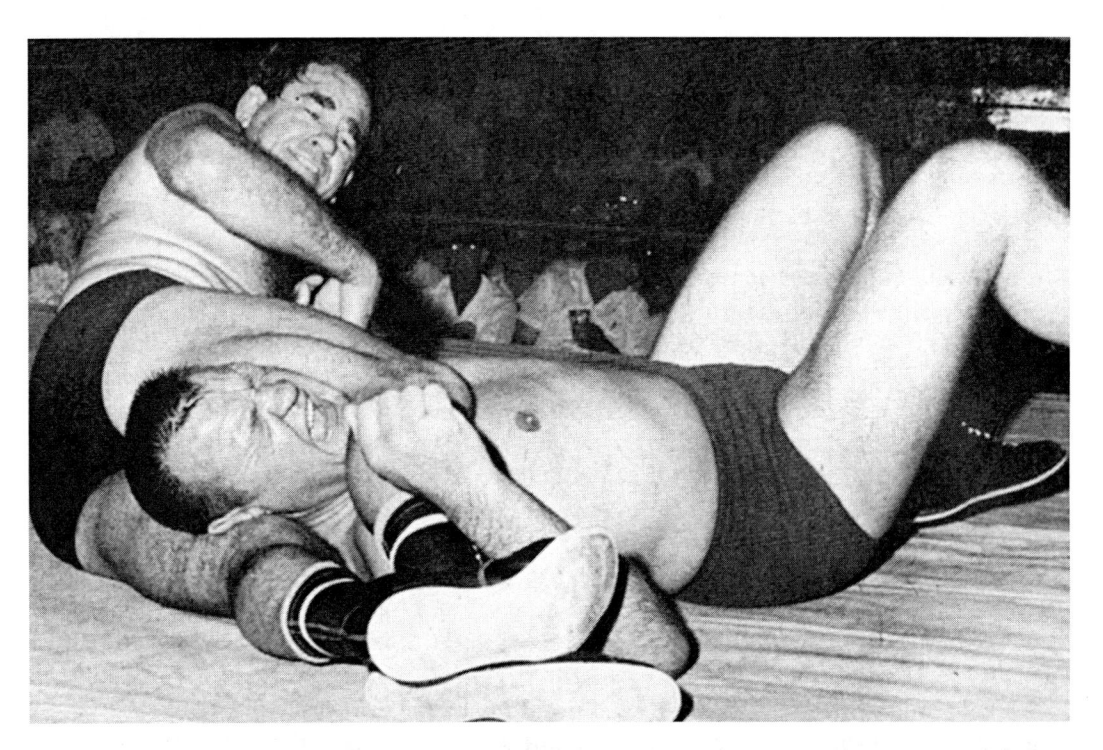

The careers of Kiniski (on his back) and all-time legend Lou Thesz were linked in many territories over many years. On January 7, 1966, Kiniski entered the golden age of his career by defeating Thesz in three falls at St. Louis' Kiel Auditorium to capture the NWA World Heavyweight championship (Vance Nevada collection).

14. Height of His Career

The match—which otherwise lived up to its billing—was stopped by the referee after nearly 50 minutes, and the victory was awarded to Kiniski, apparently after interference on Kiniski's behalf by Johnny Valentine, who had a heated feud with Bruiser in the mid–1960s. Five days after defeating Bruiser in his first NWA title defense, Kiniski scored another victory over Bruiser in Fort Wayne, Indiana, in a Texas Death Match that went five falls before Bruiser lost via countout when "Assassins" John "Guy Mitchell" Hill and Joe Tomasso attacked Bruiser.

For the most part, the remainder of Kiniski's three-year NWA Heavyweight title reign would be relatively free of the outside interference and other shenanigans often associated with heel title runs in professional wrestling. Kiniski—while seldom hesitating to bail out of the ring to regroup when it suited him—was usually presented to fans as a strong, legitimate heavyweight champion, and the vast majority of his NWA title defenses culminated in clean finishes. Most observers seem to agree Kiniski had a knack for making regional contenders look as if they were on the verge of winning the world title until a decisive finish in favor of the champion proved otherwise. In the wrestling world of the 1960s, a finishing move as basic as Kiniski's backbreaker across the knee had credibility as a finisher because it usually signaled the end of a match without stretching the credulity of fans to the degree some of the more devastating but farfetched finishing moves of current-day wrestlers tend to do. And while Kiniski was booked as an ornery heel whose job often was to look overmatched or about to drop the title, relatively few of his NWA title defenses resulted in disqualification finishes of the sort readily associated with other heel world champions. In fact, most Kiniski title defenses ending in disqualification were the result of Kiniski's opponents, and not the champion, getting disqualified.

Of course, that was generally because Kiniski's rough, sometimes illegal, tactics raised the ire of his opponents, some of whom simply got disqualified for going too far in retaliation. But that only added to the perception that a Kiniski title defense was likely to be a battle—or, as Kiniski sought to provide, an excellent value for the price of admission.

Kiniski's first extended visit to an alliance territory as NWA champion was in Florida, where he had 10 title defenses over a three-week period in January and February of 1966, broken up by visits to North Carolina, where he defeated fellow heel Hans Schmidt, and back to St. Louis, where he would check in—usually briefly—throughout his title reign to spend a little time with his family, set aside some moments for

NWA World Heavyweight champion Gene Kiniski during the height of his career (Kiniski family archive).

training dogs, and, regularly, headline cards at the Kiel Auditorium and, occasionally, appear on *Wrestling at the Chase.*

Regarding the dogs, a few years later Kiniski would tell *The Province*'s John Kirkwood, "I train my own dogs, they're two black Labs, for hunting." One of those Labs was Alberta Babe, who joined the Kiniski family in the mid-1960s and would be a favorite family pet through their years in Missouri and on until the late 1970s. Gene and Babe—trained by Gene for competition—apparently did not have any major disagreements, which was probably a good thing as far as Alberta Babe was concerned, as Kelly Kiniski reports Gene could be persuaded to spray a little birdshot into a dog he was training who wasn't a quick study. In the interview with Kirkwood, Gene Kiniski also mentioned his interest in training horses—though he didn't indicate what disciplinary measures he favored when it came to training his two Arab mares or whether avid horseman Rod Fenton had whetted his interest in horses.

In Florida, Kiniski's challengers for the NWA title during his freshman year as champion included Don Curtis, Klondike Bill, Dan Miller, Rocky Hamilton, Ron Etchison, Bob Orton, Sr., and wrestler-promoter Eddie Graham. Florida under Graham was a thriving territory, with many wrestlers vying for spots on Graham's roster and a wide range of top contenders coming into the territory at a time when there was a constant shuffling of top wrestlers from one territory to the next. Kiniski traveled the Florida loop three more times in 1966 alone, each time facing some of the same leading contenders but also a collection of newcomers to the territory since his last visit. Among contenders he would face and defeat during his second, third, and fourth tours of the Florida circuit in 1966 were Wahoo McDaniel, Buddy Fuller, Don McClarty, Jose Lothario, Hiro Matsuda, Graham, and former NWA World titleholders O'Connor and Thesz.

Other regions or centers where Kiniski played prominently as a traveling world champion in 1966 included Missouri-Kansas, Winnipeg, Southern Ontario, Tennessee-Alabama, Georgia, the Mid-Atlantic, and particularly the Pacific Northwest, where he resurfaced at times throughout the year. While touring as champion, he managed to squeeze in some hunting, as he had been doing during his travels throughout his career. He was especially known to enjoy going after grizzly and brown bears in the Canadian and American West, and by the mid-1960s, perhaps his favorite hunting destination—and one he would develop an enduring attraction to over many years—was the Flathead Valley region in the area where British Columbia, Montana, and Alberta come together.

Kiniski was an avid hunter throughout his adult life (Kiniski family archive).

Prominent challengers in Kansas and Missouri (excluding St. Louis, which was a territory of its own) included Sonny Myers, Bruiser, O'Connor, and Archie "The Stomper" Gouldie, a fellow Albertan who would evolve into a heel many long-time observers of wrestling—particularly in Stu Hart's Alberta territory—would place alongside Kiniski as the greatest heel ever to come out of Alberta. While Gouldie did not have the level of national or international success Kiniski did, he was frequently in and out of his native Alberta as Stampede Wrestling's lead villain until moving to Tennessee during the latter part of his career.

As far as St. Louis was concerned, Kiniski followed up his January 7 NWA title victory with 1966 Kiel Auditorium defenses—the majority, sellouts—against Ellis, Fritz von Erich, Bruiser, Thesz, and Funk Jr., along with occasional appearances on *Wrestling at the Chase* to build up his high-profile homecoming matches.

Challengers Kiniski faced in the Northwest during his first year as NWA champion included several names that rank high on the list of all-time wrestling attractions in the region. Heading the list is Don Leo Jonathan, probably the only wrestler in the history of Northwest Wrestling whose longevity as a regional headliner, national and international success, and historical impact would rival Kiniski's. Next would be multi-time NWA Heavyweight titleholder Thesz, who at age 50 continued to impress fans as a challenger for Kiniski's title in the Pacific Northwest and several other regions in 1966, often pressing Kiniski—who, when he wasn't fully in wrestling character, was known to refer to his legendary opponent as Mr. Thesz—to a hard-fought draw.

Kiniski faced numerous challenges in Don Owen's Portland territory, which extended into Washington, and the Fenton-Parker promotion centered in Vancouver. Among other top challengers in the Northwest were Tony Borne, an all-time favorite in the Owen territory; John Tolos, Kiniski's tag team partner in California more than a decade earlier; and popular African American contenders Shag Thomas and Bearcat Wright, both considered trailblazers when it came to paving the way for African Americans to achieve equality with whites in professional wrestling. Others challenging Kiniski in the Pacific Northwest included Haystack Calhoun, a superheavyweight "country boy" attraction and major star across North America for many years; Pat Patterson, who became a superstar especially in Northern California and the WWWF/WWF; Don Jardine, a 1960s–1980s headliner in many territories; and Billy White Wolf, who as Chief White Wolf had teamed with Kiniski in Japan in 1964. White Wolf was a Native American character played by Iraqi Adnan Bin Abdulkareem Ahmed Alkaissy El Farthie, who in the early 1990s played hated character General Adnan in a questionable WWF wrestling angle exploiting the backdrop of the First Gulf War.

In Ontario, meanwhile, Kiniski's top challengers in 1966 included Brower, Valentine, Carpentier, Johnny Powers, Ernie Ladd, and Watson, who was nearing 50 but still battling toe-to-toe with the NWA champion. Kiniski and Watson also faced off in a 1966 title match in Winnipeg that ended in a Watson disqualification. Also in Winnipeg, Kiniski had a successful title defense that year against Jonathan.

In Tennessee Kiniski had defenses in 1966 against Thesz, Snyder, Art Thomas, Etchison, Al Costello, Sam Steamboat, and Luke Graham. Kiniski also defended the NWA title against Jackie Fargo, the most popular wrestler ever based in Tennessee with the possible exception of Jerry Lawler. In neighboring Georgia, challengers included Swede Karlson, Klondike Bill, Buddy Fuller, Dick Steinborn, Alberto and Enrique Torres, and a young Bobby Shane, who would go on to challenge Kiniski for the world title in Vancouver in 1968.

A little further up the Atlantic Coast, Kiniski traveled the Virginia-Carolinas loop several times in 1966 to defend the NWA World Heavyweight title against challengers Schmidt, Karl Gotch, Johnny Weaver, Tex McKenzie, Larry "Missouri Mauler" Hamilton, Abe Jacobs, Eastern Canada's Rudy Kay, and, of course, Thesz.

Kiniski was especially active in Texas in 1966, headlining shows around the state in association with Dory Funk, Sr.'s thriving Amarillo territory; Fritz von Erich's new Dallas-based territory; and the Houston-based territory run by Morris Sigel and his assistant Paul Boesch, who would take over the promotion after Sigel passed away in December 1966. In 1966 Kiniski had at least 22 NWA World Heavyweight title defenses in Texas, where he had risen to major stardom a decade earlier and—a few years before legitimately being selected NWA champion and making it official by defeating Thesz for the title—been recognized for a time in the Amarillo territory, though nowhere else, as NWA champ. Kiniski also made several nontitle appearances in Texas in 1966.

Kiniski's 1966 title defenses in Texas included eight meetings with Fritz von Erich—a few of them draws or disqualification decisions; some outright wins for Kiniski in a best-of-three-falls format, as many major NWA title defenses would remain until the Ric Flair era; and all of them wild. At least two more 1966 NWA title defenses took place, in Dallas and Houston, between Kiniski and Fritz von Erich's "brother" Waldo.

Other contenders challenging for Kiniski's title in Texas in 1966 were Karl Kox, Jardine, Billy "Red" Lyons, Ladd, Dan Miller, Art Nelson, and Mike DiBiase. Other challengers of note were Dory Funk, Jr., who fought Kiniski to a draw in two meetings a week apart in November; Thesz, still a serious challenger in the minds of many wrestling purists of the day; and Dick the Bruiser, who lost via disqualification to Kiniski in San Antonio on November 9. A month earlier Kiniski had turned back the challenge of Bruiser in Kansas City, and on August 20 at Indianapolis' Victory Field, Kiniski and Bruiser had fought to a draw in a wild match with both Kiniski's NWA title and Bruiser's WWA belt at stake.

One characteristic of a Kiniski run through an NWA territory was fans' eagerness to see him return after he left the territory—but not, by any stretch, because he was adopted as a fan favorite. Perhaps more than any major world heavyweight champion before his time with the possible exception of Buddy Rogers, Kiniski was regarded as a touring champion who made regional contenders look like potential world titleholders, even if some of them were not among the most gifted wrestlers on the planet. As later NWA Heavyweight champion Terry Funk says in his book *Terry Funk: More Than Just Hardcore*, "The guys, the other wrestlers, make someone the world champion, and the world champion exists to make the guys seem like world-beaters. Gene Kiniski was good about that" (68).

While his first year as NWA world champion saw Kiniski mix it up with top contenders in most of the alliance's key territories, there were a few key NWA territories in which he did not set foot in 1966. These included the territories centered in Buffalo, where Pedro Martinez remained at the helm nearly a decade after Kiniski had made a big impact there; Albuquerque, where Kiniski had enjoyed success early in his career; Hawaii, where Kiniski had held titles prior to becoming NWA champion; Tulsa, where a young Jack Brisco—who would defend the NWA title against Kiniski nearly a decade later—was on the rise; and Detroit, where Kiniski, the previous year, had wrestled on some of Bruiser and Snyder's WWA shows in opposition to NWA promoter Ed "The Sheik" Farhat. While Kiniski would make title defenses in the Buffalo, Albuquerque, and

Hawaii territories in 1967 or 1968, he never defended the NWA World Heavyweight championship in Oklahoma, though he frequently did so in neighboring parts of Texas. Likewise, Kiniski never defended the NWA title in The Sheik's territory, considered one of the more "gimmicky" NWA territories of the day, with The Sheik most often headlining as the regional NWA United States champion and usually defending his title in short, sometimes bloody matches that showed little in the way of athleticism.

Kiniski apparently did not wrestle outside the United States and Canada in 1966, though he surely could have headlined shows in other parts of the world—particularly in the busy NWA territories in Mexico, New Zealand, and Japan. Mexico's Empresa Mexicana de Lucha Libre—later renamed Consejo Mundial de Lucha Libre and, in 2018, considered the world's oldest wrestling promotion—featured smaller wrestlers, and Kiniski or NWA directors likely did not view a Kiniski tour of Mexico as a potential moneymaker on the scale of continued Kiniski title defenses throughout the United States and Canada. As far as New Zealand is concerned, while there are unsubstantiated reports that Kiniski, at some point during his peak wrestling years, appeared on shows promoted by longtime NWA New Zealand promoter Steve Rickard—who made some wrestling appearances in British Columbia in the mid–1960s—there appear to be no records of any Kiniski NWA title defenses in New Zealand, and Greg Oliver's notes from his February 2002 interview with Kiniski indicate the latter had no interest in testing the waters in New Zealand. And while Kiniski was a proven commodity in Japan, he apparently never defended the NWA World Heavyweight title in that country, although he would have an impactful presence there during his title reign.

In 1967 Kiniski's pattern of tours and title defenses often mirrored his pattern of the previous year, but while continuing to make regular stops in Texas, Missouri-Kansas, the Northwest, Tennessee, Florida, Ontario, and Georgia, in 1967 Kiniski added title defenses in Iowa, Alberta-Saskatchewan, Albuquerque, and Puerto Rico.

Much of his success as a touring champion was owing to his image as a wrestler and champion who, like Thesz before him, was to be taken seriously. But while Kiniski came across to the masses and his fellow wrestlers as a tough, legitimate athlete, he was not content to get by on his gifts alone. Like Thesz, he made every effort to come across as a champion should. As Kelly Kiniski recalls, "When he went to get on a plane, he had on a suit and tie. That's what champions do—dress up."

Another aspect of Kiniski's view of what a champion should be required that he not miss any bookings for anything as trivial in his mind as pain or even injury. Strongly opposed to taking any kind of medication, even aspirin, for a little relief, Kiniski was committed to showing up for his matches—usually in time to get in a little publicity beforehand—and then delivering in the ring regardless of how he might feel afterward.

"He wrestled under so much pain," says Nick Kiniski. "He just worked through it."

It is unclear exactly when, during his NWA title reign, Gene Kiniski suffered an injury he would not fully be aware of until years later, but Kelly recalls a time his father's ankle hurt more than usual. "He just laced his boot up really tight," he says. "He said it just killed him from the dressing room to the arena, but once he got in the ring he didn't feel it anymore."

Years later in Vancouver, says Kelly, Gene was seeing his doctor, who asked, "When did you break your ankle?" Gene's response was to deny that his ankle had ever been broken—until the doctor proved him wrong and Gene was able to put two and two together.

By all accounts, Kiniski made every effort to look and act the part of the famous "Canada's Greatest Athlete" moniker that Toronto and Hamilton, Ontario, sportswriter and sportscaster Dick Beddoes is widely credited with bestowing on him. Like Kiniski, Beddoes was a native Albertan who had achieved some prominence in Vancouver fairly early in his career, and Oliver and Johnson report, in *The Pro Wrestling Hall of Fame: The Heels* (72), that Kiniski and Beddoes first met in an Edmonton gym when Kiniski was 15. A notable piece of trivia is that Beddoes hailed from Daysland, Alberta, the same tiny central Alberta community where Marion Kiniski spent her early years before making her way to Edmonton, where she met Gene in 1952 or 1953. In 1963 Beddoes moved permanently to Ontario.

Memories vary as to when Beddoes' christening of Kiniski as "Canada's Greatest Athlete" took place, but as Kiniski recalled in his November 10, 2000, *SLAM! Wrestling* chat, "I was being interviewed by Dick Beddoes on a Hamilton TV station, and he said tonight we have Canada's Greatest Athlete with us. The phone lines lit up, and they wondered what made me the Greatest. Beddoes' rebuttal was this: You have to wrestle Kiniski first, [and then] if you can play basketball, hockey, golf, tennis, then you are a great athlete. You'd be lucky to lace on your boots. By referring to myself as Canada's Greatest Athlete, it stimulated the audience. They hated that. I used to rub it in their face." As Dave Meltzer reports in the April 28, 2010, *Wrestling Observer*, "Kiniski took the name and ran with it, using it to get heat in Canada by bragging he was better than the local hockey stars, the country's biggest sport, in the major cities, as well as his opponents. In the U.S., the name was used to brag that no American star could be the equal of Canada's Greatest Athlete. He'd constantly brag that if you spent $1 to see Gene Kiniski, you would get $10 worth of value."

As quoted in *The Heels*, Dory Funk, Jr., says, "Gene Kiniski had probably the toughest attitude I've ever known. He really was Canada's greatest athlete" (Oliver and Johnson, 74). In a June 26, 2001, *SLAM! Wrestling* chat, Funk goes further in commending Kiniski—who "was like a second father to me"—for his "all-around representation of what a world champion should be. And a beautiful guy too."

Don Leo Jonathan agreed that "Canada's Greatest Athlete" was a moniker Kiniski did his best to live up to. "He played that part well," said Jonathan, who, given his long association and friendship with Kiniski—and his position, with Kiniski, atop the wrestling hierarchy of the Pacific Northwest for many years—was probably as qualified as anybody to make that assessment. "I wrestled him all over the United States, especially when he became world's champion," said Jonathan. Of his association in wrestling with Kiniski, which lasted 20 years—twice as long as Kiniski's professional association with Billy Watson—Jonathan said, "It seems like a whole lifetime." In fact, after their last meeting in a wrestling ring—in Vancouver on March 5, 1979—the two would remain friends for life.

"I would have called him Canada's Greatest Talker," said Jonathan, highlighting an aspect of Kiniski's persona that Kiniski himself always sought to play up.

Referring to Kiniski as "one of the best interviews of all time" (71), Oliver and Johnson recount how Kiniski was not only a master at delivering wrestling interviews but mainstream interviews as well, dating back to his appearances in Toronto in the 1950s, his presence on the CBC, and his rivalry with Watson. As his career developed, Kiniski, as quoted in *The Heels*, said, "I used to leave hours ahead, or even the day before, if I could just get on a radio program" (72).

Kiniski was an avid reader who was noted for delivering strong interviews geared

14. Height of His Career

toward specific markets. "My dad always read papers," says Kelly Kiniski, "so when he did interviews he knew what the latest stuff was." Unlike many wrestlers in the current day, who are usually instructed on what to say, Kiniski was noted for his ability to ad-lib as he "read" his interviewers and audiences. "I'm at my best when the pressure is on, and it's just impromptu," he explained in *The Heels* (72).

Kelly recalls, "When I was doing a speech in high school ... and I would have a hard time, my dad would say 'Here' and grab a rubber band and give me a 10-minute speech on a rubber band or a beer bottle on a desk." Kelly says his father had an amazing eye and memory for detail.

As a fierce-fighting, smooth-talking, crowd-riling, media-savvy headlining wrestler who happened to hold the NWA World Heavyweight championship, Kiniski seldom made it home to the St. Louis suburb of Bridgeton during many stretches of his NWA title reign. "My mom was king, as far as we were concerned," Kelly recalls of himself and younger brother Nick. Next in line, perhaps, was Marion's mother Emma Weller, who was staying with the Kiniskis for an extended period apparently following her divorce from Marion's father Nick Weller. Once, when his father briefly tried to assert his parental authority in between lengthy wrestling tours, Kelly, good-naturedly, says he couldn't help wondering, "Who is this miserable son of a bitch?"

NWA champion Gene Kiniski strongly believed that a champion had to look the part. Whether he was flying to the next city, doing a media appearance, or making himself available to fans outside of the arena, chances are Kiniski was dressed royally and making an effort to conduct himself in a manner befitting the top-rated wrestler in the world. "That's what champions do" is how Kelly Kiniski summarizes his father's attitude (Kiniski family archive).

Challengers in Texas in 1967 included still-familiar names such as Thesz, Funk Jr., Blanchard, Lyons, Fritz von Erich, and Claude "Thunderbolt" Patterson. Patterson had quickly risen to the top of the card in Texas after appearing in the opening match on a January 1967 show in Vancouver headlined by a Kiniski world title defense against Dutch Savage. A second Funk—Terry, coming into his own as the third legitimate wrestling superstar in his family—challenged Kiniski for the NWA title for the first time in Albuquerque on August 20, 1967.

Half a century later, Terry Funk says, by telephone, "[Kiniski] was as good a champion as there ever was." He adds, "He was loud, he was tough, he was scary, but he had a heart of gold [and] a tremendous amount of class."

Tully Blanchard, Joe Blanchard's son, echoes that sentiment, explaining how Kiniski sometimes stayed at his parents' home while coming through Texas as NWA champion. Attributing his father's lasting friendship with Kiniski in large part to the camaraderie they had established on the football field in Edmonton, Tully Blanchard says, "When

[Kiniski] stayed at my mom and dad's house he always sent my mom roses. When he left he thanked [them].... He was a very, very nice guy."

Heartland defenses in 1967 included Kiniski's encounters with Etchison and popular bodybuilder Earl Maynard in Iowa; Maynard, Etchison, Bob "The Viking" Morse, and O'Connor in Kansas; and an impressive battery of Thesz, Snyder, O'Connor, Bruiser, Carpentier, and Fritz von Erich in St. Louis. In two other 1967 St. Louis matches—though, obviously, without the NWA World Heavyweight title at stake—Kiniski was booked to stand alone in two-on-one encounters against top challengers. In May Kiniski fell to the team of Bruiser and Carpentier, and four months later Kiniski lost on television to his former partners Fritz and Waldo von Erich—in particular, Fritz, who started the match for his team and apparently earned the victory without any help from Waldo. Such booking probably did not serve the purpose that nontitle appearances by a world champion against top contenders usually sought to serve—that is, to build up an upcoming title defense by making it look as if the touring world champion was ripe for the picking and a local or regional top challenger was poised to take his place. Perhaps the only thing gained by placing Kiniski in seemingly impossible two-on-one handicap matches against top contenders was to get some fans behind the champion, who, as it turned out, returned to St. Louis to defeat Carpentier and Fritz von Erich in one-on-one title defenses in the aftermath of those odd two-on-one losses he'd suffered in the city.

At the time St. Louis—despite occasional booking of that sort by Muchnick associate Bobby Bruns—was one of the least "gimmicky" territories in the wrestling world, and even wrestlers noted primarily for outlandish gimmicks in other territories usually toned down those gimmicks considerably whenever they were brought into St. Louis. Probably the biggest gimmick in St. Louis wrestling during the Muchnick years was the popular *Wrestling at the Chase* television program, which for years, before moving to the KPLR-TV studio in the same complex, was held in the ballroom at the elegant Chase Park Plaza Hotel in west-central St. Louis before a live audience dressed in a manner more often associated with a night at the opera than a night at the wrestling matches. Whether the show was taped in the ballroom or in the studio, fans usually watched the matches respectfully, and in return, Muchnick and his wrestlers were generally careful not to do anything to insult spectators' intelligence. Kiniski—essentially, a hometown boy during the majority of his NWA title reign, although that was never really played up—had earned fans' respect over the years by delivering hard-hitting, generally believable, athletic matches whenever he came into St. Louis.

He was also well remembered for some sharp early 1960s verbal exchanges with Joe Garagiola, a former St. Louis Cardinals catcher who had been the inaugural host of *Wrestling at the Chase* before going on to national broadcasting fame while remaining a close friend of Kiniski's in later years. By telephone, Matysik recounted an early 1960 episode in which, during a tag team match that saw Kiniski partnered with Rip Hawk, "[Garagiola] would be needling them and they'd needle him back" until Kiniski and Hawk "chased Joe Garagiola around the ring." In the dressing room afterward, Matysik said, "Sam blasted them" for acting so unprofessionally with a local celebrity who in Muchnick's view was doing the promotion a service by announcing the show.

Later that night, Matysik said, Muchnick stopped off for a bite at the Redbird Lanes bowling alley, whose owners included St. Louis baseball personalities Garagiola and future Major League Hall of Famers Stan Musial and Red Schoendienst. According to Matysik, it was when Muchnick saw Kiniski and Hawk bowling with Garagiola that he realized he'd been taken and, after a few tense moments, admitted, of the chase around the ring, "Yeah, it was a great spot."

Without a doubt, St. Louisans saw many other "great spots" from Kiniski and appreciated the wide display of his efforts and talents in their city over many years. As a result, long after his title reign was over, Kiniski remained one of the wrestlers—along with a few others including Bruiser, Thesz, and O'Connor—that fans of his era in St. Louis most respected.

In Tennessee during his second year as NWA champion, Kiniski turned back the challenges of Thesz, Fargo, Alex Perez, Don Greene, and Steve Kovacs. Kovacs—legally, Vince Bryant—was a Texas native who had been moderately successful in several territories dating back to the 1950s. But his greatest career success would come a few years after his failed challenges for Kiniski's NWA World Heavyweight title in Nashville and Chattanooga in the summer of 1967 when Kovacs—as Native Canadian Steven Little Bear—would become a frequent opponent of Kiniski's, a multi-time regional singles and tag team champion in the Northwest, and an NWA world title challenger in the early 1970s.

In the Mid-Atlantic and Southeast regions of the United States, Kiniski was an active NWA titleholder. In North Carolina and Virginia in 1967, he turned back challengers including Tex McKenzie, Klondike Bill, Johnny Weaver, and Larry "Missouri Mauler" Hamilton. In Georgia Kiniski stopped the challenges of Thesz, Enrique Torres, Ike Eakins, and El Mongol. In Florida, meanwhile, Kiniski defended his title 23 times in 1967, facing challengers including Thesz; Eddie Graham; Wahoo McDaniel; Dromo; Sam Steamboat; Sailor Art Thomas; and Joe Scarpa, who in the early 1970s would take a similar route as Steve Kovacs' to greater success by adopting a Native American character and, in Scarpa's case, going on to wrestle for many years in the WWWF/WWF as Chief Jay Strongbow. In 1967 Scarpa and Thomas would also fall to Kiniski while challenging for the NWA world title in Puerto Rico.

As far as world title defenses in Canada in 1967—Canada's centennial year—were concerned, key challengers included Valentine, Brower, Mighty Igor, and Tiger Jeet Singh, all facing Kiniski for the title in Toronto. Though all among that group except Valentine would be considered "gimmick" wrestlers, Brower was a tough headliner in several territories, Igor had already had a brief AWA title run and was getting established as a big favorite in the Detroit-Toronto region, and Singh would become something of an ethnic hero in Ontario and a very successful villain in Japan. Valentine, meanwhile, was a tough, no-frills wrestler whose rugged approach, ability to agitate fans, and level of success in many territories over a long career could be seen to rival Kiniski's.

In the Canadian Prairies, Kiniski turned back the challenges of Stan Stasiak, Jonathan, and fellow Alberta native Dave Ruhl during the summer of 1967. Further west in British Columbia, Kiniski defended the title against Savage, Abdullah the Butcher, John Tolos, Chris Tolos, and Jonathan over the course of the year. He also had additional defenses in Seattle and Tacoma, Washington, against Abdullah, both Tolos brothers, Jonathan, and Rocky Johnson. A bit further south—in Oregon's only NWA Heavyweight title defenses in 1967—Kiniski went to a draw with Jonathan and earned a disqualification victory over Lonnie Mayne.

Barry Owen, Don's son, who saw many NWA titleholders come through Oregon during his years of helping run Pacific Northwest Wrestling, says, of Kiniski, "I remember he was a great champion … a big, tough brawler."

While Kiniski had more than 150 successful title defenses in the United States and Canada in 1967—with nontitle or tag team matches and plenty of media appearances sprinkled in between—the professional highlight of 1967 for the NWA World Heavyweight champion quite possibly took place over a four-day span in August when he did not defend the NWA title yet put on a couple of performances that mesmerized fans in Japan and helped pave the way for Shohei "Giant" Baba to become one of the legendary performers, personalities, and power brokers to a generation of Japanese fans.

Since his debut in 1960 under the tutelage of Rikidozan, Baba showed signs of being destined to one day take the reins of the wrestling industry in Japan. Rikidozan's death in 1963 accelerated Baba's rise, and in 1964 and 1965 Baba made numerous appearances in major U.S. territories and in Toronto and had opportunities to challenge Thesz and Sammartino for their world titles. Back in Japan, a series of hard-fought draws between Baba and Kiniski during the latter's 1964 tour with the Japan Wrestling Association helped establish Baba as a top-tier attraction.

In November of 1965 Baba defeated Dick the Bruiser via disqualification in Osaka and was named NWA International Heavyweight champion, a title that had been vacant since Rikidozan's death nearly two years earlier. Over the course of 1966 Baba defended his International title with victories over Killer Karl Kox, Gorilla Monsoon, Fritz von Erich, and Thesz, but it was really a couple of short title-challenge series in 1967—each just two matches, both resulting in draws—that helped convince fans in Japan that Baba was as good as any wrestler in the world.

In March of 1967 WWWF champion Sammartino had several matches in Japan, including two one-on-one matches with Baba in which Sammartino's WWWF title was not at stake. On the line instead was Baba's NWA International Heavyweight title. That title was normally defended once every month or two against a top foreign wrestler brought in by the JWA, which was headed by Yoshinosato, who replaced Toyonobori as JWA president early in 1966.

On March 2, 1967, in Osaka's Prefectural Gym, Sammartino won the first fall via bear hug submission and lost the second via pinfall before he and Baba were both counted out not long into the third fall after a wild exchange. Five days later the two met again in Tokyo's Kurumae Kokugikan—Tokyo's Sumo Hall at the time—again splitting the first two falls via Baba pinfall and Sammartino bear hug. But this time the third fall went nearly half an hour before the match ended in a 60-minute draw that convinced many fans Baba could hold up his end of an epic match against a wrestler widely considered equal to any other in the world.

Baba next defended the NWA International Heavyweight title in April and May against two more top opponents, Dick "The Destroyer" Beyer and Fritz von Erich—the latter having defeated Baba in a nontitle match three days before losing his May 27 title challenge in Sapporo. Putting his title on the shelf for the next two months, Baba faced a variety of North American stars—most notably, Kiniski associates Dutch Savage and Don Leo Jonathan—in the lead-up to his showdown with the NWA World Heavyweight champion, who was generally the top-rated wrestler in the world given the size and international scope of the National Wrestling Alliance.

Although the Japan Wrestling Association was an NWA member in good standing, the Kiniski-Baba megamatches in 1967 did not have the NWA world title at stake. While Baba was a shrewd wrestler and businessman who would work out deals with the NWA allowing him to win and lose the NWA World Heavyweight championship during brief periods when an NWA world titleholder was touring Japan in the years following Kiniski's reign, Baba was not a wrestler who was ever considered a serious candidate for a lengthy world title run that would expose his limitations as a wrestler in territories around the alliance. His was an act that could get over—and stay over—in Japan, but elsewhere, he was at best a wrestler who could be expected to entertain fans only as a short-term novelty act. Although an NWA touring world champion usually moved in and out of territories quickly and did not have to entertain the same fans week after week, the world champion was expected to put on athletic and legitimate-looking matches that could convince fans he was a serious wrestler at the top of his profession. Rogers had been something of an exception to that general rule—especially during the period when most of his NWA title defenses took place in the Northeast—but wrestlers like Thesz, O'Connor, and Kiniski made a strong statement in the 1960s regarding what an NWA World Heavyweight champion was expected to be.

Though not the sort of wrestler most fans outside of Japan would have taken to as a touring world champion, Baba fit his niche in Japan almost perfectly as a rare example of a Japanese wrestler who, though not having the sort of muscularity or proportions usually associated with top athletes, was larger than most of his foreign opponents and had a level of in-ring charisma that at the time was probably second only to Rikidozan's among Japanese wrestlers—or those pretending to be Japanese—since the advent of pro wrestling in Japan. While Baba in later years was involved in three quick, back-and-forth NWA title switches in Japan, in 1967, as Baba was still rising to legendary status, there was probably no interest from Yoshinosato or the JWA in having him lose the second match of a back-and-forth title series. Instead, the preferred route seemed to involve simply building up Baba's NWA International Heavyweight title as a championship that was second to none in the world. Bringing in a respected NWA World Heavyweight champion and booking Baba to be his equal in the ring—especially with memories of Baba's stalemate series with Sammartino still fresh in fans' minds—seemed the surest way to do that.

Kiniski did his part, going to a tough one-fall-each draw with Baba on August 10 in Tokyo's Den'en Coliseum. Major wrestling events in Japan at the time were covered in detail by sports newspapers—available throughout the country to crowds of commuters at train stations—and many fans were salivating for the rematch that would take place four days later at Osaka Stadium.

The second Baba-Kiniski match was no more decisive than the first—except in how it did precisely what it was supposed to do. Before an estimated 25,000 fans, the two larger-than-life gladiators in the ring fought it out for more than an hour in the summer heat. Baba took the first fall, nearly half an hour in, after a flurry finishing with a big boot to Kiniski's chest. Nearly 18 minutes later, a methodical Kiniski beatdown capped off by a backbreaker and two knee drops off the top rope squared the match at a fall apiece. The third fall was a brutal back-and-forth exchange, with Kiniski getting the better of things when the bell rang to signal that the one-hour time limit had elapsed.

From there, Kiniski paced the ring, showing five fingers on his right hand to signal that he wanted five more minutes in his quest for Baba's NWA International Heavyweight title—a simple move no doubt designed to elevate Baba's title to one an NWA world champion would covet. Officials conferred, and Baba, by agreeing to give his challenger a second chance to win the title, established himself as a proud, fighting champion who would back down from no one—and the fans in attendance ate it up.

Baba's first offensive move in the five-minute "overtime" period was a standing drop-kick—hardly a standard move in the Baba repertoire—that staggered Kiniski and led off a flurry of action inside and outside the ring that established beyond any question how important this match was to both men. Kiniski was relentless in his attack until missing a top-rope knee drop and hitting only canvas. Baba took over, attacking Kiniski's injured right knee and locking his right leg in a half Boston crab until the time limit bell rang a second time.

This time Kiniski, "selling" or conspicuously favoring his injured knee, did not ask for another five minutes in which to claim victory. Instead, he limped out of the ring, leaving Baba to don the championship belt both men had just worked so hard to elevate. The match was remembered for years afterward as an all-time epic in Japanese wrestling, and it greatly boosted Baba's credibility as a big-time wrestling champion. Many observers consider the Baba-Kiniski 65-minute classic the best performance of Baba's career—and, for the action it delivered and the purpose it served, it can probably be considered one of the best all-around performances of Kiniski's career as well.

15

Passing the Torch

Following a brief tour of Florida in December of 1967, highlighted by NWA world title defenses against Valentine and Thesz—who seemed to challenge Kiniski almost everywhere the champion turned up—Kiniski apparently took a three-week break from the ring to reconnect with family and friends and to lay the groundwork for a chapter in his life that would extend far beyond his days as NWA champion.

By most accounts, Kiniski had a hand in running the Vancouver-based Parker-Fenton promotion since sometime in advance of his winning the NWA World Heavyweight title in 1966. From there, according to Vance Nevada's *Wrestling in the Canadian West*, "In addition to his marquee status [while NWA champion], Kiniski is believed to have been a [secret] partner in the promotion while Rod Fenton was at the helm" (46). Some wrestlers who appeared in British Columbia in the mid–1960s refer to Kiniski as the booker, or planner, of their matches.

It was not uncommon during Kiniski's era for leading wrestlers to be involved in running promotions in ways that fans were not aware of. Among Kiniski's circle of friends and partners throughout his career, Snyder and Bruiser quietly co-owned the WWA promotion in Indianapolis. Dory Funk, Sr., and Fritz von Erich, marquee wrestlers like Kiniski, were guiding forces in running successful territories covering large areas in and around Texas. Lord Blears was heavily involved in booking and promotion in Hawaii in the 1960s and beyond. Verne Gagne was firmly established as an owner and leading wrestler in the AWA from the early 1960s to the 1980s. In earlier years, Thesz and Watson, unbeknownst to fans, held ownership stakes in the St. Louis promotion, and Watson also owned a share of the Seattle promotion in the mid–1950s.

While Kiniski and Cliff Parker appeared to have roles or stakes in helping run the Vancouver promotion, wrestling in British Columbia during most of the 1960s was firmly in the hands of Fenton, who had given Kiniski his start in Arizona. But then, as Patrice Fenton reports, Rod Fenton decided to sell his share in the promotion when his wife, facing a diagnosis of terminal cancer, asked that the Fenton family of four return to the United States. "He would have done anything to make my mom happy—to try to save her life," says Patrice, whose admission to Mills College in Oakland, California, was the key factor in determining where the Fenton family would go.

As the dust settled, by early 1968 full ownership of Vancouver-based Northwest Wrestling Promotions/All-Star Wrestling was in the hands of Sandor Kovacs, Gene Kiniski, and Don Owen, and after apparently helping the new owners, over the course of a few months, to make a smooth transition, Fenton traveled to California with his wife and two daughters during the summer of 1968 to take up residence in Atherton, an affluent community about 35 miles south of Oakland. Though Fenton would never promote another wrestling show in Canada after that, he would briefly resurface a few years later as a promoter in Tucson, where his journey as a wrestling promoter had begun.

Kovacs was a veteran wrestler who, like Kiniski, had been active in the Fenton-Parker promotion for several years, both in the ring and behind the scenes, before buying into the company. In British Columbia under Parker-Fenton, Kovacs—who had some experience as a booker in Quebec and Alberta—did some refereeing and matchmaking while, essentially, serving an apprenticeship under Fenton. While there is some disagreement as to exactly how power was divided among the new ownership triad in British Columbia, there seems little doubt that Kovacs—like Kiniski, a close friend of Lord Blears'—was the key player early in the new administration, while Kiniski was usually out of the territory meeting his numerous obligations as NWA World Heavyweight champion.

Owen, who had run a successful territory down the Pacific Coast in Oregon since World War II, is an interesting study when it comes to the role he played as part-owner of the promotion in British Columbia. While Owen, like Kiniski, was a secret owner of the promotion as far as fans were concerned, even wrestlers of the day are not in agreement as to what Owen's role was with regard to the actual operation of Northwest Wrestling Promotions/All-Star Wrestling. Although some wrestlers who appeared in Vancouver at the time did not see Owen as contributing greatly to the day-to-day operation or direction of the company, others recall seeing him regularly during wrestling events in Vancouver and suggest Kiniski respected his achievements across the border and valued his input greatly.

While a grueling schedule usually kept Kiniski away from his family during the first two years of his NWA world title reign, much of his focus in 1968 clearly was on establishing a foundation for the sort of life he hoped to pick up after his world title reign ended. Kiniski wore many hats while sitting atop the wrestling world from 1966 to 1968. He was a successful, money-drawing, and credible world champion who never shrank from the spotlight, but he was also the father of two boys in elementary school, the husband of a mother who usually had to double as a father to the couple's sons, and a world traveler who had already adopted the Pacific Northwest as his home. Moreover, he already had some behind-the-scenes experience in helping run the Vancouver wrestling promotion, and he was a shrewd man who had done well with his money and didn't run from opportunity.

"I had my family and I just wanted to stay in one spot so I could be with my family when they were growing up. So we bought Rod Fenton [out]," Oliver quotes Kiniski as saying in an April 14, 2010, *SLAM!* report. "I knew Fenton for a long, long time. He was pretty well burnt out."

In 1968 Kiniski had another busy year of title defenses along with other obligations imposed on an NWA champion. In early February, by telephone, he told Canadian syndicated journalist Jim Coleman, "I just got home from South Carolina. Tonight, in St. Louis, I'm defending my world title against Édouard Carpentier, from Paris.... Then I'm flying to Lethbridge for one of those sports celebrity dinners on Saturday night. I imagine that they'll want to make me the main speaker. The next night I'm wrestling in Fort Worth, Texas. The following day I begin a tour of whistle stops in the Caribbean." Yet, as much as Kiniski continued to travel in 1968, he put in fewer miles than the previous year, when he likely earned in the range of $100,000 while spending, as he said in the

Coleman article, a total of $12,800 on air tickets—though much of that was no doubt covered by promoters.

Kiniski's increased presence at home in 1968 helped him and associates Kovacs and Owen—the latter an NWA promoter in good standing since 1951—quickly establish the British Columbia territory as an NWA promotion, which, in effect, it had already been for years, even though Fenton, who had been admitted to the alliance while promoting in Arizona, never fully brought his Vancouver promotion under the NWA umbrella. Apparently with NWA approval, Kiniski managed to juggle the demands of maintaining a strong home territory with his obligation of touring various territories run by fellow promoters, some of whom wanted the touring world champion to make himself available for as many dates in their territories as possible. While this was by no means a replay of the situation several years earlier that saw NWA promoters feel shortchanged when Buddy Rogers was booked to defend his title primarily in the Northeast, alliance promoters saw the potential for big payoffs when Kiniski came to defend the title against local challengers fans were strongly behind, and promoters wanted as many of those paydays as possible.

In fact, only about a fifth of Kiniski's NWA world title defenses in 1968 took place in the Pacific Northwest, and overall, the number of his title defenses in all territories that year was reduced by about a fifth from the previous year. But Kiniski had earned a share of goodwill from the NWA, which as a whole continued to see him as a proven champion who was good for the alliance.

Setting out most of the year from his family's new home base in Blaine, Washington—just across the international border and about an hour southeast of downtown Vancouver—Kiniski hit most of the promotions he had traveled to in 1967, along with one or two others. Although the number of Kiniski's NWA title defenses may have been reduced somewhat from the previous two years, 1968 was nonetheless an amazing year for a wrestler who, at age 40, was still near the top of his game.

Over the course of 1968, Kiniski was frequently in and out of Texas, facing the likes of Lyons, Jardine, Aurelian "Grizzly" Smith, Argentina Apollo, Pat Patterson, Nick Bockwinkel, Waldo von Erich, Funk Sr., and, most notably, Ernie Ladd, Thesz, and, six times, Fritz von Erich.

Ladd was an all-pro football player who had spent several seasons with the then–AFL San Diego Chargers before getting traded to the Houston Oilers in 1966. He had started in pro wrestling in San Diego almost immediately after the 1962 AFL season and since then had been a frequent traveler as a big-time wrestling attraction and an unusually gifted athlete for someone of his 6'9", 300-pound-plus stature. Ladd had spent part of every off-season since 1963 wrestling in Texas, and had been a world title challenger going back to his rookie year, when he faced Thesz in Houston. Territories where Ladd was a popular attraction included British Columbia, where for a brief time in 1967 he formed a powerhouse team with the similarly sized and skilled Don Leo Jonathan. In 1968 Kiniski and Ladd—who had paired off in three title matches during the first year of Kiniski's reign as NWA Heavyweight champion—wowed fans with hour-long draws on consecutive nights in Corpus Christi and Houston that showed the amazing stamina and athletic prowess each man possessed. Six weeks later—on May 13, 1968—a Kiniski-Ladd title rematch in Houston ended in a double disqualification. Their next rematch took place the following month in Toronto, where Kiniski, in the pair's final meeting with the NWA Heavyweight title at stake, earned the victory after 19 minutes.

Kiniski's meetings with Thesz and Fritz von Erich in 1968 demonstrated those proven rivalries were still of great interest to fans. More than a tenth of Kiniski's title defenses that year were against either Thesz or von Erich, and on one occasion in 1968—in Houston on August 30, when Thesz refereed a Kiniski-von Erich title match—fans got the rare chance to see all three in the ring at once.

In Toronto in 1968 Kiniski dispatched a few familiar challengers—namely Ladd, Carpentier, Brower, and Guy Mitchell, under a mask as The Assassin. In nearby Buffalo, where he had been a major attraction a decade earlier, Kiniski successfully defended his NWA world title against Hans Schmidt in April.

Decades later, in a 2006 interview with Oliver, Kiniski identified Schmidt as a heel he held in high regard. "He kept himself in great, great shape," Kiniski said. "He was a big, rugged, lean-boned guy with a brush cut. He had the persona of being a stormtrooper, I would think" (Oliver, Files).

In a variety of other NWA territories and regions including the Mid-Atlantic, Florida, Georgia, Missouri-Kansas, and Tennessee, Kiniski faced other familiar challengers such as Ron Etchison, Klondike Bill, Joe Scarpa, Sonny Myers, Bruiser, Johnny Weaver, Eddie Graham, Watts, O'Connor, Jose Lothario, and Valentine—with the latter pair also challenging Kiniski in Puerto Rico and the Bahamas, respectively. Among first-time challengers Kiniski faced in those territories in 1968 were Red Bastien, Tim "Mr. Wrestling" Woods, George Scott, Steve Bolus, Paul Jones, Bill "Bobby Red Cloud" Wright, Richard "Chief Little Eagle" Bryant—the brother of Vince "Steve Kovacs" Bryant—and Aurelian Smith, who, as The Kentuckian, challenged Kiniski, in early 1968, in Macon, Georgia, where Kiniski would be presented the key to the city by Mayor Ronnie Thompson later in the year.

Smith would challenge Kiniski again in summer, in Texas, as Grizzly Smith. In between his NWA title challenges against Kiniski, Smith appeared, as Ski Hi Jones, for about two months in the British Columbia territory Kiniski had just bought into. Though it appears Jones—or Aurelian Smith in any character—never wrestled Kiniski in the Northwest, his son, future WWF star Jake "The Snake" Roberts, would arrive in Vancouver to face Kiniski a decade later—and would have much to say about it.

Kiniski's challenger during a pair of 1968 NWA title contests in Honolulu—the first going to a 60-minute, one-fall-each draw—was Jim Hady, who had been a regular opponent of Kiniski's earlier in the 1960s mainly in the Midwest. Kiniski and Hady also faced each other at least once in Newfoundland and Labrador, in August of 1963, and at least once more in the Northeast the following year during Kiniski's stay in the WWWF.

Hady was as a member of Vancouver's All-Star Wrestling roster during much of 1965, when Kiniski was in and out of the territory. At least twice in British Columbia in 1965 Hady teamed with Kiniski, though he partnered more often with, first, Red Bastien and then Don Leo Jonathan—both coholders, with Hady, of the territory's NWA Canadian Tag Team championship in 1965. The following year Hady settled in Hawaii, where, as a popular babyface, he held a variety of regional titles leading up to his challenges for Kiniski's NWA World Heavyweight title in 1968. Sadly, Hady passed away, as a result of a heart attack following a match in Hawaii, just a few months after his second and final challenge for Kiniski's title.

It appears Kiniski made only two brief swings—at least, for wrestling purposes—through the Canadian Prairies in 1968. In Alberta, Saskatchewan, and Manitoba during the summer of that year, he successfully defended his title with victories over Archie Gouldie, Stan Stasiak, and Bill Watts.

15. Passing the Torch 127

In the Pacific Northwest, meanwhile, All-Star Wrestling generally drew healthy crowds and plenty of attention as Kiniski defended the NWA title on his home turf against the likes of Tex McKenzie, Paddy Barrett, Calhoun, Savage, Bobby Shane, and Jonathan. Perhaps his most persistent challenger based out of Vancouver in 1968 was John Tolos, coholder of Kiniski's first professional wrestling championship 14 years earlier in Southern California. After his pairing with Kiniski had run its course early in both men's careers, Tolos earned many titles and accolades with real-life brother Chris, and the Tolos Brothers were a dominant tag team in British Columbia as late as 1967. From there the brothers went their separate ways, with John landing on his feet as a top singles contender and, eventually, emerging as a major heel back in Southern California in the 1970s. As far as 1968 was concerned, John Tolos, with a no-nonsense ring style and a gift of gab seen by some to rival Kiniski's, helped draw some large crowds to Monday night wrestling shows in Vancouver, especially on consecutive weeks in late October and early November when he challenged Kiniski for the NWA world title. Tolos was also the challenger in Kiniski's only 1968 British Columbia title defense held outside of Vancouver, as the two battled for the NWA title on a December 17 show in the provincial capital of Victoria.

Besides defending the title 13 times in British Columbia in 1968, Kiniski was able to squeeze several other matches on BC's Lower Mainland and on Vancouver Island into his schedule that year. Most notable were a tag team appearance in March in which the powerful Kiniski-Jonathan tandem reunited and lost to the Assassins (no connection to John "Assassin" Hill, aka Guy Mitchell); a couple of losing efforts in battle royals on shows in which Kiniski defended his NWA title; and a few appearances on the lifeblood of the promotion: the popular *All-Star Wrestling* TV show.

By 1968 *All-Star Wrestling* was seen across much of Canada, in effect replacing the old CBC wrestling broadcasts from Toronto as the closest thing to a nationally televised wrestling product in Canada. As a result, Kiniski was back on a national stage in his native country, usually providing many of the highlights of any episode on which he appeared. In many cases, even more memorable than his work in the ring on *All-Star Wrestling* broadcasts were his interviews and interaction with the long-time voice of *All-Star Wrestling*, BCTV (CHAN-TV) personality Ron Morrier. Greg Oliver writes, at the *SLAM!* Wrestling Hall of Fame website—where Kiniski is also honored—"Simply put, [Morrier] WAS wrestling to anyone who grew up on Canada's West Coast, hosting *All-Star Wrestling* on BCTV for more than 20 years." While Morrier had some detractors who questioned his knowledge of wrestling and his ability to "sell" upcoming matches, he and Kiniski had an excellent on-camera rapport—and in many ways, the face of *All-Star Wrestling* during Kiniski's NWA title reign and for years afterward would best be represented by a combination of both men's features. To this day many older Canadians can recite the tail end of a typical Kiniski interview conducted by Morrier, who hosted *All-Star Wrestling* from the early 1960s to the early 1980s. After thanking his "fellow Canadians and American viewing audience for allowing me into your homes via TV," Kiniski typically closed by saying, "And as usual, Ron, you did a great job of interviewing me."

Kiniski traveled down the West Coast in 1968, defending the NWA title in Washington State against Jonathan, McKenzie, John Tolos, and Shane. In Oregon he defended the title on consecutive nights in September, going to time-limit draws with Jonathan and Luther Lindsay, and then defeated Jonathan and Pepper Martin in November. Also in November, Kiniski traveled to California, where he was the first NWA champion to defend the title in Los Angeles in more than a decade, as Southern California's regional promotion had left the alliance in the late 1950s and returned to the NWA fold only during the latter part of Kiniski's title reign. In California toward the end of 1968, Kiniski also defended his world title in the San Francisco territory run by Roy Shire.

During a few swings through California in November and December of 1968, Kiniski had title and nontitle matches against a variety of opponents. Key challengers in California in 1968 included Pedro Morales, a future WWWF World titleholder whose popularity in some arenas rivaled Sammartino's; Fred Curry, whose father "Wild" Bull Curry had teamed with Kiniski in Japan several times in 1964; and Bobo Brazil, who faced Kiniski many times over the course of both men's outstanding careers but challenged Kiniski for the NWA World Heavyweight title only once—in a December 18, 1968, match at Los Angeles' Grand Olympic Auditorium that drew more than 10,000 fans and ended in a time-limit draw after each man took a fall.

Also near the end of 1968, Kiniski returned to Japan for another tour with the Japan Wrestling Association. While his tour of Japan the previous year had been limited to major shows in Tokyo and Osaka—with Kiniski and Giant Baba going to nondecisions both times—in late November and early December of 1968 Kiniski faced a variety of opponents and teamed with several partners during a nine-day, nine-match tour of northern and central Japan.

As in 1967, Kiniski's NWA World Heavyweight title was not on the line during his late 1968 run through Japan. Although fans there were well aware that Kiniski held the NWA World Heavyweight title, Kiniski's 1968 tour of Japan saw him once more in the role of a challenger to Giant Baba, the Japanese champion and hero Kiniski had helped elevate in 1967—except this time Kiniski would be cast as a challenger for not one but two titles Baba was holding.

Since his 65-minute classic with Kiniski in 1967, Baba had continued to hold the NWA International Heavyweight championship during all but a brief period in mid-1968 when Bobo Brazil managed a best-of-three-falls victory in Nagoya before dropping the title back to Baba two days later in Tokyo. Other key challengers for Baba's International Heavyweight title in 1968 included The Crusher, Prince (better known as "King") Curtis Iaukea, Dick the Bruiser, Jess Ortega, Killer Karl Kox, and Bruno Sammartino—all tasting defeat at the hands of Baba. In Sammartino's case, five days after battling Baba to a double-countout draw in early August before a crowd estimated at 18,000 in Sendai, he lost a best-of-three-falls decision to Baba—getting counted out in the third fall—at Osaka Stadium.

In 1968 Baba also earned nontitle victories over an impressive list including Bill Miller, Fred Blassie, Killer Kowalski, Pat Patterson, Mario Milano, Ray Stevens, and Mad Dog Vachon. But Baba's success in 1968 was perhaps best illustrated by his brief title programs with The Crusher, Iaukea, Bruiser, Brazil, Sammartino, and Kiniski—with Baba emerging as the ultimate victor in each of those programs. In his pair of title defenses against Kiniski in early December of 1968, Baba retained his championship, first, by wrestling Kiniski to a no-falls decision in a best of three-falls match. The rematch, five days later in Tokyo, ended in a third-fall Baba disqualification victory after nearly an hour. The next night, in Utsunomiya, Kiniski and Baba fought to a nontitle time-limit draw.

What set the Kiniski-Baba program apart from Baba's 1968 title programs with Crusher, Iaukea, Bruiser, Brazil, and Sammartino were the length and quality of the Kiniski-Baba matches. While Crusher, Iaukea, Bruiser, Brazil, and Sammartino were top wrestlers whose stature could help solidify Baba's standing in Japanese fans' minds as the top native wrestler and one who was equal to—or even a step ahead of—the best foreign wrestlers of the day, Baba's matches against members of that group seldom went much longer than 15 minutes. Even best-of-three-falls matches with Baba's NWA International Heavyweight title on the line normally saw Baba win the deciding fall after a relatively quick succession of falls.

Kiniski's pair of challenges for Baba's NWA International Heavyweight title, meanwhile, were booked to last about an hour each. Baba was a wrestler who usually was best protected—that is, whose athletic shortcomings were easier to conceal—in shorter matches, but clearly, Kiniski was regarded as a ring general who could make Baba shine even in lengthy matches. While NWA directors surely did not want the world titleholder to look weaker than a regional titleholder such as Baba—even in a wrestling market halfway around the world from nearly all the alliance's territories—Kiniski did not have to engage in tough hour-long matches in order to do justice to his role as NWA champion or to demonstrate to Japanese fans that Baba was a world-class wrestler. Kiniski could have established parity with Baba in much shorter matches, but clearly, his pride was on display as he carried Baba to two more memorable International Heavyweight title defenses—totaling 118 minutes—during his 1968 tour of Japan. And while Kiniski's three singles matches—including the nontitle time-limit draw on December 7—against Baba were not the only lengthy contests Baba had in 1968, collectively, they were probably the most athletic and most memorable series of matches Baba had that year.

Slightly below Baba in the JWA pecking order in 1968 was another protégé of Rikidozan's, Antonio Inoki, who had spent some of his teenage years in Brazil before returning to Japan and getting into wrestling. A few years into his career, Inoki wrestled in the western United States, in Tennessee, and in Texas, where he lost to Kiniski at least twice in 1965. The following year, Inoki jumped promotions in Japan, leaving the JWA when Toyonobori cut ties with that promotion and started a new promotion, Tokyo Pro Wrestling, with Inoki as the centerpiece. But the new promotion was short-lived, and Inoki was back with the JWA in 1967, playing a rising Robin to Baba's Batman. In May of 1967 the two began teaming, and after a series of impressive victories over various combinations of North American touring wrestlers, including major names Waldo von Erich, Fritz von Erich, Don Leo Jonathan, Dutch Savage, Rip Hawk, Swede Hanson, Jess Ortega, Tarzan Tyler, Bill Watts, and Red McNulty—the future Ivan Koloff—Baba and Inoki won the JWA's NWA International Tag Team title from Watts and Tyler in Osaka on October 31. From there Baba and Inoki would hold the title most of the time until 1971, when Inoki left the promotion again.

On November 30, 1968, in Sapporo, Kiniski teamed with Paul Demarco in an unsuccessful challenge for Baba and Inoki's NWA International Tag Team title. Three days later in Osaka, Kiniski teamed with Brute Bernard in another unsuccessful challenge for the same title. In both cases it was Kiniski's partner who was pinned to end the match.

During his 1968 Japan tour, Kiniski also teamed with Joe Scarpa and Lonnie Mayne to challenge teams headed by Baba. Again, it was always Kiniski's partner or partners who took the loss for a Kiniski-led team.

In his opening match on the tour, Kiniski earned a 25-minute singles victory over Inoki in a Muroran, Hokkaido, main event that followed a seven-minute Baba-Bernard semi-main event. At the time Inoki, with a legitimate athletic background, was a serious, skilled young wrestler who, like Kiniski, tried to make his matches as athletic and believable as possible. As a result, the in-ring highlight of Kiniski's 1968 Japan tour may well have been his first match, the singles encounter with Inoki on November 29.

But as far as the entire year was concerned, the professional highlight or defining moment for Gene Kiniski had probably been a few months earlier, during the annual National Wrestling Alliance convention. Every year since the inception of the NWA in 1948, an alliance-wide convention was held—usually over a three-day period in summer—in which NWA member promoters would hammer out issues of concern, including membership, legal matters, the status of the champion and any details relating to his reign or suggestions among promoters or directors as to a possible change of direction, and any other matters of interest regarding NWA business in general.

As Dave Meltzer reports in his book *Tributes II*, Kiniski, never afraid to speak his mind, "went to the Alliance meeting in late 1968 and basically told the promoters to shove it" (179). Kiniski corroborated that story, and Oliver's April 14, 2010, *SLAM! Wrestling* report following Kiniski's death quotes from a 2009 interview in which Kiniski reportedly said, "I tell them, the way they were treating me, fucking me with my payoffs. I told them off and ... they stopped using me."

Nick Kiniski quotes his father regarding his experience with NWA promoters during his world title reign: "A whore on [Vancouver's] Davie St. can hold their head up higher than the NWA world's champion. [That's] how you screw me so bad."

Nick says, "They were screwing him out of a lot of money. That's why he bought the promotion" in Vancouver.

While Gene Kiniski remained a busy champion for a time following the 1968 NWA convention, it appears his tongue-lashing at the convention was, in effect, a strong hint that the alliance had better start looking for another champion. Kelly Kiniski concurs that his father had bought into the Vancouver promotion earlier in the year, in large part, "so he'd have someplace to wrestle" after burning a few bridges. By that time, Gene Kiniski was tiring of the grind of touring as world champion and dealing with promoters who were not always on the up and up—Sam Muchnick in his mind being an obvious exception.

As Terry Funk says in *More Than Just Hardcore*, "[In 1968] my father came to [Dory Funk] Junior and me and said, 'Gene is ready to give it up'" (53).

Funk continues, "'Gene' was Gene Kiniski, the National Wrestling Alliance world's heavyweight champion, and what he was ready to give up was the championship. Champions tended to run that route. The world champion went from territory to territory, wrestling the top stars in each, often in long, grueling matches. The grind would run through a guy physically and mentally, and they'd be ready to give it up. Some lasted longer than others. If one worked, the promoters wanted to keep him. It was almost always the champion himself who wanted to end his reign" (53).

While Kiniski was still a respected champion, the reality was that he turned 40 years old in 1968 and looked his age and more, although he could still mix it up physically as a younger man would and could still deliver long—sometimes hour-long—quality matches against a wide variety of opponents. But he was coming up on three years as NWA titleholder in late 1968, and it appears NWA directors and promoters agreed it was time for a change in the wake of Kiniski's tirade at the annual convention.

One of the few promoters, besides Muchnick, Kiniski did not seem to have a problem with was his friend and mentor Dory Funk, Sr., who had been heading wrestling operations in Amarillo since the mid–1950s. Terry Funk writes, "Kiniski wanted out, and he had told my father immediately before making it known to the NWA board because they were good friends" (53).

Selection of a new world heavyweight champion by the NWA Board of Directors usually involved lobbying by member promoters who pushed for the selection of wrestlers they thought would further the interests of the alliance and, especially, those promoters' home territories. According to Terry Funk, "after [Kiniski] told the board, and it became official that Gene would be stepping down as champion, my father told us, 'I'm going to push for [Dory Funk] Junior to be champion'" (53).

Although selection of succeeding champions was ultimately out of the hands of reigning NWA champions—who during the height of the territorial era ran the risk of forfeiting a $25,000 bond if they did not comply with directives of the Board of Directors when it came to succession—reigning champions did have some say when it came to the manner in which they would hand over the title. While Kiniski, an owner-promoter himself, did not want to get too far on the bad side of the NWA—which, despite governmental investigations into its alleged monopolistic practices more than a decade earlier, was still by far the most powerful entity in wrestling—he was not afraid to use his leverage to support what he thought was best for the wrestling business. Though it is unclear how vocal he was in his support for Dory Funk, Jr., clearly he favored passing the world title to Funk, who was a good friend who had shown great promise as a wrestler from the start of his career six years earlier. By the time Kiniski decided it was time to drop the title, Funk Jr. had already established himself in the United States, Canada, and Australia as one of the most skilled wrestlers in the world.

As Dory Funk, Sr., made the case for his elder son's ascension to the world championship, Kiniski soldiered on as a promoter-owner, regional headliner, and workhorse touring champion. Once Funk Sr.'s efforts at swaying NWA brass paid off and plans were in place to transfer the title to Funk Jr., Kiniski set about fulfilling his final obligations to the National Wrestling Alliance as the organization's touring representative and world champion.

After defending the NWA title against Bobo Brazil and unlikely challenger Lou Whitson in California in December of 1968, Kiniski returned to Vancouver, where he teamed with Stan Stasiak to lose to Jonathan and Shane, before closing out the year with world title defenses in Kansas City against O'Connor and back in Vancouver against Savage. In between those two final NWA title defenses of 1968 was a nontitle victory over Brower in St. Louis that drew far fewer fans than Kiniski had drawn in the city earlier in the year for title defenses against the likes of Carpentier, Bruiser, and Watts.

January of 1969—Kiniski's last full month as NWA champion—saw him, under a mask as the Blue Destroyer, lose a nontitle challenge in Atlanta to Doug "The Professional" Gilbert in an angle that did not go far. Kiniski also had successful title defenses that month in Georgia, as well as in Texas, California, Missouri, Tennessee, Oregon, North Carolina, South Carolina, Virginia, and Vancouver against the likes of Dominic DeNucci; Bill Dromo; Tim "Mr. Wrestling" Woods (or possibly Dick Steinborn, who reports he once, under a white mask, substituted as Mr. Wrestling for Woods when the latter was scheduled to challenge Kiniski); Johnny Walker, the future Mr. Wrestling II; Blackjack Lanza; Sam Steamboat; and Don Leo Jonathan. Kiniski's January 20, 1969, NWA title defense against Jonathan in Vancouver was apparently the pair's 16th match fought over the NWA title. Few fans in attendance likely realized it would be their last—although the two legends would go on to face each other many more times over the decade following Kiniski's loss of the NWA world title.

Kiniski title defenses in February of 1969 began with disqualification victories over Weaver in Roanoke, Virginia, and John Tolos in Vancouver and a 60-minute draw with Lanza in St. Louis. Dory Funk, Jr., appeared on the same show in St. Louis, on February 7, teaming with brother Terry in a loss to Bruiser and Waldo von Erich. From St. Louis, Kiniski and Funk Jr. headed for Florida, where both appeared on a show in Orlando on Monday, February 10. On that show Funk defeated Eduardo Perez on the undercard, while Kiniski successfully defended his world title against real-life German national Willi Kurt "Kurt von Stroheim" Rutkowsky, better known during most of his career as Kurt von Brauner.

The following night, February 11, 1969, at Tampa's Homer Hesterly Armory, Kiniski and Funk faced off in a one-fall match that would be Kiniski's last NWA title defense. Toward the end of the match—a tough, back-and-forth contest that was not a bit fancy—Kiniski delivered a falling backdrop that appeared to hurt his own back more than Funk's. From there Funk delivered a couple of body slams, and when Kiniski tried to return a slam of his own, his back gave out.

Kiniski was able to escape Funk's first attempt at applying his submission spinning toe hold finisher, but a moment later—shortly after the 25-minute mark—Kiniski fell to that same finisher as Dory Funk, Jr., kicked off a lengthy and distinguished NWA world title reign of his own by upending a competitor and friend he held in the highest regard. Afterward, Kiniski would publicly blame his loss of the title on forgetting that his defense against Funk had been scheduled as a one-fall match and not best-of-three as many of his other NWA title defenses had been.

16

Passing of Nicholas and Julia

In 1969 Gene Kiniski lost more than the NWA World Heavyweight title he had defended proudly for more than three years. That same year, on October 11, he lost his mother Julia, who passed away following a heart attack. While Gene Kiniski had spent most of his adult life outside Alberta and reunited with his parents only at irregular intervals, by all accounts he maintained, through all his accomplishments and travels, a great respect and unwavering love for his mother, who had won over the city of Edmonton through her perseverance, straight talk, and support for the working class.

Much is documented about the life of Julia Kiniski, who rose from humble immigrant, village roots to become one of Edmonton's favorite daughters, and many observers have drawn a connection between Julia's no-nonsense perseverance and the rise of her youngest son to the top of his profession. But far less is recorded about Julia's husband and Gene's father, Nicholas Kiniski, who passed away the year before Julia did. And while much is speculated about the impact Julia Kiniski had on Gene and his siblings, Nicholas Kiniski appears to have been an impactful presence in the Kiniski family as well.

The precise time or even year of Nicholas Kiniski's arrival in Alberta from Poland is unclear and appears not to have been recorded in any lasting manner. What *is* preserved as memory among various members of the Kiniski clan is that Nicholas—likely a teenager at the time—made the long trip from Poland accompanied by his brother. As Kelly Kiniski recalls, "My grandfather came over on a big boat with his brother, and when it got docked, he got separated from his brother." What complicated matters, Kelly says, is that Nicholas "couldn't read or write, so no one really knows where he was from." But even though he was suddenly on his own and facing daunting challenges, Nicholas Kiniski did not back down but instead showed much of the same dogged determination that would later be publicly displayed by Julia.

In "My Brother Is a Brute!"—which apparently appeared in an early 1960s Toronto-based broadcast industry publication—Julian Kinisky says, of Nicholas, "Father was the toughest man in our hometown of Chipman … and he came to this country from Poland, all alone. He had little education, but more plain guts than you can imagine."

According to Bruce Kinisky, Nicholas originally settled in the Lamont, Alberta, area as a homesteader. Nicholas' land was mineral-rich and located on a gas pool, and Bruce reports that his grandfather's land parcel remains in the ownership of the Kiniski clan, divided up, first, among Gene and his siblings after their parents' death and, from there, passed down to family members of the next generation. According to Kinisky, while exploration companies have expressed interest in drilling for mineral wealth on the homestead Nicholas Kiniski established more than a century ago, members of the Kiniski clan have always found a way to prevent that from happening—even though at least some have been in favor. "The Kiniskis have never agreed on anything," says Bruce.

There are several accounts indicating Nicholas Kiniski served for at time as the police chief of Chipman. Most accounts also indicate he was the only officer stationed in the village during his tenure as a keeper of the public order. According to Bruce Kinisky, Nicholas also served for a time as Chipman's fire chief.

"My grandfather, he was my favorite guy in the world," says Bruce Kinisky, whose middle name—like his uncle Gene Kiniski's—is Nicholas. "He was one rough, tough customer," Bruce continues. "When he was the sheriff in Chipman he didn't have a jail because they couldn't afford a jail there, so your punishment, if you did anything wrong in Chipman … was that Grandpa would beat the hell out of you. The punishment was immediate, and most people wouldn't repeat.… He had a temper that was very short."

While it is unclear how long Nicholas Kiniski filled in as a peace officer in Chipman and administered his brand of tough justice, Steven Eleniak confirms that, for at least a brief time, Nicholas Kiniski served as "the town cop for Chipman." Presumably, Nicholas' period of upholding law and order in Chipman did not overlap with another line of "work" Bruce Kinisky reports that his grandfather was involved in. "In the prohibition days," says Kinisky, "he was a rum runner." Nicholas is also remembered as a bartender at the local hotel in Chipman, likely after Alberta resumed the legal sale of alcohol in 1924 following a ban that was imposed during World War I.

Despite all of Nicholas' and Julia's resourcefulness and a work ethic that typified the experience of many members of the Eastern European immigrant community in a variety of villages in central Alberta, Chipman was a difficult place to eke out a living in the wake of the Depression, let alone provide opportunities to half a dozen children. As a result, the Kiniskis made the move to Edmonton, where they settled into a small house in the working-class Rossdale Flats district along the North Saskatchewan River. Arthur Roberts, the son of Gene Kiniski's oldest sibling Dorothy, recalls that the house was near a low-level bridge that crossed the river. According to Bruce Kinisky, the family of Nicholas and Julia mined their own coal on the banks of the North Saskatchewan, hauling their lodes home by canoe to fuel their home heating system during the brutal Edmonton winters. Kelly Kiniski says that scenario applied even when the Kiniskis did not have a canoe of their own to haul coal in as they set about gathering fuel for the following winter. "Uncle Julian and my dad used to swim out, beat the guys up out of their canoe, take the canoe, and then sell it," he says.

Overall, it appears the move to Edmonton served its purpose for Nicholas and Julia Kiniski. Although they still had to fashion a handscrabble existence at times, it appears none of their children lacked for education or opportunities. And while Julia's efforts in politics are better remembered, she was also a working mother who apparently tried her hand at sales and did some work—apparently teaching in some manner—at Rossdale Flats' Little Flower School.

Nicholas' business endeavors in Edmonton are far from clear, though there are reports suggesting he put his barbering skills to work in the city. While Nicholas' grandchildren are unsure about most of what Nicholas did for a living in Edmonton, Kelly Kiniski recalls learning somewhere that his grandfather worked at a garbage dump.

Nicholas Kiniski is remembered as a fiery, feisty grandfather who, despite living without many frills in Canada, "just flatly refused to ever go back to Poland," according to grandson Gene Kinisky—another male in the Kiniski/Kinisky clan who inherited the middle name Nicholas. While Julia Kiniski got into the habit, when she was able, of regularly visiting the couple's native Poland from Edmonton, Gene Kinisky recalls his grandfather saying, of Canada, "This country gave me everything I have. *That* country [Poland] gave me nothing. I'll never go back."

Kelly Kiniski says, of his grandfather, "He grew a garden, and he liked to play crib." Perhaps demonstrating—as Julia did—some of the competitiveness Gene would inherit, Nicholas, Kelly continues, "would cheat at crib."

According to Kelly, his father sometimes described Nicholas as mean. "That's what my dad would say," Kelly recalls. "I don't know what he did to Dad, but it sure wasn't very nice."

It may be possible Canada's Greatest Athlete was recalling an incident Bruce Kinisky says his father Julian brought up on occasion. According to Bruce, "The night [Gene] won the Alberta [amateur] heavyweight championship—my dad told me this story a number of times—he went out and they were partying and having a few beers and that, and he came home, and Grandpa was there in the kitchen, and Gene started to get a little bit lippy with Grandpa. Now, my grandpa was only like 5'9" [and] weighed 135 pounds soaking wet, and my grandpa didn't put up with any guff, so when Gene showed disrespect towards him, my dad said Grandpa stood up and with one punch whacked him upside the head [and] knocked him out cold on the kitchen floor. And then Grandpa stood over him and said, 'Now I'm the champion, son.' So Gene learned a valuable lesson there."

Regardless of what actually transpired during that reported skirmish between father and son, perhaps one lesson Gene Kiniski learned that day was to watch for flying fists or other unexpected objects. If so, that lesson definitely served him well during his career in the ring and his interaction with fans who might have considered pulling out weapons or mixing it up on the sly with one of wrestling's premier bad guys during an era when wrestling audiences were often known for taking goings-on in the ring seriously.

As Kiniski said in the November 10, 2000, *SLAM! Wrestling* chat, "What always bothered me was audience participation.... I always had to retaliate. I've been hit with chairs, stabbed." In a December 1967 *St. Louis Globe-Democrat* article about Kiniski, Rich Koster adds, "There are angry women with hat pins and wise guys with cigarettes [eager to do damage]. There are fans wielding chairs and knives and anonymous patrons deep within the gallery who launch missiles of various designs and material." Yet, as Kiniski told *Toronto Star* columnist Milt Dunnell a couple of years earlier, "crowds don't frighten me. [I've] been stabbed at Vancouver, knifed at Fresno, Cal., and Muncie, Indiana. [I've] been beaned with chairs and burned with cigar butts. In Japan, they showered me with sake bottles. Naw, the people don't bother me."

Kelly Kiniski says, "My dad had zero fear, you know ... with fans and riots. I've never seen a person like that to this day that had no fear when there was tons of people.... I think he liked it. Other people would have run."

While Gene Kiniski never hesitated to mix it up in venues associated with wrestling, both of his sons report that their father's discipline at home involved plenty of persuasion but never laying a hand on them. Presumably, Gene Kiniski in his younger years was just as reluctant to engage in physical confrontation with his father, who, while remembered as a tough, imposing figure, was average-sized at most and likely would not have been much of a match physically for even a teenaged Gene, who was unusually large, was well trained, and had already shown signs of matching his parents' tenacity.

As far as Nicholas and Julia Kiniski's childrearing arrangement went, "Probably, Granny was more influential," says Bruce Kinisky, "but Grandpa was always there ... to do the tough discipline."

Yet Benny Grabow, who was often at the Kiniski house, recalls Nicholas as "a grand old guy.... He always wore his hat in the house, with a cigarette dangling.... In the house Julia was the big boss. She was the boss. Nick was the nicest man. Never said a word.... I never saw a bad side of Nick at all, ever.... He just sat there. He never raised his voice. Never."

All six of Nicholas and Julia's children were on their own by the early 1950s. While four of them—Gene, Julian, and sisters Dorothy and Mary—would stay in regular contact in future years, the two other siblings, Fred and Rudy Kiniski, would reunite less often with other members of the family. The last meeting of the whole clan took place in 1965, the year Nicholas and Julia celebrated their 50th anniversary. That was also the year Julia was elected to her second term as Edmonton alderman.

Gene's oldest brother, Fred, served in the navy during World War II before settling in Salinas, California, with his wife Bunty, who is remembered as hailing from Scotland. Apparently the original adventurer among the Kiniski siblings, Fred, who worked for a railroad, once advised his nephew Kelly to "get away from the family as far as you can."

Rudy Kiniski was an accomplished musician and piano tuner who lived in Vancouver before owning a music store in Toronto. Although Fred Kiniski may have set the tone when it came to the Kiniski siblings' lust for adventure, Rudy apparently was not to be outdone by his older brother. While Fred Kiniski never had any children, Rudy, says Bruce Kinisky, had "one legitimate kid and who knows how many others. He was quite the ladies' man." Kelly Kiniski adds, "He'd come and tune your piano and probably your wife"—though former Chipman-area resident Walter Melnyk recalls, of Rudy, "He was so cross-eyed that one eye was meeting the other one."

On rare occasions when Gene and all his brothers were together, Kelly says, "They all fought each other.... [Dad] just wouldn't talk to a lot of [them]."

Grabow recalls, "The brothers ... they were all over 6'3, 6'4—good guys. [But] all the yelling and the screaming—you'd have to see it to believe it."

Nicholas had no involvement in Julia's political activities and career, and in many ways he seems to have been an antithesis to her patient persistence and her thirst for knowledge.

Gene Kiniski and his father Nicholas Kiniski. Those who knew Nicholas agree that he had a toughness far beyond his size (Kiniski family archive; thanks to Bruce Kinisky).

16. Passing of Nicholas and Julia

"Granny and Grandpa seemed to have sort of a … weird relationship together," says Bruce Kinisky, "but there was an attachment there. They'd been through everything together."

One experience they did not share, however, was to sit together in an arena and watch their youngest son wrestle. While Julia had no interest in Gene's ring career and apparently couldn't be persuaded to attend a wrestling show, Nicholas—accompanied on a few occasions by grandson Bruce—saw Gene perform in a professional wrestling ring at least several times.

Koster reports, "Once, when [Nicholas] was present, a nearby patron was overheard telling a friend that he had a rock in his pocket and was going to hurl it at [Gene] Kiniski when he entered the ring."

Then Koster quotes Gene Kiniski: "Dad was in his 60s then, but he's always been a scrapper. He really unloaded on the guy. He decked him. Now, whenever he comes to a fight, one of my brothers comes with him."

After Nicholas died, apparently of emphysema, in August of 1968—likely at age 77, although some sources suggest he was a few years younger—"Grandma couldn't live without him," recalls Bruce. "I didn't realize how much she was devoted to Grandpa, but she never really recovered once Grandpa passed away."

Venice, California, July 4, 1954. Gene's brother Fred Kiniski dwarfs Baron Michele Leone, a major 1950s attraction in Southern California and elsewhere, who for nearly two years defended the NWA Junior Heavyweight championship around the United States (Kiniski family archive).

Julia died of a heart attack—apparently not her first—on October 11, 1969, a year into her fourth term as alderman. After getting word, Gene Kiniski returned to Alberta with Marion to pay tribute to one of the forces most widely regarded as having helped mold him into the rugged competitor and unique personality he was. Less well known, perhaps, but in many ways just as apparent is the influence on Canada's Greatest Athlete of an equally feisty and fiery father who had passed away just over a year earlier, during the final six months of his son's NWA World Heavyweight title reign.

17

Still Going Strong, 1969–1973

Just eight days after losing the NWA title in Tampa, and four days after wrestling Dory Funk, Jr., to a draw in a rematch in Jacksonville, Gene Kiniski was a champion once again—this time, holding the NWA North American Heavyweight title, as recognized in the Hawaii territory.

Kiniski captured that title on February 19, 1969, in Honolulu, defeating Toru Tanaka, played by Hawaiian native Charles Kalani, a 10-year U.S. Army veteran who became one of the top Japanese heel characters of his era in the United States. While wrestlers based in Hawaii at the time typically wrestled at least a few shows per month outside Honolulu, records exist of only a half dozen Kiniski appearances in Hawaii in 1969, all in Honolulu. Given the price a wrestler of Kiniski's stature commanded—especially hot off a long, successful world title run—and his schedule of appearances in the Pacific Northwest and elsewhere, it seems unlikely Kiniski, who always liked to maximize his earnings, would have wrestled on any house shows in Hawaii outside Honolulu.

Though the Ed Francis-Lord Blears tandem held weekly arena shows and television tapings in Honolulu, running his own promotion in British Columbia prevented Kiniski from making more than monthly appearances in Honolulu—a destination he loved to visit, given the weather, the geography, and his history and friendship with Blears.

After winning the NWA North American Heavyweight title in mid–February, Kiniski defended that title—both times going to a draw—against Tex McKenzie in March and King Curtis Iaukea in April. In June Kiniski dropped the title to future WWWF World Heavyweight champion Pedro Morales, who defeated Kiniski again in a July rematch. Two months later Kiniski went to a draw in Honolulu against Giant Baba, also a close friend of Blears', who had been in and out of Hawaii as a popular attraction for several years.

Making just a few scattered but strategic arena appearances perhaps augmented by a few undocumented appearances on television, Kiniski was a big part of the Hawaii promotion's success in 1969—which is all the more remarkable given that he won only one of his six recorded matches in the Aloha State that year.

While settling for the most part into life as a homebody in Blaine, Kiniski set out for various other wrestling territories over the course of 1969.

In early March he faced Fritz von Erich and earned a disqualification victory in Fort Worth to set up an unsuccessful challenge for von Erich's NWA American Heavyweight title the following night at the Dallas Sportatorium. A few days later Kiniski traveled to

National Wrestling Alliance

A Cooperative of Wrestling Promoters in the United States, Canada, Mexico and Japan
(AFFILIATES IN OTHER COUNTRIES)

March 5, 1969

SAM MUCHNICK
PRESIDENT AND TREASURER
CLARIDGE HOTEL
ST. LOUIS, MO. 63103
TELEPHONE:
AREA CODE 314
231-7486
HOME—NO. 4 HIGHGATE ROAD
CHEVY CHASE
OLIVETTE, MO. 63132
TELEPHONE:
AREA CODE 314
993-2900

PAUL JONES
1ST VICE-PRESIDENT
310 CHESTER ST. S.E.
ATLANTA, GEORGIA
TELEPHONES:
AREA CODE 404
JA 3-6680
AREA CODE 404
JA 5-7330
HOME—"PENTHOUSE"
70 HOUSTON ST., N.E.
TELEPHONE:
AREA CODE 404
688-3880

JIM CROCKETT
2ND VICE-PRESIDENT
1111 E. MOREHEAD STREET
CHARLOTTE, N. C.
TELEPHONES:
AREA CODE 704
377-1817
AREA CODE 704
377-1818
HOME—812 QUEENS ROAD
CHARLOTTE, N. C.
TELEPHONE:
AREA CODE 704
377-4935

Mr. Gene Kiniski,
Box #907,
Blaine, Washington.

Dear Gene:-

In this rugged world of today sentiment has little backing but the fine letter you sent me proves that there is such a feeling of understanding between men and it meant a lot to me to receive it. Thanks very much.

You know, Gene, when you are in our game as long as I have been (36 years last Aug. 1) you get hardened and sometimes the dollar moves ahead of friendship. But thankfully I have managed, by God's guidance, to work for the dollar but also to want the man working with me also to make a dollar. And that has paid off via the dividend of satisfaction...a satisfaction that permits you to sleep peacefully at night.

I don't have to tell you now I felt when you lost the Belt. You should know. But that's the story of our business.

During the past 20 years I have booked Thesz, Watson, Hutton, O'Connor, Rogers and yourself and the relationship with all of those men has been good—but the relationship between you and I was the greatest and yes, Gene, they were a wonderful three years, one month and four days. I'll never forget them.

As I told you on the phone from Toronto if you should need me at any time, just pick up the telephone, and I'll be there. But I know that with your tenacity and drive you will make a success where you are and with that sweet blond at your side you have to be a very lucky man indeed.

Now as to business I would like to figure a return in Oct, especially if I can get the Arena, for Oct. 24. However, it will be necessary for you to come in a number of times before then. But there is plenty of time for all of this and God bless you.

And don't forget to put down the dates of Aug. 22 and 23 for the NWA meeting which should be bombastic. After that, as they say in our game, I will be ready to hang up my tights—but maybe I'll go a year after that.

Am going down to Florida on March 13 for about a week.

Kindest personal regards to you and the family and by the way give that efficient blonde of yours a kiss for me.

Sincerely, Sam

While Kiniski was suspicious of many promoters over the course of his years in the ring, he was known to consider St. Louis promoter Sam Muchnick above reproach. Kiniski and Muchnick had a friendship that continued beyond their years in wrestling, and Muchnick was NWA president during much of Kiniski's career and a strong backer of Kiniski's reign as NWA World Heavyweight champion. In this letter, written a few weeks after the conclusion of Kiniski's NWA title reign, Muchnick praises Kiniski for "a wonderful three years, one month and four days" as champion—adding, "I'll never forget them" (Kiniski family archive).

Toronto, where he defeated Ivan Koloff in the first of a series of matches the two would have in Toronto that year. Koloff, Ontario native Oreal Perras, had wrestled on some of the same British Columbia shows Kiniski had managed to squeeze in during the first half of his NWA world title reign, though the two apparently did not face each other during that period. Perras at the time wrestled as "Irish" Red McNulty, and though showing plenty of potential, he was booked as a preliminary wrestler who usually lost his match on the card long before the main event in which Kiniski generally appeared if he was on the show. In 1968 Red McNulty morphed into Russian Ivan Koloff, almost immediately becoming a top wrestler and headliner. Koloff remained a headliner in various territories throughout 1969 and 1970, and in January of 1971 he was the challenger chosen to end the nearly eight-year first WWWF World Heavyweight title reign of Bruno Sammartino.

Besides running off three victories over Koloff, Kiniski had five other matches in Toronto in 1969. Most notable were a pair of wild encounters with The Sheik, who, following the heyday of Whipper Billy Watson, put together a long undefeated streak—regularly cheating his way to quick victories—en route to becoming the wrestler most closely identified with Maple Leaf Gardens in the 1970s as a sideline to his owning and running the NWA territory based in Detroit. The night after a few of Kiniski's Sunday night appearances in Toronto, he was back in Vancouver, 2,500 miles away, to appear in feature matches for the promotion he had a big hand in owning and running.

In the summer and fall of 1969, Kiniski traveled from his West Coast home base to his former home base of St. Louis, where he tangled with Bob Ellis, future NWA world titleholder Jack Brisco, and reigning NWA champion Funk Jr. The October 17 show at the Kiel Auditorium, where Funk turned back Kiniski's challenge, was an unusually loaded card that saw five holders, past or present, of the NWA world title on the show, along with a few others who held regional world titles. The impressive roster on the show—including St. Louis legends O'Connor, Bruiser, and Watson—demonstrated why many observers at the time considered St. Louis the wrestling capital of the United States, if not the world.

Besides challenging Funk unsuccessfully for the title in St. Louis in 1969, Kiniski did likewise in Calgary; in San Juan, Puerto Rico; and in Vancouver. He also challenged Funk on July 29 in Tampa, where Funk had won the title in February. Kiniski lost the Tampa rematch, his last match on a weeklong Florida tour that had seen him face a couple of other notable opponents.

One was Lou Thesz, facing Kiniski yet again in one of wrestling's big-time rivalries. On the July 22, 1969, Tampa house show, one week before the Funk-Kiniski encounter, 53-year-old Thesz battled Kiniski to a time-limit, main-event draw.

Two nights later in Jacksonville, Kiniski participated in a three-on-three tag match in which a member of the opposing team was a semi-successful young wrestler who had not yet won a professional wrestling title—though he would win his first about a month later and go on to hold many more over the course of a long and colorful career. Mike Davis would continue to develop as a wrestler—though far more as a wrestling character than a ring technician—over the next few years before arriving in Oregon in mid–1972, holding the regional tag team title there for six weeks with Tony Borne, and then reuniting later in 1972 with Kiniski in Vancouver.

Although far from cured of the travel bug, Kiniski spent most of 1969 close to home in the Pacific Northwest. He wrestled occasionally in Oregon or northern Washington, but the majority of his matches were on his Vancouver promotion's featured Monday night shows, usually at the Pacific National Exhibition Gardens—and often capped off with a late meal downtown at Casa d'Italia or Hy's Encore steakhouse (the latter owned by a fellow native Albertan of immigrant stock). Kiniski made fairly regular appearances at the CHAN-TV *All-Star Wrestling* tapings on Wednesdays and, especially late in the year, on house shows in Victoria, British Columbia's second-largest market. Kiniski also did his part in running the promotion's office above a wig shop on Vancouver's West Broadway Street with Kovacs and, at least on some Mondays, going over their business approach with the third owner, Don Owen, up from Portland. Whatever formula the three owners applied to running the business seemed to work well, as 1969 was a strong year for the promotion.

Much of that, of course, had to do with Kiniski's role as a performer, which was the only aspect of his involvement in the promotion that was known to the public. As far as fans were concerned, Gene Kiniski was a former NWA heavyweight champion, a tough wrestler, and an excellent interview. The only owner or promoter of All-Star Wrestling from nearly every fan's perspective was Sandor Kovacs, and if Kovacs and Kiniski were ever spotted discussing business, in fans' minds it was almost certainly in their respective roles of sole owner-promoter and headlining wrestler.

As a headliner for All-Star Wrestling during his first year as a former NWA world champion, Kiniski repeatedly faced top regional names such as Savage, Tolos, and Jonathan, along with a variety of wrestlers who were in and out of the territory, including Greek Canadian journeyman Steve Bolus and Barbadian Earl Maynard, both given Canadian Tag Team title runs in 1969 with partner Dean Higuchi. Carpentier, Thesz, and Funk Jr. also made brief visits to British Columbia in 1969 to face Kiniski, who defeated all three, though he failed to regain the NWA world title since his October 20, 1969, victory over Funk was by disqualification in the third and deciding fall.

In the tag team ranks, two partners of Kiniski's in All-Star Wrestling in 1969 stand out. One was Canadian Football League star Angelo Mosca, who wrestled during the off-season for several years until retiring from football in 1972 and then continued to wrestle for years afterward. Though Mosca and Kiniski teamed only once in 1969, they would do so again in Vancouver in early 1970 and, from there, would feud across much of Canada in later years. Another memorable partner of Kiniski's in 1969 was Manitoba native "Bulldog" Bob Brown, a wild wrestler the Vancouver Athletic Commission fined many times for a variety of infractions. Brown, who teamed regularly with Kiniski in 1969, was a leading wrestler in the territory during much of the period when Kiniski was an owner of the promotion.

Another Manitoban of note who wrestled in British Columbia in 1969 was Al Tomko, a little-known wrestler outside Manitoba who had been active in the wrestling business, particularly in Winnipeg, going back to 1950. After making a name locally, in 1966 Tomko became the Manitoba agent for Verne Gagne's AWA.

While Tomko generally stayed close to his base in Winnipeg until 1977, he ventured west in the late 1960s, wrestling on some Stampede Wrestling shows in Saskatchewan and Alberta in 1968 and then making scattered appearances as Leroy Hirsch—namesake of a former NFL player Tomko reportedly had met—in British Columbia in 1969. Though Tomko, positioned as a midcarder, and Kiniski appeared on several of the same shows in 1969, their only recorded meeting in the ring took place at the CHAN-TV studio in Burnaby, just outside Vancouver, on the episode of *All-Star Wrestling* immediately following the October 20 Kiniski-Funk NWA title match in Vancouver. Kiniski, who would challenge Funk again in Calgary two days later, won his 1969 TV encounter with Tomko, who returned to Manitoba shortly afterward to continue promoting events for the AWA and to reestablish himself as a small independent promoter in Canada's Keystone Province. But while Tomko would book Kiniski occasionally to appear on AWA shows in Winnipeg in the 1970s, their closest association would not get underway until Tomko returned, under unexpected circumstances, to All-Star Wrestling in 1977.

In 1969 Bernie Pascall, who had come to know Kiniski in Ontario, accepted the position of sports director at *All-Star Wrestling*'s flagship station, CHAN-TV. Pascall says, "Upon my arrival in Vancouver, within days I get a call from Gene, who says, 'Welcome to British Columbia. We have All-Star Wrestling [arena shows] on Monday nights, and Bernie, I'd like you to be our ring announcer.'"

Pascall says he took the job, despite a busy schedule, out of friendship and respect for Kiniski. Besides working as CHAN's sports director, Pascall was the only member of the station's sports department when he took on his wrestling-announcing duties and, as a result, was obligated to appear on the air during the channel's dinner-hour and late sports broadcasts. He recalls, "To do it comfortably, I'd have to leave wrestling no later than 9:30 [or] 9:40, so your main event would have to start by that time for me to introduce it because I had to go back to try to get the sports ready. It was just amazing how the timing actually worked because it was always in that time period. The earlier matches would be finished and they'd have the intermission, and the main event would start in time for me to introduce it and then go back and do the late sports."

Pascall maintained his hectic Monday night schedule as long as Kiniski remained involved with the promotion. He explains, "I did it only because ... I got to know him and love him over the years."

In stark contrast to the situation during Kiniski's NWA World Heavyweight title reign, there was only one NWA world title defense—the October 20 Funk-Kiniski match—in British Columbia during the last 46 weeks of 1969 following Kiniski's loss of the NWA title to Funk. Conversely, there were two world title matches in Vancouver during the first six weeks of 1969, when Kiniski still held the title. While Funk had wrestled in British Columbia for a few months in 1964, during his NWA title reign the Vancouver promotion was no longer favored when it came to NWA title defenses. This revealed a glaring problem in the promotion, which, unlike nearly every other wrestling promotion of the time, had not had a regional championship of its own since 1963. For several years wrestlers and fans in the territory had regarded the top contendership for the NWA title—and a world title match during the champion's next visit to the territory—as the prize wrestlers in British Columbia were vying for. But when the NWA champion stopped appearing in the territory more than two or three times a year, there was no imminent prize for wrestlers in British Columbia to contend for. As a result, Kiniski, Kovacs, and Owen decided it was time to tweak their product.

In February of 1970, a year after Kiniski dropped the NWA world title, the three owners of Northwest Wrestling Promotions/All-Star Wrestling established the NWA Pacific Coast Heavyweight title as the top singles title in the territory. The trio decided Lonnie Mayne, the most popular wrestler at the time in Owen's Portland-based Pacific Northwest Wrestling promotion, would come north to defend the new championship—which he had never won in the ring—against Mark Lewin, an international wrestling star who had arrived in British Columbia in late 1969. After defeating top regional contenders such as Savage, Moose Morowski, and Bob Brown, Lewin took the title from Mayne in Vancouver on February 9, 1970. From there, the Pacific Coast title, which definitely added an edge to *All-Star Wrestling* telecasts pumping up upcoming cards, bounced among top names in the territory in 1970—namely, Bob Brown and two-time champions Jonathan and Kiniski.

On April 20, 1970, one week after kicking off his first reign as NWA Pacific Coast champion by upending Lewin, Kiniski challenged Funk Jr. for the world title in Vancouver. That match—one of just two Funk title defenses in the territory that year, with the other coming in November against Jonathan—ended in a time-limit draw. Earlier in April, Kiniski and Funk had fought to a time-limit draw in Amarillo after winning a fall apiece. Three days after that match—on April 5, one day before Kiniski defeated Pacific Coast champ Lewin in a nontitle match to set up his title victory a week later—Funk successfully defended the NWA World Heavyweight title against Kiniski in Toronto, as he had done in January.

Kiniski avoided travel for the most part in 1970 in order to unwind with his family in Blaine and devote his energy to running the promotion in Vancouver. The most significant newcomers to All-Star Wrestling in 1970 were John Quinn, a powerful, young 290-pounder who earlier in his career had been a WWWF headliner who challenged Sammartino numerous times for the WWWF title, and Vince "Steven Little Bear" Bryant, who, as Steve Kovacs, had twice challenged Kiniski for the NWA world title in Tennessee in 1966. Steve Kovacs was in no way related to Sandor Kovacs but took on the Kovacs surname—lengthening it from the "Kovac" surname he had been using—while teaming with Sandor Kovacs in the southeastern United States in the early 1960s. Another addition of some note was Matt "Duncan McTavish" Gilmour, a Scotsman who was nicknamed "The Man of 1,000 Holds" during a four-year stay in British Columbia, mainly as a dependable midcard worker and, as Greg Oliver puts it in a June 6, 2011, retrospective on Gilmour's life, "a de facto deputy to boss Gene Kiniski." All three of those newcomers to the promotion made an impact in 1970, and each held a share of the Canadian Tag Team title before the year was over.

In a story with some similarity to Kiniski's experience in the southwestern United States in 1954, Quinn—a Canadian citizen and native of Hamilton, Ontario—says he got a draft notice while living and working in the United States during the height of the Vietnam War. Rather than rolling the dice and reporting, as Kiniski had done, Quinn decided his best option lay in returning to Canada. Quinn says he had watched *All-Star Wrestling* in his home country, and in his view "the best of the best were out there." Specifically, he says, regarding his permanent move to British Columbia in 1970, "I went out there because Gene Kiniski was there."

Also appearing in All-Star Wrestling in 1970—and going through the initiation of losing singles matches to Kiniski—were two young babyfaces, British Columbia native Dan Kroffat, who would go on to become a favorite and multi-time champion in Stampede Wrestling before returning to All-Star Wrestling a few years later, and Don Morrow, who, under his real name of Don Muraco, would become a leading WWF heel and one of the most successful wrestlers in the United States in the 1980s.

Muraco, hailing from Hawaii, was a newcomer to wrestling when Lord Blears made arrangements with Kovacs to send the rookie to British Columbia for a little seasoning. "I was clueless," says Muraco. "They didn't have those schools and training centers.... It was more just getting on the mat [and learning] in Dean Higuchi's gym."

Speaking of his encounters in the ring with Gene Kiniski during his rookie year, Muraco says, "I was like a deer in headlights.... He was a buzz saw. He could go all night long.... Any style ... high spots ... working holds ... he could do anything.

"He was good to me," Muraco continues. "He gave me a little bit of a match ... probably more than I deserved at the time."

Kiniski wrestled a relatively limited schedule in 1970, averaging just one or two ring appearances per week in British Columbia or northern Washington throughout the year. Many of those appearances were on Monday night cards at the PNE Gardens, where Kiniski, before shows, would conduct business in an office upstairs from the entrance before slipping downstairs to prepare to face the likes of Lewin, Higuchi, Brown, Quinn, McKenzie, or other wrestlers who were established as credible competition for a former NWA world champion—or others who, regardless of their preparation, would be put to the test by an ex-world champ who still liked to shine in the ring and expected his opponents to hold up their end of a match. Kiniski also made frequent appearances in 1970 at the Burnaby studio where *All-Star Wrestling* was produced for a local, regional, and nationwide following. The majority of Kiniski's other appearances in the Northwest took place on the BC Lower Mainland within easy commuting distance of Vancouver, in Victoria, and in the major Washington cities of Seattle and Tacoma. A record of Kiniski's career compiled by Vance Nevada also shows Kiniski wrestled, in November of 1970, on a show in Blaine.

Kiniski's wrestling travels outside the Northwest in 1970 were limited to several favorite locations—in particular, Honolulu, Winnipeg, Toronto, the Amarillo and Dallas territories, St. Louis, and Japan. In St. Louis Kiniski appeared briefly under a mask as Crimson Knight #2—partnered with "Crimson Knight" Bill Miller—in the lead-up to Kiniski's challenging Funk Jr. for the NWA title at the Kiel Auditorium in June. Kiniski lost the challenge, refereed by Whipper Watson, in three falls before a crowd of more than 10,000. On a brief visit to Japan late in the year, Kiniski teamed twice with Johnny Valentine to split decisions with the Baba-Inoki team. In between those tag matches, Kiniski captured the NWA International Heavyweight title Baba had dominated for five years. Two weeks after winning Baba's title—and four days after teaming in Vancouver with Quinn and Brown to record a victory over Jonathan, Little Bear, and McTavish—Kiniski touched down in Los Angeles to drop the International belt back to Baba before a crowd topping 10,000 on a Friday night show at the Olympic Auditorium. Ten days after that, following a short Christmas break, Kiniski won the NWA Pacific Coast Heavyweight title from Jonathan in Vancouver.

The following year, 1971, saw Kiniski limit his travels to the Amarillo territory, where he challenged Funk three times for the world title; Winnipeg and Chicago for a few engagements in association with Tomko and Gagne; Florida, for a single recorded match in Tampa against Jack Brisco; and Hawaii, where Kiniski made periodic appearances, facing high-profile opponents such as Billy Robinson, Bearcat Wright, Pedro Morales, The Sheik, and Peter Maivia—in the process, twice winning and twice losing the NWA Pacific International Heavyweight championship. Based on a report by *Vancouver Sun* writer Jack Wasserman, excerpted in the wrestling program sold at the February 1, 1971, PNE Gardens card, it appears Kiniski also traveled to Honolulu once, early in the year—likely as a favor to Blears—when he was booked to appear on a show there but could not wrestle due to a serious thumb injury.

During his swing through west Texas late in the year, Kiniski returned to Tucson,

Arizona, where his career had gotten underway nearly two decades earlier, and fought Dory Funk, Jr., to a 60-minute draw in an NWA world title challenge. Interestingly, as Arizona wrestling historian Dale Pierce, reported by a masked wrestler named "Gene Viniski" had appeared in Phoenix just a few weeks earlier. According to Pierce, Phoenix promoter Ernie Muhammad, in his final years of promoting, was known to use wrestlers with soundalike names, in a manner earlier made famous by fellow promoters Jack Pfefer and Tony Santos.

Though it is reasonable to assume the purpose of booking a soundalike wrestler was to herald the arrival of the real Gene Kiniski in Arizona, such was not the case at all, as a change of promoters took place in the Grand Canyon State in the fall of 1971 between the appearance of Gene Viniski and the arrival of Gene Kiniski. Back in Tucson but also promoting shows in Phoenix was Rod Fenton.

Fenton had lost his wife just a few months after the Fenton family's arrival in California in 1968. Devastated, he stayed with his daughters in the Bay area until surprising them with an announcement about two years later.

"I think he was restless," recalls Patrice Fenton. "One day he just came to us and said, 'Girls, I'm thinking about moving back to Tucson. I'm thinking about starting promoting again.'"

In 1971 Rod Fenton and his daughters took their belongings, including a horse, back to Arizona, and the Fenton family resettled in Tucson, where, Patrice says, her father "tried to revive the territory." Though Tucson had changed considerably, the Fentons made a valiant effort to spread the word about their shows. Patrice recalls, "We'd go cruise Tucson and we'd put all these [posters] up." The Fentons' effort and some local buzz resulted in a promising start for the newly resurrected promotion.

Almost as soon as Fenton got back into business in Tucson, news started to get around that a local legend who had reached the top of his profession was on his way back. "I remember it was a big deal when Gene was coming back to town," says Patrice Fenton. "He maybe did it as a little bit of a favor to Dad because [the promotion] was starting up small again."

Kiniski's November 16, 1971, return was perhaps the climax of Fenton's second go-round as a promoter in Arizona, which proved much shorter than his first, as it appears he promoted his last show the following year. He had some short-lived success, but as Patrice Fenton says, "It wasn't the same as the old days.... I don't think he could draw the crowds like it was back in the fifties.... I think he was burnt out."

Interestingly, another distinguished member of the wrestling fraternity was based in Tucson in the early 1970s. As the *Tucson Daily Citizen* reported shortly after Fenton's return to the city, "Next week [Lou] Thesz"—who, the *Daily Citizen* pointed out, had faced Kiniski in Vancouver when Fenton promoted there—"is opening a decorators' and builders' supply store in Tucson." Patrice Fenton remembers Thesz' business as a furniture store—and one Thesz allowed her to list as a place of employment when her resume did not have a lot of experience to highlight. In his autobiography *Hooker*, Thesz added that he was involved in a carpeting business in Tucson (Addendum, Kindle ed.). The record also shows Thesz wrestled on at least one show Fenton promoted in Arizona in 1972.

Back in British Columbia, 1971 saw some memorable interaction between Kiniski and Wayne Cox, a BC radio and TV personality who was in the early stages of his career, working as a DJ in the province's interior. Cox says he was asked by the local wrestling promoter in Kamloops—who worked as a salesman at the radio station—to do some ring announcing along with a phone interview on the air with Gene Kiniski to hype an upcoming match.

Cox, who covered the early 1971 story about Kiniski suffering a firewood-chopping injury that required part of his thumb to be stiched back in place and put Kiniski out of action for about two months, says that, during the interview, "I went to town on that, [gibing,] 'You're so old you couldn't chop wood without almost losing a thumb.' Of course, he jumped all over me on that, [saying,] 'You're pretty brave when you're 350 miles away.' And he says, 'You just wait until I get in town.'

"Calls came in from listeners, and they were really worried about me."

The night of the show, Cox says, the arena was packed when he went into the dressing room and asked Kiniski, "What are we going to do?… The people think you're going to kill me. They've all come to see you kill me."

According to Cox, Kiniski assured him that insurance considerations ruled out that scenario. When it was time for their encounter in the ring,

> Gene came thundering down the aisle, and the place was in an uproar. He stepped one leg over the middle rope and he stared at me and he pointed at me and he says, "There you are. I'm going to take you and break you over my knee." He was stomping across the ring. I had the microphone, and he reached—he grabbed me by the tie, and he lifted me right off the ground by my tie. At the time I was, like, 5'9", 150 pounds, and of course he was about 6'4", 260 [or] 270, something like that, so it was nothing for him. As he lifted me off the ground, the first reaction was, I started thumping his forearm with the microphone. Of course, it was echoing all through this place, and the crowd was going crazy and they were all circling around the ring. [Referee Roy] McClarty jumps in and tries to separate us. I can remember him saying, "Gene, have you gone crazy?" And so he let go of me. I dropped, rolled out of the ring [into the] arms of all the fans and everything, and the match was on. From that point on, we became friends.

After the incident, Cox continued to interview Kiniski on the air prior to shows in Kamloops. He says, "I was a little more respectful after that because people knew he could kill me."

Their friendship grew after Cox moved to Vancouver in the early 1970s, and the two met regularly in Vancouver and Blaine over many years. Cox says that when he went through a divorce, Kiniski—a father figure in his life—told him, "Marriage is like a brand new, beautiful pair of shoes. Only the owners know where they pinch." And then, when Cox remarried, Kiniski, he says, made his mark on the wedding reception.

"As they were starting the speeches," he says, "all of a sudden Gene got up out of his chair and came stomping down to the front. He grabbed the microphone out of the emcee's hands, and he looked straight at me and he said in this great big, booming voice that he had, 'If you ever bring a tear to this woman's eye, I'll break both your legs.' Then he threw the microphone down and went and took his seat. So, for the people who didn't know him, there was sort of nervous laughter. But for the rest of us, it was the highlight."

In the ring, Kiniski held the Pacific Coast Heavyweight title for much of 1971, earning victories over Little Bear, Jonathan, McTavish, Higuchi, and Terry Funk before losing via disqualification to Dory Funk, Jr., in an NWA title challenge in June and then, six weeks later, dropping the Pacific Coast title to Little Bear. Kiniski also formed a formidable tag team with Brown in 1971, and the pair held the NWA Canadian Tag Team championship for seven weeks late in the year.

Yet another 1971 Kiniski pairing in British Columbia seems even more memorable. Early that year, before a sellout crowd at Madison Square Garden, Ivan Koloff had pulled off what Kiniski and numerous other top challengers had failed to do since 1963 by defeating Bruno Sammartino for the WWWF World Heavyweight title. Three weeks later, after a brief transitional reign, Koloff lost the WWWF title, also at Madison Square Garden, to Pedro Morales.

In an April 2016 telephone interview, Oreal "Ivan Koloff" Perras recalled, of his run in British Columbia from July to October of 1971, "I had just come from wrestling in New York … and ended up having a couple of months off…. My wife was from the Vancouver area, so I ended up wrestling there and being tagged up with Gene." Koloff said he already knew Kiniski well, as the two had crossed paths over the years in Alberta, Montreal, Ontario, and St. Louis, along with the Northwest.

Speaking of his stay a few years earlier, as Red McNulty, in All-Star Wrestling, Koloff said, "I was kind of a shy, introverted young man [then], and to have guys like Gene that were outspoken, you know, to tell it the way it is … they weren't afraid to do that. Consequently, it loosened me up a lot. I learned a lot from guys like Gene Kiniski."

Of his experience in 1971 teaming with Canada's Greatest Athlete for a series of matches over several weeks, Koloff said, "I can remember some really aggressive matches tagged up with Gene in the Vancouver area during that couple of months that I was there…. We had like a contest, it seemed, without coming out and saying it. Gene was like a machine in the ring. You know, he was nonstop, great shape, always go go go…. He'd take somebody and throw him in and give him a backdrop. I'd try to outdo him. A beal; I'd try to outdo it. A slam. You know, it's just like nonstop." Koloff added, "The people got into it. They loved that. They just thought it was like that's what it was supposed to have been."

Koloff, who rated Kiniski high as a booker and owner, recalled him as a lover of parties and beer but also "a heck of a warrior, a heck of a champion—to me, one of the greats, like a nonstop type of machine … a combination of a Harley Race and a Jack Brisco…. Gene, I think, filled the shoes of both. He could [apply] holds and hang on there for a long time and have the people really interested.

"I have nothing but good things to say about him," Koloff continued. "He was just one of those guys … rugged looking, with the cauliflower ears, smashed nose. He just had that look of being a fighter, a tough guy, and he showed it in the ring too."

Koloff passed away in February of 2017, at age 74.

Also teaming with Kiniski in 1971 was former CFL player representative Mike Webster. Instrumental in the creation of the Canadian Football League Players' Association, Webster had spent five years playing for the British Columbia Lions and the Montreal Alouettes until finding himself at odds with team owners who were leery of player unionization. Due to his efforts as the league's player rep, Webster found himself out of a job in 1971.

"I was without something to do for a livelihood," he says. "Gene picked me up, and I joined the circus."

Webster had done some off-season Greco-Roman wrestling while attending the University of Notre Dame, where he played football. Of his first meeting, purely by chance, with Kiniski, he says, "It was in the Broadway Gym…. [Kiniski's] office was just down the street…. He came into the Broadway Gym, and I explained to him my situation [about Webster's 'divorce' from the CFL]. He said, 'Let me make the call for you.' He called [coach] Eagle Keys [formerly an Eskimos teammate of Kiniski's] at the BC Lions … and Eagle Keys was not interested. And Gene said, 'Well, would you like to come and join the circus?' So I said yes I would, and I spent ... probably 12 years off in professional wrestling—longer than I spent playing football." Webster adds, "I made more money wrestling than I ever did playing football."

Now a well-known clinical psychologist, Webster attended Western Washington University in Bellingham, Washington, as a graduate student while wrestling in British Columbia in the early 1970s. He went on to doctoral studies at the University of British Columbia and left All-Star Wrestling, he says, when it became too difficult to juggle wrestling appearances with work on his dissertation. But before long, Webster got back into the ring—usually under a mask—and continued to wrestle into the 1980s in such places as Florida, Japan, and the United Kingdom. "I was able to pay for my graduate studies through wrestling," he says.

About Kiniski, Webster says, "Gene was an astute businessman.... He was a mentor. He was like a second father to me. He brought me into that business when my career in football had fallen apart because of my efforts to get a union going there.... I can't say enough good things about Gene Kiniski."

Webster says he was impressed particularly by Kiniski's commitment to principles. Speaking of Kiniski's effort to help him get back into football, Webster says, "Gene was adamant. He told them to go and fuck themselves, and he expressed to them that he thought [Webster's exclusion from the CFL] was entirely unfair, that players had been exploited in the league long enough, and that it was time they had a players' association." Webster says Kiniski didn't flinch despite being up "against a mountain of opposition."

He reports Kiniski hung up the phone after calling unsuccessfully on his behalf and said, "Don't worry about those guys. We'll take care of you."

Speaking of Kiniski as a businessman, Webster says, "I think Gene's heart was in the right place.... Many promoters were out for themselves, but I think he and Sandor Kovacs ... of course, they wanted to make a profit in their promotion, but I don't think they wanted to exploit any of the fellows who were working for them either."

As for the third partner in the promotion, Webster says, "Don [Owen] added a certain wisdom .... Gene would listen intently to what Don was saying ... and then he and Sandor would make a decision."

Asked what his father thought of Gene Kiniski as a business partner, Barry Owen says, "All I remember is good things said about him—[that] he was a great guy and one of the most honest guys he ever worked with."

While Kiniski and Kovacs ran the promotion, for the most part, from their third-floor office on West Broadway in Vancouver, Kovacs is remembered by some ex-wrestlers as the owner they would deal with directly about business matters.

"Gene was always busy. He wasn't always around," remembers Gil Hayes, who wrestled in British Columbia for several months in 1972.

Hayes—a Stampede Wrestling headliner in the 1970s—attributes his start in wrestling to Kiniski, whom he remembers watching on AWA television broadcasts in the early 1960s. An Ontario native, Hayes says he was living in Winnipeg when he attended a wrestling show there, apparently in 1962, headlined by a main event between Kiniski and Bill Miller. "They fought out the doors and out into the parking lot," Hayes recalls. "I just got the bug and had to do this."

Hayes' goal of becoming a wrestler drew closer a few years later when he was working as a hotel bouncer in Winnipeg and a group of wrestlers, including Kiniski, came into the bar following a show in town. "I had to usher somebody out of the bar," Hayes says, "and it was kind of rough, so Gene says, 'If you're going to fight, why don't you get paid for it?'"

Hayes says Kiniski helped set him up for a meeting with Bobby Jones, a local wrestler who had a strong amateur background and wrestled professionally for many years in Winnipeg's wrestling clubs, locally for the AWA, and in other parts of Western Canada. After training with Jones, Hayes debuted with the Madison Wrestling Club in late 1966, and the following year he started in Stampede Wrestling.

Speaking of facing Kiniski during his brief stay in British Columbia in 1972, Hayes says, "When you haven't been in the business too long … you're kind of in awe of the man once you're standing across the ring from him."

While holding the Pacific Coast title during Hayes' entire stay in British Columbia in 1972 and for much of that calendar year, Kiniski seldom wrestled in the territory outside Vancouver, Victoria, or the TV studio in Burnaby. Webster recalls, "Here in British Columbia, Gene was only wrestling part-time…. He would pick his spots, but when he put his name on the card he would draw." Others sharing top billing in the territory in 1972 were Little Bear, Lewin, Jonathan, Savage, Quinn, Higuchi, and Brown—the latter a coholder, with Kiniski, of the Canadian Tag Team title for three months early in the year—along with Dory Funk, Jr., who came in for a successful NWA World Heavyweight title defense against Kiniski at Vancouver's PNE Agrodome in early November. Slightly below the top tier in key supporting roles were names including Webster, Hayes, McTavish, Abe Jacobs, Eddie Morrow, and Buck Ramstead.

Kiniski's wrestling travels outside the Northwest in 1972 were limited to St. Louis, where he scored big wins over Bob Ellis and Jack Brisco in August and September before dropping another NWA title challenge to Funk in October, and Honolulu, where he faced wrestlers such as Ed Francis, Sam Steamboat, Billy Robinson, and Fred Curry while holding the NWA Hawaii Heavyweight title for nearly half the year despite wrestling only eight recorded matches in Hawaii in 1972. On one occasion that year, in May, Hawaii booker-promoter and close friend Blears returned the favor by traveling to the Pacific Northwest to appear on a Monday night show in Vancouver, opposing Kiniski in a tag team match.

Except for about a dozen recorded appearances in Hawaii and St. Louis in 1972, all of Kiniski's documented ring appearances that year took place in British Columbia or just across the border in Washington, and though he wrestled a limited schedule, Kiniski was the wrestler on whose shoulders All-Star Wrestling primarily rested in 1972. As Webster says, "Most of [Kiniski's] effort went into the promotion. [But] what he had riding here at home—and in Canada, really; not just in British Columbia but right across the country—was his name. And whenever Gene Kiniski was on the card, he would draw."

Kiniski held on to the NWA Pacific Coast title well into 1973—defeating top contenders such as Brown, Quinn, and Gerry "Sean Regan" Murphy—before dropping the belt in Victoria to a grappler widely considered the promotion's wrestler of the year in 1973.

Mike Davis, a few years after meeting Kiniski in Florida, had made a few appearances in British Columbia in late 1972 while based in Oregon, where—wrestling as The Skull—he briefly held the Pacific Northwest Tag Team title with Tony Borne. In early 1973 Davis established his wrestling base in Vancouver.

Davis—renamed The Brute—soon became a huge favorite in Vancouver, and he is regarded as one of the most memorable wrestling characters ever featured in British

Columbia and, especially, on *All-Star Wrestling*. In 1973 and 1974, when The Brute was a regular on the program, *All-Star Wrestling* was playing to a receptive national audience in Canada, partly thanks to favorable Canadian content broadcast regulations that had been introduced a few years earlier but also due in no small part to a strong cast of characters headed by The Brute, who delivered basic but often hard-hitting matches along with some memorable, sometimes hilarious, promos.

In January of 1973, Davis, a graduate of Purdue University, teamed with Webster to form one of the outstanding teams of 1970s All-Star Wrestling. But while Webster played up his educated side, Davis did nothing of the sort. Webster says, "My approach to being a heel was very nontraditional.... I would be the guy who would be very polite and very understanding to the fans. I would be very magnanimous and not insulting to my opponent. But when I got into the ring I attempted to portray myself as a real dastardly heel."

The Brute, meanwhile, was an old-time heel but one with a new twist. He delivered quick-witted interviews weaving together some entertaining lines, high-pitched laughs, and off-the-wall humor laced with threats against upcoming opponents. Webster and The Brute—both burly bruisers who liked to rough it up—made a memorable odd couple, and Webster recalls, "[Gene] and Sandor both confirmed that we had something there, and we ran with it, and we played it to the end." The pair held the NWA Canadian Tag Team championship from January to July of 1973.

The Brute also won the Pacific Coast Heavyweight title from Kiniski on March 29 before dropping it to Sean Regan on April 23. On June 15 in Vernon, BC—with Kiniski in St. Louis that night beating Jack Brisco—Webster defeated Regan for the title. A month later, as Webster prepared to leave the promotion as a full-time wrestler to concentrate on his studies, he and The Brute dropped the regional tag team title to Quinn and Gerry Romano. Two weeks after that, on July 30, 1973, The Brute attacked Webster following a three-on-three loss in which the pair were teamed with Kiniski. The following week, on August 6, The Brute kicked off his second NWA Pacific Coast Heavyweight title reign by pinning Webster.

Kiniski, meanwhile, was combining a limited number of ring appearances in the Northwest with appearances scattered throughout the year in St. Louis, where for seven months he held the NWA Missouri State Heavyweight title—considered by many the top regional NWA championship of the day—and defeated an outstanding list of challengers including Terry Funk, Race, Brisco, and Valentine. On October 5 Kiniski lost in a Kiel Auditorium main event to Brisco—who since July had been the NWA

Mike Webster (front) and The Brute walk to the ring during their successful NWA Canadian Tag Team title reign in 1973. Webster credits Kiniski with paving the way for him to become a professional wrestler when his activities as Canadian Football League player representative got him blackballed from the CFL (Vance Nevada collection).

17. Still Going Strong, 1969–1973

World Heavyweight champion—and eight days later, Kiniski dropped the Missouri State title to Race in three falls on a taping of *Wrestling at the Chase*.

Kiniski's October 13 loss to Race followed a slow build that got underway shortly after Kiniski—a last-minute substitute for Johnny Valentine, who was having heart problems— won the Missouri State title from Terry Funk at the Kiel on March 16. Within a few weeks, Kiniski and Race came to blows while teaming on a *Chase* broadcast to face Pat O'Connor and Abe Jacobs. When Kiniski and Race lost the match after being unable to get back on track as a team, it was announced they would face each other April 27 at the Kiel.

Kiniski successfully defended his Missouri title in that meeting when Race was disqualified by guest referee Joe Louis. Three weeks later, after the pair exchanged blows once more during an interview segment on *Wrestling at the Chase*, Kiniski beat Race in a no-disqualification, best-of-three-falls rematch at the Kiel. When Race upended Dory Funk, Jr., six days later—May 24, 1973—in Kansas City for the NWA title, Kiniski seemed positioned as a top challenger for the world title, but as it turned out, he would meet Race only once during the latter's two-month NWA title reign in 1973—battling the champion to a draw in Vancouver on July 16, just four days before Race lost the title to Brisco.

Gene Kiniski is remembered as one of the top wrestlers of his era in St. Louis, a one-city territory many observers considered the wrestling capital of the United States under Sam Muchnick. Kiniski lived in the St. Louis area during most of his NWA World Heavyweight title reign in the late 1960s, and in 1973 he had a successful seven-month reign as the NWA Missouri State Heavyweight champion. (Photograph by Dr. Mike Lano / *Wrealano@aol.com*)

Their next meeting would not be until October 13, when Race defeated Kiniski in three falls for the Missouri State title on a *Wrestling at the Chase* taping. Then, the following month, Race won a title rematch at the Kiel to complete the transition from one remarkable champion to another.

Except in the Northwest and St. Louis, Kiniski did not log much ring activity in 1973. In February he had two recorded matches in Georgia—a singles meeting with Bob Armstrong in Columbus and, two days later, a loss to Tim "Mr. Wrestling" Woods to set up an Atlanta match the following week in which Woods would challenge Funk Jr. for the NWA world title. Kiniski also had a few matches in Winnipeg in 1973, twice with Koloff on the opposing side in tag team contests. The only other territory or region Kiniski traveled to in 1973 was Hawaii, where he appeared in a three-on-three tag team match on December 19 with Giant Baba on the opposing side. It is likely Baba and Kiniski discussed business on what was a brief visit for both to Hawaii, as three months later Kiniski would work a short tour with All Japan Pro Wrestling, a promotion founded by Baba in 1972 that survives to this day.

With The Brute clearly established as the centerpiece of All-Star Wrestling during most of 1973, Kiniski, then in his mid-forties, played a strong supporting role but usually seemed content to let the spotlight shine brightest on Mike Davis, who delivered perhaps the strongest work of his long career during his stay in British Columbia in 1973 and 1974. Kiniski mainly kept out of the Northwest singles title picture after losing the Pacific Coast title to The Brute in late March 1973, though he had notable victories over John Tolos; Quinn; Savage; newcomer Larry Whistler, a Bruno Sammartino trainee who would go on to enjoy an exceptional career and two AWA World Heavyweight title reigns as Larry Zbyszko; and fellow former NWA World Heavyweight champion Dory Funk, Jr. The record shows Kiniski faced Funk twice on Saturday, November 24, earning a victory in Seattle and, likely on a matinée, battling Funk in a match in Nanaimo, British Columbia, whose result is unclear.

Shortly after the breakup of the Brute-Webster team, Kiniski took over as The Brute's partner, and on August 20 the powerful new pairing won the Canadian Tag Team championship from Quinn and Romano. Kiniski and The Brute had an 11-week title run—most notable, perhaps, for a series of matches against Samoan brothers Afa and Sika Anoa'i, a pair of wild 300-pound wrestling sophomores who would upend the Kiniski-Brute combo for the title on a November 5, 1973, show at the PNE Agrodome. Three weeks earlier in the same arena, reigning NWA champion Brisco cleanly defeated The Brute, who at the time was riding high as a dual tag team and singles champion in the territory.

Despite the loss to Brisco—and despite another unsuccessful challenge for Brisco's NWA world title five months later in Chilliwack—The Brute, though a heel, continued to ride a wave of popularity in British Columbia until leaving the Northwest in late 1974. Business was strong during the Brute's run, with $5 ringside tickets usually in high demand, and Kiniski seldom saw a need to set foot in a British Columbia ring outside Greater Vancouver or Victoria, though he made an exception with several appearances in the northern interior city of Prince George to facilitate the successful return of All-Star Wrestling there after an absence of several years. By most measures, All-Star Wrestling was at or near its peak while The Brute was a featured performer, and a strong supporting cast including Kiniski, Ron Morrier, Jonathan, Savage, Brown, and Little Bear played to a national television audience, helping drive one of the most successful periods in the history of Canadian West Coast wrestling and highlighting the ability of Gene Kiniski to achieve success in professional wrestling behind the scenes as well as in the ring.

18

The Only Woman He Ever Loved

While things were going well professionally for Gene Kiniski in 1973, not all was well in another significant area of his life that year, as 1973 saw the end of his nearly 20-year marriage to Marion.

Documents and specific details are hard to come by when it comes to the wedding of Gene Kiniski and the former Marion Weller. But while surviving relatives on both the Kiniski and Weller sides of the family apparently have no recollections or records of a public tying-of-the-knot between Gene and Marion Kiniski, coverage in the *Edmonton Journal* and the *Tucson Daily Citizen* confirms that Gene and Marion had a church wedding in Edmonton in December of 1953 before arriving together in Tucson later that month.

Patrice Fenton, at the time a young child, recalls meeting Marion for the first time not long after the newly married couple arrived in Tucson. "She really treated me nicely," says Fenton. Of the Kiniskis as a couple, she recalls, "They seemed really happy."

What is remembered by many who knew Marion is reflected in the words of her nephew Gene Kinisky: "Auntie Marion was one of the most statuesque, most beautiful women I've ever laid my eyes on. Even as a young man—as a young kid—she was just the most beautiful woman I'd ever seen."

Gene Kiniski's nephew Arthur Roberts remembers Marion as a "beautiful blonde lady." He continues, "I was riding around in a car with them before they were married, and he says to me, teasing me, 'So what do you think? She's pretty hot, don't you think?'"

Marion's attractiveness was likely all the more notable in juxtaposition with the appearance and demeanor of the young man who somehow had persisted and won her over. Eleniak recalls, "She was a very nice lady, actually. That's why it was a big joke how she got tangled up with such a beast."

Gene and Marion—the latter remembered as a smoker who favored Winstons—seemed to enjoy their gypsy life in the southern continental United States and Hawaii before returning to Canada in 1956 shortly after Rod Fenton "gave [Gene] back the contract I held on him," as Fenton recounted in a *Daily Citizen* article covering his return to promoting in Tucson in the early 1970s. Gene Kiniski quickly set about making a national name in his home country largely through exposure of the Watson-Kiniski feud to a nationwide audience and Kiniski's ability to capitalize on the exposure. During Kiniski's rise to national stardom, Alberta was a regular stop on the Kiniski tour for both professional and personal reasons, and Gene and Marion regularly connected with their families when returning to Alberta.

As much as she loved adventures with her husband, those who knew Marion well agree that her greatest joy in life came after she became a mother in 1957. Bruce Kinisky says, "I remember reading a letter that she had sent to Granny and Grandpa once shortly after Kelly was born. She absolutely loved being a mom and said she was breastfeeding and that made her feel so wonderful [to be] nurturing another human being."

In the 1960s Marion regularly brought her sons to Alberta in summer to visit relatives. Beyond summer, Kelly recalls attending elementary school for a time in Camrose, Alberta, where some members of the Weller family were living.

With Gene keeping a busy travel schedule through most of the 1960s, it fell upon Marion to do the vast majority of parenting. By all accounts she was a caring parent who took her responsibilities seriously, though it appears she sometimes resented being cooped up while her husband was out seeing much of the world. According to Kelly, his mother's mixed feelings were probably compounded by her knowledge that Gene—like many wrestlers of his day—wasn't sworn to faithfulness in marriage.

Even when Gene cut back on traveling, Kelly says, problems continued. "My dad, after he was world champion, got home and didn't want to do anything. My mom thought, 'I've been home all these years. I want to go to a nice restaurant' or 'I want to go to a nightclub,' and my dad didn't want to go. So they just grew apart."

Marion was involved to some degree in the business aspect of the Vancouver wrestling promotion in the late 1960s and early 1970s, apparently putting some of her banking and bookkeeping skills to good use and winning over many of "the boys" who were in and out of the promotion. Dean Silverstone, who wrote programs sold at Van-

Marion, Gene, and Julia Kiniski on or very close to the day of Gene and Marion's marriage in Edmonton, December 1953 (Kiniski family archive).

couver's Monday night shows before he got into wrestling promotion in his native Washington State, recalls, in his memoir *"I Ain't No Pig Farmer!,"* how he worked "with Gene's wife, Marion, who really liked me. She would regularly bake cookies for me to take back to the States. Her German noodle kugel was my favorite" (108).

Mike Webster recalls, "When Gene took me under his wing, I can remember going to the old Forum, where they used to hold the wrestling, and Marion would be sitting behind a desk, and [she] would hand out our paychecks. Now Marion, I felt like she took an interest in me that felt like she was my mother.... Marion was as interested in me and what I did with my money and my wife and children at the time as my own parents were—as my own mother was. I always felt that Marion had my best interests at heart."

Marion Kiniski was well liked outside the office as well. "She was a nifty lady," said Don Leo Jonathan. "She was always nice to [Don Leo's wife] Rose and I. She was just nice being around. She knew how to talk and make things interesting."

Marion holds a large doll she and Gene gave Rod Fenton's daughter Patrice, shown here (Kiniski family archive).

Jonathan said, echoing the observation of others, "She'd taken good care of the boys," 'Kelly and Nick. Marion's nephew Bruce Kinisky adds, "Every time I went down there to visit, she treated me wonderfully."

Bernie Pascall says, "Gene would invite my wife Judy and I down to their home in Blaine.... Marion was such an exceptional person, and [she and Gene] were just a wonderful couple. [Marion] introduced us to the Angel Kiss. It was Kaluah and whipping cream on top, and she called it the Angel Kiss. That was a famous Marion Kiniski drink anytime we went to their house."

Although Gene and Marion, in the words of nephew Gene Kinisky, were "definitely an odd couple for sure," many observers viewed Gene and Marion Kiniski less as an odd couple than a couple of pieces that appeared mismatched yet fit together to form a perfect unit. "He was a very aggressive sort of man, trying to get to do what he wanted," recalls nephew Arthur Roberts. "Auntie Marion was more soft-spoken." Yet, despite the obvious differences, some observers saw Gene and Marion as perfect complements to each other. Webster recalls, "I know that she and Gene at the time had an extremely close relationship [during Webster's early 1970s run in the Vancouver territory].... I have nothing but fond memories for Marion and for Marion and Gene together as a couple."

During that time Marion kept busy by raising her sons, refinishing furniture—a skill she had learned from Wilbur Snyder's wife Shirlee—and helping out with the promotion, but apparently that was not enough to keep her happy. Gene Kiniski said later, in *The Pro Wrestling Hall of Fame: The Heels*, "My wife was a very, very attractive girl, exceptionally attractive. The boys were growing up and she was so depressed" (75).

Some who knew the Kiniskis well attribute Marion's depression in part to her continued involvement in the wrestling business. While she came across as a cheerful, caring, and sincere woman to the wrestlers who knew her, some observers believe Marion contributed her time and skills to All-Star Wrestling more out of a sense of duty than desire and was eager to wash her hands of the wrestling business and devote her full energy to raising her sons.

For a time Marion was the proprietor of a store supplying antiques and other goods for resale in Blaine, but that endeavor was not a success, as Kelly Kiniski, who tried to help his mother make a go of the business, says customers were hard to come by.

While circumstances were definitely pulling Gene and Marion apart, what probably put a spike into the marriage was Marion's decision—amid her growing unhappiness and her full knowledge that Gene had been less than faithful over the years—to respond, at least in some measure, in kind. Marion got involved with a male acquaintance in 1972—an indiscretion Gene could not overlook. According to Kelly, while his father had had his share of extramarital companionship over the years, "he always thought women were not supposed to."

Marion Kiniski is remembered as an elegant and attractive woman who enjoyed her adventures with Gene as he climbed the ladder of his profession in the 1950s (Kiniski family archive).

Kelly was caught unawares when his mother took him to football practice not long afterward and announced she and Gene were getting a divorce. She left a new house the family had built, returned to Alberta, and then lived for a time in a condominium she bought in Bellingham, 20 miles south of Blaine, where, Kelly says, she showed signs of possible mental illness such as difficulties eating, dressing, and making decisions. That came as a shock to Kelly, who says, "I was used to a supermom."

In Marion's absence, Gene apparently did not hesitate to take on the role of a full-time parent. In *The Heels*, Nick Kiniski recalls, of his father: "He was wild and crazy, but every morning, he'd get up, make sure I had breakfast, drive me to school.... After school, I always ate good meals—vegetables and salads, there were no TV dinners; it was always a full-course meal. The house was always spotless. He did my laundry, he did my bed" (75). Gene arranged for a housekeeper to take care of Kelly and Nick whenever he traveled any distance, but for the most part he stayed close to home after becoming a single parent. Kelly, who was a tenth-grader when his parents divorced, says, "He made it just like my mom never left."

While wrestlers in the Vancouver promotion had largely been left in the dark when it came to details of the Kiniskis' marital problems, Marion's absence from the office made the situation clear, even as Gene soldiered on. "I don't know what happened," says Webster, "because I started traveling and I was off going around the world. [But] I was devastated when I heard [about the divorce] because in my mind Gene and Marion were one."

From Bellingham, Marion left for Hawaii with another male companion from Blaine, and while she and Gene had enjoyed some happy times in Hawaii, it appears Marion found no such happiness there this time around. Kelly, who paid a visit to his mother in her new condominium in Hawaii, says she reappeared briefly in Blaine in 1976, again looking little like the supermom he remembered. Kelly, who was scheduled to leave shortly for Texas to begin his freshman year in college, asked his mother to come to Texas with him. She declined, telling him, "You have your own life to live."

Marion and first son Kelly at six weeks (Kiniski family archive).

Marion and her companion left for Anchorage, Alaska, where, Kelly says, "I had no way of getting hold of her." And then, not long into Kelly's freshman year at West Texas State University, Gene Kiniski was home in Blaine when the state patrol brought the news of a tragedy that had taken place in Alaska. On September 27, 1976—while her male companion from Blaine apparently was at work—Marion Kiniski had taken her own life by gunshot.

Kelly, who roomed during his freshman year of college with football teammate Tully Blanchard, Joe Blanchard's son, says, of the night he was told about his mother's suicide, "That night was the only night we didn't go out drinking…. I just knew there was something wrong with my mom…. For whatever reason, I just knew for sure, and I told three different people. [Later that night] the head coach was waiting out in the hall, and they called Tully out first, and I thought, 'Oh, they're cutting me from the team.' All of a sudden Tully says, 'Kelly, the coach wants to talk to you.' I said, 'I know what it is. My mom committed suicide.'" Kelly flew home for a few days before returning to West Texas and soldiering on as if nothing had happened. He says it was not until the tragic event in Alaska later sneaked up and hit him hard that he learned to grieve his loss. He adds, "I don't think my dad ever grieved it properly."

Marion, who Gene and others said had developed a drinking problem, was remembered at a small, private service in Richmond, BC. Meanwhile, the Marion Weller Kiniski obituary in the *Bellingham Herald*—the local daily newspaper in Blaine—does not refer to the Kiniski divorce but simply mentions, among Marion's survivors, "her husband, Gene," who, whether he ever properly grieved his loss or not, apparently never completely got over it. While numerous friends, acquaintances, and relatives of Gene Kiniski are quick to tell about his lifelong interest in a long list of women—including a few his sons were dating—nearly as many seem convinced that the truth is that there was never another woman Gene Kiniski really loved, and several of his closest friends say he was distraught after Marion's suicide, came to regret decisions he had made that likely contributed to the breakup of his marriage, and spoke highly of Marion long after she was gone.

To that effect, in August of 2006, 30 years after Marion's suicide, Kiniski told Greg Oliver, "They ask, 'How come you never got married again?' I said, 'Nobody could ever match my ex-wife.... I had the best.'"

19

Focusing on Home

Except when he toured Japan or took a few matches in Winnipeg and a couple of high-profile main events in Hawaii, Kiniski stuck close to home in 1974 and 1975, staying in the thick of the title picture in All-Star Wrestling, pulling his weight behind the scenes, and raising his two sons—one turning 17 in 1974 and the other turning 13 that same year.

In Japan Kiniski, at age 45, lost all five of his matches, including four tag team contests in which his side opposed either Baba or The Destroyer, or both. Kiniski's only singles match on that March 1974 tour was an unsuccessful Pacific Wrestling Federation Heavyweight title challenge in Sendai against Baba, whose storied history with Kiniski now spanned a decade. A year later Baba and Kiniski would face off again when Kiniski advanced to the final of All Japan Pro Wrestling's third annual Champion Carnival tournament before losing two out of three falls to Baba on May 3, 1975. Earlier in the 1975 tour—on April 19 in Koriyama—Kiniski reunited with former partner Killer Kowalski in a best-of-three-falls effort against Baba and Jumbo Tsuruta in which Kiniski pinned Baba in the first fall before Kowalski lost the second and third via pinfall.

Singles matches in Winnipeg in 1974 and 1975 saw Kiniski face AWA wrestlers Superstar Billy Graham, a Stu Hart trainee who would end Sammartino's second WWWF title reign in 1977; Baron von Raschke, who had a long and successful career especially in the Midwest; and "Blond Bomber" Ray Stevens, who, while not noted for doing a lot of training between matches, is regarded as a top wrestler of his era. Stevens, a major attraction from coast to coast from the 1950s to the 1980s, also had a reputation as a wild and hard-living maverick, and Kelly Kiniski says Stevens was one of the wrestlers his father later advised him to stay away from.

Gene Kiniski's September 11, 1975, Winnipeg Arena match against Raschke—following up on some unfinished business when the pair were on opposing sides during a three-on-three match the previous month—saw Kiniski "[throw] the rule book right out of the window and let go with everything he had," according to a report on the previous night's matches in the September 12, 1975, *Winnipeg Free Press*. That was more the norm than the exception for Kiniski, but the report lays out the scene by suggesting Kiniski, who had earned the respect of Winnipeg fans over the years, had mellowed in his middle age and fought with such abandon against Raschke—losing via disqualification when he "mercilessly [pounded] the Baron about the head, chest, and back with [a] metal chair"—because Raschke's rulebreaking in the three-on-three match the previous month had "so upset Big Gene that he promised he'd revert to his old ways and use any means possible to get even with the German." Winnipeg fans were solidly behind Kiniski by the mid–

1970s, and promoter Tomko generally responded by matching him, when he came to town, with some top AWA villains of the day.

A similar scenario played out at times throughout Kiniski's career—particularly in its later years—as fans sometimes couldn't resist getting behind Canada's Greatest Athlete when he faced an especially stiff or vile challenge. Yet Kiniski told Greg Oliver in 2006, "To me, the boos meant more than the cheers." In the same interview Kiniski seemed to take particular pride that "I used to get so much fan mail telling me what a bastard I was. I loved it" (Oliver, Files).

Kiniski's visits to Hawaii in June and July of 1974 saw him defeat Dory Funk, Jr., and then lose an AWA World Heavyweight title challenge to Verne Gagne. The July 17 Kiniski-Gagne match was their first tangle over the AWA title since 1961—when the title went back and forth between the two—and the last time they would compete in the ring.

At home in 1974, Kiniski held a share of the NWA Canadian Tag Team title with three different partners and reclaimed the Pacific Coast title by defeating Mr. X, played by John "Guy Mitchell" Hill, one of Kiniski's championship tag team partners that same year—the others being Savage and Masa Saito. Key singles matches prior to Kiniski's reclaiming the Pacific Coast title in October included a victory against Funk Jr. at the Agrodome and a draw with Brisco in a challenge for the NWA World Heavyweight title in the same building.

After dropping the Pacific Coast Heavyweight title to Mitchell on January 20, 1975, and the Canadian Tag Team championship, with Saito, to Mitchell and Ormand Malumba six weeks later, Kiniski would recapture both titles later in the year before unsuccessfully challenging Brisco in September and October for the NWA title in Vancouver, Victoria, and apparently Prince George.

Outside the ring, Kiniski did his part in bringing new blood into the promotion in 1974 and 1975. Wrestlers coming into the territory included Pat Kelly and Victor "Mike Kelly" Arco, who played the identical Kelly Twins; George "Flash Gordon" Gordienko, a respected grappler from Winnipeg; Dan Kroffat, back for another run in British Columbia after a brief NWA United National Heavyweight title reign in Japan and several title runs in Stampede Wrestling; Tiger Jeet Singh, a major Asian Indian wrestling star in Ontario and Japan; and Dale Lewis and Bill "Siegfried Steinke" Lehman, two successful heels who would hold a share of the NWA Canadian Tag Team title with Kiniski—and with each other—during their time in British Columbia. Steinke also had a three-month run in 1975 with the Pacific Coast Heavyweight title, which he dropped to Kiniski.

Brought in during the same period were future WWF stars Jimmy Snuka and Bob Remus, later famous as Sgt. Slaughter. Both—especially Snuka—showed promise but fell short in singles encounters with Kiniski in 1974 or 1975. Among established stars appearing in British Columbia during those years—in addition to Brisco and Funk Jr.—were Haystack Calhoun, a big attraction in the territory several years earlier, and André the Giant, a hugely popular touring attraction who fought to a double countout with Kiniski in Vancouver on July 22, 1974, in what appears to have been the only singles meeting of their careers.

Two fairly young grapplers who arrived in British Columbia in 1975 were Verne Gagne trainee Dennis Stamp and Keith Franke—the latter appearing as All-Star Wrestling midcarder Keith Franks until 1976 before repackaging himself in the United States a couple of years later as Adrian Adonis, returning to All-Star Wrestling as Adonis in 1979 to capture a share of the regional tag team title, and going on to achieve major success in the AWA and WWF. Stamp—with solid amateur wrestling credentials—and Franks both had some grappling skill, which Kiniski as a boss and father was quick to put to good use.

Both of Kiniski's sons, Kelly and Nick, were avid amateur wrestlers during their teens. Kelly, a high school senior when Franks and Stamp were regulars in the territory, recalls working out with both—particularly Franks—at Gene's request. According to Kelly, his father also arranged for Franks to wise him up to the ways of the world he would be facing following graduation from high school in 1976. Says Kelly, "Before I went to university, I think Dad told him to take me out to smarten me up to life. I was pretty nurtured in Blaine."

While wrestlers based in British Columbia at the time generally considered Gene Kiniski, even in his late forties, a ring general and a shrewd businessman, few seemed to be under the illusion that they would get rich by working in the Vancouver territory. Some—like Jonathan, Tolos, Quinn, and Savage—were well established and had the ability to pick and choose their matches in the territory while also wrestling elsewhere. Some Vancouver-based preliminary wrestlers, meanwhile, hit the mat as a sideline to their day jobs, and at least a few newcomers to the territory—Snuka, Remus, and Franks among them—saw British Columbia and the opportunity to perform with All-Star Wrestling for a large Canadian audience and a smaller American one as a means toward having greater opportunity down the road.

Others came to the territory perhaps expecting more than could be delivered.

"Kiniski was robbing us blind. He was a cheap prick as a promoter," said Stamp, who passed away from cancer in March 2017.

Stamp said, "I was making about $230 a week. We were paying all our own expenses. You'd get paid on Monday, and you'd be broke by Tuesday.... I would go to the store and buy a loaf of bread—a big sandwich loaf—and I would count slices of bread and then I'd count slices of baloney and count slices of cheese to make sure we had at least two sandwiches [a day] all week long."

Stamp said Kiniski "rode with us on some of the longer trips, [but] he never bought dinner or anything. We'd bring baloney and have baloney blowouts"—a tradition among wrestlers of past eras who were on a tight budget.

Perhaps reinforcing Stamp's perception of Kiniski as a tightwad was the latter's knack, with partner Kovacs, of cutting deals with flying schools in order to secure greatly discounted travel rates when the promotion held events on Vancouver Island. According to Bernie Pascall, student pilots were eager to log flying hours as long as fuel costs were reimbursed.

Stamp said, of Kiniski, "He was a promoter, which meant that we were mortal enemies in real life." Yet he admitted Kiniski was "tough without a doubt." The two faced each other in singles or tag matches more than 20 times during Stamp's nine-month stay in British Columbia, and, as Stamp recalled, "Gene and I had good matches for sure.... His thing was to blow you up. In other words, he'd tire you out.... We had a lot of good matches. He was a good worker." Despite his differences with Kiniski over money and his perception that "Gene didn't like me," Stamp was quick to characterize his 1975–1976 stay in the British Columbia territory—complete with visits to the Kiniski house to spar with Kelly and to indulge in some of Gene's home cooking—as "a real ball," in large part due to his growing friendship with Franks.

While Stamp did not recall sparring with Gene Kiniski in Blaine, Don Leo Jonathan recalls, "[Gene] liked to wrestle with the boys and the wrestlers he brought down to help train the boys. He liked to have a go with them."

Partly as a result of their father's effort to provide strong training partners, Kelly and Nick Kiniski became accomplished amateurs. In Kelly's case, he was the third-ranked high school heavyweight wrestler in Washington State during his 1975–1976 senior year at Blaine High School, where he combined his interest in wrestling with his interest in football, as Gene had done at St. Joseph High School.

That Kelly would attend university was a given as far as his father was concerned. Even when Kelly, during his senior year of high school, told his father he wanted to follow in his footsteps and become a professional wrestler, Gene insisted his elder son go to university first—and he soon began making arrangements to ensure that would happen.

In 1976 Kelly learned he would be attending West Texas State University—now West Texas A&M University—in Canyon, Texas, close to Amarillo. West Texas State at the time was noted as a breeding ground for professional wrestlers, with a long list of wrestling alumni including Stan Hansen, Ted DiBiase, Bruiser Brody, Dusty Rhodes, Tito Santana, and the Funk brothers, to name a few.

"My dad just said I was going there," says Kelly.

Most future professional wrestlers attending the university played football for the West Texas Buffalos, and Kelly—who, thanks to Gene's arrangement, had worked out with the British Columbia Lions during his senior year at Blaine High School—was expecting a full-ride football scholarship until he arrived in Texas and quickly learned the scholarship had fallen through. But even without the expected scholarship, Kelly could depend on the support of friends in the area. Terry Funk, living in Amarillo at the time and ever since, says, by phone, "[Gene] would bend over backwards for us.... He was a super person to my brother and myself.... My father had helped him in previous times. We had the opportunity to help Kelly.

"We brought him down here," Funk says of Kelly. "He was a good football player down here at West Texas."

According to Kelly, while attending West Texas he ended up receiving a "Funk scholarship," which enabled him to pay in-state rather than out-of-state tuition.

Kelly's roommate during his freshman year was Buffalos quarterback Tully Blanchard, who was born in Alberta while his father lived there in the 1950s. While he would never play

Gene flanked by Kelly (left) and Nick Kiniski, circa 1976 (Kiniski family archive).

football professionally, Tully Blanchard went on to have a long and successful career in professional wrestling, as did a second roommate Kelly would have at West Texas: Barry Windham, another second-generation wrestler who would become a major star.

Gene Kiniski did a bit of wrestling in Amarillo in the spring of 1976, perhaps in conjunction with his effort to make arrangements for Kelly's attendance at West Texas State and to secure for Kelly the football scholarship that got away. During at least one 1976 appearance in Amarillo, Gene Kiniski wrestled under a mask as the Mighty Canadian—whose identity under the mask would have been no secret—to defeat another masked wrestler, Art "Super Destroyer" Nelson, for the territory's International Heavyweight title, which Kiniski would hold for four weeks.

Other Kiniski matches outside the Pacific Northwest in 1976 were limited to a few encounters in Toronto, Winnipeg, and Alberta and 10 matches in St. Louis. Key opponents included The Sheik in Toronto; Gouldie in Alberta; and Snyder, O'Connor, future WWWF/WWF world champion Bob Backlund, and both Funk brothers in St. Louis—particularly Terry, who had taken the NWA World Heavyweight title from Brisco in December of 1975 and successfully defended it against Kiniski at the Kiel Auditorium in June and August of 1976.

Back in the Northwest, Jonathan had a big year in British Columbia in 1976, twice winning a share of the NWA Canadian Tag Team championship and twice winning the Pacific Coast title. Yet it was Kiniski who twice challenged Funk for the NWA world championship when the latter came through BC in summer and fall, even though both times Kiniski was without a title.

Jonathan's first 1976 Pacific Coast title reign began on January 5 with a victory over Kiniski on the first wrestling show of the year in Vancouver. Jonathan's second singles title reign of 1976 got underway late in the year and ended when Kiniski turned the tables by defeating him on the second Vancouver wrestling show of 1977.

But while Kiniski enjoyed a two-month run with the Pacific Coast title in early 1977 before dropping the belt to Guy Mitchell, by far the biggest news concerning the promotion during that time was a change in the All-Star Wrestling ownership team. By all accounts Kiniski was caught by surprise when Sandor Kovacs, perhaps catching a glimpse of the hard times ahead for wrestling territories, decided it was time to give up his share of the promotion and, for a reported $100,000, stepped aside to make way for a new partner to join Kiniski and Don Owen at the reins of All-Star Wrestling—a new partner Kiniski knew well.

20

Kiniski-Tomko
An Uneasy Alliance

Al Tomko had appeared on the undercard of some 1969 shows in Vancouver that featured Kiniski, but the two knew each other mainly through periodic meetings in Winnipeg, where Tomko had been involved locally in the wrestling business most of the time since 1950, when he established a micro-promotion, the Olympia Wrestling Club, out of the basement of his home. A few years later Tomko started appearing on shows run by the Madison Wrestling Club, a larger promotion that ran weekly shows in Winnipeg and spawned some successful wrestling careers, including those of Bulldog Bob Brown and Moose Morowski. Tomko continued to appear on Madison Club shows for more than a decade, usually in the mix of top local heels, before going to work as the Manitoba agent for Verne Gagne's AWA in 1966 and purchasing the Madison Club a year later only to merge it with the AWA.

It was as the AWA agent for Winnipeg that Tomko met up with Kiniski from time to time, as Winnipeg was a destination Kiniski loved to visit. He was without a doubt one of the city's wrestling legends, and by all accounts he was always eager to reconnect with friends such as the Gagnes, Wilbur Snyder, Nick Bockwinkel, and—as he did for two wild Winnipeg matches in 1977—Angelo Mosca. While it does not appear Kiniski and Tomko struck up what could be called a friendship through their periodic business interaction in Winnipeg, there seems no evidence they had any particular disagreements over pay, booking, or wrestling philosophy.

After Tomko arrived unexpectedly in Vancouver by early 1977 and proceeded to take over Kovacs' share of All-Star Wrestling, it appears Kiniski soldiered on as the promotion went through a generally smooth transition. While there is little doubt Kiniski was unhappy Tomko had left Winnipeg without giving notice to Verne Gagne—according to Greg Gagne, because "we found out [Tomko] had been skimming [money from the gate] … and he took off"—Kiniski continued to play an active role behind the scenes while getting into the ring occasionally on some of his promotion's big shows. Kiniski's appearances outside the Northwest in 1977, meanwhile, were limited to a losing effort on June 29 in Honolulu against Giant Baba, a Calgary match in early November, and a few matches in Winnipeg, with Tomko now half a continent away on the West Coast.

Kiniski stuck to a limited ring schedule in 1978, briefly hitting a couple of his favorite territories but focusing most of his wrestling attention on the territory he owned with one mainly trusted but largely hands-off partner and another whose ideas about wrestling would later prove difficult to reconcile with Kiniski's. But as long as things were going well in the promotion—and things generally remained well until a few years into the Kiniski-Tomko partnership—Tomko appeared content to stick largely with the winning formula Kiniski and Kovacs had laid out for the promotion.

Though multiple sources report he was upset about being left in the dark regarding the Kovacs-to-Tomko transition, Kiniski was known to shed work-related stress by engaging in some of his favorite activities—most notably, hunting; trapshooting; cooking; dining out; working out; and, when the opportunity arose, mixing notoriously strong drinks for friends in his basement. Another activity Kiniski seemed to find therapeutic—according to long-time friend Larry Hamilton (no connection to wrestler Larry "Missouri Mauler" Hamilton), who owned a Texaco station in Blaine in the 1970s—was to putter around with his vehicles, which included an old Chrysler, a blue El Dorado, and an F-150 truck, all of which had British Columbia plates.

"He loved to do his own oil change," says Hamilton. "Trouble is, it would take him about six hours, and he'd tie up my rack for that long."

But Hamilton says Kiniski would make restitution by doing a job he was probably better equipped to handle.

"If [a customer] did not pay me," he says, "I would take Mr. Kiniski to their house, and he would collect the money for me."

Hamilton recounts another manner in which Canada's Greatest Athlete was known—at least on some occasions—to escape the stresses of the office.

> He called me up one day and told me to come up to his house and just walk in. I didn't know what he wanted, but he said, "You've got to come up here right away." I thought he might have a problem.
>
> I went up and knocked on the door, and he said, "Come in." I walked in, and there was a lady standing naked with a lampshade on her head. I said 'Good morning,' and he says, "Is that all you have to say? You're supposed to be excited!"

"He had something going on all the time," says Hamilton.

In January and February of 1978 Kiniski wrestled on a few Stampede Wrestling shows in Alberta and Saskatchewan against reigning Stampede North American Heavyweight champion Leo Burke, a New Brunswick native who had success in many territories and numerous title reigns in Stampede Wrestling. Late in the year Kiniski wrestled on a couple of shows in Ontario. On December 17 in Toronto, in a match to determine Maple Leaf Wrestling's inaugural NWA Canadian Heavyweight champion—seemingly a perfect fit for Canada's Greatest Athlete—Kiniski faced defeat at the hands of Dino Bravo. The next night, an hour's drive west in Kitchener, Ontario, it appears Kiniski met future multi-time world champion Ric Flair in the ring for the first time.

As far as the Pacific Northwest was concerned, while Kiniski averaged just three or four matches per month there in 1978—and only about one appearance per month on his promotion's flagship *All-Star Wrestling* TV show that was still seen throughout much of Canada—he was nonetheless a featured performer in and around Vancouver throughout the year. He occasionally headed off for a match in Victoria, Seattle, or Portland, but when he chose, for business purposes, to travel to some of the outlying towns on the All-Star Wrestling circuit, he generally left his wrestling boots at home.

In Vancouver on May 15, Kiniski kicked off what would be the final championship reign of his career when he defeated John Quinn for the NWA Pacific Coast Heavyweight title. That victory began a 10-month title run—the longest heavyweight title reign by any wrestler in the promotion during the Kiniski era—which would extend several months beyond Kiniski's 50th birthday, which came on November 23.

Besides taking center stage as the regional champion during some big Vancouver wrestling shows in 1978, Kiniski brought in some notable newcomers to play key supporting roles. One who stands out in retrospect—and who showed rare potential to be a headliner—was Aurelian "Jake Roberts" Smith, Jr., a second-generation wrestler whose father, known for most of his career in numerous territories as Grizzly Smith, had wrestled in Vancouver in 1968 as Ski Hi Jones.

Jake Roberts wrestled briefly with his father in the southern and Midwestern United States before arriving in Vancouver in March of 1978. Though cast as a heel throughout most of his career—which saw him achieve major success in the WWF in the late 1980s and early 1990s—Roberts was positioned in British Columbia as a younger alternative to lead babyfaces in the promotion such as Jonathan, Mitchell, and Savage.

Roberts won the majority of his early matches in the promotion, in the process striking a chord with fans and rising to the top contendership for Kiniski's Pacific Coast title. Roberts credits Moose Morowski—like Tomko, a veteran of the 1960s Winnipeg wrestling club scene—with helping groom him for a top position in All-Star Wrestling.

Quoted in Greg Oliver's April 14, 2010, *SLAM!* retrospective on Kiniski's life, Roberts says, "Moose basically led me through the process and made me a star, and got me over. In the process, we got to where the PNE was selling out, which they hadn't done in years. At that point, Gene says, 'Damn, I'd better come back in and wrestle again[;] they're having sellouts.' Of course, Moose put me over [i.e., lost to Roberts] in a cage match, right in the middle, made me a star. Next thing, I wrestled Kiniski and he beat me two straight [falls]."

Roberts goes on to say, "He killed it every fucking time. So why in the fuck would you do that[;] why would you murder your own business, just to grow testicles for yourself?"

Before the year was over, Roberts was out of the territory, never to look back except to question why Kiniski and Tomko missed the boat when it came to seeing his potential—or, as some see it, set out to sabotage his progress when they did recognize his potential.

Another wrestler leaving the promotion in 1978 after a notable run there was British Columbia native John Anson, whose connection with Kiniski began in the 1960s when Anson was a teenager.

Anson reports meeting Kiniski and Sandor Kovacs after amateur wrestler Bill Persack met him at the YMCA and asked whether he wanted to be a wrestler. Persack, remembered for training wrestlers at the Y, had known Kovacs since World War II, when both served in the Canadian Navy. Anson says, via Facebook messaging, "I went up to the office to meet Sandor and Gene. And when I walked in, there stood Gene Kiniski, the big monster, big, raw-boned, everything bigger than life—and very rough. You could sense he was the real deal."

Anson continues, "He decided to start training me himself before the matches Monday night at the Gardens.... A typical training session would be me getting beat up for 30 minutes at the hands of Gene Kiniski. [This] included [a] broken nose, broken ribs, etc. The best thing I remember was at the office at the Gardens, Gene getting down on his hands and knees in an amateur stance in street clothes, saying, 'Show me what you can do.'"

Anson writes, "I went behind, hooked his foot, [and] drove forward. His head hit a standing ashtray and split it open. Blood was flowing out of his face. He said to Marion, 'See what the kid did to me?' [He] was happy that I hurt him."

Anson continues, "Our next encounter, he broke my ribs. I was not happy. Sandor called me at home and said, 'You want to wrestle tonight?' I told him I could not walk, and that was the truth."

After healing, Anson did some wrestling in British Columbia early in his career. He went on to make a name in several other territories in North America and in Japan and held several titles as German heel Karl von Shotz before returning to All-Star Wrestling during the latter part of the Kiniski-Kovacs partnership. As far as the transition from a Kiniski-Kovacs partnership to a Kiniski-Tomko alliance was concerned, Anson writes, "I was there when Al Tomko bought out Sandor Kovacs.... It was not the same. Gene was not comfortable. I believe the promotion started to suffer and there were problems"—as would become apparent a few years later.

"I spent a lot of time with Gene, and we were good friends," reports Anson. "He used to summon me to his Blaine home. He had a pool table [and] loved the game with a passion." Yet, Anson adds—explaining Kiniski was unaware of his experience playing in professional pool tournaments—"I never let him win."

A potential problem ensued when Anson—by then a seasoned veteran well into a successful career—demonstrated a similar distaste for losing as he was getting ready for a wrestling match in Vancouver. "I was standing in the dressing room, looking at the ring where Gene used to beat me up," he writes. "Roy McClarty [years into his tenure as a referee and Kiniski associate] came to me and said that Gene wanted me to put him over [let him win]. We were in the main event. I told Roy to tell Gene to beat me if he can. The word came back, 'Go the distance' [to a draw]."

Kiniski was known to "work stiff" at times—that is, inflict a little unscripted punishment on an opponent or simply refuse to make an opponent look good if it meant making himself look weak or overmatched. Whether he ceded to Anson's refusal to lose the match because he respected Anson or valued their friendship—which Anson says ended over the incident—or because, at age 47, he preferred not to engage in a "shooting contest" with a young, powerful, and capable opponent is unclear, but the pair, on a September 13, 1976, show in Vancouver, went to a time-limit draw in a match whose finish apparently had the approval of both participants.

While Kiniski, even in his late forties, seemed to consider himself the alpha male of the promotion and generally liked to get his way in and out of the ring, he was known to react at times with apparent respect—whether begrudging or not—when an opponent, or a wrestler he thought had promise, stood up to him. A few years before Anson indicated an unwillingness to "lay down" for Kiniski, Dan Kroffat recalls being unhappy during a match in which he says Kiniski was not being cooperative.

"I shot Kiniski once [i.e., engaged him in some unannounced legitimate grappling]," says Kroffat. "I got tired, a little bit, of working with him, where he was just constantly dominating the match. He was the heel, and I thought, 'Okay, it's time for a comeback.' Every time I attempted to come back, he would cut if off. And I knew we had a 20-minute match, and we were running out of time, and I just felt like he was diminishing my value as a babyface."

Kroffat continues, "So I backed him up against the rope, and I slapped his face really hard, and I think that came as a shock to him.... I was sending him a message that 'It's not all about you, but it's about us working together.' And then, ironically, I had a huge comeback, and we ended it up as we should."

Kroffat, who, despite any differences they might have had, says he did not dislike Kiniski and respects Kiniski's accomplishments in the ring, reports that he suffered no adverse professional consequences following their brief skirmish. "All the boys in the dressing room were shocked that I got away with it," he says. "[But] it was almost like fighting for air sometimes, working with Gene.... His ego sometimes overrode his better judgment.... You had to push back with Kiniski. You had to let him know he can't take liberties with you."

Similarly, Anson's willingness to stand up to Kiniski did not result in any unwanted consequences. Anson would go on to become a two-time coholder of the promotion's tag team title—matching Kroffat's accomplishment a few years earlier—and while it appears Kiniski and Anson did not have any other singles matches while Anson was in the promotion, the pair formed a team on several occasions at arena shows and television tapings in 1977 and 1978. Looking back, Anson, who relocated to a mountain estate in the Dominican Republic after his wrestling days were over, says, "Gene was a mentor to me"—albeit one who was so set on projecting toughness that Anson recalls seeing Kiniski "beat up people in the ring [and] kick them so hard all 12 lace marks would be on their body." Anson says, "I said to him once, 'Why do that?' He said, 'If they can't take it, they shouldn't be in the business.' He made his point to millions of people worldwide. Nobody ever left an arena not believing in Gene Kiniski."

Ed Moretti, a California native who made a name up and down the West Coast during a lengthy career, recalls being a bit awestruck when he learned, during his rookie year as a wrestler in 1978, that his first match after arriving in the British Columbia territory would be against Gene Kiniski, who was holding the Pacific Coast title at the time. Says Moretti, "I stayed in a hotel on the King George Highway in Surrey. I just happened to buy the newspaper ... and I hit the sports page.... There's a little bitty ad, and I see 'Gene Kiniski against Ed Moretti,' and I went, 'Uh oh. What the heck is this?'"

Moretti, who had been wrestling for several months in Northern California, says, "I was green, but I still knew what I was doing." As far as his Vancouver debut against Kiniski was concerned, he says, "He wasn't very cooperative in the ring. You've got to fight for everything you get—if you get anything. And you know what the end result's going to be anyway. He's going to be the star.... He doesn't give you much unless you fight for it—and then sometimes he'll cut you off right there."

Another wrestler of note who ventured into British Columbia in 1978 was Hossein Khosrow Ali Vaziri, an Iranian native who reportedly had an impressive amateur wrestling career and worked for a time as a bodyguard for the shah of Iran.

During his four-month stay in British Columbia, Vaziri wrestled as The Iron Sheik, the name he went by during most of his professional wrestling career, including the four-week period from late 1983 to early 1984 when he was the WWF World Heavyweight champion until losing that title to Hulk Hogan, who kicked off the first of 12 world championship reigns with the victory. In British Columbia from June to October of 1978, The Iron Sheik—who had worked out amateur-style with Kelly and Nick Kiniski two or three years earlier in Blaine—teamed with Gene Kiniski several times to form a memorable tandem. According to Moretti, "Iron Sheik could stay with Kiniski, so Kiniski respected him. Iron Sheik could shoot."

Kiniski and The Iron Sheik wrestled each other outside Vancouver, Moretti says, adding, "[Kiniski] respected him, but he still beat him." The result, says Moretti, was that The Iron Sheik was "another one Kiniski put in a package and sent off."

Moretti is quick to compare Iron Sheik's departure from the territory with Roberts' during the same general period. "They killed Jake," he says. "He was getting over fantastic when I got here, and the next thing you know, he [lost to] Kiniski. It wasn't on TV, but TV would report that Kiniski beat Jake Roberts. And then people in the towns, way up north or in Victoria ... on the island ... they'd go, 'Oh, so Jake was beat by Kiniski. That's over with.'"

Moretti says that typified Kiniski's modus operandi as Canada's Greatest Athlete neared or passed 50. "Gene would come into certain towns ... and work the main events. He would go in and beat the guy who was currently working the main event—either a heel or a babyface; it didn't matter. Kiniski was Kiniski. So us guys who were working every night could never get a foothold established to get people over so we could draw money."

Gene Kiniski cut back further on his ring appearances from 1979 through the end of his association with All-Star Wrestling in 1981. In 1979 Kiniski won all but a few of his two dozen or so recorded matches in British Columbia and northern Washington, though he stayed entirely out of the title picture after dropping the Pacific Coast Heavyweight championship to Salvatore Martino in early spring and focused instead on the business of running a territory with a largely absentee partner in Owen and another partner, Tomko, with whom Kiniski was never entirely comfortable. Trying to keep the promotion fresh—though it was starting to look as though the territory had probably passed its peak—Tomko and Kiniski highlighted some new wrestlers, including Chris Colt, a bit of a wrestling cult figure from that era; Bruce Reed, who would hold championships around the United States as Butch Reed in the 1980s; Bobby Jaggers, a tough native of Washington State who held many regional titles throughout his career; 1979 Pacific Coast titleholders Jean Louis and Yaki Joe; and returning former Pacific Coast titleholder Siegfried Steinke, who would regain the promotion's title in October of 1979.

Also appearing on some major Vancouver house shows on Mondays and TV tapings the following night were two megastars from Owen's Oregon promotion, Buddy Rose and Roddy Piper, backed up by fellow Oregon wrestlers The Kiwis (future WWF tag team The Bushwhackers), Ron Bass, Matt Borne, King Parsons, and Stan Stasiak (who had been WWWF World Heavyweight champion for nine days in 1973). Following their Monday and Tuesday appearances in Vancouver and Burnaby, those wrestlers normally returned to the Portland circuit for the rest of the week, leaving fans in All-Star Wrestling's outlying areas to feel they were getting less than they had seen on television—particularly since the stars from Oregon, mainly for the sake of building up Vancouver shows, had made such a strong case for their superiority by earning victories on TV over wrestlers who were making the rounds through the smaller towns, often before dwindling crowds.

While Kiniski's presence in the ring may have helped shore up business for a time—at least in the view of some—all indications are that he knew, at that point in his career, that putting himself on center stage as a performer would not be a long-term solution. Instead, he apparently went along with the idea of shuffling wrestlers in and out of the promotion—as promoters had been accustomed to doing for decades—and bringing in more attractions from Oregon.

In 1979 Kiniski made his final visit to Japan as an active wrestler—a two-week tour highlighted by meetings with The Destroyer and Baba, with the latter defeating Kiniski by countout on May 2 in Nagasaki. Other travels in 1979 took Kiniski to Alberta for a pair of meetings with Stampede North American Heavyweight champion Big Daddy Ritter, future WWF star the Junkyard Dog; to Owen's Oregon, for a single match against future WWF wrestler Lanny Poffo, brother of 1980s–1990s WWF superstar Randy "Macho

Man" Savage; and to Toronto, where Kiniski participated in a one-night tournament for the NWA Canadian Heavyweight title, losing to tournament winner Dewey Robertson.

Kiniski also returned to St. Louis, after a three-year absence, to participate in 14 televised or arena matches between August and December of 1979. Partners or opponents included Dick the Bruiser, Ox Baker, Dick Murdoch, Ed Wiskoski, long-time All-Star Wrestling star Bulldog Bob Brown—and, most notably, Fritz von Erich's sons David and Kevin von Erich, who partnered with Kiniski in a three-on-three match on a *Wrestling at the Chase* taping in August, and reigning NWA World Heavyweight champion Harley Race, who successfully defended the title against Kiniski on the latter's 51st birthday, November 23, at the Kiel Auditorium.

The following year, 1980, saw Kiniski continue to pare down his schedule. Recorded appearances totaled fewer than 30 matches, with the majority taking place in his home territory, where wrestlers from Owen's Pacific Northwest Wrestling in Oregon continued to fill spots on major All-Star Wrestling shows and appear at the television tapings without generally following up by going on the road around the territory. Key part-timers from Oregon—in addition to Rose, Piper, and Bass—included Jay Youngblood, Rip Oliver, Fidel "Destroyer" Sierra, Jesse Barr, and Buzz Sawyer. While the addition of key players from Oregon—usually booked to overshadow the BC-based wrestlers on major shows and on television—generally did not bode well for the All-Star Wrestling core, Kiniski as a wrestler was largely unaffected, as he recorded singles victories in British Columbia in 1980 over Barr, Bass, Rose, and Piper—in the process, drawing further concern or criticism from wrestlers who thought some of those victories should have gone to younger competitors who went out on the road for All-Star Wrestling.

Critics were not limited to those based full-time in British Columbia. One of the part-timers from Oregon who wrestled in Vancouver over the course of a few months in 1980, Ed Wiskoski, says, "He was a prick.... Gene Kiniski was out for Gene Kiniski."

Despite a growing influx of wrestlers into BC from his home territory, Don Owen apparently ended his association with All-Star Wrestling before 1980 was over. That left Kiniski without a partner whose experience and success he respected, and highlighted his uneasy relationship with Tomko. Yet, while Kiniski apparently drew back somewhat from the day-to-day running of the company, he appeared periodically throughout the year on major shows on the BC Lower Mainland and, at least once, on Vancouver Island.

While it appears Kiniski was inclined to leave Tomko on his own following the departure of Owen from the promotion, he had at least one compelling reason not to cut ties with All-Star Wrestling quite yet.

Scattered throughout 1980, along with his limited ring appearances in British Columbia, were occasional bookings in other territories such as Northern California, where Kiniski briefly met up with the Funk brothers in late January; Portland, where Kiniski made a few midcard appearances in late summer and early fall; and Winnipeg, where he both served as a guest referee and wrestled in 1980. But probably the most notable wrestling junkets Kiniski made in 1980 were to the Funks' Amarillo territory and to Stampede Wrestling.

Kiniski's brief visit to Amarillo in the spring of 1980 coincided with Kelly's graduation from West Texas State. In much the manner that his father looked back on his time at the University of Arizona, Kelly has fond memories of his college experience, especially of his four years on the gridiron and his association with friends around Canyon-Amarillo who had deep roots in the wrestling business—in particular, the Funks, Tully Blanchard, and Barry Windham.

At age 51, Kiniski participated in a six-man tag match in Roy Shire's Northern California territory. Teaming with Kiniski at the Cow Palace just outside San Francisco on Jan. 26, 1980, were Ed Wiskoski (far right) and St. Louis legend Bruiser Brody (no connection to Dick the Bruiser), as the trio faced former NWA Heavyweight champions Dory Funk, Jr., and Terry Funk along with their supersized, Haystack Calhoun-esque protégé, T. John Tibbedeux, trained by the Funks in Amarillo (photograph by Dr. Mike Lano / Wrealano@aol.com).

Looking back on his football experience at West Texas, Kelly explains why coaches switched his position to center after he arrived expecting to play tackle as his father had done in the college and professional ranks:

"They said [it was] because I did a lot of wrestling moves ... and if I was in the very middle, no one could see me. If I was in the tackle position they could see me ... arm drag or whatever I was doing."

Though Kelly recalls his father making a few ring appearances in Texas while Kelly was attending university, it appears Gene Kiniski wrestled only a single match during his brief 1980 visit to Amarillo, losing by disqualification to Don "The Lawman" Slatton on May 1. Most of Kiniski's attention during his visit apparently was on paying respects, attending the Missouri Valley Conference champion Buffalos' homecoming game—and receiving the game ball—and preparing to make the long drive back to the Northwest with Kelly.

After earning his degree in mass communications with a minor in speech, Kelly stayed briefly in Blaine and worked out in the ring with his father at the Exhibition Gardens in Vancouver as he prepared for his professional wrestling debut. While Kelly had returned home and worked out with his father during the summers when he attended university, none of that training had taken place in a wrestling ring but usually involved pushups, situps, uphill running, and—always a favorite of Gene Kiniski's—plenty of neck exercises. Kelly recalls, "I used to do high bridges, and my dad would stand on my stomach and jump up and down.... My neck was bigger than my head."

When it came time for his older son to wrestle before an audience, Gene Kiniski did not immediately unveil Kelly to All-Star Wrestling fans but instead did what he sometimes liked to do with younger wrestlers under his wing and sent Kelly to Calgary, where he could develop under the watchful eye of Stu Hart. Kelly says, "My dad was a great wrestler, but he was not a good teacher." Recalling how his father knocked out one of his teeth during training, Kelly says, "He thought I needed that, I guess." Of his opportunity to train with Hart, Kelly says, "Stu wanted to work out with me," but Kelly, mindful of Hart's reputation for stretching (hurting) new or unsuspecting wrestlers, declined.

Kelly made his professional wrestling debut in Calgary on October 1, 1980, defeating Texas Red Miller but getting attacked after the match by Mike Sharpe, Jr. Stampede Wrestling at the time was an avant-garde North American wrestling promotion, featuring a mix of ring styles, athletes spanning a wide weight range, and generally strong ring work. But while demands were high in the territory and it was generally a good place for a young wrestler to get experience, Kelly says he did not get any meaningful tutelage in Stampede Wrestling—memorable to him for road trips where it was "40 below and we're all trying to huddle up in a van that doesn't have any heat in it." He adds, "I was starving to death." His father came into the territory two weeks after Kelly's debut, and the two appeared on a few cards together in Alberta and Saskatchewan, highlighted by their first-ever appearance as a tag team, October 24, 1980, in Calgary, when the Kiniskis lost to Sharpe Jr. and John Foley.

A week later, Kelly debuted in All-Star Wrestling, teaming with his father on a TV taping to defeat Morowski and Igor Volkoff, before returning to pay more dues in Alberta. Two months later Kelly returned to British Columbia for the year-end holiday, and the Kiniskis teamed on All-Star Wrestling's final show of 1980 in Vancouver to beat Morowski and Sierra.

In January Kelly was back in Alberta trading victories in Stampede Wrestling, but a few weeks later he was done with that promotion and returned briefly to the Northwest. Besides appearing on several shows in Vancouver and on TV tapings in Burnaby from late January to late February of 1981, Kelly also wrestled on at least two shows in Seattle and one in Portland on which his father also appeared, although the two did not work as a team. The Portland show, on February 24, 1981—with the Kiniskis in separate matches before returning for a main-event battle royal—appears to represent the only time Kelly Kiniski wrestled in Portland.

Explaining in part why he had no interest in establishing himself in Portland, Kelly Kiniski says, of his father's business partner in Vancouver, "Don Owen hurt me real bad as a young kid. My dad and him were drinking, and he said, 'Let me put a hold on you,' and he stretched me really good. And I went down to my bedroom crying, and I thought, 'One day I'm going to get even with that son of a bitch.' So then I grew up and I was strong and tough and beating men wrestling, and he had a few drinks and I said, 'Mr. Owen, let me show you this.'"

Kelly continues, "I gave it to him but good. My dad was screaming, 'That's Don! Let go of him! He's a promoter!' And I thought, 'You want to hurt me? It's my turn.' And I got even good."

Gene Kiniski stayed in the Northwest the entire year as Kelly wrestled primarily in the southern United States, having relatively successful runs in the New Orleans-based Universal Wrestling Federation, run by Bill Watts, and Florida, highlighted by singles matches against a young Hulk Hogan and Dory Funk, Jr., who had defeated Gene Kiniski in Florida for the NWA World Heavyweight title a dozen years earlier. Kelly Kiniski also had a promising run in Texas in 1981—rooming in San Antonio with college mate Tully Blanchard, who Kelly credits with teaching him about ring psychology—highlighted by some matches with 65-year-old Lou Thesz.

Amazingly, Kelly was not the only Kiniski the legendary Thesz would face in 1981, as on June 16 an appreciative crowd at Don Owen's Portland Sports Arena was treated to the last-ever singles match between Thesz and Gene Kiniski. That match ended in a draw.

Meanwhile, Gene Kiniski maintained some activity as an owner of All-Star Wrestling during much of the year, though his attention, as the year progressed, seemed to be more on getting out of the promotion. Wrestling only occasionally throughout 1981, he generally avoided outlying towns in the territory and limited his appearances to television tapings and some occasional Monday night shows in Vancouver, which—much like the televised *All-Star Wrestling*—were starting to show little of the luster they had shown in earlier years.

One reason the complexion of All-Star Wrestling was changing was Tomko's predilection toward featuring himself as a performer more and more as his grip on the promotion got stronger in 1981 with Owen's absence from the company and Gene Kiniski's clear intention to get out. While Tomko had wrestled occasionally from the time he bought into the promotion in 1977 through the end of 1980, 1981 was the year in which

Among decisions opening Tomko (center) up to criticism was the choice of making himself the most-decorated wrestler in British Columbia when he was in his fifties and hardly the sort of wrestler featured in the more successful, larger promotions (Vance Nevada collection).

he jumped on his growing opportunity to fill a spot as a featured wrestler in the territory. Tomko's earliest matches in British Columbia dated back to 1969, when, as Leroy Hirsch, he was on the undercard for a few months and lost most of his matches. Not surprisingly, he fared better in his matches after returning to the promotion in 1977, when he had the power of ownership in his corner; and by 1981—when full control of All-Star Wrestling was becoming concentrated in his hands—Tomko had graduated to becoming a regular main eventer in the territory.

By that time Tomko had been involved in wrestling for more than three decades, mainly in Manitoba, where he had been active as a trainer, wrestler, and promoter going back to 1950. During his years of wrestling in Manitoba, he had held one title—a share of Winnipeg's Madison Wrestling Club tag team title, apparently for several months in the mid-1960s—and he never won another championship or headlined a show outside Manitoba before buying out Sandor Kovacs' share of All-Star Wrestling in 1977. Yet, apparently getting a taste for being in the spotlight in his own promotion, Tomko captured the second championship of his career when he and Igor Volkoff won the NWA Canadian Tag Team title from "Klondike" Mike Shaw and Dan "Danny O" Pettiglio in September of 1981. Gene Kiniski was not on that show.

Tomko, who turned 50 during that tag title reign, went on to enjoy 11 more title reigns—including six runs as his promotion's Canadian Heavyweight champion—when he folded what little was left of All-Star Wrestling in 1989. Opinions of wrestlers and others associated with All-Star Wrestling during the Tomko regime seem somewhat mixed with regard to Tomko's abilities as a promoter. Although many see his shortcomings, some point out that numerous other regional promoters were put out of business in the 1980s and early 1990s by the expansion of the WWF and the increased presence on television of U.S.-based promotions whose production values and wrestling personnel greatly surpassed what smaller regional promoters such as Tomko had at their disposal. But when it comes to questions about Tomko the wrestler—especially during most of the 1980s when, in his fifties, he booked himself to be the wrestler of the decade in British Columbia—Tomko is generally not viewed favorably.

Moretti, says, "It was tough. It was his decision to be a main-event wrestler. We pretty much worked around him. We knew what he wanted. He'd explain himself, and sometimes it didn't make sense. But we'd say, 'Okay, Al, you're the boss,' so we'd do it."

Kiniski had no part in Tomko's string of title runs in British Columbia, and most indications are that Kiniski and Tomko were never fully on the same page when it came to their co-ownership of All-Star Wrestling. Greg Oliver quotes Kiniski in the August 6, 2009, Tomko obituary on the *SLAM!* website: "[Tomko's] idea of promoting wrestling was different. But then this gets into a business deal, and I'd rather not talk about it. I'm one of these people, my word is my bond. It ended up costing me a big bunch of money because of my stupidity. I trusted people. It just didn't work out that way."

Kiniski was an old-school wrestler who took a similar approach to his role as an owner-promoter. Apparently never quite at ease with Tomko's more experimental approach to promoting, it appears Kiniski had minimal interest in helping run the promotion after Owen's departure and Tomko took full advantage by implementing more of his own ideas, some of which—according to Dutch Savage, quoted in Oliver's Tomko obituary—"sounded like a Jerry Springer program."

In a similar vein, perhaps—at least in terms of potential for injecting a little turmoil in the life of Gene Kiniski—was a drawn-out episode involving British Columbia con man Allan Ammerlaan. At about the same time the Kiniski-Tomko alliance was in its final chapter, Ammerlaan was living it up around Vancouver—as the *National Post* reported on February 15, 2010, following Ammerlaan's death—"by pretending to be famous Canadian wrestler Gene Kiniski." According to the *National Post*, "It got him meals at fine restaurants and free hotel rooms and cab rides."

Nick Kiniski says one of those cab rides ran up a charge of $800. As far as hotels were concerned, Nick says Ammerlaan, over the course of close to a year, had a habit of making reservations by phone, saying he was Gene Kiniski, requesting that the hotel staff take good care of his friend Ammerlaan, and promising he would pick up the tab. Nick says, of Ammerlaan, "He would come into the hotel and do everything like he's friends of Gene Kiniski. The guy would go there and check in, stay for three days, order cigarettes, booze, steak, everything, and just eat high on the hog." According to Nick, charges run up by Ammerlaan during the time he posed as Gene Kiniski or Gene Kiniski's friend totaled as much as $80,000.

Vancouver native Verne Siebert, who wrestled for All-Star Wrestling during most of the 1980s, says he went to high school with Ammerlaan and was well aware of his illegal tendencies.

Siebert says, "He would contact the BC Lions and tell them he was the Vancouver Canucks and tell them he wanted *x* amount of tickets. He'd send somebody to get the tickets at the box office, and he'd have them stand out in front of the football stadium and sell the tickets. Then he'd try to phone the Canucks and tell them he was the Lions."

According to Siebert, Gene Kiniski was not the only wrestler's name Ammerlaan adopted in carrying out some of his shadier activities. "I know Kiniski and [Nick] Bockwinkel were two of the main ones he used to defraud hotels and bars," he says.

As Siebert recalls, Ammerlaan's luck ran out and "he ended up in prison." The *National Post* reports, "Ammerlaan spent most of his twenties in institutions for a variety of frauds."

Nick Kiniski recalls that some businesses defrauded by Ammerlaan contacted Gene Kiniski, who, not surprisingly, replied, "Fuck off. I'm not paying anything. You never got a credit card from me." Nick says a Vancouver court wanted his father to come and answer a few questions, but Gene Kiniski, as adamant as he was innocent, walked away from the Ammerlaan episode unscathed, though presumably and justifiably angry.

As bold as his father was when it came to defending his reputation and his pocketbook, Nick recalls a detail suggesting Ammerlaan had a degree of boldness to match his intended victim's. According to Nick, Ammerlaan sent Christmas cards to Gene Kiniski while he was incarcerated.

Siebert says Ammerlaan later "turned his life around," and a letter to the editor, written by inmate Paul Dempsey, in the September 12, 2005, edition of the *B.C. Catholic* newspaper, says contact with a prison chaplain "set Allan on a course that would lead to him establishing Luke 15 [Halfway] House in Burnaby. It would also lead him into studies for the priesthood." A few years after his release from prison, Ammerlaan turned his attention toward helping fellow ex-convicts make a successful transition out of prison. The *National Post* reports that Ammerlaan ran Luke 15 House for more than a decade before passing away due to diabetes-related complications in early 2010. Over eight years after Ammerlaan's death, Luke 15 House is still operating at a new location in Surrey, BC.

Though probably as eager to extricate himself from his partnership with Tomko as to ride out the Ammerlaan complication, Kiniski nonetheless stayed around until the end of 1981, just long enough to team with Kelly—who was in Blaine for the holidays—one last time in front of a home audience. The Kiniskis defeated Art Crews and Terry Adonis in Vancouver on a December 28 show with Tomko in the main event.

A few days later, Kelly would kick off a month-long tour with Giant Baba's All Japan Pro Wrestling—an opportunity that normally would not come to a wrestler so early in his career. Definitely recognized in Japan as his father's son, Kelly recalls, "When I got there, mafia people [and] real rich people would take me out and wine and dine me every night."

As far as Gene Kiniski was concerned, December 28, 1981, marked his last appearance in an All-Star Wrestling ring, as he walked away from the promotion and ended his professional association with Tomko—although both would live out their final decades in Blaine, where they would cross paths from time to time, though they never, according to people in Blaine who knew both, let their professional differences get the better of them.

21

Slowly Winding Down

While 1981 saw the end of Gene Kiniski's association with All-Star Wrestling, it did not spell the end for the ring career of Canada's Greatest Athlete. Through much of 1982, while Tomko's All-Star Wrestling focused exclusively on running shows in British Columbia, Kiniski wrestled occasionally on shows in Washington and Oregon for Owen's Pacific Northwest Wrestling. He also made a single appearance in Calgary in June and engaged in a rugged series of encounters in Toronto that same month and into July with Angelo Mosca.

Clearly, much of Kiniski's attention during that period was focused on his adult sons. One, Nick, was now attending Simon Fraser University in Burnaby, BC, on a football scholarship, playing center and, off the field, studying geography and kinesiology while enjoying great success as an amateur wrestler. Gene Kiniski, credited as one of Nick's early trainers, liked to keep in contact with the Simon Fraser wrestling team and, at least to some degree, amateur wrestling in general. Alberta Sports Hall of Famer Mike Eurchuk, a notable name in Canadian and international amateur wrestling at the time, recalls, "I was refereeing a Canadian championship in Vancouver [sometime in the 1980s], and Gene came out and sat with his old colleagues to watch the thing. He didn't play any active role, but he paid his admission and came in and he was a spectator." In the early 1980s Kiniski was particularly conspicuous as a supporter of Nick—an elite superheavyweight wrestler who would became a member of Canada's national wrestling team and an alternate for the 1984 Olympics—and Nick's teammates at SFU.

Nick recalls a visit home from college that put a new spin on what many people already knew about Gene Kiniski: that he was as fearless as they come.

He says, "I came home … and see his arm's all taped up. I go, 'Dad what did you do?' He was playing with my neighbor's dogs. They had two great big Shepherds, over 100 pounds apiece…. They were pretty aggressive … [and] weren't trained that good. He jumped over the fence to wrestle with the dogs.

"Who does that?" says Nick, adding, "He was fearless of people—and dogs."

Kelly Kiniski, meanwhile, was paying his dues as a professional wrestler throughout 1982. Besides touring Japan, Kelly wrestled that year mainly in Jim Crockett's NWA Mid-Atlantic territory, which spilled over into Ontario.

Kelly recalls following a young wrestler's protocol by introducing himself to fellow wrestlers in the dressing room before the matches. "They wouldn't shake my hand," he says. "Then they'd find out I was Gene's son"—at which point, he says, nearly every wrestler was quick to extend a hand.

One exception, Kelly says, was Jake Roberts—still stinging, perhaps, from what had transpired with Gene in Vancouver a few years earlier. "I don't know what my dad did to him," says Kelly, who recalls that Roberts seemed to have no interest in mending fences.

In June and July, Gene Kiniski wrestled a series of at least a dozen matches for the Crockett promotion in Virginia, Upstate New York, and Southern Ontario, apparently emerging undefeated except against Mosca, who beat him three times in Toronto, where Crockett owned a share of the promotion. Kiniski's opponent on a show in Buffalo was Roberts—who'd won a few regional heavyweight titles since leaving British Columbia in late 1978—but on June 7, 1982, in the city he'd helped set ablaze a full quarter century earlier, Kiniski got the better of Roberts once more.

One reason for Gene Kiniski's visit to the Mid-Atlantic territory in 1982, of course, was the opportunity to spend time with Kelly. The two got to see each other often, as both Kiniskis appeared on several of the same shows throughout Gene's brief stay in the Crockett territory in 1982.

The most memorable show on which Gene and Kelly Kiniski appeared in 1982, however, was an April 30 card at the Kiel Auditorium in St. Louis. In 1982 Gene Kiniski made several arena appearances in St. Louis, which, to no one's surprise, he identified in a November 10, 2000, *SLAM!* chat as "a tremendous wrestling city" and his favorite place to wrestle in the United States. Kiniski's St. Louis matches in 1982 included a tag team pairing with Dick the Bruiser in January and singles matches against von Raschke (not usually known as a "baron" in St. Louis) and Funk Jr. later in the year, but the highlight of Kiniski's activity as a wrestler in 1982 was his appearance on the April 30 show at the Kiel.

On New Year's Day 1982 Kiniski had been special referee for a Ric Flair NWA title defense against Dusty Rhodes on a card marking Sam Muchnick's retirement that drew nearly 20,000 to the St. Louis Checkerdome. Long-time wrestling manager, promoter, and commentator Jim Cornette reports, at www.jimcornette.com, "Also on the card were St. Louis icons Dick the Bruiser, Pat O'Connor, and Harley Race.... Special guests at the presentation to Sam at intermission included the sports editors of the daily newspapers, the sports directors of the local TV stations, representatives of the mayor's office, the Missouri Senate and House of Representatives, and local team owners from the baseball and hockey worlds. Also on hand were wrestling promoters Verne Gagne, Wally Karbo, Frank Tunney and others, as well as Joe Garagiola himself." According to Larry Matysik—St. Louis booker at the time—Kiniski and Garagiola reprised their memorable 1960 verbal exchange at the Muchnick retirement show. "They were hilarious together," he said, adding that an equally unforgettable moment for him—as he also recounted in his book *Wrestling at the Chase* (228)—came when Kiniski, after delivering a touching in-ring tribute to Muchnick and his late wife Helen, broke into a chorus of *There's No Business Like Show Business* with long-time friend Verne Gagne as Matysik drove the pair back to their hotel—the Chase.

Kiniski was back in St. Louis when Flair made his return to the city two months later and turned back challenger Dick the Bruiser under questionable circumstances. Next in line for an NWA title challenge in St. Louis was 53-year-old Gene Kiniski, who had been appearing regularly on *Wrestling at the Chase* and, according to the April 22, 1982, St. Louis Wrestling Club bulletin, "has been piling up victories right and left [and] is clearly primed for an all-out effort to grab the gold belt for the second time in his illustrious career."

The St. Louis Wrestling Club bulletin credits the Kiniski sons, Kelly and Nick, with "helping to revitalize their father Gene's career." The bulletin points out that Kelly, scheduled to wrestle Jerry Brown in the fourth match on the card, would be in his father's corner during Gene's main-event title challenge. Meanwhile, the report continues, "waiting by a telephone in his college dorm will be Nick, possibly the best amateur grappler in Canada. Nick expects to get a call from Kelly saying their father is again the world champion."

Though that call never came, Kelly recalls things getting out of hand in the crowd during his father's match against Flair. "I thought people were slapping me on the back, like 'Way to go; your dad's doing good.' But there was a riot going on. I was watching the match and they were actually hitting me in the back…. Dad stood out of the ring. He said, 'Turn around and fight, you dumb bastard.' We were fighting, kicking fans and punching them, and I said, 'This is a fine way to raise your son!'"

Southern Illinois wrestling promoter Herb Simmons, who had a close connection to the St. Louis wrestling office, was on hand for the Kiniski-Flair match. Simmons, with more than four decades of involvement in wrestling promotion dating back to the 1970s—as well as a 34-year incumbency as the mayor of East Carondelet, Illinois, where he continues to promote monthly independent wrestling shows—says, of 53-year-old world title challenger Kiniski, "He never missed a beat, as far as the fans were concerned. They remembered him as Big Thunder."

Simmons continues, "I remember [after the match] they went to a place over in Sauget, Illinois—a place that the wrestlers would go to—and I remember Flair saying, 'Boy, he's a tough son of a gun.' Of course, those weren't the words he used. Flair gave him all the respect in the world."

The match was a best-of-three encounter in which Kiniski took the first fall before succumbing to Flair's signature figure-four leglock to end the second fall. A two-minute rest period was scheduled between falls, and Kiniski, "selling" an injured knee, did not answer the bell to start the third fall.

The match was Gene Kiniski's final challenge for a world title—or for any wrestling championship. It also marked the end of Kelly's involvement in St. Louis wrestling, where his father had been such a key player for a quarter century.

In 1983 Kelly wrestled primarily for Jim Crockett Promotions and held a share of the NWA Mid-Atlantic Tag Team title for a time with George "One Man Gang" Gray, a gigantic wrestler who would later achieve some success in the WWF. Key wrestlers on the Crockett roster made regular visits to Toronto for Sunday night shows at Maple Leaf Gardens, and while Kelly appeared in Toronto at least 10 times in 1983, he was not there on May 15, when Canada's Greatest Athlete, at age 54, made his only appearance of the year—and the last of his career—at Maple Leaf Gardens, wrestling in a tag team match on the undercard five days after the death of long-time Toronto promoter Frank Tunney, whose funeral was the reason for Kiniski's brief visit to Ontario. Kelly was booked that day to wrestle a total of three matches on afternoon and evening shows in Asheville and Charlotte, North Carolina.

Gene Kiniski made a brief return to St. Louis in 1983, battling Dick Murdoch to a no contest and participating in a battle royal on June 10. By that point St. Louis, sorely missing the leadership Sam Muchnick had provided for decades, was in the process of unraveling as a leading wrestling center.

In late 1983 Kiniski returned to the Crockett promotion as a guest referee to oversee a cage match pitting NWA champion Harley Race against challenger Ric Flair, who had dropped the title to Race in mid-year. The cage match was the main event of Jim

Crockett Promotions' inaugural Starrcade extravanganza, held November 24, 1983, in Greensboro, North Carolina, with close to 16,000 fans in attendance. Though Kelly Kiniski, who was still active in the promotion, did not appear on the show, several wrestlers who had some history with Gene Kiniski—namely, Mike "The Brute" Davis as Bugsy McGraw, Mark Lewin, Abdullah the Butcher, Wahoo McDaniel, Angelo Mosca, Roddy Piper, Jay Youngblood, and, of course, both combatants in the main event—were on the card.

While Kiniski's relative inexperience as a referee led to some awkward-looking moments, he was cast as a fair-minded ref who generally called things down the middle, frequently mixing it up with the wrestlers as he sought to keep them in line. The end came after Race, who had the upper hand through much of the match, accidentally headbutted Kiniski, who was slow to get up. As Kiniski recovered, Flair delivered a flying bodypress off the top rope onto his opponent, and Kiniski, still down after taking the headbutt, counted the pin after about 24 minutes. Following the match Kiniski had a few words with both bloody combatants, handed the NWA title belt to Flair and shook his hand, and quietly left the ring as Flair celebrated his victory with fellow wrestlers.

Kiniski made no other documented ring appearances in 1983—and, most notably, none in the Pacific Northwest. The decision to walk away from All-Star Wrestling and turn over absolute control to Al Tomko was, in Kiniski's mind, irreversible, and his estimation of Tomko as a promoter dictated that he would never set foot again in an All-Star Wrestling ring.

But Kiniski was not yet finished putting his imprint on the wrestling industry in the Northwest—even if the manner in which he did so in 1983 likely caught many followers of wrestling in the region by surprise.

Stu Hart's Calgary-based Stampede Wrestling was a much stronger promotion overall than All-Star Wrestling was in the early 1980s, and Stampede Wrestling had a superior roster of wrestlers and a far more entertaining TV program when booker Bruce Hart and his father Stu made the call to pull the promotion out of the NWA in 1982, relieving the Harts of a professional commitment not to encroach on a fellow NWA promoter's territory. Before the end of 1982, Stampede Wrestling could be seen weekly on television in the BC Lower Mainland, and a West Coast invasion by Stampede Wrestling seemed imminent.

While it is widely believed Kiniski maintained a wariness with regard to Stu Hart—partly because his of general suspicion of promoters but also because he felt Hart had long taken undue credit for training him to be a wrestler—Kiniski clearly was supportive of Hart's expansion to the West Coast in April of 1983. By some accounts Kiniski—who had displayed a photo of himself, Hart, and Joe Blanchard in his office for years—was the key force in convincing Hart the time was right to expand to Vancouver.

"Gene pretty much begged him to come out there," says Bruce Hart.

Bruce Hart continues, "Gene [did] virtually nothing other than inviting my dad out there to get rid of Tomko." While Kiniski took on the role of West Coast promoter for Stampede Wrestling, Hart says Kiniski's efforts at promoting Stampede's early shows on the coast involved nothing more than placing ads in the local paper. Yet, he says, "I heard [Gene was getting] anywhere from 10 to 20 percent of the gate."

Hart continues, "My dad probably could have gone out there without Gene at all.... We had a hell of a crew at that time—Dynamite [Kid], Davey [Boy Smith], Bret [Hart], and all the other guys. We were really doing good business."

According to Hart, Kiniski's failure to hype Stampede's shows in the local market—combined with his habit of "coming into the dressing room and kind of making snide remarks about 'midgets' [when he referred] to [the size of] Dynamite and some of the Japanese wrestlers on the card"—disappointed or alienated many of the wrestlers. Hart says his father, after West Coast personality and talent manager Bruce Allen expressed an interest in helping promote Stampede Wrestling shows on the coast, "started letting Allen do all the promoting there and the hyping on CFOX [Radio and] the newspapers and [media] like that." Allen's efforts, says Hart, enhanced Stampede's standing as "a really hot ticket out there." Hart adds that while Allen took over virtually all of the local promotion for Stampede Wrestling's shows, Kiniski continued to receive his share of the gate.

"My dad was a man of his word," he says.

According to Hart, Kiniski and Allen proved incompatible when Kiniski presumably saw the latter as stepping on his toes and, as some observers report, seemed to resent Allen's success in spiking Stampede's attendance in Vancouver—and effectively driving Tomko's floundering promotion out of the city to a smaller venue in Surrey/Cloverdale. During a show in Vancouver, says Hart, "Davey came running to my dad and me. He said that Bruce Allen just left in a huff and Gene tried to physically throw him out of the building."

Hart continues, "There was a big standoff, almost like a mini mutiny with wrestlers. Davey and Dynamite and Ron Starr and a few others basically said, 'If Gene doesn't go, we're quitting,' or something like that…. Stu was going to have to make a choice between Bruce Allen or Gene. My dad was pissed off with being forced to make a decision. [He had] longstanding ties with Gene from the 1940s till that time. He ended up telling Gene he had to bow out."

Hart says events of that evening took a heavy toll on a 36-year-old wrestling promotion and on a friendship of similar longevity. In 1984 Stu Hart sold Stampede Wrestling to the expanding World Wrestling Federation. "That was kind of predicated on the Gene and Bruce Allen thing," says Hart. "I wouldn't necessarily blame [Gene], but there was a lot of resentment." As far as the Stu Hart-Kiniski friendship was concerned, Bruce Hart says, "I don't know if they ever really spoke after that."

In February of 2002, Kiniski, recollecting events of 1983–1984, told Oliver that Hart was "not one of my favorite people…. I didn't have anything in writing, and again, I'm not mad at him, I'm mad at myself for being so stupid. I trusted him. Him and Vince made a move and all of a sudden I'm sitting on the outside looking in."

But even during his 1980s fling with Stampede Wrestling, most of Kiniski's attention in semiretirement was not on professional wrestling but on activities such as working out, reading, socializing, and supporting Nick's efforts on the amateur mat. Gene Kiniski had a single recorded match in 1984, though it was a memorable one, as he teamed one last time with Dick the Bruiser on a Kiel Auditorium show as the pair lost to AWA Tag Team champions Jerry "Crusher" Blackwell and Ken Patera. Kiniski was flown to St. Louis for that show as a replacement for the injured Ted DiBiase. The only other ring appearances for Kiniski in 1984 appear to have been a couple of bookings as a guest referee on AWA shows in Manitoba, where he officiated tag team matches on March 21 in Brandon and October 18 in Winnipeg.

Kiniski kept a close watch as Nick wound up his amateur wrestling career with an alternate spot on Canada's 1984 Olympic freestyle wrestling team. Gene Kiniski is also credited with helping Bob Molle, Nick's roommate at Simon Fraser, bounce back from a serious back injury and surgery after barely two weeks—just in time to compete as a freestyle wrestling super heavyweight at the 1984 Los Angeles Olympics.

Although Molle's coach at the time, Mike Jones, says on the Simon Fraser University Clan website, "The head surgeon for the Olympic team said it would be impossible for Molle to wrestle," Steve Frost reports, on the Clan website entry about Molle, "With friend Gene Kiniski at his side pushing him on, Molle found the resolve, and three days before his first match he arrived in Los Angeles." Molle, who Jones, on the website, says had lost 20 pounds and could barely walk shortly before the Olympics, won the silver medal in Los Angeles—in the process, according to Frost, displaying "a courage that wowed audiences."

Molle, who later starred for the CFL Winnipeg Blue Bombers, recalls, more than three decades after his silver-medal effort at the Olympics, "About three weeks before the Olympics I found out I [needed] a back operation.... I had what was called a sequestered disk.... A piece of the disk had broken away, and so they had no choice but to operate because it was protruding in my nerve and was just going to get eventually worse."

In his book *Get Comfortable Being Uncomfortable: Improving Your Performance*, Molle reveals that his back problems seemed to be the result of intense training with future super-heavyweight pro wrestler John Tenta, who outweighed him by more than 150 pounds.

Molle says, by phone, "I had no choice but to do the surgery.... It was just starting to embed in my nerve, and I was losing function in my left leg." At that point, thoughts of participating in the 1984 Olympics were fast slipping away from Molle.

Also by phone, Jones recalls, "I had no thought that he would even be able to come close to being able to wrestle."

Molle had met Nick Kiniski four years earlier, in 1980, when "Nick beat me at the Canadian national wrestling tournament in my hometown of Saskatoon, Saskatchewan. He beat me in the finals, so he was a bit of a—excuse my expression—a prick at the time because he beat me in the final in front of my parents and all the family and everybody.... [But] weird enough, at the end of the tournament, when we were sitting around the locker room later on, he came up to me and we started chatting.... I'd never met the guy before and, personally, hated him because, to tell the truth, I lost to him. And he recruited me to Simon Fraser."

At the time, says Molle, "I didn't even know who Gene Kiniski was."

Molle first met Gene Kiniski after arriving on the West Coast in mid-1981 to take up his place at Simon Fraser University. A primary training partner of Nick's and both a football and wrestling star at SFU, Molle quickly became "part of the family"—alternating between time on the SFU campus with roommate Nick and long spells at the Kiniski residence. "We'd spend our off-season with Gene in Blaine," says Molle. "I think we had four or five summers there with him"—typically, training in the morning, attending SFU wrestling practice in the evening, and working nights at a bar.

Gene played an active role in Nick's and Molle's training in Blaine, says Molle. "Gene would beat the shit out of us, like, you know, 'Wake up! How many eggs do you want? Do you want 8 ... 10 ... 12?' He was always trying to get you bigger and stronger. Everything was old school—you know, more is better. He was like an egg and steak guy, meat and potatoes kind of guy, and just wanted [us] to get bigger and stronger."

Describing Kiniski as his "second dad," Molle outlines a tender side of the man he refers to as his mentor. "He'd say, 'I love you.' He'd kiss you on the lips good night. When we lived in Blaine, it was just the way he'd tuck you in."

Not surprisingly, Molle says Kiniski was also able to deliver a tougher brand of love when necessary. Molle, who worked with Nick just across the border at the Tudor pub in White Rock, BC, recalls, "If we ever got caught drinking and driving, we were dead. We knew that."

Molle says Kiniski sometimes took preemptive measures to ensure the two young amateur wrestling stars under his wing stopped short of drinking too much. At times, says Molle, "Gene would jump in the car at two in the morning … [and] come walking in [the bar] in pajamas and slippers…. 'What are you guys doing?' No one would screw with us. Nick and I were two big wrestlers that everybody knew … and Gene would walk in and grab us by the earlobes. So you've got these two big, supposedly tough guys…. Gene would be half asleep. He'd be rubbing his eyes. He's in his housecoat, pajamas, and slippers in a bar … grabs us by the earlobes, and takes us home."

Once, when he missed a workout after drinking too much the night before, Molle says, "Gene grilled me. I never forgot that."

The same Tudor pub where Molle and Nick worked had been a favorite destination of the Kiniski family for years, and friends of Gene's recall how he used to walk across the border to enjoy perogies—a Ukrainian specialty and long-time favorite food of his—fresh out of the Tudor kitchen. Nick remembers how, as a boy at the Tudor, he would sometimes get physical with patrons who didn't show his father proper respect.

"Dad was always afraid of getting sued," he says, so "when guys were mouthing off to my dad, I'd just pop 'em … knock 'em down … sucker punch 'em. What are they gonna do—sue a 12-year-old kid?"

When his father asked why he'd roughed up a customer, Nick says, "[I'd explain,] 'I didn't like how he talked to you.' And we'd continue like nothing went on. That was just normal life for us."

Training with Gene Kiniski was intense, says Molle. As an example, he recalls, "Gene was crazy about neck exercises. First thing in the morning … we had to do neck exercises because he didn't want any of us [to get] hurt in football or wrestling and be paraplegic. It was like a morning ritual. You had to lay down … where the pool table was, and you'd have to do neck exercises every morning. And he'd stand there and he'd put his big mitts across your face, and then you'd have to go all different ways…. You had four sets of reps, and he stood there every morning, and you know what he used to do? Measure your neck…. He was all prevention—that you'd never get your neck damaged because you'd have a good support system."

After his back injury shortly before the 1984 Olympics saw him hospitalized in New Westminster, BC, Molle says, "I wake up the next day after surgery and I'm all whacked out on drugs and everything else, and guess who's there at the bedside? Gene." Molle recalls Kiniski greeting him: "'Bob, how you doing? We've got to get training.'"

> He goes, "What do you want to do?" … I've got a catheter in. I'm trying to get rid of the catheter just to go to the bathroom…. So he goes, "Yeah? Well, let's try. Let's get rid of the catheter, and let's walk to the bathroom." I said, "Is it okay to walk?" He said, "We can do anything."
>
> So I take my first step, and I don't have enough balance [and] fall flat on my face. I didn't even get my hands up in front of my face. I hit the cement, and my nose popped…. The nurse [heard and] comes running. "What's going on? What's going on?"
>
> "Oh, we're just going to the bathroom."
>
> "You just got out of back surgery. What are you walking for?"

Molle continues, "And Gene kind of looks at me. He goes, 'I guess we'll try that again tomorrow.'"

The next day, Molle recalls, "He held on to me. We got to the bathroom." During his weeklong stay in the hospital, Molle says, "Every morning [Kiniski] would drive up from Blaine" to help him to the bathroom and lead him in walking, stretching, and doing whatever exercise his mentor thought Molle could handle. "He pushed the boundaries … to see how fast I could recover. [He said,] 'Bob, we're not average people. We're going to recover.'"

As Gene Kiniski later recounted in an article by Richard E. Clark, "I had to get him up…. The surgery cut through massive muscles. Ice packs were applied. But we couldn't use any drugs because those would prove positive and disqualify him."

Molle says Kiniski wouldn't be deterred from taking the lead at the hospital. He recalls Kiniski offering instructions—"Nurse, we're going to do this and that"—to those entrusted with Molle's care.

Molle recalls getting in a week of "training" under Kiniski while in hospital, followed by a week of training at SFU and some final training in Los Angeles before the freestyle wrestling competition got underway at the Olympics—fortunately, Molle says, near the end of the Games, giving him time to get in just enough training. To emphasize how close he came to missing out on his dream, Molle says he watched the opening ceremony of the 1984 Los Angeles Olympics from his hospital bed in British Columbia.

But less than three weeks later, Molle was an unlikely silver medalist in freestyle wrestling—and he gives full credit to Gene Kiniski.

"The biggest thing he changed for me," says Molle, "was the fear of failure…. When you came out and talked to him, you felt you could take on the world."

Molle recalls how he and Nick—enrolled at a small NAIA college that didn't meet NCAA standards—were sometimes regarded as "David taking on Goliath" when they participated in major wrestling competitions in the United States. Referring to a tournament which both he and Nick were scheduled to face former NCAA champions in the semifinals, Molle recalls Gene Kiniski asking, "How can they call themselves champions if they haven't wrestled you guys yet?"

Molle says, "That was Gene … the way he taught us."

As it turned out, both Molle and Nick won their semifinals. Then, in the tournament final, Molle came from behind to beat Nick.

After graduating from SFU, Nick made his debut as a professional wrestler. "It was something I just always wanted to be," he says. Nick credits Erich Froelich, who worked with him at the bar, with helping train him to be a pro wrestler.

Molle's interest, meanwhile, lay in another area, and he fulfilled a second dream by playing seven seasons of professional football as an offensive lineman and, eventually, team captain for the Winnipeg Blue Bombers. He was on two Grey Cup-winning squads and remains the only person to have won a Grey Cup and an Olympic medal. In 2016—long after being inducted to the British Columbia and Saskatchewan Sports Halls of Fame—Molle was named to the Blue Bombers Hall of Fame.

Molle, who remained close to the Kiniskis, says of his mentor, "My kids used to call him Grandpa Gene." When Molle's family visited the West Coast from Manitoba and Molle had plans of his own, "We'd just dump the kids off at Grandpa Gene's…. He'd feed them all up and play with them in the water." And, while Grandpa Gene is gone now, Molle, who lives again on the coast, in Victoria, BC, remains close to his children's "Uncle Nick," who regularly travels to Victoria by boat from his home on Orcas Island, Washington.

21. Slowly Winding Down

> **Province of British Columbia**
> OFFICE OF THE MINISTER
>
> **Ministry of Provincial Secretary and Government Services**
>
> Parliament Buildings
> Victoria
> British Columbia
> V8V 1X4
>
> August 9, 1984
>
> Mr. Gene Kiniski
> Box 1297
> Blaine, Washington 98230
> U.S.A.
>
> Dear Mr. Kiniski:
>
> It has been brought to my attention, as Minister responsible for sport in British Columbia, that you have had a significant influence on the athletic development of one of our top athletes.
>
> Please accept my heartiest congratulations for the part you have played in Bob Molle's preparations for the 1984 Olympics in Los Angeles.
>
> For these Olympics, British Columbia has qualified more athletes than ever before and it is largely due to individuals such as yourself who have generously given their time, talent and experience.
>
> On behalf of all the British Columbians who will be watching our athletes at the Olympics in Los Angeles with rapt attention, I thank you for your contribution to amateur sport.
>
> Yours sincerely
>
> James R. Chabot
> MINISTER

Gene Kiniski was a great supporter of amateur sport who played a huge role in helping 1984 silver-medalist wrestler Bob Molle get ready for the Olympics after Molle suffered a serious injury three weeks before the Games. Molle says it is an "understatement" that Kiniski helped him recover in time for the Olympics, adding that "the beautiful thing that Gene brought everybody, I think, was confidence" (Kiniski family archive).

As far as Nick's pro wrestling career was concerned, after making his debut in early 1985 he spent much of the year in Texas, appearing regularly on shows run by World Class Championship Wrestling (WCCW), the promotion owned and operated out of Dallas by Fritz von Erich. According to Nick, he had the opportunity to team with his father twice during his rookie year in the Lone Star State. Kelly also spent much of 1985 wrestling in Texas, and according to www.wrestlingdata.com, the Kiniski brothers had the opportunity to team there on a few occasions that year, and at least once in neighboring Louisiana.

On October 6, 1985, Gene Kiniski made an appearance at WCCW's major show of the year—a much-hyped extravaganza that drew upwards of 25,000 fans to the Cotton Bowl in Dallas. Gene Kiniski did not wrestle on the show but seconded Kelly—sporting a crewcut and a strong resemblance to his father—before climbing into the ring after the match to celebrate Kelly's victory, set up with a backbeaker, over Tommy Montana in what was Kelly's last match with the promotion. Prior to that, Kelly says, he and Gene—who got a good reception from the Cotton Bowl crowd—had the opportunity to team up in Texas. Meanwhile, Gene Kiniski made two other documented ring appearances in 1985—one, a loss in St. Louis on February 15 to Wahoo McDaniel, and the other, a Christmas night disqualification loss to Billy Two Eagles on a Portland, Oregon, show on which Nick Kiniski—about to become a regular in Don Owen's Pacific Northwest Wrestling—was also booked.

Other than a "legends" battle royal two years later in New Jersey and a totally unexpected series of matches when he was 63, Gene Kiniski's Christmas 1985 undercard appearance in Portland is the final entry in the Gene Kiniski record book. He would remain close to a few friends in the wrestling business and leave Blaine on occasion afterward to make wrestling-related appearances, but by the time he returned home from that brief visit to Portland in late 1985, every indication is that Gene Kiniski was a very happily retired man.

22

Endgame

Gene Kiniski's association with the wrestling business remained intact long after his days as a serious wrestler were over in the early 1980s. Recognized by fans and media as a luminary in his profession, Kiniski—relieved of the pressures of actively owning a share of the British Columbia territory he had helped run for a decade and a half—was free to focus on promoting the interests of other wrestling promotions when the opportunities came.

Along with his association with Stampede Wrestling in 1983 when the Hart family saw the opportunity to knock Al Tomko's declining All-Star Wrestling out of the Vancouver market, Kiniski also had a hand in promoting AWA shows in Vancouver in early 1985. Ed Moretti, who wrestled on one of the AWA shows in Vancouver, confirms that Kiniski was a front man for Verne Gagne's American Wrestling Association, which at the time had designs on competing with Vince McMahon's WWF as a national and international wrestling promotion. Despite his ambitions, Gagne could never match McMahon's ability to change with the times, and by the early 1990s the AWA would be just one more competing company the WWF would put out of business. As far as Vancouver was concerned, Neil Drummond, a key player on camera and behind the scenes with All-Star Wrestling in the 1980s, says Kiniski delivered promos on AWA television programming viewable in British Columbia to tout the arrival of that promotion's product in Vancouver.

The WWF had already established itself in Vancouver when the AWA ran its Vancouver shows in January, March, and April of 1985. While the AWA's debut in the market was semi-successful, outdrawing a WWF card in Vancouver the previous month, crowds declined over the course of the three AWA shows—in part, because of no-shows by key wrestlers—and the AWA cut its losses and never held a fourth event in British Columbia. From Kiniski's perspective, while any contributions he made when it came to helping promote the AWA's expansion to British Columbia were no match for what was afoot with the WWF, he likely derived some satisfaction from putting his name and some effort behind one more attempt to promote an alternative to the product Tomko was presenting in British Columbia by 1985—featuring Tomko himself as a main-event wrestler.

While the WWF was well on its way to dominating all aspects of North American professional wrestling by the early stages of Gene Kiniski's retirement, he would never play a significant role in that organization.

But on August 28, 1987, in Houston, he appeared on a retirement show for a legendary wrestling promoter, as he had done in St. Louis on New Year's Day 1982. The Houston show, which drew 12,000 to the Sam Houston Coliseum, honored Paul Boesch, who had been active in Houston wrestling when Kiniski headlined shows in the city in the 1950s. Shortly before retiring three decades later—most of that time as the owner-promoter of Houston Wrestling—Boesch formed a brief promotional partnership with the WWF, and his August 1987 retirement show was a WWF event.

Appearing on the show—either as dignitaries or wrestlers—along with Kiniski were many of his associates over the years, including Verne Gagne, Lou Thesz, Stu Hart, Ernie Ladd, Billy "Red" Lyons, Jack Tunney (Frank's brother, who had taken over the Toronto promotion), Terry Funk, Mark Lewin, and Bruno Sammartino (who, at 52, wrestled on the show).

While Sammartino and Kiniski had sold out arenas together in the 1960s, Sammartino recalled in 2017, "When we were wrestling, the only time I saw him, practically, was in the ring.... In those days you didn't socialize ... or be seen with an opponent." Though they apparently met only twice after the prime of their careers—in Houston for the Boesch tribute and a dozen years later, in Japan, where they would participate in a tribute to another legendary promoter—Sammartino said, of Kiniski, "Outside the ring, as I got to know him after we were retired, he was a great guy."

On November 1, 1987, about two months after the Boesch tribute show, Kiniski participated in a "legends" battle royal on a WWF show at the Brendan Byrne (Meadowlands) Arena in East Rutherford, New Jersey, just outside New York City. Also participating in the match were former Kiniski associates and fellow "legends" including Bobo Brazil, The Crusher, Nick Bockwinkel, Pat O'Connor, Édouard Carpentier, Ray Stevens, Al Costello, Art Thomas, Joe "Chief Jay Strongbow" Scarpa, Dominic DeNucci, Killer Kowalski, and Lou Thesz, who won the battle royal. According to Nick Kiniski, who had been

On Oct. 5, 1997, the World Wrestling Federation paid tribute to some key figures in St. Louis wrestling history during a WWF pay-per-view event in the city. Honored were former NWA champions (back row, left to right) Lou Thesz, Jack Brisco, Gene Kiniski, Dory Funk, Jr., Harley Race, and Terry Funk. Also honored was long-time St. Louis promoter Sam Muchnick (front row center), flanked by WWF agents Jerry Brisco (front left) and Pat Patterson (photograph by Dr. Mike Lano / *Wrealano@aol.com***).**

on the WWF roster for nine months before jumping to the AWA in mid–1987, Gene Kiniski, despite his differences with Vince McMahon, Sr., and the WWWF more than two decades earlier, had no reservations about appearing on the show. "He let bygones be bygones," says Nick.

Gene Kiniski's only other recorded post-retirement appearance on a WWF show would not take place until a decade later, when he participated in a ceremony at the Kiel Center (now Scottrade Center), a larger, upgraded facility built on the site of the former Kiel Auditorium in St. Louis. In a ceremony hosted by the WWF's Jim Ross on an October 5, 1997, pay-per-view event attended by more than 21,000, Kiniski was honored in the ring along with other St. Louis wrestling luminaries Thesz, Muchnick, Race, Jack Brisco, Dory Funk, Jr., and Terry Funk—all friends Kiniski was proud to share the ring with—before returning to the Northwest to participate in a "parade of sports heroes" during halftime of a BC Lions game at BC Place Stadium on October 10, 1997.

Two years earlier, in August of 1995, Gene and Nick Kiniski had traveled to St. Louis to participate in a red carpet celebration honoring Muchnick, who was turning 90. A letter Muchnick's daughter sent to Kiniski two weeks before the celebration says, "Gene, my father has many so-called friends, but not true friends like you!" Other than the Kiniskis, only a few people involved in wrestling—most notably, Thesz and Larry Matysik—were invited to the celebration.

Kiniski and Lou Thesz (right) met a few times in the 1990s at events usually honoring the achievements of one or both. Each was known to hold the other in high regard, and their professional careers were inextricably linked on January 7, 1967, when Kiniski defeated multi-time champion Thesz in St. Louis to capture the NWA World Heavyweight championship (Vance Nevada collection).

Nick recalls, "[Dad] just thought the world of Sam Muchnick."

A decade after his appearance as a referee at Starrcade, Kiniski participated in Slamboree, a 1993 wrestling extravaganza hosted by World Championship Wrestling (WCW)—the Atlanta-based rebranded version of what, essentially, had been Jim Crockett Promotions until that promotion was acquired by the Ted Turner communications empire in the late 1980s. At the May 23, 1993, Slamboree event, legends Kiniski and Verne Gagne seconded Dory Funk, Jr., and Nick Bockwinkel, respectively—legends themselves—who wrestled to a 15-minute draw which saw Kiniski get involved by jogging in and out of the ring as he delivered a stomp to Bockwinkel, who had caught Funk in a figure-four leglock in the waning moments of a match that fans in Atlanta's Omni Coliseum seemed to appreciate.

Billed as a legends' reunion, Slamboree 1993—the first of eight annual WCW Slamboree shows to be held before WCW was acquired by the WWF in 2001—honored or featured an impressive list of big-name wrestlers and wrestling personalities with ties to

Kiniski, including Lou Thesz, Eddie Graham, Lord Blears, John Tolos, Mike "Bugsy McGraw" Davis, The Crusher, Stu Hart, Don Owen, Johnny Valentine, and Bob Geigel. Wrestling on the show, besides Funk and Bockwinkel, were several competitors whose careers had intersected with Kiniski's, including Ivan Koloff, Baron von Raschke, Thunderbolt Patterson, Don Muraco, Dick Murdoch, Wahoo McDaniel, and Jimmy Snuka.

Besides making occasional appearances in the St. Louis area and elsewere in the United States after his retirement from the ring, Kiniski continued his long association with Giant Baba by appearing from time to time with All Japan Pro Wrestling, a promotion noted at the time for continuing to honor and even feature familiar legends such as The Destroyer, Mil Mascaras, Abdullah the Butcher, and the Funks. Concerning Kiniski's continued association well into retirement with All Japan Pro Wrestling, Benny Grabow recalls, "For many years they would send him a first-class ticket to come to Tokyo. They remembered him for years and years, and he said, 'Benny, it's so damn easy. They fly me business class, and I get here and then they hand me US$10,000 just to get into the ring and wave to the crowd and shake some hands.'"

A few months after Baba passed away in early 1999, recalled Sammartino, "They brought back some of the so-called legends, and [Gene] and I were there at the same time" to pay tribute to Baba. Others on hand to help fill the Tokyo Dome included The Destroyer and Lord Blears. Looking back on his chance to socialize a bit more with Kiniski, Sammartino said, "He had a great personality. He could be funny, you know, and serious, but he was just different from what you saw in the ring."

In 2000 Kiniski was selected to play the ceremonial role of interim commissioner of the Pacific Wrestling Federation, All Japan's storyline governing body, after Blears stepped down as commissioner. Kiniski stayed only briefly in the ceremonial post, appearing on a single tour in October, though clearly he enjoyed one last generous payday in Japan and the opportunity to connect once more with fans who remembered him from his heyday.

Another wrestling center Kiniski returned to after retirement was Winnipeg, where he had headlined many shows over the course of two decades. Tony Condello, a longtime Manitoba promoter who ran shows in opposition to Tomko and the AWA for many years, recalls, "As a kid I used to watch [Kiniski] at the Winnipeg Arena." Following Kiniski's retirement in the 1980s, Condello, who owned several hairdressing salons in Winnipeg, booked Kiniski to sign autographs at a shopping center. According to Condello, a long line waited to get Kiniski's autograph.

Several years later, still running independent shows in Winnipeg that were televised locally, Condello had a conversation with one of Kiniski's friends and fellow wrestling greats.

"Nick Bockwinkel was an agent for Vince McMahon at that time in the WWF," says Condello. "When Bockwinkel was in Winnipeg he asked me, 'Tony, do you need a special guest referee? Maybe you should give a call to a good friend of mine, Gene Kiniski.' I said, 'That's a very good idea.'"

Condello recalls calling Kiniski, who was 63 at the time. "I asked if he'd like to come meet his friend Nick Bockwinkel in Winnipeg and be a special guest referee for television here."

Condello says Kiniski responded, "Sure, Tony. No problem. I'd like to see Winnipeg again and meet Nick."

But then, on February 25, 1992, the day of the show, the unexpected happened.

22. Endgame

"While [Kiniski] is putting his boots on to referee the event," recalls Condello, "Nick Bockwinkel called me [aside] and said, 'Tony, you should ask Gene if he wants to be, instead of being a referee, if he wants to wrestle.' So I go to Gene [and] I say, 'Gene, the young guys here … they respect you, the legend Gene Kiniski. You know, if you put your boots on and your trunks to wrestle instead of refereeing, you know, they'd be more … appreciative.' … He says, [good-naturedly,] 'Hey Tony, Nick Bockwinkel put you up to this!' I said, 'You know what? You're right. But I'm asking you.' And he did. That time on the card we had Chris Jericho … Lance Storm … young guys that became famous later on."

Condello adds, "That's how I got Gene Kiniski on video," referring to the last video recording of Kiniski as a wrestler, viewable on YouTube in 2018.

Gene Kiniski made few wrestling-related appearances after serving briefly as All Japan's commissioner in 2000. In his *SLAM!* chat posted on November 10 of that same year, he said, "I do a lot of TV, radio, [and] newspaper interviews." But he acknowledged, with regard to "[w]hat is happening in wrestling today, I don't think I could add anything to it. I would distort the TV picture for them."

Later in the same chat, however, Canada's Greatest Athlete added, "I'm 72 now. If my knees were good, I could still wrestle."

23

You couldn't help but love the guy"

While Gene Kiniski met some of the demand for his presence at wrestling events and made himself available for interviews from time to time, the vast majority of his time after retiring from wrestling was spent in the comfort of the spacious three-bedroom home in Blaine's Harbor View Heights that he and Marion had built in 1972, the year before they divorced. While Gene and Marion Kiniski's marriage did not survive long after the Kiniskis moved into their new home, Kelly Kiniski says his father, even when he was well into retirement, never entertained thoughts of living anywhere else.

Kelly, who lived with his father and brother Nick at the Harbor View Heights home for nearly four years before leaving for college in Texas in 1976, says, "[Dad] always said he would never move out of it." Referring to the tragic event that took place during his freshman year at West Texas, Kelly continues, "That's probably because when my mother committed suicide, he buried the ashes right outside his bedroom door."

Speaking of his father, Kelly continues, "He was a tough ass and all of that, but after she committed suicide … that was the only woman my dad, I think, ever really loved."

According to Kelly, the Kiniski house, after Marion's departure and death, "stayed exactly as my mom decorated it. Nothing was changed."

Grabow, who moved from Edmonton to Vancouver around 1966 and says he met Kiniski in Blaine "at least once a week when he wasn't traveling," recalls that Marion used to shop at auctions for items of furniture that needed work. Recalling that Marion had a gift for finishing furniture, Grabow says, "Many, many years after Marion died, [Gene] never changed one bit of furniture…. Gene never changed one thing in the house…. All the furniture—everything that Marion bought—that wasn't Gene's bag. Marion built a beautiful home for them."

While the house the Kiniskis built in 1972 is no longer in the family's hands, the current owners speak effusively of the old-school home—notable, before getting updated in the 2010s, for being heavy on shag carpet Gene Kiniski was known to rake, and highlighting such colors as avocado green and harvest gold. "He really thought things through," says one of the owners, citing the house's positioning on a hill allowing main entry, unlike other houses in the neighborhood, to the main floor upstairs. "That's a lot easier on me and my wife," he says.

"It's a million dollar view," he adds, with fetching views of the mountains and Boundary Bay and even Puget Sound viewable in the distance. "The whole back of the house is literally all glass. It's like a panorama view, [and] you get this amazing cross breeze. The whole house has totally got a cross breeze, which, in my opinion, is a masterpiece."

Speaking of his first impressions of the Kiniski residence, the current owner says,

"It just reminded me of my youth. It was very nicely decorated.... When you come up the street you can tell it's a nice house. It's a ranch type of a home, but it's got a unique appeal. It's a classy ranch."

Neither owner knew who Gene Kiniski was when they purchased the home, but both say they learned plenty about the ex-owner from talking to neighbors—a few of whom preferred to keep their silence rather than directly offer comments for this book. Both owners say a neighbor confirmed a story others in Blaine were aware of concerning Kiniski's love of guns and his right to fire off a few rounds, even in the comfort of home.

"He had a storage room which we have turned into a bedroom," says one of the owners. "He would stand in that storage room and shoot to the other end, where there's a big rec room [now a bedroom]. He would shoot down at that end, and then they'd go down to the other end and shoot back ... down the hallway.... It's not that big. It's just a hallway."

The co-owner adds, "He would shoot from one end of the downstairs to the other end of the house and open up the door on either end. I think that's just kind of crazy, you know, but I guess he was having fun.... Just hearing what type of person he was, it didn't surprise me.

"He was a carefree person," she says of Kiniski, who was a staunch supporter of the Second Amendment to the U.S. Constitution and a life member of the National Rifle Association.

More than firing bullets across the basement—where Bernie Pascall says Kiniski liked to make ammunition for his hunting trips—Canada's Greatest Athlete devoted much of his time in retirement to keeping in rare condition for a man his age. Kelly Kiniski recalls that his father normally went for about a three-mile run—part of it up the hill in his neighborhood—most days of the week when he was retired. According to Pascall, "He enjoyed running up the hill backwards" to build up his leg muscles. Gene Kiniski was also known for cycling around Blaine, and he frequently found refuge in the basement gym of his home, where, Grabow says, he had taught Kelly and Nick to wrestle. Partial to pushups and neck exercises long after last trading holds in a wrestling ring, Kiniski made time to work out almost every day, usually in the comfort of his modest home gym. "He loved his privacy, first and foremost," Grabow says.

But as much as he valued the quiet and relative privacy of his retired life in Blaine, Gene Kiniski was a gregarious individual who enjoyed socializing—particularly during the years when both of his sons were off making their own names as professional wrestlers—and he liked to get out of town regularly to do some mingling. Grabow recalls, "I would pick Gene up at least once every three weeks. I'd pick him up, and we'd go to the different casinos ... buffets.... Everybody knew him in the state of Washington ... and he'd be signing autographs, and we just had a ball."

Kiniski was not a gambler, Grabow says, explaining that the former NWA World Heavyweight champion would play for small stakes—often sitting at the $3-limit blackjack table—"and his maximum was $20."

Grabow continues, "The people all recognized him. We would sit down and have lunch, and everybody was coming up to him for his autograph, and Gene was good at that. Gene was good with people. And every time we came into the casino the second or third time, he always gathered a crowd. Always.... He loved it. He loved the interaction with the people."

As if to further dispel the image Gene Kiniski had presented for decades on television, Grabow tells about how a nephew of his, suffering from muscular dystrophy, sometimes came along on those casino outings.

"Gene took to him immediately," Grabow says, "and they became immediate friends.... Gene had such a soft heart. He made my nephew's life so livable. He wouldn't do anything [without saying,] 'Bring Bernie. Bring Bernie down.' And Bernie loved him."

But Kiniski mainly lived out a quiet existence in Blaine while his sons were out on the road—as he would continue to do in later years. While Kelly and Nick agree that their father didn't seem ecstatic that his sons were making the same career choice he had made, both younger Kiniskis achieved some success in pro wrestling in the 1980s before deciding to pull the plug on their pro careers while they were still in their twenties.

Both younger Kiniskis spent periods wrestling for a few of their father's friends—Joe Blanchard, Fritz von Erich, and Verne Gagne—in Texas and the Midwest. Nick also spent a period wrestling in the WWF for owner Vince McMahon, Jr., whose father Gene Kiniski felt had shorted him on money when Kiniski helped boost attendance in the Northeast during his run in 1964 and 1965 as the top challenger for Sammartino's WWWF World Heavyweight title. Both younger Kiniskis also toured Japan—Kelly with Baba's All Japan Pro Wrestling and Nick with the rival New Japan Pro Wrestling company owned and headlined by Antonio Inoki.

Kelly decided to call it quits with wrestling, he says, when bookings started getting fewer and fewer, and he suspects his father may have been a factor in his growing difficulty making a living in wrestling.

Kelly says, "I'm pretty sure my dad did not want me to wrestle at all—or my brother. He knew, if you have a house payment and get hurt ... what are you going to do?" Citing the problems between his parents and the likelihood his father had the ear of promoters Kelly was working for, Kelly says, "My dad never told me not to wrestle, but I think behind the scenes, he had a lot to do with it."

Nick Kiniski adds, "I feel my dad didn't really want us in the wrestling business. In hindsight, I don't really blame him. All my buddies are dead—heart attacks, suicide ... [or in] pain."

After retiring from the ring in 1986, Kelly took a job as an electrician in Irving, Texas, near Dallas. Speaking of his transition in and out of wrestling, he says that due to his exposure to the wrestling business and mindset from birth, "wrestling was not a shock to me. When I got *out* of wrestling and found out how normal people live, that's what was ... overwhelming to me."

After a few years in Irving, Kelly, drawn back by his family's roots and the splendor of the region, returned to the Pacific Northwest with his wife at the time. After staying about a year in a Blaine condo, Kelly divorced after his wife returned to Texas, and he relocated to Point Roberts, Washington, a scenic little enclave on the North American mainland having no direct land connection with the rest of the United States. While Blaine and Point Roberts are both in Washington State's Whatcom County, getting from one to the other requires a 25-mile drive and two international border crossings, as Point Roberts juts out below the 49th parallel separating Canada from the United States on a mini Baja-like peninsula and is separated by the waters of Boundary Bay from the rest of the border separating British Columbia from Washington State. During most of the 28 years since Kelly's return to the Northwest, he has specialized in construction, and he owns a small business in Point Roberts. Kelly remarried following his divorce and, in 2018, has been happily wed for more than a quarter century.

Kelly's wife Joyce Kiniski says, of Gene, whom she knew only "as a wrestler on TV" when she met Kelly in the summer of 1990, "He never lost his eye for young, pretty women." Joyce says, "I did not fit the perceived correct mold. I'm not tall, blonde, young … money … slim …. I'm the polar opposite." Yet, she says, once Gene got to know her, "he was okay with me…. I never had any problem with him."

Still, as Kelly reports, Gene Kiniski never got close to Joyce's daughter from a previous marriage. Kelly, now a grandfather of two through his stepdaughter, recalls that there was some tension in the air when it came to his father's relationship with Kelly and Joyce as a couple, which resulted in a situation where Gene Kiniski did not really get to know Joyce's daughter or the couple's grandchildren well. As a result, there was none of the "Grandpa Gene" dynamic Kiniski friends such as Molle, Cox, Pascall, and others observed between their children and Gene Kiniski when it came to Kiniski's relationship with the children best considered his actual grandchildren or great-grandchildren.

"My dad and I butted heads all the time," says Kelly, explaining that the fallout had at least some effect on Gene's relationship with Joyce during a period in which communication between Kelly and his father was strained. As far as his own relationship with his father was concerned, there probably still existed some tension stemming from several years earlier, when Kelly, still wrestling and based at the time in Louisiana, suffered a serious illness that he says put him out of commission for more than three months.

"I thought I was going to die," he says.

Though barely able to speak, Kelly asked his father to come to Louisiana to help him get back on his feet. Gene's response, he says, was simply to advise him to tough it out.

"To this day I don't understand why he didn't come help me," Kelly says. "I wasn't the type of kid to just say 'I need help.' He knew I was a tough kid. I don't know if he was just pissed off at me…. I don't know. I'll never know."

Even so, Kelly—when he was back in the Northwest building a new life—followed his brother's advice to go the extra mile rather than let his relationship with an aging father go sour. "I finally bent over backwards," he says.

Nick Kiniski, meanwhile, was already back in the Northwest when Kelly returned. After closing out his professional wrestling career in 1988, Nick quickly purchased a bar, called it Kiniski's Reef, and began a 30-year run, as of 2018, serving thirsty patrons. From 1996 to 2000 Nick also owned The Breakers, a fish cannery converted into a Point Roberts club noted for live music. Kiniski's Reef remains a popular local oceanside watering hole and eatery, although, with the Canadian dollar having fallen on hard times in recent years, the Reef does not attract the amount of Canadian clientele that it used to.

Nick, a paramedic and battalion chief on Orcas Island, Washington, as well as the proprietor of Kiniski's Reef, recalls that his father enjoyed spending time at the bar, where he mingled with clients and often mixed drinks. By that time Gene Kiniski's drinking days were well in the past, largely due to his sons' insistence that he stop when a few episodes of overindulgence caused him to black out.

"He was here a lot," says Nick. "That's why a lot of people thought he probably owned it."

Long-time Kiniski family friend Mike Hill shares a similar story. Hill, whose father owned some bars around Blaine, says, of Gene Kiniski, "He volunteered at my dad's tavern. Every Tuesday they'd have Gene Kiniski [there]. He did it for 10 or 12 years."

Hill's brother Dennis, who took over the family's Pastime Tavern, recalled "Gene Kiniski's Pool Shoot," which became a well-known weekly event around Blaine, transforming what had been a relatively quiet night of the week at the tavern to one of the most popular.

"He just did it for fun," said Dennis Hill, who passed away in 2017. "He would walk through the bar, pick up ashtrays, clean them up. 'How you doing; how you doing?' ... talk to people, give the ladies hugs."

As far as the waitresses were concerned, Dennis said, "He wouldn't go over the line, but he would just blow smoke about how beautiful they were." One of Kiniski's favorite lines, Dennis said, was, "You're intoxicatingly beautiful. How do *I* look?"

Kiniski was also known to put his cooking skills to use from time to time at the Pastime, which was known to attract some of the professional wrestlers based in Vancouver, several of whom lived in Blaine. Mike Hill recalls Kiniski suggesting, "Let's make perogy night." Hill says, "He'd show up at two in the afternoon, and we'd be there until midnight eating perogies.

"When he cooked it was always huge. If we needed perogies, he'd bring a 50-pound sack of potatoes." And when Kiniski got it into his mind to do a little social cooking at home and not at the bar, Mike Hill says, "It was Thanksgiving every time you went over there for dinner."

The Hills first met the Kiniskis in the late 1960s, when the Kiniskis—after trying tenancy at a few rental properties in Blaine and nearby Birch Bay, and a few years prior to building their home in Harbor View Heights—lived in the first home Gene ever bought, a 1,269-square-foot house on Blaine's G St. Nick Kiniski says the modest residence raised the suspicion of the IRS, which apparently had some difficulty believing it was the first house such a high-profile, world champion wrestler had owned. According to Nick, when the IRS audited his father and asked about the modest nature of his residence, Gene Kiniski answered, "Well, one shot and it's over for me."

Nick says that explanation satisfied the auditor—as did another, when Gene, on a separate occasion, apparently was investigated for claiming drinking tabs as publicity expenses. According to Nick, after his father explained to the auditor that his drinking with reporters or other influential players was not for fun but because "I have to buy drinks for this guy for publicity," he intercepted any objection by asking, "Do you know how much it would cost for me to buy an ad?"

Mike Hill, who is Nick's age, remained close to the Kiniskis throughout their years in Blaine, and after becoming owner of Blaine's Chevron service station off busy I-5 in 1992, Mike Hill assumed a key role in the retirement routine of Gene Kiniski.

Nearly every morning, as long as his health permitted, Kiniski dropped by Hill's Chevron for his daily coffee, along with a little schmoozing. Kiniski's visits usually began around eight in the morning and lasted about an hour. "He had his routine," Hill says. "We even had on the coffee pot, where it says 'brew,' it would say 'Gene Kiniski's brew.' You couldn't help but love the guy."

On mornings when Kiniski couldn't make it in by eight, Hill says, he would call the station and ask, "Mike, do you think it's okay if I come in a little late?"

Hill continues, "I'd laugh my ass off. He was just not your typical person. People would know him after meeting him a few times. I'd always hear 'I've never met a person like that in my life.' He was bigger than life.... What a character. When you say 'Think outside the box,' he's the guy on the outside of the box."

Coming down for his morning coffee was part of Kiniski's fitness program in retirement, as he often covered the two miles each way by cycling or jogging. "It was like a workout for him," says Hill. "Once he got his routine down, you just don't mess with it."

Hill recalls seeing Kiniski jogging through Blaine over a period of many years. Providing vivid evidence to support his view—which few would contest—that Kiniski stood "outside the box," Hill says, "He would always run down H Street, down Harvey Hill, up Sweet Road. Everybody knew him. You'd swear sometimes [he was out] in a one-piece, running in his freaking underwear … he's sweating … ass crack's wet … [like an] escapee out of a prison."

At the Chevron station, just to turn the tables on Kiniski, who was so noted for his quick wit, Hill says that after Kiniski made a morning pot of coffee, "once in a while [we] would send somebody in there who'd say, 'Who made this shit?'"

Needless to say, Kiniski let the critic have it every time. "He was such a character once you got to know him," says Hill, who to this day has a 10-foot-tall picture of Canada's Greatest Athlete on the wall inside the Chevron station.

Kiniski was as steady a visitor as Hill's Chevron had over the better part of two decades. If Kiniski didn't pull into the service station on his bike or in his truck, or come jogging through the door, two or three mornings in a row, chances are he was out of town.

While his morning visits with Mike Hill played an important part in the satisfaction and well-being of a retired Gene Kiniski, Kiniski probably played an equally important role in nurturing the well-being of his friend. Stories abound in Blaine and Vancouver about the impact of Gene Kiniski on the lives of others—encouraging young people to pursue their education, set high standards, and work toward achieving goals; making his name and his presence available for charitable awareness, public causes, and fundraising; sharing his resources with people he trusted who were in need; and impressing on many the importance of keeping in good physical condition—but one of the most striking stories concerns Kiniski's effort, during his early years of retirement, to help Mike Hill lose weight.

Hill says he stayed at Kiniski's house for 17 days in what was essentially a weight loss camp. At the outset, Hill says, Kiniski laid down the ground rules: "This is a fucking democratic household. It's my way or get the hell out here, no questions asked. Do what I say and listen."

Hill continues, "All I could have was a baked potato, nothing on it … cold corn … juice in the morning [but] he took care of me. He'd come down and have sliced carrots for me. He didn't want me to get too hungry, right? But every day we'd do our walk, and after a while I was eating breakfast … orange juice and, like, a hardboiled egg … every night dinner [was] a potato, tomato slices with pepper, a little olive oil on it, and I finally asked him, about the seventh night…. I was getting a little growly … [so] I said … 'I don't think I can eat any more of that.'"

Hill says Kiniski exploded and "kicked me out the door. I was scared." He says Kiniski explained, "You're not eating for flavor. You're eating for effect."

Hill returned, and while it may not have been pleasant, he reports, "I lost 47 pounds in 17 days"—a claim few participants at more traditional weight loss camps would likely make. Kiniski's ability to inspire the seemingly impossible—as Hill, Bob Molle, and others would attest—inspired profound respect from his friends.

Another athlete Mike Hill respected was Muhammad Ali, and Hill recalls attending a fundraising event at Seattle's Olympic Hotel well into Kiniski's retirement. When he saw Ali with his entourage at the hotel, Hill decided to go over and shake the boxing legend's hand. When he did so, Hill says, Ali asked where Hill lived, and it came up in the conversation that Hill and Gene Kiniski lived in the same town.

"Is that old Polack still alive?" Hill recalls Ali asking.

Ali asked that question not merely as a wrestling fan but as someone who had crossed paths with Kiniski, in a significant way, years earlier.

Kiniski was on top of the wrestling world as NWA World Heavyweight champion when Frank Tunney—who promoted boxing shows as well as wrestling—had the opportunity of a lifetime and hosted a Muhammad Ali title defense at Maple Leaf Gardens on March 29, 1966. Ali found a mainly receptive population in Southern Ontario during the height of his opposition to the Vietnam War, and his opponent was Canadian George Chuvalo, known as a determined fighter but not an elite one. In order to drum up interest in the Ali-Chuvalo encounter—which took place, amid the 1960s turmoil, on just 17 days' notice—Tunney turned to the best mouth he knew: world heavyweight wrestling champion and long-time Toronto headliner Gene Kiniski.

Kiniski and Ali engaged in a series of radio "debates" aimed solely at a Canadian audience. Ali, following his conversion to Islam, his denunciation of U.S. policy in Vietnam, and his refusal to be drafted, was on the outs with American media, and his fight with Chuvalo would not be broadcast in his own country. And while no recording of the 1966 "Battle of the Mouths" debates seems to have survived and it is unclear how many of the 13,540 spectators' tickets or thousands of closed-circuit tickets Gene Kiniski helped to sell, his role in the "Battle of the Mouths" is well-remembered.

Though overmatched, Chuvalo managed to become the first boxer to last 15 rounds with Ali, and he received a big payoff six years later when he got a second chance against Ali, in Vancouver. By that time, Ali—who had been stripped of his title and sentenced to prison for refusing to be drafted—was back in the good graces of the U.S. mainstream and was on fire as a boxing attraction in pursuit of the heavyweight title that had been taken from him. Chuvalo, meanwhile, was hugely popular in Canada and known throughout boxing as someone who could tough out a beating against the best.

Ali-Chuvalo II was a fight that definitely could sell itself in the Canadian market. Even so, local promoter Murray Pezim must have been delighted when he learned Ali-Kiniski II would be occurring as a preliminary to Ali-

This is the photograph—10 feet tall—that continues to greet customers at Hill's Chevron in Blaine years after Gene Kiniski made a daily habit of stopping by the station in the morning for a little coffee and a lot of socializing (Kiniski family archive).

Chuvalo II, which took place May 1, 1972, at the Pacific Coliseum and ended with a result not too different from that of Ali-Chuvalo I.

Sports Illustrated writer Robert F. Jones reported, on May 15, 1972, that Ali, just prior to his rematch with Chuvalo, "appeared on a [CKNW Radio] talk show emanating from [Vancouver] in what was billed as the 'Battle of the Windbags.' His opponent was Gene Kiniski, a Vancouver wrestler whose cauliflower ears and zigzag nose belied his quick wit and quicker tongue. After an hour and a quarter of outrageous hyperbole from both contestants, the show's host, a jolly Scot named Jack Webster, declared himself the winner. Ali smiled and shook his head. 'Kiniski,' he said, 'if only there was a white heavyweight boxer like you from Alabama or Mississippi, we could make us a skillion dollars.'"

Wayne Cox says a highlight of the show came after Ali said wrestling was phony and challenged Kiniski to take it outside. "Gene said, 'I would love to once you release me from the handcuffs that are holding me down in this chair,'" recalls Cox. "[Right after that,] there was a whole bunch of thumping noise on the desk, and then the show was over."

Bernie Pascall says Webster, who later joined him at BCTV, "always mentioned that one of the biggest moments and highest-rated radio programs [he ever did was when] Ali and Gene were the featured guests." Concerning Kiniski's part in the promotion of a boxing show in Vancouver, Pascall adds, "Even when Muhammad Ali was front and center, they were leaning towards Gene to help promote Muhammad Ali"—who was perhaps the highest-profile athlete in the world at the time.

Kiniski was known to be generous with his time and money, supporting a variety of causes and lending a hand to friends when they needed help (Kiniski family archive).

As far as charitable activities were concerned, Kiniski was known to support several organizations and causes—Big Brothers, Easter Seals, and Schmockey among them—with his pocketbook, his presence, or both.

Schmockey nights (a variation on "hockey nights") were held over many years in parts of Western Canada to support people with disabilities, and Kiniski—a long-time skater who, as a young Edmonton Eskimo, had taken to the ice regularly with friend and future NHL Canuck General Manager Bud Poile's Western Hockey League Edmonton Flyers squad—participated in more than one Schmockey event in British Columbia during the height of his popularity.

Pascall recalls Kiniski's participation in one Schmockey night in particular, which attracted some premier athletes and 15,000 fans who came out to support the cause of disabled children. One of Kiniski's fellow athletes on hand for the Vancouver event was Angelo Mosca, and Pascall says the appearance of Kiniski and Mosca with a disabled child drew "just a thunderous ovation" from the crowd.

He says, "Here were two mean characters…. Tears were rolling down their cheeks, and these were mean, tough guys…. The people in the stands saw that, and they saw the other side of these two characters in their respective fields—[that] they had a real soft side too."

Summing up Gene Kiniski's motivation to participate in charitable events, Pascall says it often boiled down simply to "If it's for the kids, I'll be there"—though by no means was Kiniski known to withhold his charitable efforts or contributions from others on the basis of age.

24

A Largely Retired Life

Even though Kiniski, in retirement, cherished his privacy in Blaine and his time in Point Roberts tending bar or visiting with his sons, he occasionally left home to attend a funeral or, more often, gave in to the demand for his presence at social events or fundraisers. Making public appearances well into his seventies, Kiniski continued to find receptive audiences, and he regularly stole the show. The wrestling world had not forgotten Kiniski either and made a point of honoring him with a prestigious award from time to time.

Among the accolades Kiniski received in retirement was an award by the Cauliflower Alley Club, a nonprofit organization established in 1965 to honor and support the wrestling industry in general and retired wrestlers in particular. The Cauliflower Alley Club exists and thrives to this day and is now open to wrestlers, ex-wrestlers, others connected with the wrestling industry, and fans. In 1992, just a few weeks after the unexpected series of matches in Winnipeg that closed the curtain on his grappling career, Kiniski was honored by the Cauliflower Alley Club for his outstanding contributions to wrestling.

Washington State native Dean Silverstone got to know Gene Kiniski in the mid–1960s when Silverstone, who had written and sold printed programs at Seattle wrestling shows since his teens, started traveling to Vancouver on Monday nights to sell programs at the major weekly wrestling events in Vancouver. Silverstone later struck out on his own, running his own promotion for two and a half years in the 1970s in Washington State, part of which was viewed by Kiniski and his partners at the time, Kovacs and Owen, and by the NWA as falling within the Northwest Wrestling Promotions/All-Star Wrestling territory. Speaking of his friendship with Kiniski, Silverstone reports in *"I Ain't No Pig Farmer!"* that "it definitely ended in 1973 when I began promoting the state of Washington. He didn't like the fact that I was infringing on what he felt was his to do with as he pleased" (101).

In 1992 Silverstone was a Cauliflower Alley Club director when the club's executive committee voted to honor Kiniski at its annual convention that year. According to Silverstone, Kiniski agreed when Lou Thesz called to ask whether he'd be willing to pay his own way to California to receive the award, as was required of honorees. Silverstone also reports in his book that while Kiniski did not seem disposed toward him at the convention, the two conversed amicably when they ran into each other right afterward at the John Wayne Airport in Orange County before catching the same flight back to Seattle—though that would be the last conversation Kiniski and Silverstone ever had (101).

A decade after being honored by the Cauliflower Alley Club, Kiniski did not speak favorably of the experience or the organization, telling Greg Oliver, "I was there once.

You've got a bunch of assholes who never did anything. TV people that talk about wrestling, wrestlers, and all that. Fuck, it's an insult to my intelligence" (Oliver, Files).

In 1996 Kiniski was inducted as a member of the Wrestling Observer Hall of Fame's inaugural class. While not a traditional, brick-and-mortar hall of fame, the *Observer* institution reflects high standards when it comes to induction and is overseen by *Observer* editor Dave Meltzer, widely regarded as the English-speaking world's leading wrestling journalist—in the true journalistic sense and not the laxer, more fanciful sense often associated with wrestling "journalism." Meltzer, in the August 19, 1996, inaugural Hall of Fame issue of the *Observer*, describes Kiniski as "a hard-nosed big man" who was considered "one of the great workers of his era" and "a top headlining heel [everywhere] he appeared."

While Kiniski would receive further recognition in retirement for his accomplishments in wrestling, he was never inducted into a "sports" hall of fame. Most conspicuous, perhaps, is his absence from the inductee lists of the British Columbia, Alberta, Washington State, St. Louis, and Canada sports halls of fame.

As far as British Columbia is concerned, Pascall, a BC Sports Hall of Famer in the media category who has been the voice of many sports in his adopted province over the course of a distinguished broadcasting career, says there have been efforts to get Kiniski inducted to the BC hall, which is located at Vancouver's BC Place Stadium. While previous efforts to get Kiniski inducted have fallen short, Pascall says, "There's a move afoot now to have him included in some capacity just for his involvement. So many young wrestlers from Simon Fraser and from [the University of British Columbia] were friends of Nick and Kelly Kiniski, and they came down to Gene's home and Gene would spend so much time with people like Bob Molle."

Pascall cites "Gene's commitment to the betterment of young wrestlers that were combining their academics with wrestling" as one reason he is worthy of consideration for a place in the BC hall. "He was very respected and high-profile," says Pascall. Referring to leading sports figures of Kiniski's day in or from Canada such as Jackie Parker, Eagle Keys, and Gordie Howe, Pascall says, "I think if you included Gene's name in that group, people knew who he was. They may not admit that they were wrestling fans, but they certainly knew the name of Gene Kiniski."

Another British Columbia Sports Hall of Famer in the media category, Greg Douglas, worked in public relations for the Western Hockey League's Vancouver Canucks (not to be confused with the later NHL Canucks) in the late 1960s. In

(Left to right) Dick Hutton, Hard Boiled Haggerty, Verne Gagne, and Lou Thesz pose for the camera while attending the 1994 Cauliflower Alley Club convention in Studio City, California. Two years earlier, Kiniski attended his only CAC convention and received an award (photograph by Dr. Mike Lano / *Wrealano@aol.com*).

Danny Hodge (left) and Verne Gagne flank Billy Robinson, recipient of a 1994 Cauliflower Alley Club award and a noted shooter of his era. Hodge, an outstanding amateur wrestler, was recognized as NWA World Junior Heavyweight champion during most of the 1960s and at times in the 1970s (photograph by Dr. Mike Lano / *Wrealano@aol.com*).

1968–1969, Douglas recalls, the Canucks had a strong season but were expected to hit a brick wall when facing the league-leading Portland Buckeroos in the WHL final.

Douglas says, "They were heavily favored to sweep Vancouver.... I talked to Gene and ... asked him if he would come down to our dressing room. I thought, 'Bring Gene Kiniski into a dressing room and heads are going to turn, right?' He was more than willing and went into that room and captivated it, just as I was hoping he would. He wasn't acting.... He was telling them how important it [was] to believe in themselves .... The players just sat there in stone silence, looking at him, and they all knew who he was. These guys were from all over North America." Douglas continues, "The story is that we swept Portland in four games and won the championship—and that team is in the British Columbia Sports Hall of Fame."

Kiniski was a regular and popular guest on a KVOS-TV sports talk show Douglas cohosted with long-time *Vancouver Sun* sports columnist Jim Taylor for the Vancouver market; and, like Pascall, Douglas is one of several notable figures to have written letters or emails on Kiniski's behalf in an effort to get him inducted to the hall. Another is Bret Hart, a brother of Bruce Hart, son of Stu Hart, and one of the most famous wrestlers Canada has ever produced. In his 2007 email supporting the induction of Kiniski to the BC Sports Hall of Fame, Bret Hart calls Kiniski "one of the greatest NWA champions I ever watched" and concludes, "I can't think of any Canadian wrestler more deserving than he is at being inducted into the BC Sports Hall of Fame."

October 7, 1997

Dear Gene:

On behalf of the BC Lions I would like to take this opportunity to thank you for taking the time from your busy schedule to join our parade of sports heroes on October 10 when we celebrate the notion that "This is a Sports Town". With your attendance, we are guaranteed a successful event.

Enclosed are your tickets to the Premier's suite at BC Place for you and your guest. To access the suite, Gate H (near Terry Fox Plaza) would be your best choice for entry into the stadium. Upon your entry, please have the members at the concierge desk direct you to the Premier's suite to begin your evening.

At the start of the 2nd quarter you will be escorted by BC Place security onto the field in preparation for the halftime show. Upon the conclusion of the parade, you will escorted back to the suite to enjoy the remaining two quarters of the game.

Should you have any questions, please do not hesitate to contact my asssitant, Lillian at 930-5483. Thank you once again. Your willingness to join this celebration is greatly appreciated.

Regards,

Glen Ringdal
President

Kiniski was a well-respected member of British Columbia's sporting community over the course of his career and during his retirement. In 1997 the British Columbia Lions recognized Kiniski and other "sports heroes" during halftime of a football game at BC Place Stadium—location of the British Columbia Sports Hall of Fame, to which Kiniski has been nominated for induction several times (Kiniski family archive).

Jason Beck, curator of the BC Sports Hall of Fame since 2006, reports that Gene Kiniski has been nominated for induction three times. Each nomination to the BC hall remains active for three years, followed by a year of inactivity before a nomination can be reintroduced.

The selection committee, which changes from year to year, comprises 15 members: five representing the British Columbia sports media; five from the sporting community; and five BC Sports Hall of Fame trustees or inductees. Seventy-five percent support from the committee—translating to thumbs up from 12 of the 15 members—is required for induction.

"It's a pretty high hurdle," says Beck, "so even if you have two or three individuals that are on the fence or against it, it's pretty tough for any nomination to get in."

Asked how the British Columbia Sports Hall of Fame views professional wrestling, Beck says, "We're not discriminating against any sports. We get nominations for sports that are far more obscure than professional wrestling." Yet he adds that some selection committee members may ask, "Is it a legitimate sport, or is it entertainment? I think that's the point that is kind of a hang-up for professional wrestling."

But Beck says Kiniski "always gets strong support…. He's one of those nominations that always gets votes, and I do know in some years he's been a finalist, which means he's made it to the top 10" of the 50 or 60 nominations to the hall during an average year.

"He definitely is someone I think we should consider fully," Beck says. "At one time he was very likely one of the most well-known British Columbians in any field, and I think that does count for something."

While never a member of the BC hall, Kiniski definitely wasn't out of place when he attended a British Columbia Sports Hall of Fame dinner and sat beside prominent Vancouver businessman and long-time friend Moray Keith, who was a director of the organization and, according to Douglas, "led the charge" to get Kiniski inducted. Keith recalls that Kiniski was introduced to those on hand for the dinner as a Canadian sports representative around the world and "Canada's Greatest Athlete."

"The crowd goes wild," Keith recalls, and Kiniski got a standing ovation.

Kiniski's undeniable presence, quick wit, smooth tongue, and ease in front of a camera led to his making occasional television and film appearances during retirement. He was a proven commodity on television, of course, dating back to the mid–1950s when he made his TV debut in the land of television, Southern California. From there he made numerous television appearances on wrestling shows in locations such as Hawaii, Buffalo, Japan, Alberta, Quebec, Indianapolis, Minnesota, and Texas. Most prominently, he was a featured performer for years on *Wrestling at the Chase* from St. Louis and on broadcasts airing across Canada that featured some of his early matches from Toronto and, later, his performances from Vancouver over a period exceeding 15 years.

Kiniski's name recognition, unique features, and crowd-pleasing aura made him a popular guest on mainstream media aimed at an audience far broader than those who bought wrestling tickets. And from time to time, Canada's Greatest Athlete was called on to speak his mind on the air about sports other than wrestling.

Douglas recalls how Kiniski liked to talk football when he made appearances on Douglas and Taylor's Sunday night KVOS show. Kiniski also did some cohosting of the British Columbia Winter Games on BCTV, mingling with young athletes, as he liked to do, and showing television viewers yet another twist in a character they thought they had figured out years earlier.

Without a doubt, Gene Kiniski was as memorable to the A-listers who ever met him as he was to the people who simply sat high in the stands to watch his matches or to listen to his mastery on the microphone. Arthur Roberts, Kiniski's nephew, who lived for many years in California, says he met Clint Eastwood in a Carmel bar decades after the actor reportedly was a neighbor of Kiniski's for a time in Southern California. According to Roberts, Eastwood didn't say much in the bar but made it clear, when asked, that he remembered Gene Kiniski.

Along with his radio debates with Ali and appearances on mainstream local and regional TV, Kiniski, over many years, appeared occasionally on television programs broadcast across Canada, including *Front Page Challenge*, *Tabloid*, the *Sports Hot Seat*, and the *Alan Hamel Show*. But Kiniski's best-remembered appearance on Canadian network television was probably his exchange on Peter Gzowski's CBC show *90 Minutes Live* in early 1978.

Gzowski, like Kiniski a prominent Polish Canadian, reached a large audience as a leading radio and television host and interviewer on the CBC from the 1970s to the 1990s. And though Gzowski was known to many as Mr. Canada, he met his match the day he hosted Canada's Greatest Athlete.

As R. B. Fleming reports in *Peter Gzowski: A Biography*, "When Peter interviewed former world-champion wrestler Gene Kiniski on March 8, 1978 … the guest took over the show. The big guy, dressed in a vibrant red suit, dwarfed Peter. Kiniski began by talking about his skills as a cook. Peter wanted, instead, to talk about wrestling as theatre. Kiniski wasn't about to agree that professional wrestling was scripted. 'Your hands are shaking,' noted the wrestler. 'Something the matter?'" (229). In reality, Gzowski seemed wise to the nature of the man sitting beside him in the red suit, and his interview with Kiniski (CBC Digital Archives), introduced by Gzowski as someone who "may be the meanest man in Canada," had many of the characteristics of a wrestling interview except specific mention of an upcoming match. Early in the interview, after informing Gzowski that, whether Gzowski mentioned his name or not, the audience would know exactly who he was, Kiniski drove his point home by saying, "If Prime Minister Trudeau and I walked down the street, they'd say, 'The guy with the crewcut is Kiniski. I don't know who the other guy is.'"

After extolling the beauty of Vancouver, offering advice on cooking pork sausage, and talking about high school wrestlers who came to his house, Kiniski recalled his days of wrestling in Toronto and fans there reacting violently to his matches.

"On numerous occasions they've gotten back to me," said Kiniski, "but that is one of the hazards of my chosen occupation and profession."

Kiniski followed up by standing and staring down the studio audience. But when Kiniski returned to his seat, Gzowski got him to break character momentarily by noting, "You'd do better if you could get that twinkle out of your eye, you know."

A moment later, while recalling a series of sellout matches, ending in riots, with Whipper Billy Watson in London, Ontario, Kiniski returned the favor, catching Gzowski off guard by asking, "Has anyone ever told you you have beautiful eyes?"

Kiniski also made a couple of appearances in movies, though the most recognizable film in which Gene Kiniski is credited with appearing is one he never appeared in at all.

In 1978, after achieving fame for writing and starring in *Rocky*, Sylvester Stallone followed up with *Paradise Alley*, a film he wrote, directed, and starred in, about three New York brothers who enter the world of professional wrestling. Stallone, who wrote the script for *Paradise Alley* before hitting it big with *Rocky*, used a collection of professional wrestlers in filming *Paradise Alley*. Among wrestlers credited with appearing in the film were Terry Funk—playing a key role as wrestler Frankie the Thumper—along with Dory Funk, Jr., Ted DiBiase, Don Leo Jonathan, Dick Murdoch, Ray Stevens, Bob Roop, Dennis Stamp, Rock Riddle, Reg Parks, Larry Lane, Don Kernodle … and Gene Kiniski.

But while every list of *Paradise Alley* credits and almost every account of Gene Kiniski's life listing his film appearances seems to confirm that Canada's Greatest Athlete briefly appeared in the film, Kelly Kiniski says that did not happen. A Kiniski did appear in *Paradise Alley*, Kelly says, but it wasn't Gene.

At the time *Paradise Alley* was filmed, Kelly Kiniski was attending West Texas State and playing football there. After hearing that Stallone needed wrestlers to appear in an upcoming movie, Kelly recalls, "I really wanted to do it."

With onerous restrictions on amateur athletes, Kelly says he talked to his football coaches about the possibility of appearing in the movie.

"They said, 'You can't, because you're an amateur athlete. You can't get paid.'"

Displaying some of his father's doggedness, Kelly found a solution: "I just used my dad's name. I gave them my dad's Social Security number."

Asked how he got away with passing himself off as Gene Kiniski despite his father's reputation and unmistakable face, Kelly explains, "My part was, like, half a second. It was so fast, you wouldn't even know who it was."

Despite his brief appearance on camera, Kelly says he had to get a 1940s-style haircut to play his part in the film. "I looked really strange," he says. To explain his changed appearance to his coaches back at West Texas, he says, "I told them, 'I lost a bet with my dad. He made me get a haircut like this.' I didn't know what else to say."

Movies in which Gene Kiniski did appear were *Double Happiness*, a 1994 Canadian production about a Chinese Canadian family in which Kiniski got billing simply as "Man at Bus Stop." A few years earlier, Kiniski's talents were put to better use in the 1990 Canadian independent movie *Terminal City Ricochet*, filmed in Vancouver and described as a dystopian comedy, in which Kiniski played Commander Crutcher, a gravelly-voiced cop who roughed up a suspect, delivered a few funny lines, and shot a van that wasn't moving.

"He enjoyed that," recalls Nick Kiniski.

Besides his movie appearances and occasional interviews, Gene Kiniski made a few public affairs announcements, including a "Buckle Up for Safety" spot in British Columbia. But his most memorable public service spot—at least, to Wayne Cox, who appeared on camera with Kiniski—was one promoting blood donation to the Red Cross.

Cox recalls how he and Kiniski got into a shtick where "the big gruff awful mean old wrestler" kept stumbling while reading off the teleprompter and "the little TV guy" kept scolding him. "The crew in the studio froze," Cox says. "They didn't know we knew each other, and they thought, 'He's going to kill him.'"

When the shooting was over, says Cox, "[Gene] says, 'You know, I can't give blood…. I'll pass out.'" After he reminded Kiniski that he had been in many bloody matches, Cox says, Kiniski explained, "It's not the blood. It's the tube sticking in my arm…. I'd pass out if they did that to me."

When Kiniski showed up about a week later to meet Cox at work,

> he had a big brown envelope. I opened it up, and there's [a picture of] Gene in a reclining chair with a blood tube coming out of his arm and a nurse sitting beside him holding his hand. I said, "Wow, Gene. Fantastic. I thought you were going to faint or something." He says, "Sometimes you've got to just step up and be a man."
>
> And then this big smile broke out on his face, and he started to laugh, and he said, "No, I just taped that on me for the picture."
>
> He had me right to the very end.

Kiniski also appeared occasionally in ads and on commercials—with his best-remembered work likely an ad showing Kiniski "torture-[testing]" a pair of jeans in a 1975 Eaton's Department Store catalog (thanks to Greg Oliver) and a commercial for Parker's Mattress City in Vancouver. He probably would have made more commercials had he found the work more engaging. Kelly Kiniski recalls, "I went with him on one commercial. We ended up playing crib most of the day. It was a really long day." For his part, Gene Kiniski, quoted by Tom Hawthorn in *The Globe and Mail*, voiced some displeasure over the cattle calls associated with casting for commercials. "Who needs it?" he said.

A less taxing means—at least for Gene Kiniski himself—of keeping the Kiniski name relevant to television viewers came when comedian Ryan Stiles, a native of the Northwest, displayed his intelligent but underachieving Lewis Kiniski character to national audiences in the United States and Canada via nearly a decade of performances, beginning in 1995, on *The Drew Carey Show*. While it is unclear whether Gene Kiniski thought Stiles was

Gene Kiniski, who apparently acquired a taste for southern climes after living through childhood blizzards in central Alberta, enjoyed his visits to California during his later years (Kiniski family archive).

doing him any favors by adopting the Kiniski name for his sometimes bumbling character, Kiniski preserved in his collection a clipping focusing on trivia about Stiles. Meanwhile, Stiles, in a 2001 interview at www.comedycouch.com, said, regarding Lewis Kiniski, "I was always a big Kiniski fan, so it's kind of an ode to Gene.... He was always my [favorite] wrestler."

Perhaps Gene Kiniski's unlikeliest appearance on screen came in 1993, when he appeared on CBUT-TV in Vancouver, joining host Christine Lippa on the arts and entertainment show *Zero Avenue* to visit a local art gallery and to discuss art. According to Kelly Kiniski, if his father's ability to talk his way through anything were ever put to the test, that was it. But as Kelly recalls, his father passed the test, in the process impressing the show's staff and viewers with his "knowledge" of art.

Kelly continues, "It was just a big swerve. He just went there and everyone after that said, 'Oh, we didn't know you were such an art critic.' My dad said, 'What a bunch of shit.' Dad came home and he was just laughing, [saying,] 'I don't know shit about art.'"

Asked what some of his father's legitimate interests were during his retirement years, Kelly quickly replies, "He liked girls and guns."

His father's interest in the former, Kelly admits, hadn't done his parents' marriage any favors. Throughout his wrestling career, Gene Kiniski wasn't known to shy away from women, especially in Japan, where Kelly says his father was normally provided female companionship to tide him over until his tour of the islands was over.

Nick Kiniski says, "He loved the women.... The better looking they were, the quicker he'd be on them." Nick, who keeps a second home in California, says, "I got to spend quite a bit of time with him in Palm Springs"—a location where Kelly says some older women showed a lot of interest in his father. Gene, however did not return the interest. Kelly recalls his father commenting that "I don't want [any] women my age."

Moray Keith recalls,

> Gene would sit with the boys and swear with the best of them, but I don't think there was anybody that ever charmed ladies quite as well as Gene did. I mean, he had a face like a road map, but he was just—he had all these wonderful lines. My son told a story [at Gene Kiniski's "celebration of life" memorial service] about being in a ferry line and Gene going over to talk to two young girls so that he could introduce them to Greg and his friend that were going fishing together.
>
> Greg said when [Kiniski] finished charming these girls by saying, "You look like a star from heaven" and "Did you get a ticket coming here?" the girls said, "What do you mean, a ticket?" [Kiniski answered,] "Well, because you've got 'Fine' written all over you." Just so many lines like that Gene always had. You [can] say those are cheesy lines and everything, but the girls would love it. I mean, they'd absolutely love it.

Here is evidence making it hard to refute the latter half of Kelly Kiniski's answer to the question of what particularly interested his father: "He liked girls and guns" (Kiniski family archive).

Keith adds, "When a lady was at a table, if she got up to powder her nose or whatever, Gene would run around the table to get her chair for her. It would be a young lady.... He was just always a charmer and a gentleman."

Skye Hill, Mike Hill's wife and a Blaine native, recalls, during her student years, observing Kiniski, from her school bus, out running in a "little tiny Speedo." Once she got to know him, she says, "He always made me feel special. Anytime I was getting into a car he would lean in and buckle my seat belt and try to get a kiss." Once, under some Christmas mistletoe, she says, "I went to kiss his cheek and he turned his head [and] gave me the tongue, and ever since then ... handshakes [were] good enough."

Mike Hill reports seeing Kiniski, an incorrigible kisser, take part in a kissing contest at the Tudor pub—of course, with a much younger partner—when he was in his seventies. "They'd been locking lips for, like, 40 minutes," he says. "Everyone was [cheering], 'Come on Kiniski! Go Gene go!'

"That guy never changed."

As far as Kiniski's other primary interest—guns—was concerned, aside from firing across his basement on occasion, he was an avid gun collector and trapshooter. But more than that, says Benny Grabow, "he loved to get out in the wilderness. He loved his big game hunting. That was his passion." Pascall says, however, that while his friend loved every other aspect of hunting and, especially, drawing on his resourcefulness in the great outdoors, Kiniski once told him, "I love putting the powder in the bullets and getting all ready to go, but I don't like to shoot any wildlife."

Yet Nick Kiniski says his father was adept at all stages of going out and bagging game, right down to preparation for the table. "He could carve up a deer [or other animal]," says Nick. "He could wrap it and cut it up." Presumably, that skill could be traced in part to some tutelage a young Gene Kiniski had received from a butcher back in Edmonton. And, of course, as he made clear on the Gzowski show and as his friends were well aware, Kiniski loved to cook.

During the Kiniski family's early years in the Pacific Northwest, Gene and his young sons used to enjoy visiting a vacation property near Princeton, BC, owned by 1950s–1960s Vancouver wrestling promoter Cliff Parker.

"[Parker] owned the Sky Blue Lodge," Kelly recalls, "and that's where we used to go deer hunting and black bear hunting and grouse hunting." Those getaways were treasured, Kelly says, because "we didn't have many vacations. Dad was always wrestling."

In later years Gene Kiniski regularly visited the Flathead Valley in southeast British Columbia, an area abundant with pristine forests, lakes, mountain views and parks—and a hunter's and fisherman's paradise.

Though he fulfilled engagements and went to see friends on occasion—and, of course, lent a hand at his favorite bars when he wanted to—Gene Kiniski loved nothing more than staying at home when his wrestling days were over. "He never even went to Bellingham," says Kelly. "He pretty much stayed at home, other than he would go up to the Flathead, which is [near] the Montana-BC-Alberta border.... There was a little cabin with all wood floor and bunks ... and Dad just loved it there"—especially when he had occasion to go hunting with his sons.

Kiniski's love for the outdoors spilled over into fishing, and Georgia native Jerry Jernigan, a friend of Kiniski's dating back to the early 1970s, recalls that, while he and Kiniski went hunting a few times over the years in Washington State, they spent more time out on the water together fishing. Jernigan, who had been a commercial fisherman, recalls, during the early period in which he knew Kiniski, "He used to come down to the boat, and he'd look down on the boat and go downstairs and look at the engine and all that stuff, and the boys would be with him."

Jernigan continues, "We'd go out pleasure fishing too. I had a pleasure boat, and we'd go out pleasure fishing sometimes."

Jernigan says he met Gene Kiniski when the Kiniskis were in the process of building their home in Harbor View Heights. Jernigan, whose journey in life had taken him from commercial fishing to real estate development, was building a few homes in the area, and he and Kiniski got on well, though, Jernigan says, "I didn't get to know him real well until later."

When Kiniski and Jernigan were neighbors in Blaine, the latter—an avid motorcyclist at the time—attracted neighborhood boys who were eager to do some biking. "[Kelly and Nick] used to come over to my house all the time and ride motorcycles with me," says Jernigan. Dennis Hill, who rode motorcycles with Jernigan and other neighborhood boys, recalled that Kelly and Nick liked to pop "wheelies at 60 mph down the road."

After hosting Nick and Kelly, Jernigan says, "I'd go back home with them to make sure they made it all right, and I just kept meeting [Gene] and his wife, and I always got along with them good."

Over time—before and after the loss of Marion—Kiniski and Jernigan developed a close friendship and spent many hours enjoying each other's company.

"We'd shoot pool an awful lot at his place," says Jernigan. "[Once] we shot all night long until daylight the next day. We had a deal going that one had to get three games ahead of the other one, and we never could do that all night long. We shot pool for hours and hours, day after day."

Jernigan, who recalls going on three- and four-day motorcycle trips with Kelly and Nick when they were old enough, made his business know-how available to the Kiniskis and, over the years, provided advice and help to Gene and his sons when he thought they could benefit from it.

Not long into their friendship, Jernigan and Kiniski became business partners, buying and developing some properties around Blaine. The partnership began over a game of pool, when, Jernigan says, "I was telling him about a deal downtown, and he said, 'If you want, I'll go with you and we'll buy it,' and I said okay."

The Jernigan-Kiniski holdings included some homes to flip and a hotel across the road from what would later be Mike Hill's Chevron station. The hotel housed a few businesses in the basement, including a shop selling sex toys and a massage parlor, where Kiniski was known to enjoy visiting the staff. "It was not a high-class hotel by any means," says Kelly Kiniski.

Among the tenants for a time was the proprietress of a shop specializing in antiques and assorted goods bought in bulk in Seattle to be sold for a profit in Blaine. The proprietress was Marion Kiniski, still married to Gene, but she found it a difficult task to lure customers into the basement of a seedy hotel. Jernigan says he bought out Marion's inventory when she saw no future for the business.

As far as Gene Kiniski's approach to business was concerned, Jernigan recalls, "He left most everything to me. He never handled the books. He never looked at the books all the time I was business partners with him."

Jernigan summarizes a conversation the two partners had when he suggested Kiniski look at the books.

"Well, *you're* looking at 'em, aren't you?"

"Yeah."

"Well, that's good enough for me."

There is little to suggest Kiniski was ever that trusting of his business partners when it came to ownership of the wrestling promotion in Vancouver. A close friend of Kiniski's observed that Kiniski had at least some skepticism when it came to Sandor Kovacs, and by all accounts, that skepticism increased dramatically when Al Tomko came in.

Jernigan says, "I knew Al very well. I built a house for him."

According to Jernigan, early during the Tomko-Kiniski partnership, "We used to go over to Denny's and we'd have coffee with Al and Gene and a couple more of the guys around town." But later on, Jernigan says of Kiniski and Tomko, "They would run into one another, but they didn't have much to say at all."

Being short on words, of course, was not all the norm for someone who could go toe-to-toe on the microphone with Muhammad Ali. Going back to his early wrestling years, Kiniski had drawn notice as a money-drawing interview—one who could speak directly to fans and entice them to buy tickets to his matches. Known to arrive early in a city where he was scheduled to wrestle, Kiniski read the local newspapers and was prepared for almost every interview or publicity opportunity that came his way.

His preparation was hardly limited to brushing up on local issues, as Kiniski's practice of reading widely was often credited with helping him speak intelligently or convincingly on just about any subject. That ability, of course, sold many tickets and kept Gene Kiniski front and center during most of his wrestling career, but it served him equally well outside the ring.

"He played the rough, tough wrestler," says Moray Keith, "but he could sit down and he would talk. When my dad was the vice president of a bank here in Canada when there was only a few of them, I mean, Gene could sit and talk one-to-one with senior guys in almost every walk of life. And I mean he would be impressive because he was so well read."

In an interview with John Kirkwood in the November 19, 1971, Vancouver *Province*, Kiniski said, "I read everything from rasslin' magazines to books about wolves becoming extinct. But what I like reading must be honest stuff. I enjoy fiction but it must be stuff done with a lot of research. Based on fact. *The Godfather*. I enjoyed that. I couldn't put it down. I like stuff on aircraft and flying."

Kiniski continued to read widely in retirement, favoring *The Wall Street Journal* and political biographies—none more than *Plain Speaking*, Merle Miller's account of Harry Truman's life.

Steve Petersen became a friend of Kiniski's—receiving plenty of practical advice as a perk—after landing north of Bellingham in 1982 following his high school graduation. Petersen, who "knew [Kiniski] as a wrestling fan as a kid" while growing up in the Seattle-Issaquah, Washington, area, says Kiniski continued to read several newspapers a day long after his years of match-hyping promos were over.

Kelly Kiniski says, of his father, "He kept well read because he didn't want to feel like a dummy."

Don Leo Jonathan agreed that the Kiniski tongue continued to pack a punch long after his days in the ring were over. Jonathan said, "After we both retired and we were called to go on [radio] shows, I never had to worry a bit because I'd just go and sit down and Gene would take over [and say,] 'Isn't that right, Jonathan?' [and I'd say,] 'Oh yeah, that's right, Gene.'"

As Mike Hill puts it, "[Kiniski] could talk a shoe salesman out of shoes." Petersen adds, "He'd talk about any subject [under] the sun.... [He was] pretty strongly opinionated, but he'd listen to other people's opinions."

While Kiniski may indeed have been a good listener, Dennis Hill said, "if he thought you were full of shit about something, he'd let you know it."

When he wasn't putting his persuasive skills to use, Kiniski sometimes used his gift of gab simply to set up a good laugh. Mike Hill recalls attending a cancer benefit in Vancouver in the 1990s with Gene and Nick Kiniski. Although fellow attendees included hockey legends Wayne Gretzky and Bobby Hull, Hill says Gene Kiniski—as he nearly always did—stole the show.

As Hill recalls, a doctor from Australia addressed the crowd to speak about prostate cancer. During his address, Hill reports, the doctor said, "'We used to believe that the sneeze was the closest thing to the male orgasm, with the contractions [and] the release of the body.' I'm sitting there, and I'm watching Gene. [And the doctor] goes on, 'But now they've looked into it, and now they say that the bowel movement is the closest thing to the male orgasm.' All of a sudden you [see] Gene stand up. The cameras sway over on us. Gene [calls out,] 'Doc! Doc! Repeat yourself.' And this doctor says the same thing."

Hill continues, "I never laughed so damn hard in my life. And then they handed him the mike. [Gene said,] 'Explain it to me. This is all facts and figures.' He was playing like he was just as serious as hell."

After the doctor went into greater detail, Hill says, Kiniski closed out the exchange with a punch line the crowd of several thousand ate up: "Doc, either you don't know how to fuck or I don't know how to take a shit!" According to Hill, "The place just erupted. I mean, he was just quick-witted."

Keith, who used to accompany Kiniski to most of his post-retirement West Coast media appearances, adds, "From time to time [he'd appear on] a talk show or something like that…. He'd absolutely steal the show. He was so good at that. He made everybody feel comfortable, and the reporters and people just loved him."

While compromising his privacy on occasion to grant an interview, make an appearance, or attend to his properties or social interests, "When he retired he truly retired," Grabow says of Kiniski. Kiniski valued his time and his relative freedom in retirement, and by all accounts he enjoyed living a relatively simple life during his later decades and did not miss the spotlight.

One of his simple pleasures was to continue following and watching football long after his—and his sons'—days on the gridiron were over. According to Larry Donovan, head coach of the BC Lions from 1986 to 1989, a shared interest in football played a part in helping Donovan and Kiniski forge a strong and lasting friendship.

"He prided himself in the fact that he played football," says Donovan.

Fellow ex-pro footballer Bob Molle—whose career Kiniski followed closely—says his mentor liked to analyze plays when the two got together to watch a game.

Other simple pleasures of Kiniski's in retirement—such as watching *The Sound of Music* or listening to violinist André Rieu—revealed a softer side of Gene Kiniski to those who knew him well. Bernie Pascall recalls another simple pleasure of Kiniski's that revealed a tender side that seemed entirely at odds with the character the public had come to know.

"He'd feed the bluejays in his backyard," Pascall says. "He would always show us the salt block out in the backyard. He'd feed the deer, and we'd sit at the window there and watch the deer come by. He had a hummingbird feeder by his kitchen window, and he took great pride in that."

He continues, "Here's the big, mean Gene, who'd want us to be quiet and tiptoe to the window to look at the hummingbirds feeding at the feeder outside the kitchen window. There was the mean Gene side, but there was also the very mild Gene side, and we got the opportunity to know him well and see a lot of that."

Though he didn't closely follow the more modernized form of wrestling represented by the WWF/WWE, Kiniski outwardly kept a respectful attitude with regard to professional wrestling, grateful for the opportunities his profession had given him. While he may not have related to some of the changes the sport had undergone since his retirement—and while sometimes critical, in private, of what pro wrestling had become—he almost never publicly denigrated those who had made such a spectacle out of wrestling or revealed the inner workings of the business that he and other wrestlers of his generation had sought to protect. But it appears he let his guard down when, at age 71, he told Dennis

Kane of *The Powell River Peak*, "[Wrestling's] not better than it used to be, that's for sure …. It seems like it goes on every night, and they don't know how to wrestle[;] it's just show. It's all tits 'n' ass now, and it looks like Jerry Springer up there." Yet Kiniski went on to acknowledge, "I will say, though, that they're giving the people what they want. The name of the game is money, and it's a billion-dollar business."

While Kelly Kiniski says his father seldom talked about other wrestlers when he was retired, Gene Kiniski did keep in contact with a few good friends from his working years—particularly Jonathan, who lived 45 minutes away in Langley, BC; Joe Blanchard in San Antonio; George Scott, a long-time wrestler in territories where Kiniski appeared who went on to play a major role behind the scenes for Jim Crockett Promotions and, later, the WWF; Sam Muchnick, who Kelly says phoned his father every week for years; and Lord Blears, whose daughter Laura Blears reports, "I know they talked frequently … probably at least once or twice a month."

She says, "He was one of my dad's closest friends when I was little. I remember Gene Kiniski and his family at our house." Laura Blears—formerly a championship surfer, like other members of her family—adds that the Kiniski and Blears families had a great deal of fun on Waikiki Beach, although she is unsure whether her father, who introduced many fellow wrestlers to surfing over the years, ever managed to get Gene Kiniski on a board.

Another close friend from Kiniski's early years in the ring was suffering the effects of cancer in the 1990s—having already suffered the untold tragedy of losing five of his six sons to accidental death or suicide. According to Kelly, his father made one last visit to see Fritz von Erich not long before cancer claimed his friend's life in 1997.

It is unclear whether, while discussing von Erich's condition during that final visit, Kiniski brought up his own brush with cancer—which took place at about the same time or not long before. For Kiniski, previous medical concerns during retirement had pretty much been addressed by a few hernia surgeries, but when he neared 70 he was diagnosed with early-stage prostate cancer. His prostate was removed, and he made a speedy and full recovery—though Nick Kiniski says his father, for some time afterward, still seemed convinced he was destined to fall to the cancer that had been detected. Yet Gene Kiniski preferred to keep quiet about the diagnosis and surgery, and many people who knew him seem unaware that he had any history of cancer, or any concerns about it, dating back to about 1996 or 1997—likely because he kept a positive outlook overall and barely seemed to hit a bump as he dealt with the disease.

Jonathan recalled making the short trip across the border to Blaine on occasion when Kiniski was retired.

"I used to stop by his house occasionally to say hi," he said. "I'd go down and talk to him. For some reason, we got along good, and I know that every time I would go down that way or I would stop to see him, he would be happy."

Asked how he observed his friend keeping busy in retirement, Jonathan said, "All I know is that he'd chop wood…. And he would work at [Nick's] place in Point Roberts…. He liked that because he liked to talk to people if he could pick them out."

Asked to explain, Jonathan said Kiniski always favored interesting people. Even in Kiniski's retirement, Jonathan said, "There were some people he really liked talking to and some he didn't want to talk to at all."

Joyce Kiniski notes, of her father-in-law Gene, "He valued intelligence. Young, pretty women were attractive, but we had an elderly lady friend who was very intelligent, and he would sit and talk with her and they had good conversations…. He [valued] intelligence in anybody."

When he wasn't tending bar, Kiniski liked to do some of his socializing at home. Pool playing was always a favorite activity, even well into the night—or through the night, as when Kiniski and Jernigan kept trading victories and weren't willing to settle for a draw.

Nick Kiniski recalls a lesson his dad—perhaps taking a cue from his experience playing cribbage with his own father Nicholas decades earlier—taught him over a game of pool during his amateur wrestling days at SFU. Nick says he was facing away from his father and chalking his cue when he happened to look into a mirror.

"I can see that he's cheating," says Nick. "I turn around and catch his hand [and say,] 'Dad, you're cheating!' He said, 'Son, let that be a lesson. If your own father would do that, just think what others will do to you.'"

Despite a serious weakness for maple nut ice cream, Gene Kiniski tried to eat healthily, and he worked out religiously during his retirement years. Besides stretching, cycling, running, and doing weight exercises and calisthenics most days at his home gym, he swam twice a week at an aquatic center just across the border in White Rock—to the tune of 50 laps per visit, according to a *Vancouver Sun* column by Greg Douglas, whose career in sports has extended far beyond broadcasting and public relations. Part of Kiniski's workout regimen apparently involved jawing the young border guards when he made the short drive to White Rock. Typically, says Jernigan, who often made the crossing with Kiniski, "They'd say something to him at the border and, boy, he would blast them back."

The guards—sometimes, Jernigan says, college students filling in—would ask Kiniski whether he had anything to declare upon entering Canada. To each specific item they would quiz him about, such as apples or guns, Kiniski would reply, "I have nothing to declare"—at least, Jernigan says, until he'd had enough. Jernigan says,

> After several questions, Gene got mad [and] cursed [and asked,] "What else am I supposed to tell you?"
>
> Then they would tell us, "Okay, park your car and go in the office." So he'd park the car and we'd go in the office and see the supervisor, and he would just throw up his hands or wave at us and motion for us to go out the door. [The supervisors] knew Gene well. They knew he didn't have anything.

Yet Mike Hill recalls one instance when Kiniski's jawing at the border got him handcuffed—though, when the dust settled, everything turned out well. "They actually ended up writing him a letter one time and apologizing to him: 'We're sorry for the way you were treated,'" Hill says.

As Kiniski recalled in an interview with Greg Oliver on July 17, 2004, "Every once in a while you get some new [border guard], some fucking asshole…. If you give up your central rights for some security, indeed you're losing both of them" (Oliver, Files).

Despite Kiniski's determination to stay fit, until almost the end of his life he was never able—or quite motivated—to shake off an unhealthy habit many athletes of his generation had fallen into. During most of his life Kiniski was an avid partaker of smokeless tobacco. "He loved the snuff," says Grabow, recalling how Kiniski, during his morning visits to Hill's Chevron, would "put on the coffee pot, have his coffee, and have this little cup with him. He loved his chewing tobacco, and he'd spit it into the cup."

Dennis Hill recalled Gene Kiniski once getting a young Nick to spit out a wad of gum he was chewing. "Chew *this*," Hill said Kiniski told his son—"*this*" being a wad of tobacco.

Referring to the white F-150 truck Gene Kiniski liked to drive, Hill said, "The whole side of it just had a streak of brown on it" where Kiniski used to spit.

Kelly Kiniski, who fell into the smokeless tobacco habit himself before quitting when he understood the potential health costs, says his father dipped Scoal and Copenhagen most of his life. Kelly says his father also had a taste for good cigars.

As much as Gene Kiniski loved his life of simple pleasures and privacy in Blaine, he frequently defaulted to being the gregarious individual the public had come to know.

Keith says, "I'd take many stars from hockey and everything else to our box at GM Place.... I can tell you, Gene was the number one [attraction]. Fans at the hockey arena would always want Gene's autograph because they'd see Gene, and it was all ages. It was just absolutely amazing. Everybody loved him."

As Nick Kiniski puts it, "Dad had charisma. People just seemed to like him. It could be a priest, or it could be the nuns, or it could be in a strip club. He just had that personality that people were drawn to."

Nick recalls, when he was nominated for BC Athlete of the Year during the height of his amateur wrestling success, he and his father were among 1,000 or so attendees at a dinner when the speaker, a prominent broadcaster, fired off a Polish joke.

"My dad stands up and says, 'John, you know what's black and blue and doesn't breathe? It's you if you should tell another Polack joke.' Everyone laughed ... and at the end of the night, the pro hockey players line up out in the hall [and] my dad's signing autographs. These guys wanted autographs from my dad."

Regarding jokes about his Polish heritage, Gene Kiniski's objections may have been aimed more at the messenger than the message. Grabow recalls, "Wherever Gene went, I got phone calls from [anywhere] he wrestled ... always with a Polish joke."

In between his occasional appearances at fundraisers, sporting events, and ceremonies—where he always made himself accessible to fans—Kiniski liked to lie low in the company of his friends, his regular crowd, and members of his family. While Gene Kiniski was closer to Nick than to Kelly during their adult years—though personalities clashed and observers report Gene and Nick were barely speaking for a time—Grabow, a confidant of Kiniski's until the end, says Kiniski loved his sons greatly and was "very, very, very, very proud of his two boys. He became much closer to his sons [as] time progressed. He had an extremely good relationship with his boys."

Despite the potential for conflict, Kiniski also valued opportunities to spend time with his siblings when such opportunities arose. Though the last meeting of all six children of Nicholas and Julia Kiniski was on the occasion of Nicholas and Julia's 50th wedding anniversary shortly before the NWA World Heavyweight title reign of Gene Kiniski got underway, Gene remained close to Julian, Mary, and Dorothy. Mary made her career in banking on the West Coast and lived a short drive from Blaine in Richmond, BC, and she and Gene always had a close relationship.

Julian Kinisky and Dorothy Roberts, Gene's oldest sibling, were prominent Albertans. While Julian—as a regional television personality and political figure—was the better known, Dorothy made her career as a nurse in Westlock, Alberta, about 50 miles north of Edmonton.

According to Justice Allan Wachowich, "Mrs. Roberts was a prolific woman and a very, very highly regarded person who represented our community.... She was wise and just a very nice lady." Over the course of 53 years in Westlock, Dorothy Roberts served as a town councilor, provincial president of the Catholic Women's League, public speaker, and president of the local nurses' chapter, and in 2003 she was awarded a Queen's Golden Jubilee Medal for her long record of community service. Later that year, Dorothy Roberts, then a widow for nearly two decades, moved to British Columbia to be near loved ones—including baby brother Gene, whom she would see regularly during his last seven years.

A December 22, 2009, *Edmonton Journal* article by Keith Gerein reports that Dorothy Roberts, an avid bridge player, "saw her brother wrestle only once and was never tempted to return."

"Once was enough," Gerein quotes Roberts as saying. "It was really scary because he fell out of the ring.

"I didn't realize that he didn't hurt himself."

Gene and Julian remained close until Julian passed away in 2004, although Kelly says his father and uncle could never quite overcome the Kiniski/Kinisky family members' penchant for sparring with words. As Dorothy Roberts' daughter Julie-Anne Stone recalls, "The whole Kiniski family spent all their time hating each other and loving each other. I remember as a kid we'd often go to my grandmother's for Christmas, and they'd be at the table fighting, and then they'd be singing."

Decades after those Christmas get-togethers in Edmonton, Kelly and Nick Kiniski went on a hunting trip with their father and their uncle Julian. As Kelly recalls, "They were just miserable with each other."

Kelly continues, "We were out hunting ... and they were fighting like cats and dogs. [I thought,] 'Really, you guys are 70, and you're acting like that?' My brother and I, we looked at ourselves, and we just shook our heads."

He adds, "It was just ridiculous, like a cartoon."

Yet, as feisty as Gene Kiniski could be during his early seventies, he was deeply appreciative of all the rewards his hard work in earlier years and his generally good fortune in later years provided in retirement: the opportunity to enjoy the company of his sons; to enjoy time with other relatives when the occasion arose; to tend bar and mingle with the regulars at the Reef; to get away to Palm Springs with Nick on occasion; to escape to the Flathead now and then to commune with nature; to meet his friends for morning coffee; to talk regularly with a few big names from his wrestling days; to work out in a manner most men half his age wouldn't even attempt; to make appearances or do interviews only when it suited him; to continue putting his acerbic wit to good use whether he had an audience of two or two thousand; and to enjoy his usually quiet life in Blaine, in the home that remained precisely as Marion had laid it out.

25

Final Decade

The majority of Gene Kiniski's eighth decade saw him enjoy relatively stable and good health as he continued to go about his favorite pursuits of reading, working out, socializing, and getting away from Blaine briefly to see friends or family or to enjoy the great outdoors.

Of course, the wear and tear of a high-impact career in wrestling took its toll on an aging body, and the knee that had cut short his football career—along with the other one—was giving Kiniski a lot of trouble by the turn of the 21st century. Yet he continued to work out, stretching to relieve the joints that had taken such a beating over the years and often focusing on calisthenics and work with lighter weights to go with low-impact aerobic activities such as swimming and cycling. As quoted in his April 14, 2010, *SLAM! Wrestling* obituary, Kiniski explained, "Everyone calls it working out, but I call it doing my physiotherapy." Or, as Kiniski was known to tell friends in one variation or another, "Young men choose to work out; old men must."

Former BC Lions coach Larry Donovan says Kiniski, even in his advanced years, wasn't satisfied to keep the benefits of exercise to himself. "Within the friendship group, if someone was letting himself go, he would certainly mention it and try to help get them back on track," Donovan says.

There were few wrestling-related engagements after Kiniski made his final trip to Japan, alone, in 2000 to serve as All Japan Pro Wrestling's storyline commissioner, but during his final years Kiniski continued to stay in touch with some of his closest friends from the wrestling world—particularly Blears, whose stepping down as All Japan's commissioner opened up the role for Kiniski; Jonathan, who continued to visit on occasion; George Scott, retired from a post-wrestling career in real estate and living in Florida; Blanchard; and Dutch Savage, like Kiniski a long-time mainstay of professional wrestling in the Pacific Northwest.

The latter two are particularly interesting, as Blanchard and Savage were devout Christians, while Kiniski, according to Grabow, "wasn't a religious person." Kelly Kiniski goes further, saying of his father, "He was absolutely against religion"—at least, religion as it is commonly construed.

Kelly says, "We were not allowed to go on church grounds" while growing up. But just the same, Gene Kiniski made sure his sons were baptized early in life "just in case we got into politics."

Gene Kiniski himself would tell Greg Oliver, in 2004, "Every time I think of religion it makes me throw up" (Oliver, Files).

Yet people who knew Gene Kiniski well overwhelmingly seem to agree that, despite

Gene Kiniski, pictured here with family friend Greg Keith (center) and Nick, loved few things more than the outdoors (Kiniski family archive).

his views on religion and all his off-color or seemingly uncensored behavior, he most definitely lived by an unmistakable moral code. Savage, who became a born-again Christian and an ordained pastor after his wrestling days were over, said, on Oklahoma wrestling personality C.M. Burnham's oklafan.com website, following Kiniski's death, "There's about three thousand guys who owe an awful lot to Gene that he's helped monetarily [and] spiritually. He was a complete agnostic and atheist, but I loved him and would defend his right to believe whatever he wants to believe. Gene helped so many people."

Indeed, during much of his life Kiniski was known—though he sought no recognition for it—to pick up the phone or write notes on occasion to offer words of encouragement to friends or acquaintances coping with difficult circumstances. One recipient of such a message from Gene Kiniski was Don Getty, who spent a decade playing for the Edmonton Eskimos, starting two years after Kiniski left the team for good in 1953. In 1988 Getty, then premier of Alberta, went through a tough stage following the arrest of his son on a drug trafficking charge, and in September of that year he sent Kiniski a letter thanking him "for taking the time to convey your message of hope and encouragement."

Kiniski was perhaps even quicker to offer support to members of his community close to home. Bob Drake, who serviced Kiniski's tobacco spit-stained white F-150 at his service station in Blaine, is among those who say Kiniski was quick to lend them money when it was needed. Dennis Hill weighed in with a story about how Kiniski quickly put up about $100,000 when the Hills decided it was time to remodel the Pastime, with Kiniski adding, almost as an afterthought, "Just pay me back when you can get it." Though

Kiniski apparently was a good judge of character, as Drake, Hill, and others paid him back quickly, Hill said, "If he trusted you, he would give you whatever [you needed]."

Nick Kiniski, confirming that his father lent money to many people, says, "He never said anything [about it]. I think that shows a lot of character." Yet a friend of the Kiniskis reports that Gene's largesse did not extend to Nick when he was in the process of purchasing his bar—though perhaps out of confidence, possibly expressed also during Kelly's illness in Louisiana, that his sons were equipped to meet whatever challenges life threw at them.

Kelly says, "He would always tell me, 'If there are old people ... shovel their walks. If they're sick, you need to go over there and bring them a pot of soup.... That's what

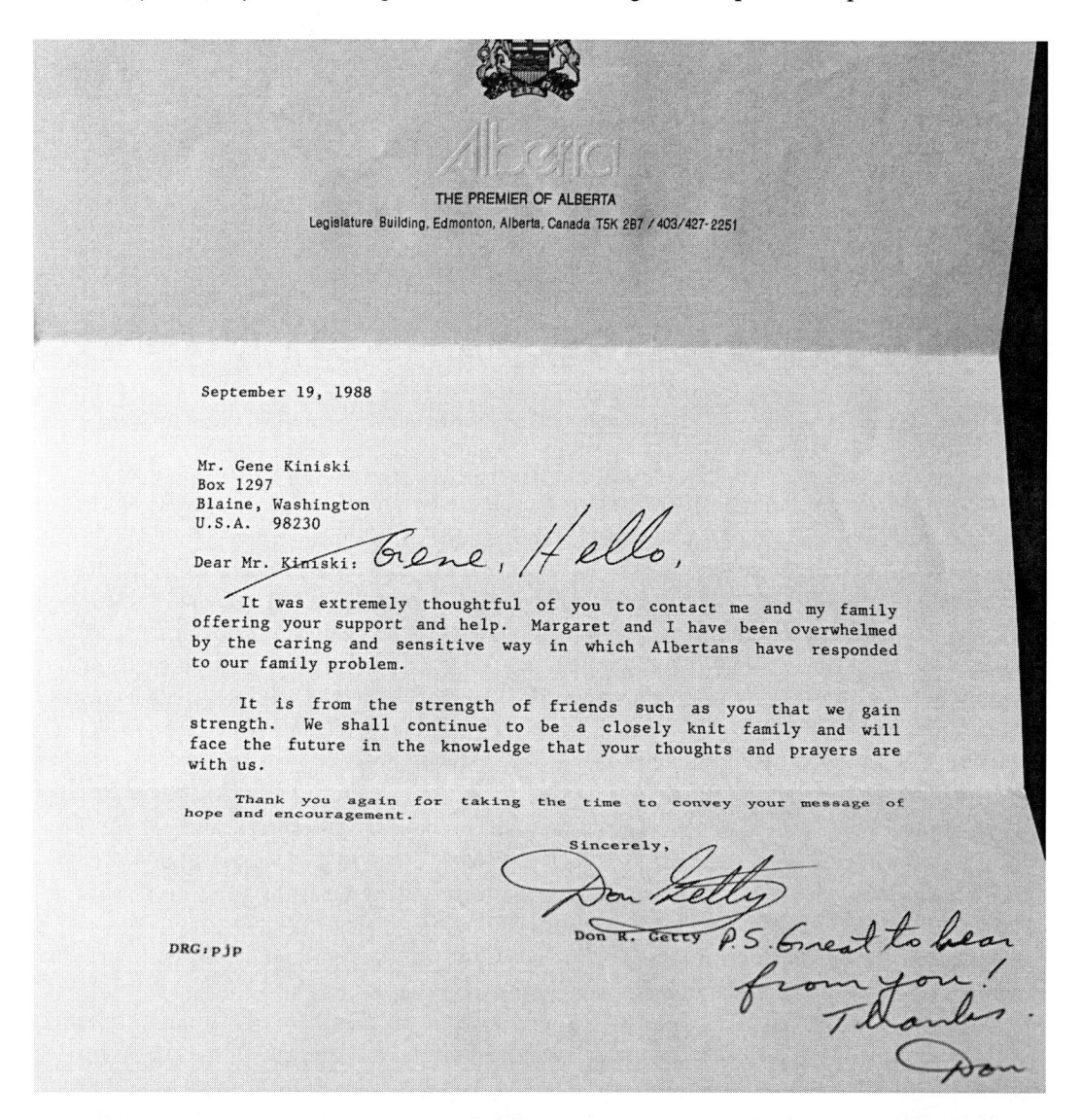

THE PREMIER OF ALBERTA
Legislature Building, Edmonton, Alberta, Canada T5K 2B7 / 403/427-2251

September 19, 1988

Mr. Gene Kiniski
Box 1297
Blaine, Washington
U.S.A. 98230

Dear Mr. Kiniski: Gene, Hello,

It was extremely thoughtful of you to contact me and my family offering your support and help. Margaret and I have been overwhelmed by the caring and sensitive way in which Albertans have responded to our family problem.

It is from the strength of friends such as you that we gain strength. We shall continue to be a closely knit family and will face the future in the knowledge that your thoughts and prayers are with us.

Thank you again for taking the time to convey your message of hope and encouragement.

Sincerely,

Don R. Getty

DRG:pjp

P.S. Great to hear from you! Thanks. Don

Kiniski was known to offer support and encouragement to friends and acquaintances facing difficulty—including former Edmonton Eskimo and 1980s–1990s Alberta Premier Don Getty (Kiniski family archive).

religion is.' He said, 'You need to go take care of people,' and he'd be quite set in that, but he hated religion."

While unsure why his father had disdain for organized religion, Kelly speculates, "I think probably when he was young something happened…. I think he had to go to church and be an altar boy or something."

Though Gene Kiniski as an altar boy is an image many wrestling fans would find hard to grasp, serving in that capacity was typically a rite of passage for boys enrolled in Catholic schools such as St. Joseph. While St. Joseph, specifically, does not appear to have been regarded as the strictest of Catholic educational facilities, Gene Kinisky—a son of Julian Kinisky, who also attended St. Joseph—says, "I remember Dad telling me many times the nuns and the fathers at St. Joe's were extremely strict; very, very strict." Asked whether the environment at St. Joseph in the 1940s could potentially have scared a free-spirited young man such as Gene Kiniski away from religion, Kinisky says, "No doubt about that."

Bruce Kinisky, Julian's other son, adds, "The priests were teachers, and there were some pretty tough ones there. If you did something wrong, Dad often told me that you had to go and do three rounds of boxing with one of the priests after school. That was your punishment for doing something wrong. I don't think Uncle Gene was particularly attached to the church. That might have been the reason."

Whatever the impetus was, Gene Kiniski—while raised in a family that was active and prominent in the local Catholic church—kept his distance from organized religion during his entire adult life. Yet, says Kelly, his father loved religious music, and he had a taste for watching some religious programming on television—likely seeing a parallel between televangelism and the professional wrestling business. "He would watch religion all the time," Kelly says. "He loved the way they drew crowds and how the guys could turn on the tears and stuff. He just loved that."

Gene Kiniski made some final television appearances during his seventies—in particular, an interview, looking back at his wrestling career, on a March 2001 episode of the Canadian Comedy Network series *Wrestling with the Past*. The April 14, 2010, *SLAM! Wrestling* retrospective on Kiniski's life reports that when making "one last round of the Canadian media in 2001 [to help promote] *Wrestling with the Past* … Kiniski charmed a whole new generation of writers and TV hosts, including interviews with the *Toronto Sun* [and] *Toronto Star*. [He also made] an appearance on the Mike Bullard show"—*Open Mike with Mike Bullard*, a late-night talk show broadcast nationally on CTV.

While clearly enjoying the journey back through his wrestling days, Kiniski was in no way one to live in the past. He retained little memorabilia other than some reel-to-reel tapes and a bit of ring wear—in particular, the "Canada" jacket he'd been so noted for wearing throughout his career. Yet Steve Petersen says Kiniski once commented, when it dawned on him that there seemed to be a market hungry for artifacts of his career and the glory days of Vancouver wrestling, "If I'd known people wanted to buy this stuff 30 years later, I would have taken care of it."

Kiniski briefly returned to the spotlight in mid–2004, when he was inducted into the George Tragos-Lou Thesz Professional Wrestling Hall of Fame, located at the time in Newton, Iowa, but now in Waterloo, Iowa. Tragos was an Olympic wrestler from Greece and a noted shooter who had trained Thesz in his early years, and the Tragos–Thesz Hall of Fame was established in 1999—three years before Thesz' death—primarily to honor wrestlers who were successful in both the amateur and professional ranks. Early inductees, besides Thesz and Tragos, included prominent Kiniski friends or colleagues Verne Gagne, Dick Hutton, Bobby Managoff, Jack Brisco, Bob Geigel, Dick "The Destroyer" Beyer, James "Baron von" Raschke, and Billy Robinson, along with former Olympic wrestler and fellow Canadian pro wrestling legend Maurice "Mad Dog" Vachon, who, according to Oliver and Johnson in *The Pro Wrestling Hall of Fame: The Heels*, faced Kiniski at the 1947 Canadian amateur wrestling championships (73). In a July 17, 2004, interview with Oliver days before the induction ceremony, Kiniski revealed that Hutton—who passed away in November of 2003—had originally been slated to introduce him as an inductee (Oliver, Files).

Honored by the Tragos-Thesz Hall of Fame in 2004 along with Kiniski were former NWA champion and long-time Kiniski opponent Pat O'Connor, honored posthumously; Leroy McGuirk, a major wrestling star before Kiniski's time who went on to be a successful promoter in Oklahoma, also honored posthumously; Brad Rheingans, a 1976 Olympian who went on to wrestle primarily in the AWA and Japan for over a decade; and George Scott, whose friendship with Kiniski spanned many years. On hand for the ceremony was close friend and 1999 inductee Gagne.

Of his friendship with Kiniski, Scott told Oliver, "He's a great guy. We talk at least every week. Just the old times. Him and I did a lot of traveling together" (Oliver, Files).

Gene Kiniski was showing more of his age by 2004, and this time he didn't travel alone as he had done a few years earlier when he was booked to appear in Japan. Accompanying him to Iowa for his Hall of Fame induction were sons Nick and Kelly, who, despite a few ground transportation and hotel reservation problems in Iowa, were proud to have the opportunity to see their father get some deserved recognition from the wrestling community before all three headed back to their post-wrestling lives in the Northwest.

The death of Julian Kinisky several weeks after his brother's induction in Iowa—following the passing of sister Mary a few years earlier—left Gene Kiniski with only one surviving sibling. Gene and Dorothy had always been close, and that would not change as long as Gene lived, despite their polar views on religion and their ability to argue. Of her uncle Gene, Dorothy's daughter Julie-Anne Stone recalls, "He was very kind to my mother. They were both very fond of each other. She was the oldest and he was the youngest in the family."

Bobby Managoff was a well-respected wrestler, former world champion, and an opponent of Kiniski's in Central Canada and the Midwest during the late 1950s and 1960s. After Managoff's death in 2002, Kiniski assisted *Chicago Tribune* journalist Rick Hepp, who wrote Managoff's obituary (Kiniski family archive).

In 2004 Gene Kiniski traveled with sons Kelly and Nick to Newton, Iowa, to attend Gene's induction to the George Tragos-Lou Thesz Hall of Fame. Of Thesz, who lent his name to the institution before passing away in 2002, Nick Kiniski says, "My dad thought the world of Lou" (Kiniski family archive).

She adds, "He would come up to see my mom every now and again, and they'd go out to dinner or whatnot."

During the last several years before his death in 2010, Canada's Greatest Athlete was going through most of the transitions of a man in his seventies and finding it increasingly difficult to maintain a large, shag-carpeted house on a lot on a hill. But he remained determined never to leave the home he had built with Marion—and had preserved just as she had set it up and furnished it before tragedy struck in the 1970s.

As far as the inside of the home was concerned, Kiniski had a housekeeper. But as for the outside, Kiniski made a determined effort not to back down.

"He was stubborn," says Mike Hill. "He'd go out there and he'd be pushing his mower, a single little … the wheels weren't even powered…. He'd be out there just sweating his ass off."

When Hill surprised Kiniski by mowing his lawn for the first time, Kiniski responded, surprisingly perhaps, in religious terms: "The Lord sent me to heaven." But Hill says Kiniski added an afterthought: "I hate that fucking yard."

Hill, who went on to cut Kiniski's lawn regularly, refused any money when Kiniski wanted to pay him. After that, says Hill, "We'd have this ongoing thing that if I'd see him out somewhere [I'd say], 'That cheap bastard. I mow his lawn [and] he never pays me.'"

Another friend of Kiniski's in Blaine who provided him a lot of help during his last years was Jeff Kennedy, a North Carolina native Kiniski always called "Carolina"—and who spent time with Kiniski almost daily during the latter's final years.

Kennedy, who got to know Kiniski by taking on some jobs for him, says, "I saw him [wrestling] when I was a kid in the Carolinas. I didn't think at the time I'd end up meeting him."

The two became friends, and Kennedy says, "the drinks would never stop if I didn't say no. He was the ultimate host."

As their friendship developed, Kennedy says, "He'd call me up on my birthday and sing me *Happy Birthday*."

Kennedy is frequently cited by members of Kiniski's circle of friends as the one who probably did more on a day-to-day basis to make life as palatable as possible during the final years of the man Kennedy calls "the ultimate youngster."

In a March 1, 2006, *SLAM! Wrestling* report by Greg Oliver titled "Health Lessons from Gene Kiniski," the subject of the report confides, "I'm all beat up. My joints and stuff are all worn out." Yet, while unable to run any longer and fully aware of his growing limitations in his late seventies, Kiniski continued to make the most of his life and circumstances, particularly the opportunity to enjoy time—when he wanted to—with family members, friends, and the crowd at Nick's bar, and, at other times, the pleasure of relative solitude at home in Blaine. Of course, in Blaine he had his share of visitors, including close friends such as the Hills, Kennedy, Jernigan, Grabow, and a few friends from his All-Star Wrestling days, including Jonathan, Moose Morowski, and Duncan McTavish. Though the wrestling world seemed far removed from Kiniski's world as he got closer to 80, he remained loyal to his friends from the wrestling business and usually spoke respectfully, when asked, about the industry in which he had made an international name.

That respect was returned in kind when Kiniski was named to the inaugural class of the St. Louis Wrestling Hall of Fame in 2007, along with other St. Louis legends including Thesz, O'Connor, Race, Bruiser, Fritz von Erich, Flair, Valentine, Longson, and Muchnick. The following year, at 79, Kiniski was inducted into the Professional Wrestling Hall of Fame (PWHF), chartered in 1999 and currently located in Wichita Falls, Texas, but at the time of Kiniski's induction in 2008 located in Amsterdam, New York.

According to the hall's mission statement, the facility aims to preserve "the dignified history of professional wrestling" and "to enshrine and pay tribute to professional wrestlers who have advanced the national pastime in terms of athletics and entertainment." The institution has a distinguished selection committee composed of successful ex-wrestlers from many regions, along with several prominent wrestling historians. PWHF honorees prior to Kiniski's induction in 2008 included many top-shelf wrestlers he faced over the course of his career, including Lou Thesz, Gorgeous George, Buddy Rogers, Bruno Sammartino, André the Giant, Killer Kowalski, Antonino Rocca, Nick Bockwinkel, the Fabulous Kangaroos, The Destroyer, Ilio DiPaolo, Fred Blassie, Verne Gagne, Terry Funk, Harley Race, Jack Brisco, Dory Funk, Jr., Dick the Bruiser, Bill Longson, Don Leo Jonathan, Johnny Valentine, Ric Flair, Ray Stevens, Pat Patterson, Rikidozan, Pat O'Connor, Karl Gotch, and the Tolos Brothers. Inducted with Kiniski on May 24, 2008, were two more of his most distinguished career opponents, Giant Baba and Bobo Brazil, both posthumous inductees, and fellow Canadian legend Bret Hart.

Although honored by his selection, Kiniski, by 2008 a certified homebody who didn't like to travel far from Blaine, was not eager to cross the continent for his induction. As Greg Oliver would report two years later in his April 14, 2010, retrospective on Kiniski's life, Kiniski said, on the topic of flying to Upstate New York for his PWHF induction, "To be honest and truthful, this is just a pain in the ass. That's all I've done all my life, getting on a fucking airplane. Where are you going? Take off your shoes. It's a bunch of shit, that security shit. For 50 fucking years I've been traveling all [around. All] of a sudden, they want to protect me. Protect me from what?"

Yet Kiniski made the trip to Amsterdam, New York, with Nick at his side and, by all accounts, was elated to mix with friends and fans during a series of weekend events culminating in the Hall of Fame inductions. A photograph in the Schenectady, New York, *Daily Gazette* on May 24, 2008, shows Kiniski—accompanied by two Nicks, Kiniski and Bockwinkel—flashing a broad smile that fans who knew Gene Kiniski only as a wrestling character may not have recognized.

The final inductee to be given the podium at the Pro Wrestling Hall of Fame's seventh annual induction ceremony, Kiniski, a main eventer throughout his career, acknowledged fellow wrestlers who may not have enjoyed equal recognition but, in his mind, were equally worthy of the honors accorded wrestlers such as himself.

One such wrestler Kiniski was known to respect was Jack Bence, a well-traveled athlete who wrestled in preliminaries in British Columbia for many years and never held a title. According to Kelly Kiniski, his father—who usually restricted genuine compliments to the likes of such elite wrestlers as Watson, Jonathan, and André the Giant—thought highly of Bence's ability in the ring and held the journeyman in high regard.

Oliver, who attended Kiniski's induction, reports, in a *SLAM! Wrestling* article posted on May 24, 2008, just after the ceremony, that Kiniski went on to tell his audience, "The oldest profession in the world is the art of deceiving yourself. I am not going to deceive myself this evening…. The reason that I'm here standing in front of you is because of my peers, and because of the people who made it all possible, wrestling fans. Without you, we wouldn't be here. Thanks for making my life so special, so enjoyable."

In 2009 Kiniski was selected for induction to the National Wrestling Alliance Hall of Fame. Though the NWA by 2009 was only a shell of what it had been a generation earlier, many long-time fans and old-time wrestlers continued, as many do to the present, to value the NWA name and its association with the organization's glory days from the late 1940s to the early 1980s—during most of which Gene Kiniski was a prominent player. The NWA Hall of Fame was established in 2005, and some of its early inductees included Thesz, Race, Muchnick, and Dory Funk, Jr. Among those selected for induction with Kiniski in the summer of 2009 were Terry Funk and Tully Blanchard.

Like the Wrestling Observer Hall of Fame, the NWA Hall of Fame is not housed in a building. Announcement of inductees most often takes place during the annual convention of the Cauliflower Alley Club, the organization that honored Kiniski in 1992, and early inductions took place in Nashville, Atlanta, and Las Vegas—the latter the site of the Cauliflower Alley Club's annual conventions since 2000. In 2009, while a date in September was set aside for honoring Kiniski and the other members of his class of inductees, no NWA Hall of Fame induction ceremony ended up taking place that year, so Kiniski and his fellow honorees were simply added to the roll of NWA Hall of Famers.

Had the 2009 NWA Hall of Fame ceremony taken place as scheduled in September in a city such as Las Vegas or Atlanta, it is unlikely Kiniski could have made the trip, as much as he might have wanted to. A few months earlier, he had been unable to follow through on an agreement to attend a wrestling show in the St. Louis area that was billed as a tribute to the debut, 50 years earlier on St. Louis' KPLR-TV, of the hugely popular *Wrestling at the Chase* television program that had seen Kiniski as a featured performer for many years. Yet, despite Kiniski's inability to attend the tribute wrestling show—on May 23, 2009, in East Carondelet, Illinois, 10 miles south of St. Louis—that same show appears to have been Gene Kiniski's final "appearance" to fans attending any kind of wrestling event.

The show was promoted by East Carondelet mayor Herb Simmons, who had been in attendance in St. Louis on April 30, 1982, when Kiniski last challenged for the NWA title. Regarding the wrestling event he promoted in East Carondelet on May 23, 2009, ten and a half months before Kiniski's death, Simmons says, "We tried to have him in [but] his health was failing…. Gene really wanted to [come] because St. Louis was a good place for him over the years. He had a lot of main events at the Kiel Auditorium and at the Checkerdome, and then, of course, he was a fixture on *Wrestling at the Chase*."

Also scheduled to take part in the show was Kiniski's good friend and fellow former NWA champion and St. Louis legend Harley Race. Kelly Kiniski, pointing out a similarity between his father and Race, says both were determined, night after night, to deliver fans every bit of the entertainment they deserved. Recalling a show during his stint as a wrestler in Texas, Kelly says, "There was a snowstorm, and there were more wrestlers than audience. All of the wrestlers wanted to go home, and Harley said, 'Well, you're not going home. The matches are going on. These people bought ringside seats. You're having a match.' Harley wrestled an hour that night."

Gene Kiniski displayed a similar perseverance on the night of the *Wrestling at the Chase* tribute show in East Carondelet. Though Kiniski's health did not allow him to make the trip, Simmons says, "We had him hooked up on a speaker phone in the building." A third big name in 1960s–1980s St. Louis wrestling, von Raschke, also participated in the show, and Simmons says, "It was worth the price of admission just to hear those three talking about the old days."

Simmons continues, "They got to telling road stories. I think there wasn't a fan in there that wasn't excited about it…. It was a good night and something I will remember forever."

Kiniski, says Simmons, told the audience over the intercom that he was "regretful that he couldn't join us" in person, though he didn't talk about what had prevented him from making the trip. And, though his health was failing, Kiniski, described by Simmons as "one of the best interviews there ever was," delivered one last time for an eager wrestling audience. "When we hooked him up on the phone," says Simmons, "you could have heard a mouse crawl across the floor."

While Kiniski was aware Race would be participating in the show, he did not learn about Raschke's participation until the phone hook-up was in progress. "You could just hear it in his voice how excited he was about that," Simmons says.

James "Baron von" Raschke, an accomplished amateur wrestler and, like Kiniski, a member of the Tragos-Thesz and St. Louis Wrestling Halls of Fame, recalls first meeting Kiniski when Big Thunder was passing through Texas as the NWA champion.

"Gene was a very loquacious guy," says Raschke. "I'm kind of a quiet guy, so I sat back and listened to a lot of stories he told."

Of the show in East Carondelet, Illinois, on May 23, 2009, Raschke says Kiniski, despite his declining condition, sounded like "the same old Gene Kiniski…. I didn't know that he was sick."

But he was—though the exact nature of what was ailing Kiniski around the time the final year of his life got underway in April of 2009 was not yet known. Though Kiniski was feeling all of his age by then and did not get around too easily, there did not seem to be many signs that the end was imminent. On Canada Day—July 1, 2009—he sounded about as energetic and opinionated as ever in a CJOB radio interview with Winnipeg's Marty Gold, although that would be Kiniski's final media interview. Friends continued to visit him in Blaine, and he is described as a host who never lost his graciousness. Don Leo Jonathan, an occasional visitor until Kiniski's final year, said, "The last time I saw him I didn't know he was sick." When he later got word that Kiniski was ill, said Jonathan, "I was having my own problems, so I never got to go see him in the hospital."

Kiniski was in and out of the hospital as 2009 played out, usually for a tuneup of sorts to address the challenges of aging. Still determined to avoid medication, he toughed out the difficult periods—as he had done all his life—and, when his health allowed, tried to get back into the swing of doing what he enjoyed doing as much as he could. He continued to enjoy spending time with his sons; with Dorothy and her children; and with his closest friends from Blaine and Vancouver—perhaps most frequently Kennedy, Mike Hill, and Grabow. He continued to enjoy reading, driving, and working out—to the degree he could—as long as health and circumstances allowed. He did, however, make a decision—and stuck to it—to give up his long-time habit of chewing tobacco.

Though he didn't travel much during his final year except to Point Roberts and Vancouver when he felt like it, Kiniski did make one last trip, in spring, to Palm Springs, with Nick and Bob Molle. "I could tell he was not feeling well," Nick recalls.

Back in Blaine, Gene Kiniski was diagnosed with lymphoma and began chemotherapy treatments, even though it was determined his cancer was at an advanced stage.

According to Nick, in earlier discussions about what to do in the event of such a scenario, "[Dad] said he would never take any cancer medication … but when he had it he sure wanted the treatment." In interviews and elsewhere during his seventies, Kiniski had voiced frustration—though generally graciously—over some of the difficulties or perceived indignities of aging. Now, at age 80 and facing a difficult prognosis, it appears he was hoping for a little second wind, if not a chance to turn back the clock, at least momentarily.

"I tried to talk him out of it," Nick says of the chemo treatments. "I said, 'Dad, it's too late.'"

Gene Kiniski fought on bravely, though the chemotherapy weakened his vision and made it impossible for him to read. When Nick took his father to the eye doctor, Gene Kiniski was told, diplomatically, that his sight wouldn't allow him to drive but he could come back for another eye examination after his chemotherapy was over. According to Nick, his father believed he would drive again, but that never happened.

Through the ordeal of cancer treatments, Kiniski continued to work out regularly. Simmons recalls "talking to him on the phone [not long] before his passing. He was doing pushups while he was talking to me on the speaker phone. And I'm thinking, 'This guy is unbelievable.'"

Larry Matysik, who phoned Kiniski regularly during his illness, said, of Kiniski's demeanor on the phone, "You'd never have known [about the illness] because he had all of these stories. He didn't want you to feel bad…. He wanted to make you laugh."

Yet the truth soon became apparent—even over the phone—to those who were close to Kiniski. Bernie Pascall, another regular caller when Kiniski was battling cancer, says, "Some days [the phone] would ring and ring and ring, and he wouldn't answer. Then the next day he'd answer it, and he'd say, 'Bernie, I'm losing my eyesight. I hear the phone, but I don't know where the hell it is. This is the toughest time of my life.'"

The spread of cancer to Kiniski's brain coupled with congestive heart failure in early 2010 signaled that the end was near. According to Kelly, when his father was hospitalized it was also determined that he had an aortic puncture that could well have ended his life, suddenly, decades earlier.

Gene Kiniski was moved from St. Joseph Hospital in Bellingham to the Stafholt Good Samaritan Center's assisted living facility in Blaine when it became obvious that he was facing a foe that he would not be able to defeat.

Kelly says, "He went straight from the hospital to the old folks' home, which he said he would never go to. They treated him so well there. I asked him, 'Nick and I will pay for nurses or whatever, and you can go home.' He said, 'Hell, no, I'm staying right here.'"

When he asked whether his father wanted anything to be brought from home, Kelly says, the response was equally decisive: "Hell, no. I've got everything I need right here."

Even during his father's final weeks, says Kelly, "There were tons of people coming. It was amazing. There'd be six to eight people in his little room trying to visit him. A lot of people came and saw my dad. Right up to the end, if someone came up and was a wrestling fan, he would get up and shake their hand and [ask,] 'Where are you from?' He always did that."

Friends say Kiniski found a somewhat kindred spirit in a fellow resident who had served in World War II, and the two spent some time together talking about guns.

Arthur Roberts, who often brought his mother Dorothy to see her baby brother during Gene's final months and weeks, recalls, "All the people … were totally amazed by him … how nice he was. But the cancer just slowly ate him away, you know. The boys would come and pick him up and lift him into the truck and take him out for a cigar."

No longer able to exercise and, for the first time in his life, depending on painkillers for a little relief, Kiniski was well aware, by late winter or early spring of 2010, that his days were numbered. Eager for his father to fill in some blanks or missing details from his life—particularly regarding his early years—Kelly recalls his father being tight-lipped and responding, "No one gives a shit. There's nothing for me to tell."

Yet Kiniski's friends say he continued to display grace despite the most difficult conditions. "I hated to see him go like that. It wasn't that long, but it was tough," says Nick, adding, "He was always a gentleman."

Gene Kiniski passed away on April 14, 2010, the same day he acknowledged to 67-year friend Benny Grabow how important their friendship—dating back to the "phenomenal times" Grabow says Kiniski recalled the pair sharing in Edmonton—had been to him.

"He was holding my hand," Grabow says, "and he says, 'You know, Benny, you and me have had a lot of acquaintances in our lives, but … you can count all your friends on one hand.' He said, 'Just think about it. We had a lot of acquaintances, you and me, through our careers, but the good friends we can count on one hand.'

"I could never forget that," says Grabow, who adds—speaking for many others, whether they were fortunate enough to make Kiniski's shortlist of good friends or not—"To this day I miss him terribly. I really do."

26

Celebration of Life

On April 25, 2010, a celebration of life get-together in memory of Gene Kiniski—announced and open to the public—was held at Kiniski's Reef Tavern. It was the only memorial event for Gene Kiniski, and attendees were advised, "Please dress casual, as Gene would have liked."

Nick Kiniski, who oversaw the celebration, says, "Dad didn't want anything [in the way of a memorial], so he probably would be pissed off. But it's not for the person that died. It's for the people alive…. It was a great night. We probably had 1,000 people here."

Attendees included family, friends, wrestling fans, people who knew Kiniski from his years of tending bar, and, Nick says, people "from every walk of life." Also in attendance were wrestlers from Simon Fraser University, where Nick had been a star athlete, and his father, a major booster. Donations made in Gene Kiniski's memory were earmarked for the Simon Fraser wrestling program. As Nick explained following his father's death, "For a guy who never finished college, he sure believed in education, you know, and we're going to start an endowment fund for the Simon Fraser wrestling program under his name" (SFU Online). Former SFU wrestling coach Mike Jones reports that the Gene Kiniski Endowment Fund survives to this day.

As 2000s/2010s British Columbia wrestling personality Scotty Sweatervest reports in a May 4, 2010, *SLAM! Wrestling* report on the Gene Kiniski celebration of life, "The program included about half a dozen speakers sharing their stories about Gene Kiniski, the performer, the gentleman, the ribber, the father."

Apart from Kiniski's sons—who paid tribute to their father at the event—on hand to represent the Kiniski clan was Gene's sister Dorothy, who provided perspective on her baby brother's early years. Dorothy herself would pass away just a few months later at age 94. Her memorial service would be held in Westlock, Alberta, where she had been an active figure in community service work during the half century she lived there. Hundreds of people attended Dorothy's memorial service, says her son Arthur, who adds, "Around the town of Westlock, they put up memorials to her."

Also speaking at the celebration of life in honor of Gene Kiniski were Moray Keith, Bernie Pascall, and Wayne Cox. Looking back at his friend of nearly 40 years, Cox says, "He was such a big bear of a man, but he had this teddy bear heart."

Other speakers at the celebration were perhaps less prominent in the community but had entertaining or compelling stories to tell about their experiences with Gene Kiniski.

Sweatervest tells about one, "a [Kiniski] family friend, introduced simply as 'Bubbles,'

[who] let the crowd know that at 81 years old, Gene 'still had it' when she was visiting him in the nursing home and he lifted her into his bed in a playful moment."

Also sharing a message was Jeff "Carolina" Kennedy, whose respect for Kiniski has not waned in the years since his friend's death.

Looking back, Kennedy—who received Kiniski's 1972 F-150 and promptly equipped it with "KINISKI" plates—relates a story about how, when he was doing everything he could out of concern for his dying friend, Kiniski turned the tables by saying he was worried about Carolina.

"Worried about *me*?" Kennedy responded. "*I* should be worried about *you*. Why are you worried about me?"

Kennedy says Kiniski replied: "I just wonder, when you get old, are you going to have a Carolina?"

Steve Petersen says he learned at the celebration how deeply Kiniski had affected many people.

"I thought I had this really deep relationship with Gene," Petersen says. "[I found out] there was 100 guys up there that he touched the way he touched my life. What a big person he was."

Eugene Nicholas "Gene" Kiniski died April 14, 2010 at the age of 81. He leaves two sons, Nick and Kelly and daughter in law Joyce of Pt. Roberts, WA, and sister Dorothy Roberts of Maple Ridge. He also leaves a long list of true friends and a legion of fans who followed his storied professional wrestling career in Canada, the United States and Japan over a span of five decades. Gene was born near Edmonton on November 23, 1928, the youngest of six children to Nicholas and Julia Kiniski.

He was scouted as a football player by the late Annis Stukas and followed that path through the University of Arizona to a signing with the Edmonton Eskimos. An injury ended his professional football career so he turned full time to his other passion, wrestling. His professional wrestling debut—and win—in Tucson Arizona on February 13, 1952 lead to a career that saw him win individual and tag team championships through all major wresting organizations in North America and Japan. His outgoing and vibrant personality made him a favorite of radio and television broadcasters as well as millions of fans who enjoyed "Big Thunder" as the "villain" in more than 200 matches every year. He was Canadian Tag Champion nine times and became World Wrestling Champion when he defeated the legendary Lou Thesz in St. Louis, Missouri on January 7, 1966. Gene is the only wrestler ever to hold both the NWA and AWA Wrestling World Championship Titles. When a radio interviewer referred to Gene as "Canada's Greatest Athlete" he gained an identity that would follow him throughout his career. The title remained with him to the end. Gene was a wrestling promoter in Vancouver, other parts of Canada, and in Japan in later years, stepping into the ring himself as late as 1992.

In lieu of flowers, the family requests donations be made to Simon Fraser University, earmarked for the "Gene Kiniski Endowment Fund", and can be mailed to SFU, 8888 University Drive, Burnaby, BC, V5A 1S6.

Nick, Kelly and Joyce would like to thank everyone for attending this Celebration of Life, and for sharing your stories and memories of Gene.

A celebration of life in honor of Gene Kiniski was held at Kiniski's Reef Tavern in Point Roberts, Washington, on April 25, 2010. Nick Kiniski, who owns the Reef, estimates 1,000 people attended the celebration, where Kiniski stories were shared freely and it became apparent to all who attended what an impact Canada's Greatest Athlete had had on numerous people from many walks of life (Kiniski family archive).

BRITISH COLUMBIA
The Best Place on Earth

April 21, 2010

A Message from the Premier
to the
Family and Friends of Gene Kiniski

Canada has lost another great one – Gene Kiniski – an avid football player and an incredible wrestler who had a dream, pursued that dream and lived that dream.

Gene Kiniski had a wonderful life. He travelled a lot and experienced a lot and people, over the years, have learned a lot from him. He was known as *Big Thunder* and *Canada's Greatest Athlete* and *King of the Ring*. He taught us that we can win some and we can lose some, but we always get back on our feet to face another day.

After his wrestling career ended, he remained involved and instructed and encouraged others, like his sons, Kelly and Nick, who followed their father's lead and also became wrestlers.

Gene brought wit and excitement to the sport and he was the kind of wrestler people loved to hate. He loved to tease his fans as he boasted about future mayhem in the ring. He was a true and colourful entertainer and his character will never be forgotten by anyone who knew him as a wrestler, a businessman and a friend.

May he rest in peace knowing that he enlightened and enriched the lives of many.

Sincerely,

Gordon Campbell
Premier

Province of British Columbia
Office of the Premier
www.gov.bc.ca

PO Box 9041 Stn Prov Govt
Victoria BC
V8W 9E1

After Kiniski's death, tributes poured in from all corners recognizing Gene Kiniski's abilities and contributions as an athlete, entertainer, businessman, and friend. Here, sitting British Columbia Premier Gordon Campbell wrote, "He taught us that we can win some and lose some, but we always get back on our feet to face another day…. May he rest in peace knowing that he enlightened and enriched the lives of many" (Kiniski family archive).

Several years after his passing, Gene Kiniski's legacy remains apparent in the lives of people like Petersen, Kennedy, Cox, Bob Molle, and many others who came to know Kiniski as a father figure. As far as professional wrestling is concerned, while the industry today may barely resemble the wrestling world in which Gene Kiniski cut such a wide swath more than a generation ago, Canada's Greatest Athlete remains a standard of excellence and a revered figure to many fans and practitioners of pro wrestling in the 21st century. Mark "Gorgeous Michelle Starr" Vellios, since 2007 the head of the modern-day incarnation of British Columbia-based All-Star Wrestling, attended the celebration of life and says, "I brought my [wrestlers] out to pay respect to a legend who paved the way for others in this area."

The life of Gene Kiniski is a remarkable story of the journey of a strapping son of hardy immigrant stock—the scion of a family that scrapped as much as it loved—who blazed a trail from tiny Chipman, Alberta, to a major college and the pro gridiron before making his way to packed arenas and into the hearts of wrestling fans from coast to coast and beyond before settling into the simpler, small-town life he loved above all else. It was a wonderful journey—but one in which a final leg remains.

Kiniski made it known to his sons that he wanted his ashes spread in the Flathead, where he loved to go hunting. Perhaps not eager to say goodbye just yet, Kelly says, "I'm going to have to take a week and go up and do that." When he does, the amazing journey of Gene Kiniski will be complete.

Bibliography

Alberta Rose Historical Society. *Pride in Progress: Chipman, St. Michael, Star, and Districts*. Alberta Rose Historical Society, 1982.

amarillowrestling.wikia.com. "An encyclopedia about professional wrestling in the Amarillo and West Texas territory." A report on the July 19, 1962, show at the Amarillo Sports Arena is at amarillowrestling.wikia.com/wiki/Amarillo,_TX_-_July_19,_1962. Last accessed 28 Jan. 2018.

Anderson, Robert. Otherwise unidentified newspaper article on WBBM-TV's *Chicago Championship Wrestling*. (Source: Gene Kiniski's personal collection.)

Anson, John. Interview via Facebook messaging. 15–18 May 2016.

Beck, Jason. Phone interview. 24 Apr. 2017.

Beekman, Scott M. *Ringside: A History of Professional Wrestling in America*. Praeger, 2006.

Berton, Pierre. *The Last Spike: The Great Canadian Railway, 1881–1885*. Anchor Canada, 1971.

Blackburn, Bob. "The Wrestling Game." *The Telegram* (1 June 1963).

Blanchard, Tully. Phone interview. 19 Feb. 2018.

Blears, Laura. Phone interview. 17 Mar. 2017.

Bradbury, Tavish. "Big Thunder Elected to Hall of Fame." *All Point Bulletin* (Feb. 2004).

Burnham, C M. "Gene Kiniski Was the Real Deal." Oklafan.com website. Article is at www.oklafan.com/news/view/3336/. Last accessed 3 Nov. 2017.

Carbury, Joe. "Many Hometown Football Players Are in Poor Bargaining Position." (Source: Gene Kiniski's personal collection. Further identifying information is unavailable.)

CBC Digital Archives. Peter Gzowski's Mar. 8, 1978, *90 Minutes Live* interview with Gene Kiniski, www.cbc.ca/archives/entry/wrestlings-gene-kiniski-stirs-the-pot. Last accessed 3 Nov. 2017.

Clark, Richard E. "Silver Medalist Shares Secret." News article on Bob Molle's unlikely path to Olympic success. (Source: Gene Kiniski's personal collection. Further identifying information is unavailable.)

Coleman, Jim. "Kiniski the Diplomat Selling Canada to the U.S." Article apparently published in Southam newspapers in early February of 1968. (Source: Gene Kiniski's personal collection; exact date of article unknown.)

Condello, Tony. Phone interview. 18 Apr. 2016.

Cox, Wayne. Phone interview. 20 June 2016.

Crews, Art. Phone interview. 3 June 2016.

Dempsey, Paul. "Allan Ammerlaan takes his message into a prison." Letter to the Editor in the *B.C. Catholic* newspaper (12 Sept. 2005), bcc.rcav.org/05-09-12/index2.htm. Last accessed 3 May 2017.

Dennis, Daniel. "Giant Who Conquered Aussie Hearts: King Curtis Iaukea, 1937–2010." *The Sydney Morning Herald* (25 Feb. 2011), www.smh.com.au/comment/obituaries/giant-who-conquered-aussie-hearts-20110224-1b70p.html. Last accessed 3 Nov. 2017.

Dilschneider, Donna. "Julia Kiniski Wins in 'Last' Attempt." *Edmonton Journal* (Oct. 1963). (Source: Gene Kiniski's personal collection; exact date of article unknown.)

Donovan, Larry. Phone interview. 14 Aug. 2016.

Douglas, Greg. Phone interview. 11 Apr. 2017.

Drake, Bob. Phone interview. 31 Mar. 2017.

Drummond, Neil. Phone interviews. 25 Jan. 2017; 21 Feb. 2017.

Dunnell, Milt. "Speaking on Sport" column. *Toronto Star* (3 Sept. 1965).

Edmonton City Website. "Biographies of Council Members" at www.edmonton.ca/city_government/documents/Chapter_18_-_Biographies.pdf. Alphabetical link to biographies of Julia Kiniski and Julian Kiniski (*sic*). Last accessed 3 Nov. 2017.

Edmonton Journal. Various articles on Gene and Julia Kiniski.

Eleniak, Steven. Phone interviews. 24 Jan. 2016; 28 Feb. 2016; 27 Apr. 2016; 20 May 2016. In-person interview and tour of Chipman, Alberta. 25 Nov. 2016.

Eurchuk, Mike. Phone interview. 30 Jan. 2016.

Fenton, Patrice. Phone interview. 17 Mar. 2017.

Fleming, R. B. *Peter Gzowski: A Biography*. Dundurn Press, 2010.

Bibliography

Flowers, Tim. Phone interview. 1 May 2018.

Fort Frances Times. "Gene Kiniski, Pleased by Reception, Turns Cheers to Jeers" (5 June 1961). (Source: Gene Kiniski's personal collection.)

Fox, Margalit. "Verne Gagne, Wrestler Who Grappled through Two Eras, Dies at 89." *New York Times* obituary (1 May 2015), www.nytimes.com/2015/05/01/sports/verne-gagne-wrestler-who-grappled-through-two-eras-dies-at-89.html?_r=1. Last accessed 3 Nov. 2017.

Froelich, Erich. Phone interview. 9 Nov. 2016.

Frost, Steve. "Lasting Impressions of Clan Olympians." Simon Fraser University athletics website. Bob Molle entry is at athletics.sfu.ca/sports/2015/6/29/50th_0629150903.aspx?path=50th. Last accessed 3 Nov. 2017.

Funk, Terry. Phone interview. 14 Apr. 2016.

———, with Scott Williams. *Terry Funk: More Than Just Hardcore.* Sports Publishing, 2006.

Fussman, Cal, and Killer Kowalski. "What I've Learned: Killer Kowalski." Online edition of *Esquire* (31 Aug. 2008), www.esquire.com/sports/interviews/a3195/kowalski0807/. Last accessed 3 Nov. 2017.

Gagne, Greg. Phone interviews. 22 Feb. 2016; 16 Feb. 2017.

Gagnon, Erica. "Settling the West: Immigration to the Prairies from 1867 to 1914." Canadian Museum of Immigration website at www.pier21.ca/research/immigration-history/settling-the-west-immigration-to-the-prairies-from-1867-to-1914. Last accessed 3 Nov. 2017.

Gerein, Keith. "Wrestler's sister puts her best foot forward." *Edmonton Journal* article about Dorothy Roberts. 22 Dec. 2009. (Source: Greg Oliver, Files.)

Goldstein, Marty (aka Marty Gold). Phone interview. 7 May 2018.

Goldstein, Richard. "Killer Kowalski, Wrestler, Dies at 81." *New York Times* obituary (31 Aug. 2008), www.nytimes.com/2008/09/01/sports/01kowalski.html. Last accessed 3 Nov. 2017.

Grabow, Benny. Phone interviews. 11 May 2016; 11 June 2016; 16 Jan. 2018.

Hamilton, Larry. Phone interview. 31 Mar. 2017.

Harding, Jessica. "Weekend should provide thrills for wrestlers and fans." Schenectady, New York, *Daily Gazette* article on the Professional Wrestling Hall of Fame's class of 2008 inductions (24 May 2008).

Hart, Bruce. Phone interview. 10 Sept. 2016.

Hawthorn, Tom. *Deadlines: Obits of Memorable British Columbians.* Harbour Publishing, 2012.

———. "Gene Kiniski a Proud Canadian Fans Loved to Hate." *The Globe and Mail* (20 Apr. 2010), www.theglobeandmail.com/news/british-columbia/gene-kiniski-a-proud-canadian-fans-loved-to-hate/article4352840/. Last accessed 4 Nov. 2017.

Hayes, Gil. Phone interview. 19 Feb. 2016.

Hepp, Rick. "Chicago pro wrestler was champion in 1940s." Bobby Managoff obituary in the *Chicago Tribune* (20 Apr. 2002).

Heritage Community Foundation. "Albertans: Who Do They Think They Are?" from the HCF Alberta Online Encyclopedia, accessible at www.albertasource.ca. Account focusing on Alberta's Polish community is at wayback.archive-it.org/2217/20101208165300/http://www.abheritage.ca/albertans/people/polish.html. Last accessed 4 Nov. 2017.

Hill, Dennis. Phone interview. 1 Apr. 2017.

Hill, Mike. Phone interview. 15 June 2016. In-person interview. 12 Aug. 2016.

Hill, Skye. In-person interview. 12 Aug. 2016.

Hornbaker, Tim. *National Wrestling Alliance: The Untold Story of the Monopoly That Strangled Pro Wrestling.* ECW Press, 2007.

Jernigan, Jerry. Phone interview. 18 June 2016.

Johnson, Steven, and Greg Oliver, with Mike Mooneyham. *The Pro Wrestling Hall of Fame: Heroes & Icons.* ECW Press, 2012.

Jonathan, Don Leo. Phone interview. 19 Feb. 2016.

Jones, Mike. Phone interview. 28 May 2018.

Jones, Robert F. "The Blast Was One Big Bust." *Sports Illustrated* article on Ali–Chuvalo II (15 May 1972), www.si.com/vault/1972/05/15/612857/the-blast-was-one-big-bust. Last accessed 4 Nov. 2017.

Julia Kiniski School. Website at www.epsb.ca/schools/juliakiniski/. Last accessed 28 Dec. 2017.

Kane, Dennis. "Wrestler Strove to Be the Villain." "Kane's Call" column published in *The Powell River Peak* in about 2000. (Source: Gene Kiniski's personal collection.)

Kearney, Jim. "'Self-Help'—the new order." (Source: Gene Kiniski's personal collection. Further identifying information is unavailable.)

Keith, Moray. Phone interview. 18 June 2016.

Kennedy, Jeff. In-person interview. 12 Aug. 2016.

Kiniski, Gene. Personal collection of news clippings, photos, and other mementos. Shared electronically by Moray Keith and Jodi Cobden.

Kiniski, Joyce. In-person interview. 11 Feb. 2017.

Kiniski, Kelly. In-person interviews. 16 Jan. 2016; 11 Feb. 2017; 9 Dec. 2017. Phone interviews. 6 Mar. 2016; 12 June 2016; 29 Jan. 2017; 29 Apr. 2017; 30 June 2017; 30 Oct. 2017; 7 Dec. 2017.

Kiniski, Nick. Phone interviews. 14 June 2016; 17 June 2016; 28 Jan. 2017; 1 July 2017. In-person interview. 9 Dec. 2017.

Kinisky, Bruce. Phone interview. 25 Jan. 2016. In-person interview. 26 Nov. 2016.

Kinisky, Gene. Phone interview. 24 Jan. 2016.

Kinisky, Julian. "My Brother Is a Brute!" Exact date and name of publication in which story appeared are uncertain. (Source: Gene Kiniski's personal collection.)

Kirkwood, John. "Meet Gentleman Gene." *The Province* (19 Nov. 1971).

Koloff, Ivan. Phone interview. 1 Apr. 2016.

Koster, Rich. "Women with Hat Pins Can Make Kiniski Meek." *St. Louis Globe-Democrat* article from Dec. 1967. (Source: Gene Kiniski's personal collection; exact date of article unknown.)

Kroffat, Dan. Phone interview. 20 May 2016.

Lewis, Glyn. "Buddy, Gene set to shake the Stadium." *The Columbian*. (Source: Gene Kiniski's personal collection. Further identifying information is unavailable.)

MacLean, Dick. "Why Kiniski [Julian Kinisky] Quit TV." *TV Week*, Edmonton, Aug. 26–Sept. 1, 1961, edition. (Source: Gene Kiniski's personal collection.)

Maimann, Kevin. "Legendary Al Oeming dies." *Edmonton Sun* (30 Mar. 2014), www.edmontonsun.com/2014/03/30/legendary-al-oeming-dies. Last accessed 4 Nov. 2017.

Manson, Bill. Phone interview. 6 Feb. 2016.

Matysik, Larry. Comprehensive audio series with Gary Cubeta on the history of St. Louis wrestling. 57Talk, 2009.

_____. Phone interview. 25 Apr. 2017.

_____. *Wrestling at the Chase: The Inside Story of Sam Muchnick and the Legends of Professional Wrestling*. ECW Press, 2005.

Melnyk, Walter. Phone interview. 15 July 2016.

Meltzer, Dave. *Tributes II: Remembering More of the World's Greatest Professional Wrestlers*. Sports Publishing, 2004.

Meltzer, Dave, ed. *Wrestling Observer Newsletter*. Weekly newsletter covering the pro wrestling industry. Current and archived issues are available to subscribers at www.f4wonline.com. Last accessed 28 Jan. 2018.

Molle, Bob. *Get Comfortable Being Uncomfortable: Improving Your Performance*. Kindle ed., Amazon Digital Services LLC, 2011.

_____. Phone interview. 6 June 2016.

Mooneyham, Mike. "Tex McKenzie Dead at 73." *The Wrestling Gospel according to Mike Mooneyham* (16 June 2001), www.mikemooneyham.com/2001/06/16/tex-mckenzie-dead-at-73. Last accessed 4 Nov. 2017.

Moretti, "Moondog" Ed. Phone interviews. 5 Feb. 2017; 14 Mar. 2017.

Moser, Chuck. Phone interview. 18 Feb. 2016.

Muraco, Don. Phone interview. 19 Feb. 2018.

National Post. "Ex-con opened halfway house to help others in need." Article on Kiniski impersonator Allan Ammerlaan (15 Feb 2010) accessible at the PressReader website, www.pressreader.com/canada/national-post-latest-edition/20100215/283326108502442. Last accessed 4 Nov. 2017.

National Wrestling Hall of Fame. Website at nwhof.org. The Bobby Managoff page is at nwhof.org/blog/dg-inductees/bobby-managoff. Last accessed 4 Nov. 2017.

Nevada, Vance. *Wrestling in the Canadian West*. Crowbar Press, 2009. (Thanks to Nevada also for sharing historical materials concerning All-Star Wrestling.)

Odem, Benjamin "Boo." "Boo Odem Nearly Made Fatal Mistake in 1951." (Source: Gene Kiniski's personal collection. Further identifying information is unavailable.)

Ohira, Rod. "Iaukea reminisces about 50th-state wrestling." *Honolulu Advertiser* article (24 July 2005) featuring recollections by King Curtis Iaukea is at the.honoluluadvertiser.com/article/2005/Jul/24/il/507240325.html. Last accessed 4 Nov. 2017.

Oliver, Greg. "Al Tomko—a true original—dies." *SLAM! Wrestling* website article (6 Aug 2009), slam.canoe.com/Slam/Wrestling/2009/08/06/pf-10379921.html. Last accessed 4 Nov. 2017.

_____. "Duncan McTavish dead at 80." *SLAM! Wrestling* website article (6 June 2011), slam.canoe.com/Slam/Wrestling/2011/06/03/18235286.html. Last accessed 4 Nov. 2017.

_____. Files containing interview and research notes and writings pertaining to Gene Kiniski. (Special thanks to Oliver.)

_____. "Gene Kiniski Dead at 81." *SLAM! Wrestling* website article (14 Apr. 2010), slam.canoe.com/Slam/Wrestling/2010/04/04/13464196.html. Last accessed 4 Nov. 2017.

_____. "Health lessons from Gene Kiniski." *SLAM! Wrestling* website article (1 Mar. 2006), slam.canoe.com/Slam/Wrestling/2006/02/24/pf-1460939.html. Last accessed 4 Nov. 2017.

_____. "Kiniski ends Hall of Fame induction on high note," *SLAM! Wrestling* website article (24 May 2008), slam.canoe.com/Slam/Wrestling/2008/05/24/pf-5660011.html. Last accessed 4 Nov. 2017.

_____, and Steven Johnson. *The Pro Wrestling Hall of Fame: The Heels*. ECW Press, 2007.

_____. "Remembering Al Oeming's days as a wrestler and promoter." *SLAM! Wrestling* website article (3 Apr. 2016), slam.canoe.com/Slam/Wrestling/2014/04/05/21582606.html. Last accessed 4 Nov. 2017.

_____. "Rod Fenton: Rough wrestler, respected promoter." *SLAM! Wrestling* website article (30 June 2010), slam.canoe.com/Slam/Wrestling/2010/05/30/14193521.html. Last accessed 21 Dec. 2017.

_____. "*SLAM!* Wrestling Canadian Hall of Fame: Ron Morrier." *SLAM! Wrestling* website article (3 Apr. 2016), slam.canoe.com/SlamWrestling BiosM/morrier.html. Last accessed 4 Nov. 2017.

_____. "Verne Gagne recalls glory days: The man behind the AWA on promoting, Hogan, and wrestling today." *SLAM! Wrestling* website article (20 Apr. 2000), slam.canoe.com/SlamWrestling Features/gagne_2.html. Last accessed 4 Nov. 2017.

openparliament.ca. Private website housing tran-

scripts and other materials relating to the activities of Canada's Parliament. MP Jean Charest's message in the House of Commons following the death of Steve Paproski, along with thoughts on Paproski by other parliamentary colleagues, can be found at openparliament.ca/debates/1994/1/20/john-loney-1/. Last accessed 28 Jan. 2018.
Owen, Barry. Phone interview. 16 Mar. 2017.
Paproski, Pat. Phone interview. 14 Aug. 2017.
Parks, Reg. Phone interview. 30 June 2017.
Pascall, Bernie. Phone interview. 14 Apr. 2017.
Patola, Roger. "Villains Retain Mat Crown as Kiniski, Haggerty Win." *Port Arthur News-Chronicle* (27 June 1961).
Pavlovich, Lou. "On the Beat." (Source: Gene Kiniski's personal collection. Further identifying information is unavailable.)
Peck, Doug. "Television" newspaper column reporting on CBUT-TV's *The Manly Art of Mayhem.* (Source: Gene Kiniski's personal collection. Further identifying information is unavailable.)
Petersen, Steve. Phone interview. 1 Apr. 2017.
Pierce, Dale. *The History of Arizona Wrestling.* Lulu, 2015.
Professional Wrestling Hall of Fame and Museum. Website at www.pwhf.org. The Don Leo Jonathan page is at 0362dc8.netsolhost.com/halloffamers/bios/jonathan.asp. Last accessed 22 Apr. 2017.
Proudfoot, Jim. "Speaking on Sport" column in the *Toronto Star.* Mid-1960s piece on Gene and Julia Kiniski. (Source: Gene Kiniski's personal collection; exact date of column unknown.)
Quinn, John. Phone interview. 20 May 2016.
Quinsey, Mike. Phone interview. 31 July 2018.
Ranger, Joe. "Julia Kiniski made a lasting impression on city council." *The Edmonton Examiner* (12 May 2000).
Raschke, James (Baron von). Phone interview. 6 June 2016.
Rinke, Chris. Phone interview. 21 July 2018.
Roberts, Arthur. Phone interview. 18 Feb. 2016.
Robinson, Dana. Phone interview. 14 Aug. 2016.
Robinson, Jerry. Phone interview. 15 Aug. 2016.
Romanowski, Pawel. "A Short History of Polish-Canadians in Alberta." Article, posted at Polish-Heritage.ca, is accessible at www.polishheritage.ca/page.aspx?page_id=89. Last accessed 24 Feb. 2017.
Sammartino, Bruno. Phone interview. 23 Apr. 2017.
Santa Cruz Sentinel-News. Brief, untitled piece, hand-dated Nov. 23, 1955, reporting on Gene Kiniski's rescue of a dog. (Source: Gene Kiniski's personal collection.)
Schire, George. Phone interview. 26 Jan. 2018.
_____. *Minnesota's Golden Age of Wrestling: From Verne Gagne to the Road Warriors.* Minnesota Historical Society Press, 2010.

Scott, Stephen. "Kiniski on Wrestling: 'You've Got to Build Up Crust.'" Canadian Press article. (Source: Gene Kiniski's personal collection. Further identifying information is unavailable.)
SFU Online. "SFU People in the News—April 16, 2010." Brief mention of Gene Kiniski's death, quoting Simon Fraser alum Nick Kiniski, is at www.sfu.ca/archive-sfunews/news/sfu-people-in-the-news-april-16-2010.shtml. Last accessed 4 Nov. 2017.
Siebert, Verne. Phone interview. 28 Jan. 2017.
Silverstone, Dean, with Scott Teal. *"I Ain't No Pig Farmer!"* Crowbar Press, 2014.
Simmons, Herb. Phone interview. 29 May 2016.
SLAM! Wrestling website. "SLAM! Wrestling Dory Funk, Jr. Chat." Chat, dated 26 June 2001, is at www.canoe.ca/SlamWrestlingChats/funkdory_jun01-can.html. Last accessed 4 Nov. 2017.
_____. "SLAM! Wrestling—Gene Kiniski Chat." Chat, dated 10 Nov. 2000, is at www.canoe.ca/SlamWrestlingChats/nov10_kiniski-can.html. Last accessed 4 Nov. 2017.
_____. Gene Kiniski career overview, dated 30 Apr. 2008, is at www.canoe.com/Slam/Wrestling/ResultsArchive/Wrestlers/kiniski.html. Last accessed 4 Nov. 2017.
Smith, Maurice. "Unsung Lineman Kiniski Now Earns $90,000 in Ring." (Source: Gene Kiniski's personal collection. Further identifying information is unavailable.)
Snyder, Mike. Email interview. 28 Aug.–6 Sept. 2016. (Thanks to Richard Vicek.)
Stamp, Dennis. Phone interview. 13 Feb. 2016.
Stamp, Robert M. "Alberta." The Canadian Encyclopedia website at www.thecanadianencyclopedia.ca/en/article/alberta (26 Mar. 2009). Last accessed 4 Nov. 2017.
Steinborn, Dick. Phone interview. 30 June 2017.
Stone, Julie-Anne. Phone interview. 18 Feb. 2016.
Sweatervest, Scotty. "A final sellout crowd says goodbye to Kiniski." *SLAM! Wrestling* website article (4 May 2010), slam.canoe.com/Slam/Wrestling/2010/05/04/13826521.html. Last accessed 4 Nov. 2017.
Thesz, Lou, with Kit Bauman. *Hooker.* Kindle ed. Crowbar Press, 2014 (based on 1995 bound manuscript edition).
Thomas, Allen. Phone interview. 2 Dec. 2016.
Tselentis, Tony. "Minor Riot Caps Bizarre Mat Play." (Source: Gene Kiniski's personal collection. Further identifying information is unavailable.)
Tucson Daily Citizen. Various articles pertaining mainly to the early years of Gene Kiniski's professional wrestling career, particularly from 1952 to 1954, when he was based mainly in Tucson.
Vicek, Richard. *Bruiser: The World's Most Dangerous Wrestler.* Crowbar Press, 2016.
_____. "Mike Snyder: Proud of his wrestling days, but prouder of his Dad's legacy." *SLAM! Wrestling*

website article (3 Apr. 2016), slam.canoe.com/Slam/Wrestling/2013/03/25/20683936.html. Last accessed 4 Nov. 2017. Vicek was also instrumental in setting up the author's email interview with Mike Snyder.

_____. Phone interview. 10 May 2016.

Village of Chipman website at www.chipmanab.ca. Includes a "Village History" link. Last accessed 4 Nov. 2017.

Wachowich, Allan. Phone interviews. 17 Apr. 2016; 10 May 2016.

Warren, John. "Julia Kiniski is Colorful Addition to City Council." Canadian Press article in the *Winnipeg Free Press* and other newspapers (30 June 1964).

Watson, Hugh. Brief article reporting on a Gene Kiniski job offer in Peru. (Source: Gene Kiniski's personal collection. Further identifying information is unavailable.)

Watts, "Cowboy" Bill, and Scott Williams. *The Cowboy and the Cross.* ECW Press, 2006.

Webster, Mike. Phone interview. 16 Feb. 2016.

White, Dave. "'Gene Is Good Boy'—Julia … Opponents Disagree." *Edmonton Journal.* (Source: Gene Kiniski's personal collection; exact date of article unknown.)

Whitehead, Eric. "Fanfare" column. *The Province* (12 Mar. 1960).

Whiting, Robert. *Tokyo Underworld: The Fast Times and Hard Life of an American Gangster in Japan.* Vintage, 2000.

Wilson, Jim, with Weldon T. Johnson. *Chokehold: Pro Wrestling's Real Mayhem outside the Ring.* Xlibris, 2003.

Winnipeg Free Press. "Kiniski Shows His 'Metal'" (12 Sept. 1975). Article on the previous night's matches in Winnipeg, including Kiniski's disqualification loss to Baron von Raschke. (Source: Gene Kiniski's personal collection.)

Wiskoski, Ed. Phone interview. 7 Oct. 2016.

Wood, John. "Champ versus Chump?" Newspaper article (25 Aug. 1957). (Source: Gene Kiniski's personal collection. Further identifying information is unavailable.)

www.legacyofwrestling.com. Tim Hornbaker's "Los Angeles Wrestling Television History," which reports on the cancelation of the 1954 CBS network wrestling program from Hollywood Legion Stadium, is at www.legacyofwrestling.com/LosAngelesTV.html. Information about Dick Hutton, researched by Hornbaker, J Michael Kenyon, Don Luce, and Steve Yohe, is at www.legacyofwrestling.com/Hutton.html. Hornbaker's article on Rod Fenton's tenure as an NWA promoter in Arizona is at www.legacyofwrestling.com/TucsonOffice.html. Hornbaker's article on Rikidozan is at www.legacyofwrestling.com/Rikidozan.html. Hornbaker's report on the career of Gene Kiniski is at www.legacyofwrestling.com/Kiniski.html. Last accessed 21 Dec. 2017.

www.jimcornette.com. Website of long-time wrestling manager, promoter, and commentator Jim Cornette. Cornette's article recalling Sam Muchnick, *Wrestling at the Chase,* and the Muchnick retirement show is at www.jimcornette.com/fighting-spirit/meet-me-stlouis-fsm106. Last accessed 4 Nov. 2017.

www.onlineworldofwrestling.com. The Shag Thomas page is at www.onlineworldofwrestling.com/bios/s/shag-thomas. Cody Metcalf's "Hawaii: The Forgotten Wrestling Territory" (22 Nov. 2006) is at www.onlineworldofwrestling.com/columns/misc/codymetcalf01.html. Last accessed 28 Dec. 2017.

www.comedycouch.com. Interview (1 June 2001) with comedian Ryan "Lewis Kiniski" Stiles is at www.comedycouch.com/interviews/rstiles.htm. Last accessed 4 Nov. 2017.

www.wrestlezone.com. "Dory Funk, Jr. Shares His Memories of the Late Gene Kiniski," www.wrestlezone.com/news/180629-dory-funk-jr-shares-his-memories-of-the-late-gene-kiniski. Last accessed 4 Nov. 2017.

www.wrestling-titles.com. A storehouse of searchable information pertaining to pro wrestling history. Contains extensive information about wrestling promotions and championships over the years. A year-by-year listing of NWA title defenses by Gene Kiniski and other titleholders can be accessed at www.wrestling-titles.com/nwa/world/nwa-h-matches/. Last accessed 4 Nov. 2017.

www.wrestlingclassics.com. Information about Wilbur Snyder and about the 1954 CBS network wrestling television program from Hollywood, posted by wrestling historian Steve Yohe, is at www.wrestlingclassics.com/.ubb/ultimatebb.php?ubb=get_topic;f=7;t=000548. Last accessed 28 Jan. 2018.

www.wrestlingdata.com. Website contains substantial historical data concerning wrestling promotions around the globe and at least partial career records of most wrestlers of any significance worldwide, including Gene Kiniski. Last accessed 28 Jan. 2018.

Yetter, Earle F. "Kiniski: Big Thunder in Buffalo!" *Wrestling Life* magazine (June 1957).

Index

Abbott, Ace 28
ABC-TV 43
Abdullah the Butcher 119, 180, 190
Achtemychuk, Tom 15
Adkisson *see* Von Erich
Adonis, Adrian 160; *see also* Franks, Keith
Adonis, Terry 176
Agrodome *see* PNE Agrodome
Alan Hamel Show 205
Alberta, early history 9–11, 13–14, 19
Alberta Sports Hall of Fame 25, 65, 177, 202
Albuquerque, New Mexico 28–29, 114–115, 117
Ali, Muhammad 198–199, 205, 211
Ali-Chuvalo I 198–199
Ali-Chuvalo II 198–199
All Japan Pro Wrestling 151, 159, 176, 190–191, 194, 218
All Point Bulletin 20
All-Star Wrestling (promotion) 5, 7, 59, 76, 79, 123–124, 126–127, 141–143, 147–150, 152, 156, 159–161, 163–167, 169–170, 172–177, 180, 187, 201, 224, 232
All-Star Wrestling (TV program) 5, 72, 87, 127, 141–144, 150, 165, 173
Allen, Bruce 181
Amarillo, Texas 29–30, 39, 54, 84–86, 88, 102, 114, 131, 143–144, 162–163, 170–171; Kiniski recognized as NWA world champion (1962–1963) 84–85, 88, 102, 114
Amarillo Sports Arena 84
amarillowrestling.wikia.com 84
amateur wrestling *see* wrestling, amateur
American Wrestling Association (AWA) 68, 72–79, 86–87, 98, 105, 123, 141–142, 148–149, 159–161, 164, 181, 187, 189–190, 222; events in British Columbia 187
Ammerlaan, Allan 175
Anaya, Cyclone 46–47
Anderson, Ox 104
Anderson, Robert 72
André the Giant 160, 224–225
Anoa'i, Afa and Sika 152
Anson, John 166–168

Apollo, Argentina 125
Arakawa, Mitsu 87
Arizona Daily Star 27
Arizona Wildcats 23–28, 30, 40
Armstrong, Bob 151
army, Kiniski's brush with 40–42, 143
The Assassins (British Columbia) 127
The Assassins (Indiana) 111
Atkins, Fred 68
Ault, James "Great Mephisto" *see* Great Mephisto
Austin, Buddy 103
Australia 54, 67, 99, 106, 131, 212
AWA United States Heavyweight title 74–75, 77–78
AWA World Heavyweight title 45, 50, 61, 73, 77–78, 87, 109, 119, 152, 160; Kiniski's title reign 50, 76–78
AWA World Tag Team championship 75–78, 181

Baba, Shohei "Giant" 96–98, 102, 120–122, 128–129, 138, 144, 151, 159, 164, 169, 176, 190, 194, 224
Backlund, Bob 163
Baker, Ox 170
Barend, Johnny 47–49, 103
Barnett, Jim 67, 71, 106
Barr, Jesse 170
Barrett, Paddy 127
Bartlett, D.W. 80
Bass, Ron 169–170
Bastien, Red 102, 126
"Battle of the Mouths" 198
"Battle of the Windbags" 199
B.C. Catholic 175
BC Lions 147, 162, 175, 189, 204, 213, 218
BC Place Stadium 189, 202, 204
BC Sports Hall of Fame 184, 202–205
BCTV 127, 199, 205
Beck, Jason 6, 204–205
Beddoes, Dick 116
Beekman, Scott 73
Bell, Bert 32
Bellingham, Washington 148, 156–157, 210, 212, 228

Bellingham Herald 157
Bemis, Ernie "Mr. Kleen" *see* Kleen, Mr.
Bence, Jack 225
Bernard, Brute 103, 129
Berton, Pierre 10–11
Beyer, Dick "The Destroyer" *see* The Destroyer
Big Brothers 200
Big Thunder 67, 71, 179
Big Time Wrestling (Alberta) 34, 59–60, 80
Big Time Wrestling (British Columbia) 80
Blackburn, Bob 86–87
Blackwell, Jerry "Crusher" 181
Blaine, Washington 125, 138, 143–144, 146, 155–157, 161–162, 165, 167–168, 171, 176, 182, 184, 186, 192–198, 201, 209–211, 214, 216–219, 223–224, 227–228
Blanchard, Joe 34–35, 44, 50, 59, 64, 71, 104, 117, 157, 180, 194, 214, 218
Blanchard, Tully 117–118, 157, 162–163, 170, 173, 225
Blassie, Fred 44, 96, 103, 128, 224
Blears, Jimmy 50
Blears, Laura 50, 214
Blears, "Lord" James 45–51, 98, 123–124, 138, 143–144, 149, 190, 214, 218
Blue Destroyer (Gene Kiniski) 131
Bockwinkel, Nick 45, 71, 86, 106, 125, 164, 175, 188–191, 224–225
Bockwinkel, Warren 45
Boesch, Paul 54, 114, 187–188; retirement show 187–188
Bogni, Aldo 73
Bollas, George 49
Bolus, Steve 126, 141
Borne, Matt 169
Borne, Tony 113, 140, 149
Boston, Massachusetts 53, 67, 73
Bradbury, Tavish 20
Bravo, Dino 165
Brazil, Bobo 44–46, 48, 67–68, 96, 102–104, 128, 131, 188, 224
The Breakers 2, 195
Brendan Byrne Arena *see* Meadowlands Arena

239

Index

Brisco, Jack 114, 140, 144, 147, 149–152, 160, 163, 188–189, 222, 224
Brisco, Jerry 188
British Columbia 5, 9–11, 15, 22, 40, 67, 69, 71, 80–81, 84, 88, 95, 99, 103, 106–107, 112, 115, 119, 123–127, 138, 140–144, 146–150, 152, 160–161, 163, 165–170, 172–174, 177–178, 183–184, 187, 194, 200, 202, 204, 207, 210, 216–217, 225, 229–230, 232
British Columbia Winter Games 205
British Empire Heavyweight title (Toronto) 63, 68
British Empire Heavyweight title (Vancouver) 77, 86, 88
Brody, Bruiser 162, 171
Brower, Bulldog 78, 86, 95, 113, 119, 126, 131
Brown, Bulldog Bob 5, 141, 143–144, 146, 149, 152, 164, 170
Brown, Jerry 179
Bruiser: The World's Most Dangerous Wrestler 6, 110
Brunetti, Joe 87
Brunetti Brothers 58, 68
Bruns, Bobby 47, 118
The Brute 140, 149–150, 152, 180, 190
"Buckle Up for Safety" 207
Buffalo, New York 52–64, 66–67, 69–70, 84, 114, 126, 178, 205
Buffalo Memorial Auditorium 52–53, 58
Buffalo News 64
Burke, Leo 165
Burnaby, British Columbia 5, 141, 144, 149, 169, 172, 175, 177
Burnham, C.M. 219
The Bushwhackers *see* The Kiwis

Calgary, Alberta 10–11, 13, 19, 21, 34, 60, 67–68, 76, 83, 104, 140, 142, 164, 177, 180
Calhoun, Haystack 67, 87, 96, 102, 104, 113, 127, 160, 171
California 34, 47–48, 50–51, 56, 59–60, 68, 76, 96, 98, 102, 106, 127–128, 131, 136–137, 145, 168, 201–202, 205, 208–209; Northern California 45–51, 113, 168, 170–171; Southern California 39–41, 43–45, 47–50, 53, 58, 127, 137, 205
Calypso Hurricane 98
Campbell, Gordon 231
Canada, 19th century 9–11, 13
Canada's Greatest Athlete (nickname) 1–2, 5, 116, 205
Canadian Football League (CFL) 22, 32, 34, 141, 147–148, 150, 182, 184
Canadian Open Tag Team championship (Southern Ontario) 58, 60–61, 63, 68–70
Canadian Press 22, 79, 91, 93
Capitol Wrestling Corporation 101–102
Carbury, Joe 22
Carlson, Cowboy 87
Carpentier, Édouard 63–64, 67–68, 72–73, 80, 83, 102, 113, 118, 124, 126, 131, 141, 188
Cauliflower Alley Club 201, 202, 225; Kiniski receives award 201–203
CBC (Canadian Broadcasting Corporation) 57, 63, 116, 127, 205
CBS-TV 43–44
CBUT-TV 72, 208
celebration of life 209, 229–230, 232
CFOX Radio 181
CFRN-TV 65
CFTO-TV 82, 86
CHAN-TV 72, 87, 127, 141–142
Charest, Jean 30
Charleston *Post and Courier* 54
Checkerdome 178, 226
Chicago, Illinois 46, 49, 60, 69–70, 72–74, 76, 83, 106, 110, 144
Chicago Championship Wrestling 72
Chicago Tribune 56, 222
The Chilliwack Progress 87
Chipman, Alberta 6, 14–15, 17–19, 37, 89, 133–134, 136, 232; Kiniski's early years 17–18
Chokehold: Pro Wrestling's Real Mayhem Outside the Ring 80
Cholak, Moose, 102, 107
Christy, Ted 47
Christy, Vic 44, 47
Chuvalo, George 198–199
CJOB Radio 226
CKNW Radio 199
Clark, Richard E. 184
Coleman, Jim 124–125
Colt, Chris 169
The Columbian 26
The Comedy Network (Canada) 221
Comiskey Park 101
Commander Crutcher (Gene Kiniski) 207
commercials 207
Condello, Tony 190–191
Co-operative Commonwealth Federation 90
Cornette, Jim 178
Cortez, Hercules 85–86
Costello, Al 113, 188; *see also* Fabulous Kangaroos
Cotton Bowl 186
The Cowboy and the Cross 88
Cox, Wayne 145–146, 194, 199, 207, 229, 232
Cretoria, John 39
Crews, Art 176
Crimson Knight #2 (Gene Kiniski) 144
Crockett, Jim 177–179
Crosby, Len *see* Montana, Lenny
Crowbar Press 6
The Crusher 68, 86, 102–103, 128, 188, 190
CTV 221

Cubeta, Gary 109–110
Curry, Bull 97, 128
Curry, Fred 128, 149
Curtis, Don 112
Cyclone Negro *see* Calypso Hurricane

The Daily Gazette (Schenectady, New York) 225
Dallas, Texas 29, 59, 62, 114, 144, 185–186, 194
Dallas Sportatorium 29, 52, 138
Danny O 174
Davis, Karl 44
Davis, Mike *see* The Brute
Daysland, Alberta 37, 116
Deadlines 89, 94; *see also* Hawthorn, Tom
Delormier Stadium 64, 83
DeMarco, Mario 37
Demarco, Paul 129
Dempsey, Paul 175
Dennis, Daniel 99
DeNucci, Dominic 131, 188
Depression, Great 15, 17–19, 27, 29, 46, 89, 98, 101, 134
The Destroyer 49, 96, 120, 159, 169, 190, 222, 224
Detroit, Michigan 54, 71, 74, 104, 106, 114, 119, 140
DiBiase, Mike 45, 51, 114
DiBiase, Ted 51, 162, 181, 206
Dick the Bruiser 71, 74, 106–111, 113–114, 118–120, 123, 126, 128, 131–132, 140, 170, 178, 181, 224
Dilschneider, Donna 91
DiPaolo, Ilio 56–58, 60, 64, 68–70, 104, 224
Dixon, Dory 102
Donovan, Larry 213, 218
Double Happiness 207
Douglas, Greg 202–203, 205, 215
Doyle, Johnny 43–44, 46, 67, 101, 106
Drake, Bob 219–220
The Drew Carey Show 207
Dromo, Bill 108, 119, 131
Drummond, Neil 187
DuMont Television Network 34, 46, 101
Dunnell, Milt 135
Dusek, Joe 73
Dynamite Kid 180–181

Eakins, Ike 119
East Carondelet, Illinois 179, 225–226
Easter Seals 200
Eastwood, Clint 205
Eaton's Department Store advertisement 207
Edmonton, Alberta 6, 10–11, 14, 17–25, 28, 32, 34–38, 44, 65, 74, 76, 78, 80, 83, 89–95, 104, 116–117, 133–136, 153, 192, 210, 216–218
Edmonton Eskimos 21–23, 27–28, 32–38, 41, 44, 59–60, 64, 108, 147, 200, 219–220

Index

Edmonton Examiner 15, 91
Edmonton Journal 22, 35, 78, 91–93, 153, 217
Edmonton Maple Leafs 22
El Paso, Texas 28–30, 37, 40
El Paso Herald-Post 32
El Paso Times 29
Eleniak, Steven 6, 37, 78, 90–92, 134, 153
Ellis, Cowboy Bob 71, 83, 86, 102, 107, 113, 140, 149
Esquire 82
Etchison, Ron 47, 87, 112–113, 118, 126
Eurchuk, Mike 20, 89, 91–92, 177
Evans, Moose 104

Fabulous Kangaroos 59, 104, 224
fans, interaction with 74, 79, 87, 117, 135, 228
Fargo, Jackie 113, 119
Fenton, Jackie 80, 123, 145
Fenton, Patrice 26, 81–82, 123, 145, 153, 155
Fenton, Rod 25–27, 38, 40, 44–45, 59, 72, 80–82, 85, 87–88, 95, 112–113, 123–125, 145, 153, 155
Filchock, Frankie 28
fines, suspensions, legal issues 62, 64, 68, 71, 74, 141
Flair, Ric 77, 114, 165, 178–180, 224
Flathead 112, 210, 217, 232
Fleming, R.B. 205
Fliehr, Dr. Richard 77
Florida 75, 111–112, 115, 119, 123, 126, 132, 140, 144, 148–149, 172–173, 218
Foley, John 172
football 4, 7, 20, 22–28, 30–34, 42, 56, 59–60, 65, 71–72, 74–76, 95, 99, 105, 117, 125, 147–148, 156–157, 162–163, 170–171, 177, 182, 184, 206, 213, 232; Kiniski's football career 6, 21–22, 32–36
Fort Frances Times 74
Fox, Margalit 72
Francis, Ed 51, 98, 138, 149
Franke, Keith *see* Franks, Keith
Franks, Keith 160–161; *see also* Adonis, Adrian
Frazier, Bill 104
Freeman, Ace 29–30
Froelich, Erich 85, 184
Front Page Challenge 205
Frost, Steve 182
Fuji, Mr. *see* Fujiwara, Mr.
Fujiwara, Mr. 99–100
Fuller, Buddy 112–113
Funk, Dory, Jr. 86, 95, 106, 108, 113–114, 116–117, 130–132, 138, 140–146, 149, 151–152, 160, 162–163, 170–171, 173, 178, 188–190, 206, 224–225
Funk, Dory, Sr. 26, 29–30, 38–40, 45, 77–79, 84, 86–87, 95, 104, 114, 123, 125, 130–131, 162
Funk, Terry 114, 117, 130–132, 146, 150–151, 162–163, 170–171, 188–190, 206, 224–225

Gagne, Greg 76–77, 164
Gagne, Verne 58, 60, 67, 72–78, 83, 98, 105, 123, 141, 144, 160, 164, 178, 187–189, 194, 202–203, 222, 224
Gagnon, Erica 13
Garagiola, Joe 118, 178
Garza, Dick *see* Mighty Igor
Geigel, Bob 29, 78, 108, 190, 222
Gerein, Keith 217
Get Comfortable Being Uncomfortable: Improving Your Performance 182; *see also* Molle, Bob
Getty, Don 219–220
Gilbert, Doug "The Professional" 131
Gilmour, Matt *see* McTavish, Duncan
The Globe and Mail 89, 94, 207
The Godfather 75, 212
Gold, Marty 226
Gomez, Pepper 51–52
Gonzales, Lupe 104
Gordienko, George 85–86, 160
Gordon, Flash *see* Gordienko, George
Gorgeous George 46, 57, 68, 224
Gotch, Karl 78, 104, 114, 224
Gouldie, Archie "The Stomper" 113, 126, 163
Grable, Dr. Lee 29
Grabow, Benny 6, 19–20, 25, 30–32, 91, 136, 190, 192–194, 209, 213, 215–216, 218, 224, 227–228
Graham, Bobby "Hercules" *see* Marauder #1
Graham, Eddie 104, 112, 119, 126, 190
Graham, Jerry 103–104
Graham, Luke 104, 113
Graham, Superstar Billy 159
Graham Brothers 104
Grand Olympic Auditorium 45–47, 128, 144
Gray, George "One Man Gang" *see* One Man Gang
Great Mephisto 87
The Great Zimm 88, 103; *see also* Von Erich, Waldo
Greene, Don 119
Gretzky, Wayne 212
Grey Cup 32, 36, 184
Gunkel, Ray 51
Gzowski, Peter 205–206, 210

Hady, Jim 75, 126
Haggerty, Hard Boiled *see* Hard Boiled Haggerty
Hamilton, Larry 165
Hamilton, Larry "Missouri Mauler" 114, 119
Hamilton, Ontario 45, 54, 56, 68, 116, 143
Hamilton, Rocky 112
Hansen, Stan 162
Hanson, Swede 129
Harbor View Heights 192, 196, 210
Hard Boiled Haggerty 68, 74–78, 83–85, 202

Hart, Bret 180, 203, 224
Hart, Bruce 35, 180–181, 203
Hart, Stu 21, 25, 34, 59–60, 65, 80, 99, 113, 159, 172, 180–181, 188, 190, 203
Hawaii 28, 48–51, 56, 59, 95–96, 98–100, 115, 123, 126, 138, 143–144, 149, 151, 153, 157, 159–160, 205
Hawk, Rip 103, 118, 129
Hawthorn, Tom 89, 94, 207
Hayes, Gil 76, 148–149
Heffernan, Roy *see* Fabulous Kangaroos
Hennig, Larry 73
Henning, John Paul 71
Hepp, Rick 56, 222
Higuchi, Dean 99, 141, 143–144, 146, 149
Hill, Dennis 196, 210, 212, 215–216, 219–220, 224
Hill, John *see* Mitchell, Guy
Hill, Mike 195–198, 209, 212–213, 215, 223–224, 227
Hill, Skye 209
Hill's Chevron 196–198, 211, 215
Hirsch, Leroy *see* Tomko, Al
Hito, Mr. *see* Shibuya, Kinji
Hnatyshyn, Ray 30
Hodge, Danny 203
Hoffman, Duke 103
Hogan, Hulk 168, 173
Hollywood, California 42–47, 49, 51
Hollywood Legion Stadium 43–44
Holmback, Eric *see* Yukon Eric
Homer Hesterly Armory 132
homesteading (Alberta) 10, 13–14
Honolulu, Hawaii 28, 49, 98–100, 126, 138, 144, 149, 164
Honolulu Advertiser 49, 99
Hooker 145
Hornbaker, Tim 6, 43, 73, 80, 101, 109
Houston, Texas 51–52, 54, 114, 125–126, 187–188
Houston Chronicle 23
Howe, Gordie 202
Hudson's Bay Company 9–10, 19
Hughes, Curly 28
Hull, Bobby 212
hunting 77, 112, 165, 193, 209–210, 217, 232
Hutton, Dick 58–59, 61–67, 71–72, 80, 202, 222

"I Ain't No Pig Farmer!" 155, 201; *see also* Silverstone, Dean
Iaukea, King Curtis 72, 96, 99–100, 128, 138
Indianapolis, Indiana 67, 71, 106–107, 109, 114, 123, 205
injuries 144, 146, 182, 185; from football 22, 32–38, 40, 42, 218; from wrestling 44, 78–79, 115, 135, 166
Inoki, Antonio 97, 108, 129–130, 144, 194
International Heavyweight title (Amarillo) 163

Index

The Iron Sheik 168
Ivan the Terrible 28
Ivy, Pop 36

Jacobs, Abe 114, 149, 151
Jaggers, Bobby 169
Japan 49, 54, 92, 96–99, 113, 115, 119–122, 128–130, 135, 144, 148, 159–160, 167, 169, 176–177, 188, 190, 194, 205, 208, 222; Kiniski tours 96–98, 120–122, 128–130, 144, 151, 159, 169, 190, 208, 218
Japan Wrestling Association (JWA) 96–98, 120–121, 128–129; All-Asian Tag Team title 98
Jardine, Don 113–114, 125
Jericho, Chris 191
Jernigan, Jerry 210–211, 215, 224
Jim Crockett Promotions 177–180, 189, 214
Johnson, Rocky 119
Johnson, Steven 46, 116, 222
Johnson, Weldon T. *see* Chokehold: Pro Wrestling's Real Mayhem Outside the Ring
Jonathan, Brother 68
Jonathan, Don Leo 5–6, 59, 68–70, 72, 80, 85, 88, 90, 94–96, 104, 108, 113, 116, 119–120, 125–127, 129, 131, 141, 143–144, 146, 149, 152, 155, 161–163, 166, 206, 212, 214, 218, 224–225, 227
Jones, Bobby 149
Jones, Mike 182, 229
Jones, Paul 126
Jones, Robert F. 199
Jones, Ski Hi *see* Smith, Aurelian "Grizzly"
Julia Kiniski School 93
Junkyard Dog *see* Ritter, Big Daddy

Kalmikoff, Ivan and Karol 67
Kane, Dennis 213–214
Kangaroos *see* Fabulous Kangaroos
Karasick, Al 28, 48, 98
Karbo, Wally 73, 76, 178
Karlson, Swede 113
Kay, Rudy 114
Kearney, Jim 27
Keith, Greg 209, 219
Keith, Moray 205, 209, 212–213, 216, 229
Kelly, Gene (Gene Kiniski) 51–53
Kelly Twins 160
Kennedy, Jeff "Carolina" 223–224, 227, 230, 232
Kenneth, Ken 54
The Kentuckian *see* Smith, Aurelian "Grizzly"
Keomuka, Duke 51
Kernodle, Don 206
Keys, Eagle 147, 202
Kiel Auditorium 71, 103–104, 109–110, 112–113, 140, 144, 150–151, 163, 170, 178, 181, 189, 226
Kiel Center 189
Kiniski, Bunty 136

Kiniski, Dorothy 16–17; *see also* Roberts, Dorothy
Kiniski, Fred 16–17, 47, 136–137
Kiniski, Joyce 195, 214–215
Kiniski, Julia 16–19, 24, 89–95, 133–137, 154, 216; political activity and career 90–95, 134, 136; *see also* Warshawski, Julia
Kiniski, Julian *see* Kinisky, Julian
Kiniski, Kelly 1, 3–4, 6, 20, 37–38, 40, 50, 52, 61–62, 66, 98, 107–108, 112, 115, 117, 130, 133–136, 154–157, 159, 161–163, 168, 170–173, 176–180, 185–186, 192–195, 202, 206–212, 214, 216–218, 220–223, 225–228, 232
Kiniski, Lewis (Ryan Stiles character) 207–208
Kiniski, Marion 3, 6, 37–39, 41–42, 54–55, 61–62, 77–78, 98, 100, 116–117, 137, 153–158, 166, 192, 211, 217, 223; wedding 37–38, 153–154
Kiniski, Mary 16–17, 136, 216, 222
Kiniski, Nicholas 15–19, 24, 89, 92, 94, 133–137, 215–216
Kiniski, Nick 1–3, 6, 77, 98, 105, 109, 115, 117, 130, 155–156, 161–162, 168, 175, 177–179, 181–186, 188–189, 192–196, 202, 207, 209–212, 214–217, 219–220, 222–225, 227–230
Kiniski, Rudy 16–17, 136
Kiniski Gardens 93
Kiniski's Reef and Tavern 2, 195, 217, 229–230
Kinisky, Bruce 15, 65–66, 78, 89, 91–92, 94, 133–137, 153–155, 221
Kinisky, Gene 66, 90, 94, 135, 153, 155, 221
Kinisky, Julian 16–18, 22, 37, 65–66, 89, 94, 133–136, 216–217, 221–222
Kirkwood, John 20, 23, 112, 212
The Kiwis 169
Kleen, Mr. 83, 86
Klondike Bill 103–104, 112–113, 119, 126
Klondike Mike 174
Knox, Buddy 30
Kohler, Fred 46, 74, 101
Koloff, Ivan 129, 140, 146, 151, 190
Koster, Rich 135, 137
Kotal, Ed 32
Kovacs, Sandor 47–50, 59, 64, 85, 87, 123–125, 141–143, 148, 150, 161, 163–167, 174, 201, 211
Kovacs, Steve *see* Little Bear, Steven
Kowalski, Killer 50, 62–64, 67–68, 82–83, 86, 96, 102–103, 128, 159, 188, 224
Kowalski, Stan 73
Kox, Killer Karl 114, 120, 128
KPLR-TV 118, 225
Krauser, Karl *see* Gotch, Karl
Kroffat, Dan 143, 160, 167–168
KTLA-TV 43
KVOS-TV 203, 205

LaBelle, Pierre 26–27
Ladd, Ernie 108, 113–114, 125–126, 188
LaDue, Monte 26
Lamont, Alberta 15, 17, 133
Lane, Larry 206
Lano, Dr. Mike 58
Lanza, Jack (Blackjack) 87, 131–132
Larsen, Elmer 40
Laskin, Jack 68
Laurier, Sir Wilfred 13
Lawler, Jerry 113
Lee, Daffy Don *see* Ivan the Terrible
Lehman, Bill *see* Steinke, Siegfried
Leone, Baron Michele 39, 44, 137
Lethbridge Herald 28
Lewin, Mark 5, 102, 142–144, 149, 180, 188
Lewis, Dale 160
Lewis, Ed "Strangler" 35
Lewis, Glyn 26
Lindsay, Luther 99, 127
Lippa, Christine 208
Lisowski, Reggie *see* The Crusher
Lisowski, Stan 68
Little Bear, Steven 5, 119, 126, 143–144, 146, 149, 152
Little Eagle, Chief 126
London, Ontario 57, 70, 206
Longson, Bill 43, 67–68, 71, 224
Los Angeles, California 42, 45, 54, 58, 72, 127–128, 144, 182, 184
Los Angeles Rams 32–33
Lothario, Jose 112, 126
Lougheed, Peter 22
Louis, Jean 169
Louis, Joe 96, 151
Luce, Bob 110
Luke 15 House 175
Lyons, Billy "Red" 55, 67, 114, 117, 125, 188

Macdonald, Sir John A. 10
Mackenzie, Alexander 10
MacLean, Dick 22
Madison Square Garden (New York, New York) 101–103, 146
Madison Square Garden (Phoenix, Arizona) 80
Madison Wrestling Club 149, 164, 174
Magnificent Maurice 103
Magrill, Leo 20
Maiava, Neff 99–100
Maivia, Peter 144
Malcewicz, Joe 46, 48
Malenko, Boris 103
Malumba, Ormand 160
"Man at Bus Stop" (Gene Kiniski) 207
Managoff, Bobby 56, 68, 106–107, 109, 222
Manitoba 9, 107, 126, 141–142, 174, 181, 184, 190
The Manly Art of Mayhem 72
Manson, Bill 65–66

Index

Maple Leaf Gardens 54–55, 61, 63, 68–69, 78, 86, 140, 179, 198
Marauder #1 109
Marauder #2 (Gene Kiniski) 109
Marciano, Rocky 64
Marigold Arena 34; *see also* Wrestling from Marigold
Martin, Pepper 127
Martinez, Pedro 52–54, 57, 63, 114
Martino, Salvatore 169
Mascaras, Mil 190
Masked Marvel 30
Masters, Joe 64
Matsuda, Hiro 112
Matysik, Larry 6, 107, 109–110, 118–119, 178, 189, 227
Maynard, Earl 118, 141
Mayne, Lonnie 119, 129, 142–143
McClarty, Don 79, 83, 86, 104, 112
McClarty, Roy 73–74, 79, 82–83, 85–86, 97, 146, 167
McClarty Brothers 79, 83, 84
McCready, Earl 35
McDaniel, Wahoo 95, 104–105, 108, 112, 119, 180, 186, 190
McGraw, Bugsy *see* The Brute
McGuirk, Leroy 222
McKenzie, Frank "Tex" 54–55, 87, 114, 119, 127, 138, 144
McKenzie, Merv 62
McLemore, Ed 62
McMahon, Jess 101
McMahon, Vince, Jr. 98, 101, 181, 187, 190, 194
McMahon, Vince, Sr. 101–102, 105, 189
McMahon, Vincent J. *see* McMahon, Vince, Sr.
McMahon, Vincent K. *see* McMahon, Vince, Jr.
McNulty, Red *see* Koloff, Ivan
McShain, Danny 44
McTavish, Duncan 143–144, 146, 149, 224
Meadowlands Arena 188
Melnyk, Walter 16–17, 136
Meltzer, Dave 36, 60, 62, 116, 130, 202
Menacher, Sam 29
Mesa, Arizona 37, 80
Metcalf, Cody 98
Metropolitan Stadium 76
Mexico 30, 41, 115
Mid-Atlantic Championship Wrestling 177–178
Mighty Canadian (Gene Kiniski) 163
Mighty Igor 87, 119
Mighty Ursus 83, 128–129
Milano, Mario 128
Miller, Bill 50, 57, 67–68, 85–86, 128, 144, 148
Miller, Dan 85–87, 112, 114
Miller, Ed 68
Miller, Merle 212
Miller, Texas Red 172
Mills, Tiny 73, 75
Minneapolis, Minnesota 60, 72–74, 76–77, 79

Missouri Athletic Commission 71, 110
"Mr. X" Frank Townsend *see* Townsend, Frank
"Mr. X" Guy Mitchell *see* Mitchell, Guy
Mitchell, Guy 104, 109–110, 126–127, 160, 163, 166
Miyaki, Taro 71
Molchan, Anna 15
Molle, Bob 181–185, 195, 197, 202, 213, 227, 232
Mondt, Toots 101–102, 105
El Mongol 119
Monsoon, Gorilla 103–104, 120
Montana, Lenny 51, 74
Montana, Tommy 186
Montreal, Quebec 21, 43, 50, 54, 59–60, 63–64, 67–68, 72–73, 82–83, 147
Montreal *Gazette* 63
Mooneyham, Mike 54
Morales, Pedro 103, 128, 138, 144, 147
Morelli, Tony 26–27, 38–39, 49
Moretti, Ed "Moondog" 168–169, 174, 187
Morgan, Toar 34–35
Morowski, Moose 143, 164, 166, 172, 224
Morrier, Ron 5, 127, 152
Morrow, Don *see* Muraco, Don
Morrow, Eddie 149
Morse, Bob "The Viking" 118
Mortier, Hans 103
Mosca, Angelo 141, 164, 177–178, 180, 200
Moto, Mr. 44, 83
Muchnick, Helen 178
Muchnick, Sam 67, 73, 107, 109–110, 118–119, 130, 139, 151, 178–179, 188–189, 214, 224–225; 90th birthday celebration 189; retirement show 178
Muhammad, Ernie 145
Muraco, Don 143–144, 190
Murdoch, Dick 170, 179, 190, 206
Murphy, Gerry *see* Regan, Sean
Murphy, Skull 103
Musial, Stan 118
Myers, Sonny 113, 126

Nagurski, Bronko 28
National Football League (NFL) 23, 28, 32–33, 41, 59, 71–72, 105, 141
National Post 175
National Rifle Association 193
National Wrestling Alliance (NWA) 29, 46, 53, 62, 73, 76, 78, 80–83, 101–102, 105, 107, 109–111, 114–115, 120–121, 125–131, 139–140, 150, 180, 201, 225
National Wrestling Alliance Hall of Fame 225
National Wrestling Alliance: The Untold Story of the Monopoly That Strangled Pro Wrestling 73, 80, 101; *see also* Hornbaker, Tim

National Wrestling Hall of Fame *see* Tragos-Thesz Professional Wrestling Hall of Fame
Nelson, Art 114, 163
Nevada, Vance 6, 81, 123, 144
New Brunswick 9–10, 63, 165
New Japan Pro Wrestling 194
New York, New York 47, 53, 101, 147, 188, 206
New York Times 72, 82
Newfoundland and Labrador 63, 86, 126
90 Minutes Live 205
Nomellini, Leo 28, 46–50, 74, 76
Northwest Wrestling Promotions *see* All-Star Wrestling
NWA American Heavyweight title (Texas) 138
NWA Canadian Heavyweight championship (Toronto) 165, 170
NWA Canadian Heavyweight title (British Columbia) 174
NWA Canadian Tag Team title (British Columbia) 85, 87–88, 104, 126, 141, 143, 146, 149–150, 152, 160, 163, 174
NWA Canadian Tag Team title (Calgary) 60
NWA Hawaii Heavyweight title 99–100, 149
NWA Hawaii Tag Team championship 49
NWA International Heavyweight title (Japan) 120–122, 128–129, 144
NWA International Tag Team title (Japan) 129
NWA International Television Tag Team title (Southern California) 44–46
NWA Mid-Atlantic Tag Team title 179
NWA Missouri State Heavyweight title 150–151
NWA North American Heavyweight title (Hawaii) 138
NWA Pacific Coast Heavyweight title (British Columbia) 142–144, 146, 149–150, 152, 160, 163, 165–166, 168–169
NWA Pacific Coast Tag Team title (British Columbia) 83–85
NWA Pacific International Heavyweight championship (Hawaii) 144
NWA Southwest Tag Team championship 84
NWA Texas Heavyweight title 29, 51
NWA Texas Tag Team championship 29, 51, 74
NWA World Heavyweight championship 29, 34, 44–45, 47, 51–52, 56–58, 61–68, 71, 73, 76, 83–84, 88, 95, 99, 101–102, 105–107, 109–115, 117–121, 123–133, 138, 140, 141–146, 151–152, 160, 163, 170–171, 173, 178–180, 188–189,

193, 203, 222, 226; Kiniski's title reign 7, 109–115, 117–121, 123–133, 137–140, 142–143, 151, 189, 198, 216, 226
NWA World Tag Team championship (Northern California) 47

O'Connor, Pat 58–63, 65, 67–68, 71–73, 76, 80, 83, 101, 104, 108, 112–113, 118–119, 121, 126, 131, 140, 151, 163, 178, 188, 222, 224
Odem, Benjamin "Boo" 23–24
Oeming, Al 21, 25, 34–35, 42
Ohira, Rod 99
Oki, Kintaro 97
Oliver, Greg 23, 34, 45–46, 51, 55, 64, 67, 73, 80, 86, 115–116, 124, 126–127, 130, 143, 158, 160, 166, 174, 181, 201–202, 207, 215, 218, 222, 224–225
Oliver, Rip 170
Olson, Cliff 80, 87, 95
Olympia Wrestling Club 164
Olympic Games 58, 72, 177, 181–185, 221–222
Omni Coliseum 189
One Man Gang 179
O'Neill, Marty 76
Open Mike with Mike Bullard 221
Ortega, Jesus *see* Mighty Ursus
Orton, Bob, Sr. 46, 68, 112
O'Toole, Tommy 103
Owen, Barry 119, 148
Owen, Don 46, 55, 59, 113, 119, 123–125, 141–142, 148, 163, 169–170, 172–174, 177, 186, 190, 201

Pacific Coast Tag Team title (British Columbia) 82–84
Pacific Coast Tag Team title (Northern California) 45
Pacific National Exhibition (PNE) Gardens 79, 82–84, 141, 143–144, 166, 171
Pacific Northwest Wrestling 55, 119, 142, 149, 169–170, 177, 186
Pacific Scandal 10
Pacific Wrestling Federation (Japan) 159, 190
Pacific Wrestling Federation Heavyweight title 159
Palm Springs, California 209, 217, 227
Paproski, Pat 30, 34, 52
Paproski, Steve 19–20, 22–23, 26–27, 30, 34, 37, 52
Paradise Alley 206–207
Paramount Television Network 43–44
Parker, Cliff 72, 80, 82, 85, 87, 113, 123–124, 210
Parker, Jackie 202
Parker's Mattress City 207
Parks, Reg 206
Parsons, King 169
Pascall, Bernie 87, 142, 155, 161, 193–194, 199–200, 202–203, 210, 213, 227, 229

Pascall, Judy 155
Pastime Tavern 196, 219
Patera, Ken 181
Patterson, Claude "Thunderbolt" 117, 190
Patterson, Pat 113, 125, 128, 188, 224
Pavlovich, Lou 27
Peck, Doug 72
Pender Wrestling Club 80
Perez, Alex 119
Perez, Eduardo 132
Perez, Miguel 104
Persack, Bill 166
Peter Gzowski: A Biography 205
Petersen, Steve 212, 221, 230, 232
Pettiglio, "Danny O" *see* Danny O
Pezim, Murray 198
Pfefer, Jack 145
Phoenix, Arizona 28, 37, 40, 45, 80, 145
Pico, Roberto 52
Pierce, Dale 145
Piper, Roddy 169–170, 180
Plain Speaking 212
Plechas, Danny "Golden Terror" 45, 51, 53
PNE Agrodome 149, 152, 160
Poffo, Angelo 109
Poffo, Lanny 169
Poile, Bud 200
Point Roberts, Washington 2, 4, 20, 194–195, 201, 214, 227, 230
Poland 7, 14, 19–20, 89, 91, 94, 133–135; immigrants from 13–15, 19, 46, 133; Kiniski's Polish background 6–7, 53, 82, 89–90, 94, 105, 133–135, 205, 216
Port Arthur News-Chronicle 74
Portland, Oregon 113, 141–142, 165, 169–170, 172–173, 186
Portland Buckeroos 203
The Powell River Peak 214
power generation 22–23
Powers, Johnny 108, 113
Pride in Progress 15; *see also* Chipman, Alberta
The Pro Wrestling Hall of Fame: The Heels 46–47, 116–117, 156, 222; *see also* Johnson, Steven; Oliver, Greg
Professional Wrestling Hall of Fame (PWHF) 68, 224–225
Professional Wrestling in the Pacific Northwest 5
Proudfoot, Jim 91–93
The Province 20, 22–23, 72, 112, 212
public service announcements 207
Puerto Rico 99, 115, 119, 126, 140

Quebec (province) 9–10, 59, 63, 124, 205
Quinn, John 143–144, 149–150, 152, 161, 165

Race, Harley 147, 150–151, 170, 178–180, 188–189, 224–226
Radovich, Bill 23

railroads: Canadian Northern Railway 14, 19; Canadian Pacific Railroad (CPR) 11, 14–15; *The Last Spike: The Great Railway, 1881–1885* 10–11; transcontinental railroad, building of 10–11
Ramirez, Benny "The Mummy" 98
Ramstead, Buck 149
Ranger, Joe 15, 91
Raschke, James "Baron von" *see* Von Raschke, Baron
Red Cloud, Bobby 126
Red Cross 207
Reed, Bruce "Butch" 169
Reeves, Dan, 32
Regan, Sean 149–150
Remus, Bob 160–161
Renesto, Tom 29
Rheingans, Brad 222
Rhodes, Dusty 162, 178
Rice, Tom 45
Rickard, Steve 115
Riddle, Rock 206
Rieu, André 213
Rikidozan 46, 49, 96–98, 120–121, 129, 224
Rillito Racetrack 81–82
Ringside: A History of Professional Wrestling in America 73; *see also* Beekman, Scott
riots (wrestling) 26, 64, 70, 82, 135, 179, 206
Ritter, Big Daddy 169
Robert, Yvon 62–63
Roberts, Arthur 15, 134, 153, 155, 205, 228–229
Roberts, Dorothy 134, 136, 216–217, 222–223, 227, 228–229; *see also* Kiniski, Dorothy
Roberts, Jake "The Snake" 126, 166, 168–169, 177–178
Roberts, Nick 75
Robertson, Dewey 170
Robinson, Billy 144, 149, 203, 222
Rocca, Antonino 43, 60, 67, 102, 224
Rocky 206
Rogers, Buddy 43, 47, 51, 56, 61–62, 76, 84, 86, 88, 101–102, 114, 121, 125, 224
Romano, Gerry 150, 152
Romanowski, Pauel 13–14
Romero, Ricky 84
Roop, Bob 206
Rose, Buddy 169–170
Ross, Jim 189
Rossi, Count Pietro 51–52
Rossi, Len 51
Royal, Darrell 35–36
Ruby, Martin 35
Ruhl, Dave 119

St. John's *Telegram* 63
St. Joseph Catholic School 20, 89, 162, 221
St. Louis, Missouri 7, 59–60, 67, 71, 83, 95, 103–104, 106–113, 116, 118–119, 123–124, 131–132, 139–140, 144, 147, 149–151, 163, 170–

Index

171, 178–179, 181, 186–190, 202, 205, 224–226
St. Louis Cardinals 107, 118
St. Louis Globe-Democrat 135
St. Louis Wrestling Club 107, 178
St. Louis Wrestling Hall of Fame 224, 226
St. Mary's Cathedral 37
Saito, Masa 99, 160
Sales Pavilion 35, 83
Sam Houston Coliseum 187
Sammartino, Bruno 29, 86, 102–107, 120–121, 128, 140, 143, 147, 152, 159, 188, 190, 194, 224
San Francisco, California 45–48, 50, 71, 128, 171
Sancet, Frank 23
Santa Cruz Sentinel-News 48
Santana, Tito 162
Santos, Tony 145
Sarpolis, Karl 80
Sasaki, Haru 99
Saskatchewan 9, 59, 65, 86, 115, 126, 141, 165, 172, 182
Saturday Night Wrestling 57
Savage, Dutch 5, 117, 119–120, 127, 129, 131, 141, 143, 149, 152, 160–161, 166, 174, 218–219
Savage, "Macho Man" Randy 169–170
Savich, Danny 29
Sawyer, Buzz 170
Scarpa, Joe 119, 126, 129, 188
Scarpello, Joe 75, 84
Schmidt, Hans 57, 60, 74, 102, 111, 114, 126
Schmockey 200
Schnabel, Hans 44, 49
Schoendienst, Red 118
Scott, George 74, 126, 214, 218, 222
Scott, Stephen 23, 25
Seattle, Washington 51, 119, 123, 144, 152, 165, 172, 198, 201, 211–212
Shane, Bobby 113, 127, 131
Sharpe, Ben 46–48, 50, 67, 96
Sharpe, Mike 46–48, 50, 67, 96
Sharpe, Mike, Jr. 172
Shaw, "Klondike" Mike *see* Klondike Mike
The Sheik 51, 71, 114–115, 140, 144, 163
Shibuya, Kinji 52, 55, 83, 87, 95
Shire, Ray *see* Stevens, Ray
Shire, Roy 44, 71, 128, 170
Sieber, Walter *see* The Great Zimm; Von Erich, Waldo
Siebert, Verne 175
Sierra, Fidel "Destroyer" 170, 172
Sifton, Clifford 13–14
Sigel, Morris 51–52, 54, 62, 114
Siki, Sweet Daddy 63, 84, 86–87, 102, 104
Silverstone, Dean 154–155, 201
Simmons, Herb 6, 179, 226–227
Simon Fraser University 177, 181–182, 184, 202, 215, 229
Singh, Dara 67–68
Singh, Tiger Jeet 119, 160

Sjoberg, Lou 60; *see also* Von Schober, Karl
Skaaland, Arnold, 102
SLAM! Wrestling 51–52, 69, 73, 80, 105, 116, 124, 127, 130, 135, 166, 174, 178, 191, 218, 221, 224–225, 229
Slamboree 1993 189
Slatton, Don "The Lawman" 171
Slaughter, Sergeant *see* Remus, Bob
Smith, Aurelian "Grizzly" 125–126, 166
Smith, Aurelian, Jr. *see* Roberts, Jake "The Snake"
Smith, Davey Boy 180–181
Smith, Maurice 36
Snuka, Jimmy 160–161, 190
Snyder, Mike 77
Snyder, Shirlee 77, 155
Snyder, Wilbur 34–35, 44–45, 59–60, 68, 71, 74–77, 83, 103–104, 106–108, 113–114, 118, 123, 155, 163–164
The Sound of Music 213
Southwest Championship Wrestling 34
Sports Hot Seat 86–87, 205
Sports Illustrated 199
Stafholt Good Samaritan Center 228
Stallone, Sylvester 206
Stamp, Dennis 160–162, 206
Stamp, Robert M. 9, 11, 13
Stampede Wrestling 34, 76, 113, 141, 143, 148–149, 160, 165, 169–170, 172, 180–181, 187; expansion to British Columbia 180–181, 187
Stanlee, Gene 47
Stanlee, Steve 47
Stansauk, Don *see* Hard Boiled Haggerty
Starr, Ron 181
Starrcade 180, 189
Stasiak, Stan 119, 126, 131, 169
Steamboat, Sam 68, 113, 119, 131, 149
Steeves, Clyde 85, 103
Steinborn, Dick 113, 131
Steinke, Siegfried 160, 169
Stevens, Ray 71, 128, 159, 188, 206, 224
Stiles, Ryan 207–208
Stolhandske, Tom and Betty 41
Stone, Julie-Anne 217, 222–223
Storm, Lance 191
Strongbow, Chief Jay *see* Scarpa, Joe
Stukus, Annis 22
Sweatervest, Scotty 229–230
Sydney Morning Herald 99
Szabo, Sandor 44–45, 71, 80

Tabloid 205
Tanaka, Toru 99, 138
Taylor, Jim 203, 205
television, wrestling on 5, 34, 43–46, 53, 57, 62–63, 65, 68, 72, 76, 82, 87–88, 96, 98, 101, 109, 118, 127, 138, 141–144, 148, 150–152, 165, 169–170, 172–174, 178, 180, 187, 190, 195, 205
Tenta, John 182
Terminal City Ricochet 207
Terry Funk: More Than Just Hardcore 114, 130–131; *see also* Funk, Terry
Texas 4, 28–30, 32, 37–42, 50–60, 62, 68–69, 80, 84, 86, 95, 99, 102, 104, 106–109, 114–115, 117, 119, 123–126, 129, 131, 144, 157, 162, 171, 173, 185–186, 192, 194, 205, 226
Thesz, Lou 7, 29, 34, 44–45, 47, 51, 56–58, 61–62, 64–65, 67, 73, 76, 84, 87–88, 95–96, 99, 102, 105–107, 109–110, 112–115, 117–121, 123, 125–126, 140–141, 145, 173, 188–190, 201–202, 221–225
Thomas, Allen 15, 17–18
Thomas, James "Shag" 55–56, 113
Thomas, Sailor Art 102, 113, 119, 188
Thompson, Alice 22
Thompson, Ronnie 126
Tibbedeux, T. John 171
Togo, Tosh 83
Togo, Tosh, and Great Togo 49
Tokyo Dome 190
Tokyo Pro Wrestling 129
Tokyo Underworld: The Fast Times and Hard Life of an American Gangster in Japan 96
Tolos, Chris 45, 119, 127
Tolos, John 5, 45–46, 113, 119, 127, 132, 141, 152, 161, 190
Tolos Brothers 45, 127, 224
Tomasso, Joe 111
Tomko, Al 141–142, 144, 160, 164–167, 169–170, 173–177, 180–181, 187, 190, 211
Toronto, Ontario 54–55, 57–63, 67–72, 78, 84, 86–88, 95, 97, 102, 104, 106–108, 116, 119–120, 125–126, 133, 136, 140, 143–144, 163, 165, 170, 177–179, 187, 198, 205–206
Toronto Star 135, 221
Toronto Sun 221
Toronto Telegram 86
Torres, Alberto 113
Torres, Enrique 46–48, 113, 119
Townsend, Frank 87–88
Toyonobori 98, 120, 129
Tragos, George 221–222
Tragos-Thesz Professional Wrestling Hall of Fame 56, 221–223, 226
Tributes II 130; *see also* Meltzer, Dave
Trudeau, Pierre Elliott 206
Truman, Harry 212
Tselentis, Tony 26
Tsuruta, Jumbo 159
Tucson, Arizona 23–30, 32, 36–40, 45, 80–81, 124, 144–145, 153; debut 27–28; Kiniski's transition to professional wrestling 26–27, 40, 80, 123; *see also* University of Arizona

Index

Tucson Daily Citizen 26–28, 32, 40, 42, 80, 145, 153
Tucson Garden 38
Tucson Sports Center 25–29, 38
Tudor pub 183, 209
Tunney, Frank 46, 62, 178–179, 188, 198
Tunney, Jack 188
Turner, Ted 189
Two Eagles, Billy 186
Tyler, Tarzan 129

Ukraine, immigrants from 13–15, 19
Universal Wrestling Federation 172
University of Alberta 19, 22, 89
University of Arizona 23–27, 30–31, 40, 170

Vachon, Maurice "Mad Dog" 128, 222
Valentine, Johnny 51, 83, 86, 102, 104, 106–107, 109, 111, 113, 119, 123, 126, 144, 150–151, 190, 224
Vancouver, British Columbia 5, 21, 30, 59, 65, 67, 71, 76–88, 95, 99, 102, 104, 106–108, 113, 115–117, 123–127, 130–132, 135–136, 140–149, 151–152, 154–155, 157, 160–161, 163–173, 175–178, 180–181, 187, 192, 196–201, 203–208, 210–212, 221, 227
Vancouver Canucks (NHL) 175, 200, 202
Vancouver Canucks (Western Hockey League) 202–203
Vancouver Sun 144, 203, 215
Varga, Billy 49
Vaziri, Hossein Khosrow Ali *see* Iron Sheik
Vellios, Mark "Gorgeous Michelle Starr" 232
Vicek, Richard 6, 106, 110
Victoria, British Columbia 84–85, 127, 141, 144, 149, 152, 160, 165, 168, 184
Viniski, Gene 145
Vodik, Igor *see* Mighty Igor
Volkoff, Igor 172, 174
Von Erich, David 170
Von Erich, Doris 60–62
Von Erich, Fritz 57, 59–64, 68, 71, 84, 86, 88, 103–104, 106, 108–109, 113–114, 117–118, 120, 123, 125–126, 129, 138, 170, 185, 194, 214, 224
Von Erich, Jackie 60, 62
Von Erich, Kevin 170
Von Erich, Waldo 88, 103–106, 114, 118, 125, 129, 132; *see also* The Great Zimm
Von Goering, Fritz 87
Von Raschke, Baron 159, 178, 190, 222, 226
Von Schober, Karl 60–61; *see also* Sjoberg, Lou
Von Stroheim, Kurt 132

Wachowich, Allan 89, 91, 216
Walcott, Jersey Joe 62
Walker, Johnny 131
The Wall Street Journal 212
Warren, John 91–92
Warshawski, Helen 16
Warshawski, John 15
Warshawski, Julia 14–15, 89; *see also* Kiniski, Julia
Washington, D.C. 101–104, 106
Wasserman, Jack 144
Watson, Hugh 22–23
Watson, Whipper Billy 51–52, 57–72, 74–80, 82–88, 97, 104, 107, 113, 116, 123, 140, 144, 153, 206, 225
Watt, "Big" Bill *see* Watts, Cowboy Bill
Watts, Cowboy Bill 88, 103–104, 126, 129, 131, 172
WBBM-TV 72
Weaver, Johnny 71, 114, 119, 126, 132
Webster, Jack 199
Webster, Mike 147–150, 152, 155, 157
Weller, Emma 98, 117
Weller, Marion "Bunny" *see* Kiniski, Marion
Weller, Nick 117
West Texas State University 157, 162–163, 170–171, 192, 206–207
Western Interprovincial Football Union (WIFU) 22, 32, 34–35
WGR-TV 53
Whistler, Larry *see* Zbyszko, Larry
White, Dave 93
White Wolf, Billy 97, 113
White Wolf, Chief *see* White Wolf, Billy
Whitehead, Eric 72
Whiting, Robert 96
Whitson, Lou 131
Wilson, Jim *see Chokehold: Pro Wrestling's Real Mayhem Outside the Ring*
Windham, Barry 163, 170
Winnipeg, Manitoba 21, 43, 65, 71, 74–78, 83, 85–87, 103–104, 106–108, 112–113, 141–142, 144, 148–149, 151, 159–160, 163–164, 166, 170, 174, 181, 190, 201, 226
Winnipeg Blue Bombers 35–36, 182, 184
Winnipeg Free Press 159
Winslow, Bob 25, 32
Wiskoski, Ed 170–171
Wood, John 63
Woods, Tim "Mr. Wrestling" 126, 131, 151
World Championship Wrestling (WCW) 189
World Class Championship Wrestling (WCCW) 62, 185–186
World War I 15, 18–19, 134
World War II 18–20, 48, 60, 124, 136, 166, 228
World Wide Wrestling Federation (WWWF) 51, 99, 101–106, 113, 119, 126, 143, 189; WWWF United States Tag Team championship 104, 106; WWWF World Heavyweight championship 51, 102–103, 105, 107, 120, 128, 138, 140, 143, 147, 159, 163, 169, 194
World Wrestling Association (WWA) 106–109, 114, 123; WWA Heavyweight title 107–110, 114
World Wrestling Entertainment (WWE) 87, 101, 105, 213
World Wrestling Federation (WWF) 51, 98–99, 105, 113, 119, 143, 160–161, 163, 166, 168–169, 174, 179, 181, 187–190, 194, 213–214; expansion to British Columbia 187; 1987 "legends" battle royal 186, 188
wrestling, amateur 7, 20–22, 25–26, 35, 58, 65, 72, 89, 107, 135, 147, 161–162, 166, 168, 177, 179, 181–184, 216, 221–222, 229
Wrestling at the Chase (book) 178; *see also* Matysik, Larry
Wrestling at the Chase (TV program) 107, 109, 112–113, 118, 151, 170, 178, 205, 225–226
Wrestling from Hollywood 43–44, 46
Wrestling from Marigold 46, 57, 82; *see also* Marigold Arena
Wrestling in the Canadian West 81, 123; *see also* Nevada, Vance
Wrestling Life 67
Wrestling Observer Hall of Fame 202, 225
Wrestling Observer Newsletter 36, 60, 62, 116, 202; *see also* Meltzer, Dave
Wrestling with the Past 221
Wright, Bearcat 67, 83–84, 86, 95, 102, 113, 144
Wright, Bill *see* Red Cloud, Bobby
www.comedycouch.com 208
www.jimcornette.com 178
www.legacyofwrestling.com 43, 58, 80, 96, 109
www.oklafan.com 219
www.onlineworldofwrestling.com 55, 98, 100
www.wrestlezone.com 95
www.wrestlingclassics.com 43–44
www.wrestlingdata.com 95, 185

Yaki Joe 169
Yetter, Earle F. 67
YMCA 20, 166
Yohe, Steve 43–44
Yomiuri Giants 96
Yoshimura, Michiaki 98
Yoshinosato 120–121
Youngblood, Jay 170, 180
Yukon Eric 50, 58, 60, 64, 67–69, 71, 74, 82, 86, 103

Zbyszko, Larry 152
Zero Avenue 208